FANNY & GABRIEL

Nava Semel

Translated by

Gilah Kahn-Hoffmann

Published by arrangement with The Institute for the
Translation of Hebrew Literature
Jerusalem 2021/5781

Cover Design: Amir Zelcer
Cover illustration: Amir Zelcer
Typesetting: Optume Technologies

ISBN: 978-965-7023-52-5

1 3 5 7 9 8 6 4 2

Gefen Publishing House Ltd.
6 Hatzvi Street
Jerusalem 9438614,
Israel
972-2-538-0247
orders@gefenpublishing.com

Gefen Books
c/o Baker & Taylor Publisher Services
30 Amberwood Parkway
Ashland, Ohio 44805
516-593-1234
orders@gefenpublishing.com

www.gefenpublishing.com

Printed in Israel
Library of Congress Control Number: 2020925185

To Carol and Joey Lowe, the dearest of friends

To Carol and Joey I owe the dearest of friends

Careful writing is dead writing

– *Charles Bukowski*

Contents

Sleep My Child

– By Shalom Aleichem

Translated from Yiddish into Hebrew by Nava Semel
Translated into English by Gilah Kahn-Hoffmann

Sleep my child, my beauty
My crowning glory, succor of life
Slumber my son, the day will come
When you say Kaddish for my life.

Your mother sits beside you
A little song she'll sing to you
The day will come when you will ken
Why she keens for you.

A father lives in America
Yes, your father's there
And you are yet a child
Sleep Lulinka, unaware.

It is the Promised Land
The Garden of Eden, my tiny tot
Where they eat *challah* dipped in honey
Even when it's not *Shabbat*.

Twenty dollars he will send
Father will send a photo too
We two to the Garden of Eden
He will hasten to bring us too.

Until we see a letter from him
We will wait, so he won't forget
And now close your eyes my child
In dreams find joy and no regret.

My Lulinka Li.
My Luli, Luli, Li.

Prologue

Should we call this a love story?

It depends on how you look at it. As far as the woman is concerned it's about relentless love. A love unquenchable. It oscillated along a timeline for more than fifty years, crossing real – not just metaphorical – oceans which separated the couple, and intersected with the most crucial events of the twentieth century. This love had every reason to disappear, to evaporate, to fade, to perish, and yet, against all the odds, it survived.

If for the woman the story bordered on madness, from the man's perspective it was the complete opposite. From the fulfillment of an obligation to the desecration of vows, abandonment, and alienation.

So why insist on calling this a love story, when it was apparently ongoing mutual torture, differences, and contradictions? Because despite the heartbreak a glowing ember always persisted, something mystifying and concealed which kept these two people connected body and soul, even when they were thousands of miles apart.

The woman and the man in this story are my grandmother and grandfather – Fanny and Gabriel.

I only became aware of their tempestuous drama many years after they both had died. Desire, betrayal and lies, these were swept decisively under the rug – like the one that Fanny carried with her from Europe – and were not meant for the ears of children. And yet, with the intuitions of a spy in the body of a slight, young girl I perceived the clues and arranged the discarded details like a bouquet of dry flowers, attempting in adolescence to piece them together in an orderly display with a semblance of logic. Except that love, as we know, is anything but logical and there's no point in searching for a rationale, certainly not in this story, which if it wasn't true, could easily be dismissed as elaborate fiction.

To me, Fanny and Gabriel always seemed like characters in a novel, so that the only way to understand something of what transpired between them was to transform them into one, to clutch the handful of facts at my disposal, and fill in the gaps, as instructed by my father, their only son: "If something's missing, make it up."

In the single photograph depicting them as a young couple, Fanny and Gabriel are stern-faced, their body language tense, no visible warmth between them. There are those who might say that at the time the subjects were so attuned to the formality of that moment frozen in time that they held themselves in check and did not behave freely in front of the camera. They were smitten by the fear of eternity.

It seems to me that it is actually alienation that the photograph conveys.

Both are elegant, well-groomed, every hair in place. Each item of clothing was obviously chosen with care as befitted the occasion. Gabriel with his moustache – which makes him look a little older – wears a ring that is not a wedding band, while Fanny grasps a stylized bouquet of white flowers. Despite the possible implication of an impending marriage, her elegant dress is of a dark and shiny weave and decorated with pearls. Was the photograph taken to mark their engagement or after they married? Hard to tell. What stands out are the collars, his stiffened with starch, strangles him, while hers fans out to the sides and suggests wings.

The photographer seated them in the studio on a curved bench, perhaps to make them comfortable, or maybe to add a decorative element. Fanny gazes directly at the camera, while Gabriel's expression is glazed, as he looks off into the distance, beyond the frame.

As opposed to his hand which rests on his knee, her hands are entwined in her lap, part of the bouquet. The two will be photographed in the same pose in their old age.

In that future moment I will be present.

Forgive me Fanny and Gabriel – wherever you may be – for the liberties I take as I track your first-final love and attempt to decipher your deceptive relationship; for my efforts to delve backward into your world which was so different from mine. We don't communicate with one another by means of letters in a stamped envelope, the distances between continents have shrunk to a click, and relationship troubles are a respectable source of income for therapists, psychologists, consultants, mediators, lawyers and who knows who else. A new world. And yet, the old destinies of this man and woman, like two moons in a foreign sky, continue in their strange way to beam their reflected light on me.

The older I grow the more clearly I see that they instilled in me the unavoidable connection between love and abandonment and the question about the boundaries of love and how far we are willing to go for its sake. Their scar reverberates within me.

Fanny and Gabriel – were it not for them I wouldn't exist.

Were it not for their love and their hatred I wouldn't be who I am.

PART ONE

Prohibited to Us Those Who Are Betrothed

– Jewish Betrothal Blessing

1

Once upon a time in Bukovina. A fairytale name, like a literary invention, there's no point searching for it on a map, since it isn't a state or a country, but was a province of the Austro-Hungarian Empire before the First World War. Bukovina, which exists today only in the memories of those who lived there, remains the byword for individuals of discerning taste, possessed of wit and an ironic view of the world, seasoned with an acidic humor. It was the shared starting point for Fanny and Gabriel – both of them were born there.

Fanny loved the "land of the forests" that extended to the north of the Carpathian Mountains and nestled at their feet. Snow-capped ridges, deep ravines, meadows lush with greenery, rivers and rushing streams, and an abundance of oak, beech, and especially maple trees – called "*buk*" trees in the Slavic language, hence the name Bukovina.

Outside the house they spoke a polished German, while Yiddish was the language within. Eyes were always cast longingly toward Czernowitz, a miniature copy of glorious Vienna. Abraham Katz, Fanny's father, proudly dubbed it "Jerusalem on the River Prut," and advocated for enlightened Jewish learning that would go hand in hand with German heritage. He bought books of poetry by Goethe, Rilke, and Heine, but the height of his regard was reserved for the poet Paul Celan, a native of Czernowitz, who had become the symbol of modern German poetry. They had even met once, and he had exchanged a few words with Celan. Abraham's three daughters preferred the opera singer Joseph Schmidt, who despite his short stature appeared on the finest stages and was a star of the silver screen, in addition to being the cantor of the synagogue.

"And what does he do when he has to kiss his glamorous co-star?" wondered Paula, the middle sister.

"They stand him on a special footstool," Fanny replied, asserting that she would only agree to marry a man who was taller than she was.

Marriage – that was the main topic of conversation among the sisters. On Herrengasse, the main street of Czernowitz, they promenaded up and down in their finery before the men sitting in the cafés, eating the mille-feuille, custard-layered French pastry with cream, and the Kaiserschmarren shredded pancake dipped in fruit compote. This latter dessert was named for Austrian Emperor Franz Joseph I, Fanny the cooking aficionado explained to her sisters, and he would wolf down his wife Sissi's portion as well, since she was known to watch her figure.

"Why must a woman strive to be beautiful for a man?" asked Lizzie, the youngest.

"There is no lack of men who strive to look handsome for women," Fanny retorted, although she couldn't actually think of any she knew.

Gabriel was much less impressed by the saccharine love story about Franz Joseph and Sissi. "Romantic nonsense that appeals to simpletons," was how he described it to his sister Anna, advising her not to emulate kings and movie stars.

Neither Fanny nor Gabriel came from Czernowitz proper. He was born in the village of Mihova, and she in the town of Siret.

In the competition between his village and her town she emerged victorious. Siret, which is part of Romania today, was more important than Mihova, which is now part of Ukraine, and this is because it was a crossroads on the trade routes between the Black Sea and the Baltic. A river separated the village from the town, perhaps foreshadowing things to come.

On a steamy summer's day in 1914, Gabriel crossed the river and strode along the main street of Siret, which was very similar to the main street of Mihova. Dressed in his best suit – which was reserved for the Sabbath and holidays – he passed between opposing rows of two-storey houses, surrounded by well-tended gardens with lilac bushes planted out front. Before a window adorned with a lace curtain and a line of flower pots he debated whether to pick a posy to present as a polite token to his hosts and then decided against it. He didn't want to appear too eager. If there was any excitement on his part about the step that he was about to take, he capably subdued it. To exhibit restraint at all times – that was what he had learned from his father who would reproach his mother, a native of Odessa, "Russians are an overly emotional people." The youth of twenty was on his way to propose marriage to Fanny, whom he had never met before.

The matchmaker had decreed, "She will suit you."

He listed her virtues: eighteen years old, responsible, serious, dedicated to her family – there was also a brother, a prodigy, who was at a yeshiva in Vienna – but mainly, she was industrious. Everyone affirmed how hard she toiled from morning to night in the family business. There was a filling machine in the cellar and Fanny was considered the expert at bottling the beer that came from the brewery of the German Julius Baile. She also knew how to haggle with the farmers on the weekly market day – the matchmaker embellished the praise of his human merchandise. Not to mention her cooking, which was renowned throughout the province. "You'll be licking your fingers after sampling her pickled herring in cream sauce."

Gabriel didn't care for herring. Too smelly for his taste.

And what about her appearance? He suspected that they were proposing an ugly girl, and so he asked for details about her sisters instead. Paula, the middle sister, for example. Rumor had it that she was beautiful and of a pleasant disposition. The matchmaker insisted that she was already the intended of the goldsmith Emil Stein, and in any case, Abraham Katz would never violate the order of the matches. And Lizzie, Gabriel had heard that she was all fire and flame. No, the young one's time had not yet come the matchmaker brooked no argument, and her outlook was overly modern. She tended toward the suffragette movement that demanded the vote for women, and a spouse like that was serious trouble.

He stood firm – the eldest first. It's true that Fanny wasn't celebrated for her breathtaking appearance, but it is well known that within beauty lies sin, and who wants to become entangled in temptations and jealousy which will only hinder a marriage? Besides, why do the young men of today wish to marry only pretty women? Why, when he's sleeping a man doesn't see his wife at all, and when he's dining his eyes are glued to his plate, and in the *beit midrash* he isn't obliged to opine about any woman, and when he is at work, she is not by his side. So if he meets her for only a few moments before leaving the house in the morning, and upon his return in the evening, what should he care whether his wife is beautiful or ugly? In any case, all cats are black in the nighttime, as the saying goes. Fanny is reasonable looking and even-tempered. A fair deal.

A deal – that's how it all began. A pragmatic issue and not something infused with romance or desire. That was the only model Gabriel knew – matchmaking – from the dawn of mankind. When he was a child, his father had explained to him that not only did the Creator of the world match Eve to Adam, but it was He who created her for him by special order, and it was according to his measurements that she was fashioned. Her entire being was designated solely for the man. A helpmate by his side. And until she bore him children, she didn't even have a name, and Adam referred to her as "the woman whom You gave to be with me."

A woman is given. A woman is handed over. A woman is not chosen. Marriage, offspring, a secure vocation – these were the stations in the life of every young Jew, obligations to be fulfilled. If Gabriel had dreams, they tended in a different direction. He wanted to make money. One day he would buy himself a car – what a fabulous invention – like the Ford Model T he had seen in the newsreel bulletins at the cinema in Czernowitz. Every three minutes a car was manufactured at the factory in Chicago in the state of Illinois, the narrator announced, and Gabriel learned a new concept – the "assembly line."

"Only in America," he heard a whispered sigh from behind him in the darkness.

Chicago, Illinois, America – to Gabriel these seemed to be beyond the mountains of darkness. His rebelliousness, like his dreams, was still locked deep within him. The untimely death of his father, the lumber merchant, did not permit any deviation from the mold, and he surrendered to the pressure brought to bear by his mother to establish a family and stand on his own two feet. The widow Herzig was in need of another pair of capable hands. His sister Anna was still a child and couldn't shoulder the burden of earning a living. Gabriel would marry Fanny or another, provided that she was an even-tempered woman from a decent family who would be a helpmate by his side for the expansion of the business. After all, someone had to travel to Odessa, the mother's birthplace, to sell the merchandise, and Gabriel spoke a very good Russian.

Everything was explained to him in advance. Nothing was kept from him, although the matchmaker did play down the candidate's less-endearing trait. She's stiff necked, chorused the gossips, although it was possible that the source of the rumor lay with the customers, who knew Fanny as a tough negotiator who did not give in to their pressure to register debt on credit. Either way, the matchmaker exempted himself from the obligation to report this hearsay. While stubbornness is the corridor that connects between paradise and hell, this was a young girl who had yet to complete her adolescence, and there was no doubt that a husband's instruction would steer her in the proper direction and dissolve any remnant of recalcitrance.

Still, no one coerced Gabriel to choose Fanny over any other. She was but one among the pool of options.

Beads of perspiration slid under his shirt in the heat of the day, while he wiped his damp palms on his trousers, hoping that his handshake with the father of the bride-to-be wouldn't feel too slippery. He had to convince the future father-in-law that he would be a worthy husband, who would support his eldest daughter and see to her every need.

He crossed the Ringplatz – the Ring Square – passed by the Annahof Hotel and entered the Kirchgasse, the Alley of the Church, popularly known as the "Jewish Matchmaking Market," because there as well the girls would gather in groups and walk back and forth under the gaze of the boys who surveyed the goods.

Unlike others engaged in the matchmaking process, who trembled in terror before the intimate encounter with a woman, Gabriel wasn't worried. Although the entirety of his sexual experience was derived from a visit to a whore in Czernowitz – a woman of abundant bosom possessed of a gold tooth – she had showered his performance with praise, and thrown in a few delights free of charge following the act, even though she had already received her full reward. When he left, as she promised a substantial discount for further assignations, the prostitute told her colleagues, in Gabriel's presence, that the young client was a natural. Who knew, maybe one day he would play a women's idol in the movies. He wouldn't need a stool to stand on like the heartthrob Joseph Schmidt.

Fanny's reaction to Gabriel was very similar to that of the whore's, although she saw him fully clothed. Even before he entered the house her breath caught in her throat when she peeked at him in secret through the window, from her hiding place behind the curtains. That fleeting glance at Gabriel standing in the street sealed her fate.

This was her man.

There are those who say that love at first sight is a battered concept that exists only in romantic novels, however, since Fanny was a big fan of that type of literature and was known to read at least three such volumes a week, for her the idea was real and valid.

She did not blame the wave of heat that overcame her on the spate of unseasonably warm weather that had graced Bukovina. She placed her hand on her chest, which was squashed into a corset, fluttered her fingers in the air, and without waiting for a formal invitation, descended from the living quarters while smoothing her long dress tight over her body and holding herself erect.

Gabriel, who stood in the entrance, hadn't yet had a chance to remove his hat. He was tall, just as she wished, and gave her a polite nod. She didn't see his eyes, and they also didn't have the chance to exchange a word for the matchmaker burst in at that very moment, mopping his damp, perspiring face and blaming the weather for his tardiness.

"Jews can't live in the heat," he sighed, "The Jewish brain must always be ventilated."

None of those present joined in his laughter, and so he hurried to introduce Gabriel, uttering superfluous adjectives – "an illustrious yeshiva student" – he wasn't especially gifted; "from a distinguished family" – they had no assets, and were not the descendants of a well-known rabbinic dynasty; while he described Abraham Katz as a Vizhnitz Chassid, close to the Admor, which was perfectly true.

The conversation progressed ponderously, and was filled with silences. Gabriel provided businesslike responses in economical language, fully aware of Fanny's glances. Indeed, she wasn't beautiful, but she was far from ugly. Her eyes were a shade of deep brown, and he noticed that they were framed by exceptionally long lashes.

Her silky hair was tied back, and one stray curl had escaped and fell over her temple. Her skin was fresh, as though polished, and the scent of lilacs emanated from her. She sat opposite him, rigid in her chair, her limbs taut. Ever since his visit to the prostitute Gabriel had learned to study the outline of female breasts and he registered the swell of the firm breasts within the corset, and could already imagine losing himself in her curves. He would no longer have to empty his pockets to finance a gold-toothed whore. Even her teeth did not escape him, his furtive examination leading to the happy discovery of two white, flawless rows. And the admiration that her father bestowed on her – he called her "my treasure" – convinced Gabriel that Fanny wasn't as spineless as the others who had been offered to him by the matchmaker in the past.

The German in her mouth was flawless, and she answered his questions in language as compact as his own. He asked if she played the piano that stood in the parlor. No. The German "Bechstein" had been imported specially from Vienna for Lizzie, the youngest. The fact that the greater part of his savings was invested in it, Abraham Katz chose not to mention, along with Lizzie's support for women's rights. Unconventional views in a family could easily sabotage a match.

The two younger sisters peeked into the room through a crack in the door. Paula entered with a tray upon which were arrayed glasses of brandy. She was certainly lovely, fair haired, with the same dark brown almond eyes, but too pale for his taste. Then Lizzie was invited to play a Chopin polonaise while the terms were dictated to the clapping of hands. Abraham Katz would provide the couple with living arrangements on the top floor, and the dowry would include a set of porcelain dishes made in Germany, four eiderdowns, two blankets of goose feathers, and linen sheets embroidered with monograms.

When Abraham Katz shook the hand of the intended groom – which was a bit damp – Gabriel rose from his chair. Fanny remained seated, gazing at him, her hands still folded in her lap, masking the tumult within.

There were several things he would have liked to ask her. Did she have any dreams? And what was her opinion about the wide world? Would she be willing to distance herself from her father's house for his sake? But he was twenty years old and he didn't dare to ask a thing.

Two days later they regrouped, this time in full force. Abraham Katz broke porcelain plates for luck, and the widow Herzig gave the betrothed young woman a sapphire studded ring, consigned the fee to the matchmaker's hand, and requested that the earliest possible date be set for the wedding. Fanny was already thinking ahead, and on the spot vowed to herself that she would not cut off her hair and don a wig. Gabriel would stroke her hair directly, with no barrier in between. She imagined his hand clutching her hair, intertwined in it, and his fingers penetrating with slow caresses to the very roots. She sat facing him, shuddering with the power of her imagination. That engine was set in motion inside her, with great intensity.

But Gabriel didn't have the chance to get to know his intended, not even once did he meet Fanny alone, and he never had the opportunity to ask her even one question. Two and a half million soldiers from across the empire were mobilized for the war that broke out – and he among them. A

Serbian nationalist shot the heir to the Austrian throne, the Archduke Franz Ferdinand, and his wife Sophie in the city of Sarajevo, and craving revenge Austria declared war on Serbia.

The train station in Czernowitz was decked out like a carnival. Flags and ribbons fluttered from the tops of buildings, and strains of marching music could be heard from every direction. The recruits walked in formation, waving to the cheering crowd.

The widow Herzig and little Anna accompanied Gabriel to the platform, and the girl declaimed, echoing the cries sounded in the streets, "By Christmas you'll be home!" The mother altered the festival to "by Rosh Hashanah, the Jewish New Year," wrapped a thick wool scarf around Gabriel's neck and begged him not to commit any unnecessary feats of heroism. He tore off the scarf, "Don't worry, Mother. I'll be back before the winter." He, too, was certain that he was embarking upon a short-term adventure, perhaps even one that would add some vitality to his life before he settled down. If he had known how many winters would pass before he returned home he would have smashed his leg with a hammer to evade the imperial conscription order.

A man with a first name identical to his own transformed his life completely. The assassin who changed the world order was only slightly younger than he was, and his name was Gavrilo Princip.

World War I broke out, and the marriage of Gabriel and Fanny was postponed indefinitely.

2

Gabriel hated the army, and he loathed the war even more.

He already had the commander's speech memorized: "Bukovina is the frontline against the Russians, allies of damned Serbia. And may their leader, General Aleksei Brusilov, be damned as well. But we, the Austro-Hungarians, have massed four armies against them, thirty-five infantry divisions, and eleven cavalry divisions. You, dear soldiers, are part of a mighty army waging an exalted war."

Major Klaus Von-Hoffenberg took pains to repeat these tiresome details again and again for the entire duration of the training period, and to roar,

"Our victory is assured!" when he was done. Gabriel was swept up, against his will, in the shouting, despite not being at all confident of that victory.

He was surrounded by men speaking a multitude of tongues, but fortunately for him, the members of the officers' corps spoke German, which allowed him to function as intermediary between Von-Hoffenberg and the soldiers conscripted from across the empire. Gabriel's fluency in Romanian, Hungarian, and Russian, which he had learned from his Odessa-born mother, made him the commander's official translator.

Von-Hoffenberg, a native of Salzburg and admirer of Mozart, who hailed from the same city, was deeply impressed by the polished German of the corporal from Bukovina. And especially by his ability to recite Goethe's ballad about the father and son riding through the dark forest, pursued by the cruel Elven King.

> "I love thee, I'm charm'd by thy beauty, dear boy! And if thou'rt unwilling, then force I'll employ."
> "My father, my father, he seizes me fast! For sorely the Erl-King has hurt me at last."

The major even wiped a tear from his eye as he listened to the ballad's chilling conclusion, when the child is left dead in the arms of his father, and even when Gabriel disclosed that he was a Jew, he didn't alter his attitude toward him.

In fact, there was no need for the commander to encourage the Jewish new recruits to fight, for they had received their conscription notices with enthusiasm and demonstrable patriotism. Sixty-eight years of the Emperor Franz Joseph's stable rule and the equal rights they enjoyed gave them a sense of fraternity and shared destiny. For them it was a privilege to serve their esteemed emperor and to help him to defeat Russia. Von-Hoffenberg laughed when Gabriel told him that Franz-Joseph had even been the recipient of an affectionate Jewish nickname – *Freum Yossel* – Yossel the Righteous.

The commander also had no difficulty convincing the Jews that Russia was a bitter enemy. From the start they resented the country because of the edicts about the Pale of Settlement and the countless upheavals that took place in the name of the Czar. Besides, wasn't it a mitzvah to fight to the death against an entity infected with the scourge of anti-Semitism?

However, Gabriel did not display enthusiasm about the order that had disrupted his plans. No wedding, no livelihood, and better not to even think about a secure future.

After ten weeks of training, which included military marching, firing ranges, bayonet practice, grenade throwing, trench digging, and crawling under barbed wire, he was stationed at the front. The lone Jew in the company. His uniform chafed his skin. The stink of battle and the stench of horse manure clung to him. The battle rations were inedible, and forget about keeping kosher. He didn't make any friends, was compelled to hear innumerable anti-Semitic jokes and to restrain himself from responding to the provocations about being "a man with a chopped-off organ."

The lice assailed him no less than the enemy forces, cunningly circumventing the hand grenades on his belt, and the bayoneted rifle he carried on his shoulder. He scratched until he drew blood, cursing Austria's arrogant generals and their ally the German Emperor Wilhelm II, who had dragged him into their mad game of honor and prestige.

On each day that he managed to evade another Russian shell and one more bullet he declaimed *hagomel*, the blessing recited upon deliverance from danger, and pleaded with the Holy One Blessed Be He that he wouldn't die in a war that wasn't his.

Only the connection he had forged with his commander somewhat ameliorated his daily routine. His recitations of Goethe earned him better food rations from the officers' mess, and Von-Hoffenberg even began to smuggle in high-quality tobacco for him from the supply depot. At first Gabriel smoked to mask the stench of the rotting flesh that caused him constant nausea, then he became addicted, and to his last day he skillfully rolled his own cigarettes with Chesterfield tobacco, his fingertips stained golden-brown.

He also rolled cigarettes for his commander, and their nightly smoke became their reprieve between the battles. Von-Hoffenberg still clung to the hope that the war would be over in a week, as the German Emperor had boasted.

But as the weeks lengthened into months, so did Von-Hoffenberg sink into melancholy. He started to bring bottles of schnapps along for the nightly respite and drain them one after the other. He constantly spoke of his yearning for his beloved city Salzburg, and in his drunken state would sing arias from Mozart's opera *The Magic Flute*, with grating dissonance. Despite having been born in a musical capital, he possessed not a shred of talent, and when he moved on to sing the women's roles in the opera, especially the famous aria sung by the Queen of the Night, it was clear to Gabriel that the commander had lost his hope that the war would be over soon.

His voice was hoarse from an abundance of cigarettes and schnapps, and his singing sounded like the whistle of a falling shell.

"Are you listening to me, Corporal Herzig?"

"Yes, sir. You sing beautifully. You have a future on the stage. One day you will be famous."

"Definitely. And you will be an illustrious general. The victorious Jewboy of Europe. Why do they call you Herzig, anyway? How did a Jew come by such a 'lovely' name?"

In the middle of the night, as the Russian forces opposite prepared for the next battle, Gabriel found himself telling his commander about the day when the imperial clerk, charged with choosing names for the Jewish subjects, arrived in the far-flung village of Mihova. Why, in the name of Jesus, did Jews have to be given family names at all, he fumed, when they could all be called "Jewboy son of Jewboy," and that would be that.

Weary from the vicissitudes of the long journey and downhearted at the sight of the miserable village, he hastily entered in his notebook new names for the residents according to their vocations. The shoemaker received the name "Schuster," the tailor became "Schneider," the glazier "Glaser," and the bookbinder "Buchbinder." Only the haughty town elder, who refused to host the clerk at his inn, received in revenge the name "Arsch," which means "buttocks."

Von-Hoffenberg laughed. What a serious blow, to bequeath such a demeaning surname to your descendants. Better to remain without a name at all. Gabriel was feeling no less exhausted than the imperial clerk by his family lore, but the commander demanded that he continue.

When Gabriel's grandmother heard what had happened to her husband, she panicked. The thought that her descendants would forever carry the degrading stain of a name like "buttocks" ignited a flash of inspiration. She sent her husband to the river, where he caught a fat fish. After that the grandparents invited the clerk to their home and even gave up their bed with the soft feather quilt for his comfort. They, themselves, slept outside on the hard earth in the freezing cold. The grandmother prepared a meal for the clerk that was fit for a king; fish roasted in onion, garlic, and tomatoes. The clerk licked his fingers, until all that remained on his plate was the exposed skeleton of his dinner.

"I will recommend you for the position of assistant cook in the palace in Vienna," he declared, "Even though you are a Jewess."

And so, with a full stomach and a resounding belch he bestowed upon them the family name "Herzig" and entered it in his notebook with a flourish, as though it was at the very least a title of nobility.

If he had changed just one letter and called Gabriel's grandparents "Herzog" instead, then they really could have passed themselves off as counts. But "Herzig" would have to do. That was their name from then on.

The tale concluded, Von-Hoffenberg asked Gabriel to roll one more cigarette for him, and he obeyed the order with trembling fingers. Soon it would be daybreak and the battles would recommence. If heaven forfend he should doze off during a bombardment it would be the end of him.

"Don't worry, Corporal Herzig. When the war is over I'll take you with me to Salzburg and appoint you my personal clerk. You're a man after my own heart."

Gabriel didn't view himself as someone likely to be endeared to his fellow creatures, especially in his current dismal circumstances, when he had to pick the lice off his privates, and when the stink rising from his socks could discourage even the most tenacious trench rats. Why, oh Master of the Universe, were the German soldiers the only ones to receive a change of socks in their kitbag?

"Tomorrow I will get you some clean socks," promised Von-Hoffenberg.

Gabriel crushed the end of the cigarette with the butt of his rifle and saluted his commander, hoping that the other would understand the hint. It was the last chance to grab a nap before the morning attack began.

However, Von-Hoffenberg was not ready to release his subordinate. Now he instructed him to sing him a Jewish song.

"What luck that you aren't Corporal 'Arse,'" he said. "No woman would consent to marry you with a name like that. Now sing me a lullaby."

Although Gabriel was not blessed with musical talent either, it was not possible to refuse an order from a commanding officer.

Von-Hoffenberg dragged him over to the latrine, and with his pants round his ankles, as he emptied his bowels, he listened to the only tune that

Gabriel could conjure up at that moment, "When the Rebbe sings – all the Chassidim sing."

He sang in Yiddish. And by the time he reached the last verse, the commander had picked up the melody and joined in, humming along, out of tune, with the Chassidic song, bare-assed and not comprehending a single word.

And when the Rebbe cries
When the Rebbe cries
All the Chassidim cry
Ya ba ba ba bum
All the Chassidim cry

And so Gabriel and Klaus Von-Hoffenberg sang a duet in the latrine, until the thunder of the cannons cut them off. On that particular morning the Russian artillery fire started earlier than usual. They barely made it back to the trench in time.

3

Attack, counter-attack, over and over again in a never-ending loop. More than once Gabriel played dead and cleaved to the earth. His terrified inhalations filled his lungs with dust. Once the barrage of shell-fire was over he coughed and spat mud.

The longer the battles continued, the more lost he felt. What did this war have to do with him? How had he become entangled in a snarl of foreign interests that transformed him into a pawn on the chessboard of "the corpse of the Danube," the nickname for the Austro-Hungarian empire among those who despised it. From day to day he felt that his life was hanging in the balance. Sometimes, when he awoke from a fitful sleep, he didn't know whether he was dead or alive.

At first, confronted by the corpses scattered across the crater-strewn battlefield, between the trenches and the mounds of dirt, he would murmur, "Finds a sure rest in the Divine," but he soon kept his mouth shut. No rest and no Divine.

The cries of the dying, "Mother!" "Father!" would pursue him his entire life, and when, many years later, he would see his grandson in an Israel Defense Forces uniform, he would discharge a venomous curse against leaders who send innocent youths to war, never disclosing what they should expect.

Like Gabriel, Von-Hoffenberg also appeared more lost from day to day, and his efforts to motivate and inspire his charges fell flat. The soldiers, of a range of nationalities, did not exhibit any loyalty to the ebbing empire, and in August 1914, a group of Czechoslovakians defected to the Czar's army. Soon other defectors hurried to join the French Foreign Legion.

In April 1915, two more companies of the Royal Regiment number 28, defected to the Russian side with their officers. In a gruff voice, Von-Hoffenberg read out the daily order from Emperor Franz Joseph, "No company will ever be as morally corrupt as to abandon the battlefield and betray the homeland."

Morally poisoned and a traitor is he who drags people off to an empty war in the name of a false ideal, thought Gabriel. To get away. The idea began to take root in his mind.

But the fear of the military police, with their expertise in capturing deserters, paralyzed him. He had already seen those brought handcuffed before a military judge who remained at a safe distance from the front, and sentenced them to death by firing squad. No. The risk was too great.

On the day when the commander instructed them in how to defend themselves against gas attacks, Gabriel again reflected on the idea of deserting. Artillery shells that contained tear gas were fired at the Russian forces stationed at the Rawka River, but due to the low temperature the gas froze instead of evaporating and the attack failed. The chlorine gas used in April and May 1915 was more successful in its mission of slaughter, and Von-Hoffenberg ordered those under his command to cover their noses and mouths with a handkerchief soaked in water. "Soon a supply of gas masks will arrive, made in Germany," he made the festive promise to the soldiers, while confiding to Gabriel that the effectiveness of the handkerchief defense was improved if you saturated it in urine. Every night Gabriel found himself standing by the latrine and emptying the contents of his bladder on a cloth he used to clean his gun. His body's waste is his means of defense? Maybe he should cover his skin in shit to block out the poisons? To what depths would he sink?

Damned warmongers, he cursed, if only your urine would be transformed into tears.

He rolled himself another consoling cigarette by the latrine. For rolling paper he used one of the posters that were distributed by the War Ministry on the frontlines and on the home front. It depicted a sergeant and a private attacking an enemy firing position together. The cheery-looking caption read: "An exemplary case of fortitude on the battlefield." Gabriel usually used the patriotic posters to wipe his butt, although the ink made his tattered underpants stick to his skin.

Patriotism my ass, he said to himself as he sucked on the ever-diminishing cigarette.

Suddenly a sob could be heard from behind one of the huts. At first he thought it was another miserable soldier who had drowned his terror of death in schnapps and was about to shoot a bullet through his head.

The whimpering continued, and he realized that the sobbing man was mumbling in German. He crept softly behind the hut and to his amazement discovered his commander, kneeling on the crater-pocked ground whispering fragments of sentences to a wrinkled photograph that he kissed again and again. The saliva from his lips gleamed in the beams of the searchlights that scanned the sky to expose enemy planes.

"If I should ever lose you, will you be able then to go to sleep?"

A Rilke poem. Gabriel recognized it immediately.

Even when he leaned over Von-Hoffenberg, attempting to drag him toward the officers' quarters, the major wouldn't let go of the photograph, and as if possessed by a dybbuk, continued to mumble the following lines: "…saying words as tender as eyelids that come to rest weightlessly upon your breast, upon your sleeping limbs, upon your lips?"

"Herr Major, you must control yourself."

Gabriel addressed him with authority, while at the same time taking care not to exceed the boundaries of the required distance to be maintained between an officer and a simple soldier.

However, Von-Hoffenberg eliminated all distance, pressing his fists into Gabriel's shoulders – the bayonet swinging between them – and Gabriel felt the edges of the photograph scraping against the bristles on his face.

"My love, *mein liebling*. I must return to you."

"Herr Major, calm yourself…"

"I haven't done anything…"

"Herr Major… your whole life is ahead of you."

"I have never lain with a woman. I will die a virgin."

At least I managed that, thought Gabriel. For the first time he thought of Fanny. The engagement had also been erased by the war. Only the outline of her breasts hidden within the corset remained.

On one of their rare furloughs the soldiers and officers had attended a performance in one of the neighboring villages. Gabriel was invited to join them. During the dance the captivating women kicked their legs high. Beneath the whirling dresses they weren't wearing underclothes. Unlike his fellow soldiers, Gabriel was not equipped with field glasses, and so he missed the sight of those who shaved their genitals, as was the Tatar custom. Still, the detailed description provided by the others, who saw it all as if from the front row, inspired not only his furtive masturbation when on guard duty, but the entire battalion. Von-Hoffenberg was the only officer who refused to attend the performance. There were more than a few kind souls who gossiped that the officer actually preferred men, but the truth of the matter was that he actually remained scrupulously faithful to one woman.

"Look at my *liebling*," he urged Gabriel, "Is she not the most beautiful woman in the world?"

Von-Hoffenberg held up the photograph in front of Gabriel's eyes.

The red umbrella of the bombing illuminated the portrait of a woman with a sharp nose, fleshy cheeks, small sunken eyes, and thin lips gaping in an exaggerated smile above a string of pearls adorning a high collar.

Von-Hoffenberg wasn't satisfied with the brief showing of his *liebling*, and insisted on positioning it under the next barrage of light from the sky so that Gabriel could appreciate it in improved conditions, but this did not present the woman in a kinder light. She was and remained an unlovely creature. Why, in God's name, had the major chosen her of all women?

At that very moment the sound of an explosion shook the air around them.

Even the shelling did nothing to interrupt the commander's longing for his *liebling*. He was focused on her to such an extent that he didn't bother to take cover, and Gabriel pushed the photograph away, dragged Von-Hoffenberg to the nearest trench and shielded him with his body. The shell's impact deafened them both, and in that moment the commander pulled himself together. He slipped away from Gabriel and righted his helmet that had been knocked askew as he tried to reach the photograph that had been blown outside the trench.

"You saved my life, corporal."

Gabriel was silent.

As the major promised him that he would be guest of honor at his wedding and dance a waltz with the bride, and this despite the fact that he was a Jew, a second shell exploded, this time right next to them. The ground shook with the blast as clods of earth broke apart and rained down. More splinters of fire flickered in the air. Gabriel hurled himself face first to the ground. In the grip of his terror he wet himself.

"I will come to your wedding, Herr Major," Gabriel stammered through a mouthful of earth. "Your *liebling* really is the most beautiful woman in the world."

He stood up, but in the chaos around him he couldn't make out the commander.

His outstretched arms encountered something. Gabriel cast about like a blind man, and the wetness spread from his groin down the legs of his pants, hindering his movement. Drops of urine slid down his thighs beneath his uniform and were absorbed into his filthy socks. Maybe he would manage to wash himself between this barrage and the next one. It was at just that moment, stinking of urine, when he suddenly remembered the scent of lilacs that wafted from Fanny.

When he finally managed to stand upright, Gabriel saw the ruined body of the commander, half inside the trench and half outside. The face was unscathed, the eyes open wide. They wore an expression of incomprehension, such as one might see in the eyes of a child who has received a scolding but doesn't understand what he's done wrong or why this is happening. The photograph lay close by, its edges trembling in the light breeze between attacks. Unthinking, without pausing for even a second, Gabriel snatched it up and began to run toward the darkness.

4

When he deserted he didn't even know that he had deserted.

Gabriel's next actions were pure instinct with no premeditation. With the aid of the pliers attached to his belt he cut the barbed wire and crossed over on his belly to the other side, seeking all the while to evade the non-stop patrols. He had to circumvent the fortifications and the trenches where the Russians lay in wait. A ghastly mirror-image of what he knew so well from his side. The same depths of human degradation, the same meaningless lust to kill.

He continued to crawl slowly, keeping his breathing shallow. A sniper spotting suspicious movement would kill him on the spot, for those dug-in in the opposite trenches as well, those referred to as "the enemy" by all, were as terrified as he was. Unlike his commanders, Gabriel did not view the soldiers on the opposing side as bloodthirsty monsters, but as simple, ordinary people, caught up in the inferno against their will. Exactly as he was, they were trapped in the identical horror of death and ached with longing for their previous lives. At the same time, the thought of being taken prisoner by the Russians made him shudder.

It was enough to think of those whom his own side had taken prisoner, louse-infested and starving, poking their fingers through the coils of barbed wire and begging their captors in broken language for a cigarette butt or a scrap of food.

He would not become a shadow of a man in a Russian POW camp. He had to survive, no matter what.

As he stooped close to the ground, he saw himself in the guise of the snake in the Garden of Eden, condemned to crawl along on its belly. The front raged both ahead of him and behind, making the air vibrate. The barrages continued to pound the earth and the fragments flashed above his head. He bypassed the Russian mortar positions, located behind a stand of felled poplar trees, and the supply trucks that looked like the silhouettes of animals, as his body reacted with uncontrollable shaking to the shriek of every shell.

"And by thy sword shalt thou live," the words said to Esau in the Book of Genesis reverberated within him.

The verse should be changed to, "And by thy sword shalt thou die," was the thought that flitted through his head. Verses from the Five Books of the Torah that he had memorized at heder popped into his head as he ran, and his memory filled in the words that followed, "…thou shalt shake his yoke from off thy neck," as Gabriel drew from it validation that he had done the right thing.

For hours he kept moving, paying no attention to where he was going. He tripped over blackened tree stumps and walked into smashed trees, stumbled in craters in the scarred and pocked earth, and only when he began to encounter bushy branches and an abundance of green leaves did his breathing start to return to normal. He never stopped moving. Onward and onward. Like the migratory birds with their inbuilt navigational systems, impelled toward the rural areas of Russia, far from those who hunted down deserters and a safe distance from the front.

Only when his lungs were taking in air untainted by gunpowder and the remnants of shelling did he stop, but he remained in a crouch. In fear of being discovered, he tried to quiet his breathing, but his breaths erupted like lava from a volcano. He placed his hand on his chest to quell the pounding within, not believing that he was out of danger.

Dawn rose, grey as an apron that has been washed innumerable times, and beneath the smoky sky Gabriel buried his ammunition belt and his grenades among some juniper bushes. He held onto the gun and the bullets. Who knew when he might need them?

It seemed to him that Von-Hoffenberg's gaping eyes continued to stare at him from every direction. He saw them in the fields, in the trunks of the birch and the leaves of the poplar trees, and even in the clouds rent by the planes. He murmured defiantly in their direction, "Unmerciful God."

When he stood, he barely managed to straighten his back. A sharp pain cut through him. In the coming years he was particular about his posture, walking straight and somewhat stiffly, and each time he bent to tie his shoes a dim echo of that pain would make itself felt, a souvenir of his deserter's flight on his belly. As far as he was concerned he had expelled himself, and not from the Garden of Eden but from Hell. Russia, into which he fled, would be his Tree of Knowledge.

He didn't yet dare approach populated areas, and so he chose to move in the opposite direction to the supply convoys, careful to keep to the untamed edges, and continued to cross more and more of the grey and white woods.

In a thick grove he found a blanket and a basket containing leftover bread. Perhaps they had belonged to a couple looking for a secluded spot. For an entire day he huddled under the blanket trying to get some rest but his nerves were so frayed that he didn't manage to close his eyes and he was plagued by convulsions, as if the battlefield still raged within his body.

When he rummaged in the basket searching for more crumbs he found a woman's handkerchief and a wilted bouquet. For a moment he could conjure them before his eyes. A man and a woman making love in the heart of nature, turning their backs on the mutual slaughter that was taking place nearby. He hoped they hadn't been killed on their way home.

When all the bread was gone, Gabriel placed the basket exactly where he had found it, replacing the handkerchief and the drooping bouquet. He was on the move again, surviving on blackberries, wild berries and crops that he plucked from the edges of the fields. He worked over the grains with his teeth for a long time, as though he was chewing his cud, impersonating an animal in the densest bushes. For some reason he made sure to recite the blessing, *borei pri ha'adamah* ("Creator of the fruit of the earth").

Only when he discerned the trickling sound of water did he strip off his uniform that still reeked of urine and gunpowder, and set off in search of its source. He immersed himself in the stream he discovered, scrubbing his body with bunches of leaves. "The Almighty has made me a pure mikveh," he whispered to a fish that swam by. The water that washed away the blood and the traces of urine soothed his bruises to some extent, and soon he dropped to the ground, his naked body caressed by the smooth vegetation. Only then did he manage to close his eyes and sink into a short nap.

The rank smell coming off his uniform roused him and he ripped off every sign and indication that he had ever been an Austrian soldier – he used his teeth – and just before he washed it in the stream the photograph of the commander's *liebling* fell out of one of the pockets. Gabriel was surprised. He didn't even remember snatching it up before he deserted. He examined the woman, this time in daylight. She still looked entirely unappealing.

A wave of pity washed over him for the woman who didn't know that her betrothed would never return to her. For the briefest of moments Fanny flitted through his thoughts. He placed the photograph carefully on the bank of the stream, inside a bush, so that it wouldn't fall into the water. Maybe one day he would manage to return it to the woman who Von-Hoffenberg had loved so much.

He didn't wait for his uniform to dry. Those in pursuit of the deserters never rested from the hunt. Despite his exhaustion he had to keep going, and so he wore his uniform wet. The prickly cloth stuck to his skin and hindered his movements. Still, he took the time to reclaim the photograph of the *liebling* watching him from the riverbank. He buried it in his damp pocket, turned to the fish swimming in the stream, counted ten for a minyan and said the Kaddish prayer for his commander.

Someone had to pray for his soul, even if the deceased wasn't a Jew. "He Who creates peace in His celestial heights, may He create peace for us and for all the world; and say, Amen."

5

The house in Bukovina was also transformed into a battlefront. In September 1914, the Czar's soldiers, under the command of General Evreimow, entered Czernowitz conquering Siret on their way. The Austrian army dug in to the south of the town, and there were battles in the streets. A mass exodus began. The wealthy left for Vienna, and Abraham Katz and his daughters chose to flee to the Moravia region, far from all the fronts, where they found refuge with a Christian family named Schindler, perhaps relatives of the Oskar Schindler who became renowned as a savior of Jews during the next world war.

During the months of exile as well, Fanny waited for word from the front. When the Russian forces retreated, and the Austrian army regained control of Siret, the father and his daughters also returned to the ghost town. Their income was meager, and Fanny went back to bottling beer in the cellar. At night she sat at the writing desk, by the piano that Lizzie refused to play, and filled pages with her cramped handwriting.

Fanny sent three letters to the front. The first, immediately after Gabriel's conscription, was responded to in the same economical and polite language that he had employed during their only meeting. He signed formally, "Gabriel Herzig," and made no mention of their engagement.

Her next letter, sent before the Russian takeover, returned with the stamp "address unknown," and the response to her third letter had yet to arrive.

The postal services were disrupted during those calamitous days she tried to reassure herself, and letters had been stranded for long months because of the battles. "Stubborn as a dybbuk," her father took to calling her, but she wasn't offended. She would never cry, "Out, dybbuk, out" to her stubborn nature. And when he began to look at her askance, she said, "Gabriel is a strong man. He will survive."

"How do you know? You don't know him at all."

"I know all that I need to know."

"Even if you knew more, you wouldn't really know him."

On the day when that argument took place between them, the widow Herzig and her daughter Anna suddenly appeared at their house, and the mother informed them through bitter tears that Gabriel had been declared missing in action.

People gathered round them. The mother raised her arms to the sky and beseeched that her son had not been killed, but just taken prisoner. Abraham Katz promised to pray with fervent intent to the Holy One Blessed Be He that she would soon merit the commandment of the rescue and release of prisoners, and only little Anna was silent. She was convinced that her brother was no longer among the living, or he would have sent her a sign, even from hell. Were they to sit shiva and say the Kaddish prayer for him? The rabbi refused to rule on the question.

Customers in the beer cellar shook Fanny's hand, expressed their condolences and said, "May you know no more sorrow." Others cursed the gentiles' war of Gog and Magog that had brought this disaster upon her, while she refused to grieve and held fast to her belief that Gabriel was alive and well.

In the years to come her father would speak to her about ceasing to wait for the fiancé who had vanished; urge her to break her promise and the pledge she had made. After all, she had met Gabriel only once, and they had never managed to spend any time alone. And even if by some miracle he should return, who knew what state he would be in. Maybe a cripple, stumbling along on a prosthetic limb, or mentally impaired, ridden with nightmares and scars, like those wounded who were still hospitalized across the empire, screaming into the night. Why attach herself to the fate of a damaged man? In any case he would be a different man from the one to whom she had promised her hand, and so even the matchmaker in the sky would discard His plan. The two would not be together, because they were not destined to be. No one in the world would fault her, including the matchmaker. Why, she was permitted to be with any man.

If Gabriel had seen how Fanny stood firm like a fortified wall despite the pressure brought to bear, he would have been even more impressed by that same inner tenacity that he had discerned during the only meeting that ever took place between them.

"You're stiff-necked," said her father, while she reminded him that King David had raided the Amalekite camp and allowed the prisoners to return home.

"We have no King David, and only the Amalekites are the same Amalekites," Abraham Katz hung his head in sorrow. How could he rescue his daughter, imprisoned in a delusional dream? This Gabriel or another Gabriel, if only she would finally stand under the marriage canopy, for time doesn't stand still, especially for strong-minded women.

Meanwhile, the beautiful sister Paula married goldsmith Emil Stein, while Lizzie announced that she would never marry, and vowed to dedicate herself to the struggle for women's rights.

On her sister's wedding night Fanny had a dream. She saw Gabriel standing on a riverbank, his bare feet splashing in the water. He was dressed in only a shirt, white and starched, the same one he had worn at their only meeting. Except that the buttons were undone and his chest was exposed. He aimed his rifle directly at her.

In the dream she wasn't frightened and she didn't scream, but took a step toward him, held out her hand, and her fingers crept under the shirt and caressed his flesh – something she had never done in reality to any man.

"Don't you remember me? I am your fiancée Fanny," she said.

Not only did Gabriel not lower the gun, but he moved it closer to her, and the tip of the bayonet touched her tightly corseted breast.

"I don't know you," he said.

She took the gun from him without encountering the slightest resistance and aimed it at his chest.

"You have to remember me," she said, "You made a promise to me, and you will keep your word."

At that moment the gun went off and a red stain began to spread on the white cloth. Still, Gabriel remained standing, as if nothing had happened. The gun dropped into the water – its gurgling sound in the dream intensified – and he stepped toward her with a smile, something he had not favored her with in the one and only meeting that took place between them.

Gabriel said, "Now I remember you."

Then he dipped his finger in the drops of blood trickling down his chest and wiped them with a caress upon her cheek.

"I will always recognize you," she said in the dream, and he continued to smile.

She awoke with a stabbing pain in her chest. For days she felt it there, and although there was no outward sign, the bayonet from the dream would not be dislodged.

Even when her third letter returned many months later, stamped "Addressee Missing," Fanny continued to insist that her engagement was valid, and that until Gabriel's body was found, as far as she was concerned he was alive.

Although she wanted very much to see him again, even if only in her sleep, she didn't dream about him anymore.

6

The surroundings changed. Gabriel crossed a grove of linden trees and then rows of birch, and when he didn't see a soul, dared to approach one of the villages. With the eyes of a trained soldier he surveyed the houses with the thatched roofs, built of whitewashed bricks, surrounded by vegetable gardens, orchards, and barns. He saw no weapons, nor any soldiers. The village was peaceful and the only smoke visible was curling out of a kitchen chimney.

To sleep in a barn – all his ambitions converged in that desire. And he had one other modest wish – to eat a potato, even in its peel.

He decided to risk it. He dropped to the ground again, but this time he made his way slowly, imitating an animal. Washing flapped on a clothesline, but he didn't see any men's clothes that he might steal.

Dresses swayed before him in the wind, some embroidered shirts, petticoats, and a white sheet that was stretched along the line and fastened at each corner. Gabriel felt a twinge in the presence of such cleanliness. He had become so used to filth that he had forgotten that such whiteness was even possible.

Suddenly he heard the voice of a child. Gabriel immediately retreated into the vegetable garden, crouched on all fours among the cabbage and the turnips.

The boy, who looked about six years old, paraded among the laundry with the energetic steps of a soldier, singing a marching song. Every so often he would stand upright in front of a pair of panties that the wind was furiously twisting, stretch to his full height, and salute them. A fat goose followed along behind him contributing its honking sounds.

"Kostya, come into the house," a woman's voice called from the yard. The boy ignored her and continued to sing at the top of his lungs. Gabriel recognized the marching song, *Farewell to Slavianka*, about the Slavic women accompanying their husbands to the battlefield. It was so popular among the soldiers, not only on the Russian side, but also with the Austrians, that more than once the song could be heard simultaneously from both sides of the border. He was almost tempted to hum along. "The time to part has arrived. You look into my eyes with sweet sorrow. Your voice is soothing as the storm advances."

The boy continued to sing. His voice was pleasant, although Gabriel suspected that he didn't understand the words.

"Kostya, come into the house this instant!"

When the boy didn't respond the second time either the woman burst out of the house like a whirlwind. Her hair was the color of ripe wheat, coiled in braids atop her head. She wiped her hands on her apron, still calling out to him, her voice filled with rage. Kostya continued to ignore her, marching along to the song, bumping into the laundry and hitting the clothes. With his next salute he knocked a pair of panties to the ground. They rolled along, inflated by the wind, and the boy laughed and clapped his hands.

The woman lunged at him, slapped him hard and began to pull him and the underwear into the house. The boy resisted, shouted something in Russian. The goose followed along behind them, honking for all it was worth. The marching song was broken off and only the honking of the goose could be heard. Now it was joined by the voices of other geese.

Gabriel didn't hear the child's crying.

It appears that the woman lacks fondness for both soldiers and songs, he thought as he approached the washing. He didn't dare to steal the sheet, for the woman of the house would surely notice its absence and suspect the presence of a foreign invader.

His stomach grumbled with hunger, and the smell of fried potatoes that reached him through the kitchen window nearly drove him mad. He crawled to the vegetable garden and dug in the earth with his fingers, uprooting one of the turnips and swallowing it whole with the clumps of earth still clinging to it.

As he frantically devoured the turnip he remembered a Chassidic tale about two starving men who arrived at an inn, only to find that the innkeeper had no food to give them. They begged for scraps, although there was only water and flour in the pantry. The innkeeper's wife agreed to prepare some dough for them. As she baked it, she prayed to the Master of the Universe, "Hear my voice, my Lord our God, please add some flavor from Your wealth of flavors to my bland and miserable dish."

Later she placed the cooked dough before the starving men, and wonder of wonders, they consumed it down to the last crumb, even licking the dish.

The turnip that Gabriel chewed was not endowed with a heavenly flavor. Its hard lumps dropped into him like cast lead. His bowels convulsed and his diarrhea was instantaneous. Lacking paper for wiping, he was forced to clean his rear with cabbage leaves.

As he crouched on all fours with a bare butt in the vegetable garden, he surveyed the whitewashed brick walls, the thatched roof, and the windows in which lace curtains fluttered. Now the aroma of the fried potatoes didn't whet his appetite, but they triggered unbridled longing. The sight of a warm and comfortable house, a roof over your head, a woman and a child, gave him a jolt. He felt as if he had returned from the land of the dead. A deserter with no identity, his mind jittery, his body filthy with excrement. Like the last of the beggars he yearned for shelter for the night, and a barn for animals was the pinnacle of his aspirations.

He saw one in the yard and estimated the distance. Slowly he dragged himself along on his belly, all the while hoping that the woman would be busy with the child and the frying of potatoes, and wouldn't go out to the barn.

It was warm there, and even the smell of the dung – pungent, maybe pig – was pleasant to him. With a thud he dropped down with his rifle into the hay, curled up in the stack unaware of the pinpricks, and plunged into a deep slumber. The marching song played on even as he slept. There was a woman there who soothed him with her voice and looked into his eyes with sweet sorrow.

For the rest of his life Gabriel would remember the farewell song of the Slavic women who accompanied their husbands to the battlefield, and he would hum it at unexpected moments, especially when the aroma of fried potatoes reached his nostrils.

7

He even found the tiny jabs pleasing. A feather tickled his skin and he turned onto his side, imagining that he was sinking in a soft featherbed, resting on a white sheet like the one he had seen on the clothesline. He knew he was dreaming and he tried to postpone the end of the dream.

The jabs increased, and when he finally opened his eyes he saw a goose and a boy. Confused, half-asleep, he ran his hands over his body and tried to stand up. The goose was undeterred and poked his beak at him over and over, now beating his wings in Gabriel's face. The boy's laughter reverberated in the barn. In response, Gabriel immediately burst into the *Farewell to Slavianka* song, and the boy began to skip to the rhythm, pulling him up from the straw and shouting at the top of his lungs, "Mother Homeland is summoning her sons, one can feel the wind of the marching regiments."

Gabriel joined in.

"Comrade," the boy exclaimed, "Maybe you met my father? He was also a soldier. A hero."

In a moment he had discovered the gun and tried to grab it. Gabriel immediately moved it away, to the boy's chagrin.

"Comrade, please," begged the disappointed boy. "Let me shoot. My father taught me."

"No."

"Please Comrade, I also want to fight."

"You're still a boy, Kostya."

The boy's eyes and mouth all opened wide.

"How do you know my name?"

The whole gaggle of geese entered the barn, surrounding them in a circle, while the striker continued to jab at the gun. Before Gabriel had a chance to move, the woman also came in. At the sight of a strange man she froze on the spot. Then, recovering rapidly she grabbed the pitchfork, waving it at the human scarecrow who was dotted all over with hay.

The child hung on to her, pulling at the hem of her dress. "Look what I found Matushka. Papa sent us a soldier in his place."

The woman was silent. Her knuckles whitened on the pitchfork.

Gabriel attempted to straighten his uniform. It was so worn and soiled, and it seemed to him that it still reeked of urine. He stood like a statue. Had he tried to make a move, the woman would have jabbed him with the pitchfork.

"I won't bother you *gospozha*," he mumbled in Russian. "Allow me to rest in the barn for a few days and I will be on my way."

The woman remained silent. She was older than he was, around thirty-five. Unlike the previous day, when he had seen her in the yard, this morning her flaxen hair was tied back under a kerchief, and only a few wisps escaped onto her forehead.

"Matushka," the boy tugged at his mother's dress again. "The soldier will help you in the fields instead of Papa. You won't have to work so hard."

A tear rolled down her cheek, although her expression remained frozen.

"Matushka, he even knows my name. Papa told him."

"Where are you from, soldier?" she finally asked. Her voice was so soft that he could barely make out the words.

"Odessa," the lie slipped off his tongue. Luckily, as a child he had visited his mother's birthplace. If the woman asked questions he would be able to describe the streets and town squares and to tell her that he lived near the Potemkin Stairs. Thank God he spoke fluent Russian, and what luck that he had torn off every piece of his uniform that could identify him as an Austrian soldier.

"Everyone was killed," he said softly, "I can't go back there."

The woman turned her head and he saw her furtively wipe away the tear.

The boy continued to dance around them, and the geese hopped with him. He looked so happy.

"What's your name soldier?" he asked.

"Gabriel."

The boy turned again to his mother.

"You see, Matushka, Papa is watching over us. He sent us the angel Gabriel. Where are your wings?"

And he had already jumped on Gabriel from behind and started to pull at his shirt. It was so threadbare that it came apart in his hands like a piece of paper.

The bewildered woman tried to stop her excited child, but now he tugged at Gabriel's sleeves, searching for the folded wings inside. The tattered shirt fell to the floor of the barn and Gabriel stood before the woman bare-chested.

This time she didn't turn away. He thought that she was about to reach out her finger to touch his bruised skin. He so longed for the touch of a soft hand, to make the gaping eyes of Von-Hoffenberg disappear, but the moment passed. The woman loosened her grasp on the pitchfork, leaned it against the side of the barn and took a step back.

"Until tomorrow," she said.

"*Spasiba*."

"The next day – you get out of here."

Her name was Larissa Yefimovna. Gabriel stayed with her – not for one day, but for three years.

8

In Bukovina the Russians returned, the Austrians retreated, and then they changed places again, and only Fanny kept her pledge of allegiance to her man. She interrogated every stranger who passed through town. Had anyone met Gabriel? Maybe someone had heard about the last battle he fought in? Did anyone know him? Did anyone know anything?

"Go and see the proxy," everyone advised her. He's the only one who comes and goes through the gates of the army.

They weren't referring to a wizard, but to the local blacksmith, Kalman-Zelig Hirsch, the man with the limp. Ever since the war he had supported himself less and less with his metal work and welding, and more with his deformity. He would present himself before the conscription committee in place of the conscript, exhibit his handicap and be granted an exemption. This system, referred to as "proxy," became a profitable source of income for the blacksmith, and unlike the many whose income dwindled during the war, he made a fortune.

Perhaps some word had reached him about her missing fiancé?

"He must be brought to a grave of Israel," declared the proxy.

"He's alive!" Fanny exclaimed.

"How do you know?"

"I can feel it." She touched her breast, in the place where Gabriel had jabbed her with the bayonet in her dream.

"You're young. Take another husband."

Kalman-Zelig straightened up, compensating for his limp, and almost proposed to her himself.

"I won't have another husband."

In the end she extracted a promise from him that he would keep his ears and eyes open for her.

In his heart the blacksmith wished that Gabriel had been killed, not for her sake, but for his.

Like many Jewish women during those years, Fanny was also a devoted reader of *Tseno Ureno* (Go Forth and See). which was not a romantic novel but a popular Bible for women written in Yiddish, which had been printed in 150 editions and shaped the worldview of many a young Jewess. The best-seller provoked many a tear as she identified with the matriarch Sarah, whose only son was led to the sacrificial altar, without her knowledge. But at the same time, the Biblical story had a happy ending. Fanny derived much comfort from the miracle that occurred, when the wielder of the knife did not harm the youth in the end.

Every evening, before she went to sleep, Fanny found herself returning not to the Shema Yisrael special prayer for bedtime, but rather to the liturgical poem for Yom Kippur Unetanneh Tokef or "Let Us Speak of the Awesomeness."

"For You do not wish the death of one deserving death, but that he repent from his way and live. Until the day of his death You await him."

She devoted hours to writing letters which she sent to the military headquarters in Vienna, to the dismay of her father, who worried about trouble with the authorities. Each time she received the same response: Corporal Herzig is not the only one whose body was left unrecognizable on the battlefield, and in the absence of any testimony or positive identification from his comrades in the company or from his commanders, who were killed in the same murderous bombardment at the end of 1914, we have no choice but to assume that the corporal met the same fate. The chances that he survived are slim.

And still, Fanny persisted in her expectation of a miracle. Finding no evidence in the Bible attesting to someone who had returned from oblivion, Fanny traveled to Czernowitz in search of another precedent. Surprisingly, the city was only slightly damaged the first time it was conquered and the residents continued to lead normal lives. She walked along the teeming streets, passed by the stores overflowing with merchandise, the hotels, concert halls and theaters that were still functioning, and didn't understand how the ravages of war had skipped over the capital of Bukovina. Her father recounted with emotion the story of how the sixty-three Torah scrolls in the synagogue were saved thanks to the intervention of the Archbishop Vladimir de Repta, while the Chassidic towns of Sadagóra, Vizhnitz, and Boyan were destroyed to their foundations, and Siret was licking its wounds.

Maybe there was some luck in the world. She just had to find it.

In the secondhand bookshop Fanny wandered among the shelves for hours.

"Perhaps these?" the salesman, who knew the tastes of his longtime customer, pushed a pile of romantic novels toward her. She flipped through the pages and it seemed to her that she had already read every one.

"Don't you have anything new?"

He held out a faded book, spattered with ink.

"I bought this yesterday from a family that left for Vienna."

She liked the cover. A woman wearing a robe leaned over a loom. A man stood facing her, regarding her with an expression that Fanny interpreted as an entreaty, but what sent a shudder through her body was his bare chest. She had heard of women who undressed for men, but never of the reverse.

The bookseller said, "It's a painting from an ancient Greek urn. I bought it at a bargain price. I'll give it to you for free."

It was a copy of the *Odyssey*, covered in handwritten notations. Although the reading of it posed a challenge for Fanny, who wasn't accustomed to that style of writing, she began it on the spot, and in no time was drawn to the character of Penelope, who waited eighteen years for Ulysses. However, unlike the wife of the Greek warrior from Ithaca, the fiancée from Siret did not weave during the day and unpluck her stitches throughout the night, to keep her suitors at bay. And Kalman-Zelig Hirsch didn't dare to court Fanny openly. His visits to her were always in the guise of providing assistance in her search for Gabriel. The proxy had patience. He was waiting for the right moment to supply comfort, when she finally gave in to despair.

Why didn't Penelope travel to Troy to search for her husband? Fanny asked the owner of the secondhand bookstore. In her place Fanny would have done something, would have rented a boat and sailed across the sea.

Her request to the military authorities to travel to the front – which she made via the courier Kalman-Zelig Hirsch – seemed not to merit a response. She couldn't know that he had never passed it on.

Fanny insisted on paying for the book. In addition to the *Odyssey* she bought several romantic novels that weren't recommended by the salesman. Those always had happy endings, unlike the Greek myths in which, she would learn in due time, vengefulness and intrigues in the family persisted for generations.

Her seemingly perverse refusal to give up hope earned her more than a few snickers. Many claimed that she had lost her mind. Who had ever heard of such loyalty to a prospective bridegroom who had disappeared without a trace? In Siret they shook their heads in sorrow over Abraham Katz, who had lost hope of marrying off either his eldest or his youngest daughter, for Lizzie held fast to her opinion that marriage was a tyrannical institution for the perpetuation of the inferior status of the woman.

At least there was a chance that he would see grandchildren from his middle daughter.

As a Vizhnitz Chassid Abraham Katz consulted with his Admor who ruled that "haste is from the devil." He instructed Fanny not to mourn Gabriel prematurely, for in the Bible there are two instances of people returning from the dead. And although the prophets Elijah and Elisha, known for their secret power to resurrect the dead, were not active, who knew if miracles were not being wrought in their names in our time as well.

A year after Gabriel's disappearance the widow Herzig donated a pew in the Mihova synagogue in memory of her son, and so his name was widely spoken of as that of a fallen soldier whose burial place is unknown. The rabbi even counseled the mother to recite a prayer for his soul on the tenth day of the Hebrew month of Tevet, the fast day in memory of the start of the siege of Jerusalem during the time of the First Temple.

A prayer for his soul? Out of the question. Fanny refused to accept the verdict. She made the journey to Mihova to meet with the rabbi to dissuade him from the step that would put an end to Gabriel. "Because when he returns [she didn't say 'if he returns'] he won't forgive us for burying him when he was still alive."

What harm is there in a prayer? wondered the rabbi, and Fanny snapped at him that if he didn't know the difference between a prayer in memory of the dead and a prayer for the welfare of the living, then maybe he shouldn't be a rabbi. She even compared herself to the Patriarch Jacob, who waited seven long years for Rachel.

"But Rachel was alive and well," the rabbi was enjoying the unexpected sophistry.

"Gabriel is also alive and well, until the Holy One Blessed Be He has had his say."

Anyone listening to the young woman's argument with the rabbi would have mistakenly thought that she was talking about a spouse she had known for many years, and with whom she had been physically intimate. Notwithstanding that the concept of "intimacy" was foreign to Fanny, she relied on the relationships in the cheap novels that she liked to read.

Sparring with the Torah scholar she brandished a new argument, her ace in the hole as far as she was concerned. She reminded him that the deeply religious People of Israel recite the Shemoneh Esrei prayer facing the east, and direct their hearts to the Promised Land based only on memories of days long past.

"And if, every Passover holiday, we continue to say 'Next year in Jerusalem,' who would dare to question what I believe with absolute faith?"

She promised the rabbi that he would yet hear the voice of her bridegroom declaring, "If I forget thee oh Jerusalem" before the breaking of the glass at their wedding ceremony. What is the purpose of crushing the glass if not to remind us, even at our moment of greatest joy, about how much destruction, calamity, and sorrow there is in the world.

The rabbi looked down, conceding defeat in the presence of such blind faith. The tone of rebuke in her voice had the effect of impressing him even more. What steadfastness – the same trait that Gabriel had so admired – and how articulate she was. He was mostly astonished that she didn't hesitate to speak her mind, perhaps due to the influence of her younger sister's daring outlook. The passion that overflowed augured well as to what might be expected in the most intimate of chambers. Since he been a widower for a year and his congregation was urging him to remarry, he proposed to her on the spot.

"This is blasphemy!" A shocked Fanny stormed out of the synagogue in Mihova, refusing to even glance at the memorial plaque nailed to the back of the pew donated by the widow Herzig.

The rabbi called after her, "The dead are dead and those who are alive, live," but she didn't deign to turn her head.

Fanny ran into Anna in the street. She was surprised to see how much the girl had matured since her brother had disappeared.

Anna was upset. That same morning the daughter of the neighbors, her childhood friend Luminicia Mirodan, had tried to convince her to convert to Christianity. Only the power of Holy Mother Mary could save her brother from death. And her name would shorten the process, for Anna was the mother of Mary, patron saint of women who protected them during childbirth. In her generosity the neighbor's daughter even offered Anna her own crucifix and tried to fasten it around her neck.

The girl gave it back to her friend, controlling herself so she wouldn't shout at her.

"I'm only thinking of your welfare," said Luminicia. "You recite the 'Ave Maria,' and the Holy Virgin and her mother, whose name is the same as yours, will watch over your brother."

Anna still refused.

"Who will protect him?" Luminicia asked. "What Jewish saint do you have?" The girl had no answer.

When she met Fanny in the street, Anna was sure that her brother's fiancée had come especially from Siret to the synagogue in Mihova to pay her respects to the pew in memory of Gabriel. Although her hopes of seeing her brother alive had faded, she refused to be a party to any public acknowledgement of his death.

"I will never sit in that pew!" the distraught girl announced.

Fanny said, "Maybe it will grant him long life? The memorial may bring him home."

"How do you know he's alive?" Anna asked.

Fanny didn't have an answer that would satisfy a skeptical young girl. Anna raised tear-filled eyes to her and grasped her hand tightly. The two walked away from the synagogue and stood in the center of the street.

If Homer had witnessed a young girl from a remote village in Bukovina telling her friend in fluent German about Ulysses and his return to his Ithaca, he would have been convinced of the power of the story to overcome the ravages of time, although it's possible that he might have added a comment about the Trojan war, which was an ongoing disaster even for those who somehow managed to survive it.

One way or the other, Fanny told the story of the *Odyssey* in the middle of the village street thronging with unheroic lives. Sirens mingled with horse-drawn carts, cyclopes exchanged places with farmers exhibiting their wares at market, giants and cannibals were transformed into the craftsmen at their stalls. Anna listened raptly to the adventures of the legendary warrior, all the while clinging to the hand of the woman she hoped would one day be her sister-in-law.

From that day forward, every pig herder Anna encountered was the Witch Circe, who changed men into pigs and imprisoned them in a sty. The beautiful nymph Calypso seduced Ulysses, but the thought that Gabriel might have been overcome by the charms of some foreign enchantress never crossed her mind.

"But if Gabriel only returns in another eighteen years, why, we won't be able to recognize him," Anna cried bitterly.

Fanny had an answer for this as well. The only creature to recognize Ulysses upon his return home, disguised as a beggar, was his faithful dog Argus, she told Anna. At his advanced age the dog's legs failed him and he couldn't manage to stand up to approach his master, but with the last of his strength he wagged his tail at him, and pricked up his ears. "For we have signs which we two alone know, signs hidden from others," Fanny quoted, as if the line was the conclusion of a romantic novel.

Anna wiped away her tears and for the first time since Gabriel had disappeared, she laughed.

9

In Russian, the name "Larissa" means "fortress." Gabriel had never heard of the ancient, original Larissa, a well-connected royal nymph, since he had no interest at all in Greek mythology. But the meaning of the name of the woman who gave him refuge did not escape him. Especially when the boy arrived the next morning, carrying under his arm wide trousers, a cloth shirt, a belt, and a pair of high boots. Gabriel thanked the Holy One Blessed Be He who grants a pinch of grace to His world, and asked the boy to thank his mother for him. The boy watched in wonder as the strange man turned into a Russian farmer. Gabriel fingered the soft cloth, worn from so many washings, and then dressed himself in the clothes as though they were the bridegroom's suit that he hadn't had the opportunity to wear. He tucked the wide bottoms of the trousers into the high boots, which, surprisingly, were exactly his size.

"Tell me, did you kill the enemy?" asked the boy.

Gabriel didn't answer.

"How many people did you kill?" the boy asked again.

Gabriel buttoned the shirt and discovered a tear in the embroidered collar.

"When I grow up I'll be a soldier too," the boy declared, and promptly began to search the barn for the gun. He thrust his hands into the piles of hay, spraying stalks everywhere, and only when Gabriel promised to teach him how to play football instead did he relent. Gabriel balled up his tattered uniform and sent it rolling toward the barn door. The boy ran to it right away and enthusiastically kicked it outside. They played for quite a while. If his Major had witnessed the fate of his glorious imperial uniform he would have finished him off with his bayonet, thought Gabriel.

He asked Kostya to bring him some kerosene and some matches and took advantage of his absence to stow the rifle atop one of the high beams in the barn, far out of reach.

When he prepared to throw the balled-up uniform into the flames, the boy protested.

"Don't worry Kostya. I'll bring you a real football," Gabriel promised.

He didn't forget to extract the photograph of the *liebling* from within the rag ball, and sneak it into the pocket of his farmer's trousers.

Whoever had been the owner of the clothes he wore, he was grateful to him.

Again and again the boy asked him to show him his angel's wings, and he even tried to make sure that they hadn't by some terrible chance fallen into the fire.

"Don't come too close, Kostya," Gabriel warned.

"Tell me, Gabril, do angels also shoot?"

"I've never seen them."

"Maybe you saw my father, up in the sky?"

Gabriel was silent.

Larissa looked out from the window of the house onto the fire burning in her back yard, and Gabriel, who was using a stick to push the uniform deeper into the flames, thanked her with a nod of his head, and then placed his hand on the boy's shoulder, to prevent him from moving too close to the fire.

The woman whose name was "fortress" turned her face from the window.

For the first few months Gabriel continued to sleep in the barn. Kostya brought him his meals twice a day, usually a bowl of groats, and once Larissa even sent him a *pirozhki* – a roll filled with potato. At dawn the patter of her footsteps could be heard as she went out to work in the fields. Once, when he saw her struggling under the weight of the plow, Gabriel hurried to pull on his boots and offered to do the plowing for her. At first she resisted, but he insisted. His furrows were crooked, and when he looked up from the clumps of earth, he saw her trying to hide a smile. That night she brought needle and thread to the barn and altered her husband's clothes so they would fit him better.

He stood completely still, barely breathing, as her hands fluttered around his body, mending the tear in the collar. Their eyes met, she moved her hand, and he was stabbed by the needle. Gabriel flinched. She tore the thread with her teeth and hurried to leave.

The photograph of the *liebling* rustled deep in the pocket of her husband's trousers, but Larissa didn't know it was there.

The barn was situated on the outskirts of the village yet the rumor quickly spread that the widow Yefimovna had hired a laborer to help her. According to the gossips, especially the farmer Abilov, her elderly neighbor who hadn't been called up due to his age, the reports were that it was a strong, industrious young man, and that he lived in the barn, so her reputation was safe.

Like a good student Gabriel diligently applied himself to the work in the field. He tended the potatoes and turnips, sowed the wheat and barley, and after a while Larissa allowed him to take the produce to market on the wagon drawn by a donkey. He endured kicks from the cow the first few times he milked her, and he slopped the pigs. The only animals Larissa didn't allow him to approach were the geese – the apple of her eye.

During all those days, that lengthened into weeks, and then years, Gabriel searched for a way to send a message home, but he was deep in enemy territory, the roads to Austro-Hungary were blocked, and the mail and telegraph services didn't function anymore.

He hoped that his mother and his sister had not lost hope and sat shiva for him, and as for Fanny, she had surely married another long ago. He had no grievance against her.

His former life seemed to belong to a different person, but at the same time he tried to preserve his faith in secret. He didn't touch meat, on the pretext that he was a vegetarian. He washed his hands before every meal, and silently recited, "Blessed art Thou, Lord our God... Who brings forth bread from the earth." He decided to devote one autumn day to Yom Kippur, and as he sowed the field he silently prayed the Kol Nidrei prayer. When he reached, "who by sword and who by wild beast, who by famine..." he pounded on his heart, for although he didn't engage in repentance, in prayer, or in charity, still the Creator of the Universe had protected him and rescinded the evil decree.

Whenever he mumbled a verse to himself he found the curious eyes of the boy watching him, and then he would feel his shoulder blades, hoping that the words were a magic spell that would cause Gabriel's wings to spring forth. Since he had announced to the entire village that the new farm hand was the angel who had brought Mary the news that she was pregnant with the savior, no one suspected his true identity.

He had to beware. Especially of the boy who had most certainly been taught to hate the Jews. In Bukovina as well the priest would tell his faithful about the betrayal of Jesus and demand revenge in His name, but this only happened once a year, before Easter. Gabriel would seal the wooden shutters to protect the windows from the stones that would be thrown, and move Anna and his mother deep into the recesses of the house. But in Russia the incitement was prevalent every day of the year, not only on Easter, and so he had to take precautions. Gabriel was especially careful never to relieve himself in the presence of the boy. He played with him in the yard and taught him to kick into an imaginary goal. They sang *Farewell to Slavianka* together, and dug up the turnips and potatoes, while Larissa observed them through the window. When Kostya started school, he helped him with his reading and writing. But unlike the stern teacher in the heder, Gabriel never hit him with a *kanchik*, the stick with the thin straps that sting when they make contact with a boy's skin, and patiently corrected his mistakes.

From Kostya Gabriel learned the Christian prayers, and the Pater Nostra and the Ave Maria were routinely on his tongue, while his face wore an expression of piety that he copied from Larissa. Still every time he crossed himself he asked forgiveness from the all-knowing Lord who discerns what people truly think and feel.

Larissa Yefimovna only discovered that he was a Jew when she took him into her bed.

10

Fanny did not abandon her betrothed. The belief that Gabriel was still alive was so firm within her that it became second nature. Paula the romantic spoke in praise of the Penelope from Siret, unlike Lizzie the skeptic who saw in Fanny an inability to come to terms with reality, and Kalman-Zelig Hirsch feared that she was losing her mind, since belief, in the absence of any basis in fact, often seems close to madness.

One way or the other, Fanny was of sound mind and lived a structured life, in as much as this was possible while the battlefront alternately encroached and receded.

It was the beer that kept her anchored.

Day and night she filled bottles with one of the most ancient beverages in the world, which brought comfort and oblivion to many good people, although she was not one of them. From before the war the family brewery had garnered fame among the drinkers in the area, and had financed Lizzie's piano lessons and Fanny's embroidered quilts. For his serious clients, Abraham Katz put on a convincing performance. With a flourish he would withdraw a small key from his suit pocket, unlock the door of a cupboard that stood next to the bottling machine, and reverently extract a tiny colorful bottle bearing a label with foreign letters. Taking care to obscure the writing with his hand, with maximum ceremony he would pour a few drop of the elixir into the beer. Then he would offer the customer a taste.

"It's a family secret, passed down from generation to generation."

"A taste of Paradise," the customer would smack his lips, and immediately order an entire crate.

His competitors tried everything to discover the mysterious secret ingredient that Abraham Katz used to enhance the taste of his beer, and performed their own experiments. One added essence of citrus peel, while another tried sticks of cinnamon, and Mirodan, a neighbor of Gabriel's from Mihova, traveled to Transylvania, to Count Dracula's castle, and from an old gypsy bought ginger root from his garden. Mirodan promised his customers that this not only improved the taste of the beer, but also their virility, yet nothing compared to "Katz Beer," that remained the most popular in all the taverns.

Fanny kept the magic ingredient a secret. It was simple well water. Every time she poured from the bucket into the small bottle, she wondered to herself whether her missing man had found some comfort and oblivion in some other place.

One day, two Hungarian-speaking customers visited the beer cellar. An elderly, upright man, with a well-tended white beard, whose threadbare suit still echoed its former glory, and his young companion who was his polar opposite. He was sloppy, reeking as though he hadn't bathed in a long time, and coarse in manner. When he lunged at the bottle that Fanny was filling she saw that his hand was missing, and a prosthetic hook was attached to the stump.

A wounded soldier. Her heart sank. Should she ask him where he had served? Perhaps he had come across her lost corporal?

Before she had a chance to say a word, the young man grabbed the bottle with his hook and directed it to his mouth.

She stopped herself from trying to help him, for fear that a gesture of assistance might be perceived as a blow to his self-esteem. He opened the bottle with his hook and slurped down the beer. His Adam's apple bobbed up and down and his loud swallows gurgled in his throat. After draining it to the last drop, he grabbed another bottle from the machine. He did this skillfully as well, as if he was one of the acrobats from the circus that stopped at Siret in the summers.

The old man tried to shove the young one away from the machine.

"Enough Yanush. The alcohol is bad for you. You know what the doctors said."

"The doctors? To hell with the doctors. Why didn't they let me die?" The young man ignored him. Foam dripped from his chin onto the front of his tattered shirt.

"Yanush, you are disgracing yourself in front of the lady."

The young man whirled around on the old one and it looked as though he was about to stab him with his hook.

"Too bad I wasn't killed."

"How can you say that?" the elderly man crossed himself.

"If I had died, you would be proud of me."

He turned to Fanny.

"Do I debase you, my lady?"

He took a step toward her, pressing the hook to her cheek. Strangely, she didn't flinch and didn't move away. One day Fanny would face British soldiers in the same way, brandishing a small worn carpet, when they wanted to deport her to Cyprus. Fanny's resolute nature and fortitude, that had already charmed three men – Gabriel, Kalman-Zelig Hirsch and the rabbi of Mihova – now impressed a fourth as well.

The old man was shocked. He tried to grab the younger man and move him away from Fanny. The hook twinkled in front of her eyes, but she stood immobile, feeling the cold of the metal against her skin.

What would she do if Gabriel returned to her with a deformity? Would she still keep her promise? Would she be able to wash him, to shave him, to brush his teeth, to dress and undress him? And what about the embarrassing things, like wiping his butt. How far would her devotion extend?

She took hold of the bottle and poured its contents onto the floor of the cellar. The beer bubbled and its foam spread beneath their feet.

Yanush wavered and the old man hurried to support him.

"I'm fine, Father." He shook him off and crouched down on his knees, in the puddle of beer. From there he encircled Fanny's wrist with his hook as though it was a diamond bracelet, and then wrenched it off his stump.

"My lady, please. Stab me with this."

She remained motionless.

"Please, lady, if I had any courage I would stab myself, but I am a coward."

With a decisive motion she re-attached the prosthetic hook to the stump while he bit his lips in pain. She was unapologetic, tightening the prosthesis firmly until finally a scream escaped him. The old man screamed too.

Yanush looked into her eyes. The entreaty she saw there turned her stomach. And then he took her hand and kissed it.

For the first time in her life Fanny felt a man's lips on her skin.

11

Men are always surprised when the secret world of women is revealed to them in bed. Gabriel was stunned by Larissa's sighs and moans. He hadn't known that women could climax, and he hadn't had any idea that they enjoyed sex and yearned for it as men did. After all, his erotic education was limited to the one gold-toothed professional in Czernowitz, who had executed her trade with efficiency and versatility, and then complimented his performance and granted him several favors on the house. The face that a woman was capable of taking any pleasure in "sexual intercourse" – the only concept that Gabriel was familiar with – had never entered his mind.

For him, Larissa Yefimovna was an uncharted continent. On their first night together she didn't hide underneath her nightgown but displayed herself to him. He had never seen a woman's naked body. Why was all this beauty spurned and dismissed? Was it because the Holy One Blessed Be He was a bachelor, and knew not of pleasure? Why did He create what He had created and deprive only Himself?

The contrast between Larissa during the day and Larissa at night was unfathomable. During work hours in the fields or the vegetable garden she barely spoke and avoided any contact with him, while at night she bore down on him, moaning and screaming, her writhing agitating the springs on the bed that collided with the wall.

Her body became familiar to him, and in the future he would recall her velvety skin and her soft thighs that drew him in without reservation. Larissa taught him to pleasure her with his hand, with his member, with his tongue, and even when he fell onto the bed exhausted after a day's labors, she wouldn't forego her nighttime pleasure.

Sometimes he worried that Kostya could hear the sounds, and he gently placed his hand over her mouth, but she wasn't concerned. She never mentioned her dead husband. He didn't know whether her soul was bound up with his, or whether it had been a calculated economic arrangement.

Every time he went to her bed he was grateful for his good fortune, since a bed is not something that will ever be taken for granted by one who had become accustomed to sleeping on the ground, or on a bed of straw. The soft quilts and white sheets were to him as the gates to heaven, and to the end of his days Gabriel demanded of his partners that they iron their sheets for him; even the slightest wrinkle could annoy him.

The only thing that perplexed him was that after their nightly sessions Larissa would climb out of bed to kneel on the bare floor and pray fervently, as if she was atoning for a sin.

He didn't ask her if this was because he was a Jew.

For long months before the start of the intimate chapter in their lives Gabriel was alone in the barn, his entire being occupied with his duties in the fields, as he continued to hide from any stranger who passed by. He found some comfort only in the relationship that developed between him and the boy, until the day that Kostya disappeared.

When he was late coming home Larissa began to rush around the yard and the house, the gaggle of geese waddling along behind her.

"Kostya, where are you?" she called again and again.

Her terrified voice reached Gabriel in the turnip patches. He threw down the hoe and rushed to join her. The mother's face reminded him of the faces of soldiers during a barrage of shelling, trapped in uncontrollable fear. They widened their search to the orchard where Gabriel had hidden before finding sanctuary with her.

Larissa ran around frantically. "Kostya doesn't know how to swim!" she shrieked.

Gabriel ran to the river, but there was no sign of the boy there either. He even jumped into the water fully dressed, dove into the mud, and then with his bare hands parted the high weeds and bushes growing wild on the riverbank, to make sure that no small corpse was caught there. His teeth chattered as in his sodden clothes he cleared a path deep into the thicket, and his voice echoed among the trees.

"Kostya, where are you?"

The surrounding trees were taller, their tips blocking out the sky and casting dark shade. His clothes were coated in a fine layer of ice. He had to find the boy, so none could say he had brought down disaster upon the village woman and repaid her kindness with evil.

Von-Hoffenberg's staring eyes returned, hanging in the branches, dancing before him among the leaves, as if he had never left the battlefield and was still imprisoned in the bombed out trench. At every sound he crouched and flattened himself against the ground, waiting for the shell to fall. Only when he failed to hear an explosion did he dare to raise his eyes, and he suddenly made out the boy's legs, dangling from the top of a tree.

"Don't move, Kostya, I'm coming to get you."

He was careful not to raise his voice so as not to frighten the boy who might lose his balance.

The cheerful response came from the treetops. "Gabril, will you show me how you fly?"

Gabriel didn't answer him and continued to climb slowly up the tree, until he could reach the boy's legs. Then he slid down the trunk with him as the boy held onto his back, all the while running his hands over Gabriel's shoulder blades.

"I climbed the tallest tree. I wanted to see what there is at the top."

Gabriel didn't tell the boy that there was nothing to see, but he did extract a promise that he would never climb like that again, since from down below as well you can imagine what might be at the top.

Larissa was beside herself with joy. She hugged Kostya over and over and thanked Jesus and all the saints for the safe return of her son.

Then she turned to Gabriel, "May God bless you, may Holy Mary, to whom you brought the good tidings, bless you. You really are an angel, Gabriel." It was the first time she called him by his name.

And it was on that night that she came to the barn. She wore only her nightgown and her shapely body was visible beneath the thin fabric. For some reason he thought he was dreaming about Von-Hoffenberg's *liebling*. Why was she asking him, of all people, to redeem her debt? He didn't know her at all. Gabriel sat up when he saw the blurred figure, confused and swaying.

"The Major loved you Fräulein, he loved you so much, he thought only of you," he mumbled in German.

Larissa bent over him, her breasts swinging, and only when she pulled him to his feet and pressed herself against him did he realize that the woman wasn't a mirage, but flesh and blood. She led him to her room.

The next morning she sat on the edge of the bed, pressed her joined palms to her heart in a prayer of thanks to the Holy Mother who protects young boys, and turned to Gabriel.

"Thank your Jewish God as well," she said.

12

But the Jewish God remained deep in hiding. I am like one of the conversos, Gabriel said to himself as he entered the church with Larissa and Kostya. As one who had grown up alongside Christians he was familiar with their customs and the church was not strange to him, but still, he had never passed through its gates disguised as a Christian. His glance fell on Jesus hanging on the cross above the altar, as the Roman soldiers jabbed him with their spears. Another miserable victim of the cruelty of those in pursuit of power, he kept his thoughts to himself, and attempted to justify his disguise. After all, Jesus too was circumcised and had a bar mitzvah, and lived all the days of his life as a full-fledged Jew.

He told Larissa about the masses that were held on the battlefield. Once a shell made a direct hit on the mobile altar, and the military priest was hit in the mouth with shrapnel, preventing him from speaking even one word of prayer. He was buried in haste in one of the craters that awaited him like a ready-made grave. Of all the soldiers, it was Gabriel who plunged a makeshift crucifix that he fashioned from the butts of two broken rifles into the mound of dirt.

Larissa told him, "Jesus rewards you for the grace you showed the priest."

And Gabriel replied, "Not Jesus. You, Larissa. Grace is only from human beings," and she was shocked.

The handful of men who were left in the village, most of them old or sick, looked at him suspiciously as he sat in the church, while the women, young and old alike, were secretly envious of Larissa when they took in the young laborer who was so conspicuous for his height and his handsome face. It was clear to all that he was no angel, as Kostya continued to announce with great enthusiasm, but he had brought luck to Larissa, unlike her husband who wasted all their money on cards and drink and would regularly beat her on Sunday nights when he came home from the tavern. Of course it isn't seemly to speak ill of a war hero who fell on the altar of his homeland, but let's face it, the Lord has favored her. It was plain to see that ever since the arrival of the laborer her income had increased and her produce was snapped up at the market. Even the turnip harvest that year had been unusually successful.

During this period Gabriel's commercial skills were revealed and he soon became the account manager for the farm. He taught Larissa how to improve her yields, to reduce expenses, and to invest more in turnips and less in geese. The "Larissa Chapter" of his life was a period of financial schooling for him, and the bargaining and selling would become second nature. Not to speak too soon, these would prove most impressive in the future.

At church Gabriel kept his face impassive, kneeling before the priest and opening his mouth to receive the sacrament, praying that the Holy One Blessed Be He would be understanding. Dissembling to save a life. And didn't Joseph the righteous work for his master Potiphar? And didn't Moses grow up as an Egyptian prince in the lap of Pharaoh's daughter, who drew him from the Nile, and even our forefather Abraham disguised himself and introduced Sarah as his sister, and not his wife. If the Holy One Blessed Be He allowed the tall cedars to be wrapped in foreign garb so that they would be saved, why not an insignificant man such as himself?

For the entire duration of the service Gabriel felt Larissa's body tense at his side, anxious that he would accidentally expose his Jewishness. She followed his movements during the mass, signaling to him when to cross himself and raising her voice slightly when singing the words of the psalm, to guide him. Kostya didn't let go of his hand, clutching it with pride.

As they left the church the farmer Abilov stopped them and asked where he was from.

"Odessa," Gabriel answered with certainty as he began to describe the stone staircase near the spot where the workers were murdered in the 1905 uprising.

"You saw the leaders of the rebellion with your own eyes?"

The other farmers clustered round them in a show of respect.

"Yes. The sailors from the warship *Potemkin* themselves."

"And were you part of the rebellion?"

"I was a boy. But I remember everything."

Odessa prompted fear in the hearts of Abilov and the elderly farmers. Who knew, maybe Larissa's young laborer was a member of that city's infamous gang, the group of daring criminals that even the Czar's police didn't dare to engage.

Snow began to fall. Soft and caressing.

The roofs of the village were wrapped in white. Gabriel was also accustomed to the snowy tableau, but this time he did not observe it with equanimity. A deceptive beauty, he said to himself. Who would believe that a short distance away the war was staining the snow red. He lit a cigarette, and as he squinted in the shimmering air Von-Hoffenberg's eyes returned. Had they found his remains? Had a funeral been held for him in Salzburg? And his *liebling*? Was she still in mourning, or had she already entrusted her photograph to another suitor?

Only now did he feel a lessening of the tension that had gripped him in the church. The act of pretending demands a supreme effort and perhaps that is the reason why only the tallest trees, the righteous men Joseph, Moses, and Abraham, could pass the test. He buried the butt of his cigarette in a small snowdrift that immediately melted away, and reached for the warm hand of Larissa, his fortress. But she was careful to keep a correct distance, as she adjusted her fur hat atop her coiled braids. The snow dusted her like a veil. For the briefest of moments – a fraction of a second – a memory of Fanny flickered in his mind.

"Let's go home Gabril," she instructed and she began to plow forward through the snow.

"Home," Larissa said. A word that he wouldn't allow himself to utter. If he sank into thoughts about who he had been and what he had left behind, he wouldn't be able to go on. Survival lay only in forgetting.

Kostya trailed along behind them, raising his face to the sky stretched tight as a sheet, clutching handfuls of falling snow in his fists and shouting, "Angels' feathers!"

13

Sparks of fire and particles of burning ash swirled above Fanny's head, but unlike Kostya she didn't try to catch them in her hands. Would this cycle of senseless conquests never end? Russian forces had again entered Siret, and this time they had burned down the Franz Joseph High School to its foundation.

In front of her eyes it all turned to ash. The books, the notebooks, the bench on which she once sat. Why did they choose to burn down the school, of all places? Simply because it was there. And the wooden benches and pencils and books and notebooks were the perfect fuel for the fire. The rioting Russians were wild in the streets, throwing into the flames anything that came to hand.

Despite the warning not to leave the house, Fanny had snuck outside. Maybe she could discover something about her missing man.

If only Gabriel had a grave. For the first time she thought of him as dead. She was just feeling weak, she reproved herself. She would rally, and she planned to give wide berth to the Siret cemetery, where the tombstones of Jews had marked their graves since the fifteenth century.

She pressed herself against the wall of one of the destroyed houses, her body absorbing the heat, and watched an enthusiastic soldier throwing first a chair and then a writing desk into the fire. He struggled with a thick heavy book that he also heaved into the flames.

His satisfied grunt could be heard throughout the alleyway, followed by the marching song that was familiar to all who lived in the vicinity of the battles, *Farewell to Slavianka*. Fanny detested it.

She tried to blend into the wall. Don't make a move. Lot's wife watching Sodom burn. But the tongue of fire ascending from the pages of the book revealed her presence.

"There's a woman here!" a soldier shouted, and in an instant two others burst out of the alley. In the light of the flames she watched in horror as one of them began to unbuckle his belt. And before she had a chance to try to get away he was on her, pinning her to the wall with his knees and leaning on her with the full weight of his body.

"I'm first!" he declared. He pulled her head back by the hair and groped wildly at her breasts.

It was the end of her. Why had she not heeded the warnings? Why did she have to take a risk and go out to the burning school? Maybe she really had lost her mind?

Fanny struggled. She scratched the soldier on his cheek and he responded by punching her in the face. Blood trickled from her forehead.

"I like it when they fight back," he shouted to his friends.

"Soon you'll get a taste of the Russian flavor," the second soldier joined in, "you stuck a knife in our backs, you filthy traitors. Now we'll stick you with something else."

The first soldier twisted her arm, the second ripped her dress, and the third unzipped his trousers. With the last of her strength she kicked at the legs of the one who had her pinned against the wall.

"Hold down the Jewish bitch!" he ordered his friends. They held her tightly on both sides and she saw that he had already pulled down his underwear.

She wanted to cry out "Hear, Oh Israel," but the words stuck in her throat. She didn't want to die young. She hadn't managed to get married yet. She hadn't had children.

But she wouldn't die a virgin.

Suddenly there was the sound of a shot. The soldiers immediately backed off. The coarse hands released her and she fell to the ground, trying desperately to cover herself with the pieces of her dress.

A different hand reached out to her. Someone helped her to her feet. At first she saw only the shine of his insignia, and then she recognized an officer with the rank of colonel.

"Blessed are You, Lord our God, King of the universe, Who bestows kindness upon the culpable, for He has bestowed goodness to me," she mumbled the Blessing of Thanksgiving. She was shaking so hard that she could barely stand.

The colonel barked a threat to the soldiers, and they hurried to salute and then disappeared down the alley. The school was still in flames, and the smoke that choked her triggered a fit of coughing.

The colonel gathered her to him and responded, "May He who has bestowed beneficence upon you always bestow every beneficence upon you."

The flames died down. The colonel turned his face away so that she could cover herself as best she could, and then apologized in the name of the Czar's army for the disgraceful behavior of its soldiers.

He apologized in Yiddish.

He asked if he could walk her home, and it seemed to Fanny like the longest journey she had ever made.

Inside the clouds of smoke he told her that he was born in Odessa and had been kidnapped by the Czar's soldiers. He had learned to hide his Jewish origins.

"And how did you know that I was Jewish?"

"I heard you shouting 'Hear, Oh Israel.'"

Yet she clearly remembered that she had been struck dumb.

On her doorstep he bid her farewell, wishing her peace and life.

"Life," said the colonel, "the Hebrew word is the acronym for the times when you must say the Blessing of Thanksgiving: bandage, suffering, sea, desert."

"You remember!"

"I've said the blessing dozens of times. Maybe it was the blessing that protected me."

The following morning, in the "Blessings" tractate in the Talmud, Fanny would read about the quartet of categories for which one should say thanks: for safely crossing the sea, for safely crossing the desert, for recovering from illness, and for being freed from imprisonment.

And what of she who was rescued from rape? Why didn't the *Shulchan Aruch,* a written manual containing Jewish Law, mention those brave survivors?

With his hand, the colonel wiped the blood from her lips. His touch was gentle.

"You will forget. You must forget," he whispered.

Perhaps, if Fanny had been blessed with the capacity for forgetting, she would have broken her allegiance to her missing man. Suddenly Gabriel's image seemed intangible in the presence of the flesh and blood colonel. If the door hadn't opened and Lizzie hadn't flung herself at Fanny, sobbing with relief, she would have rested her head against his broad chest and sought solace in his arms. He was a good looking, powerful man, no shorter than her betrothed, maybe even taller. If he had remained in Siret, there might have been a surprising plot twist, and Fanny's entire life would have been utterly changed. Such things happen, and an emotional connection between rescuer and rescued is hardly improbable. But the battles with the Austrians started up again, and the Russian knight was ordered to return to the front. He never returned to Siret.

On the following Sabbath in the synagogue, when Abraham Katz stood by the Torah scroll and recited the "Blessing of Thanksgiving" for the miracle that had occurred to his daughter, Fanny sat in the women's section and tried to convince herself that one day she would see Gabriel through the partition and hear his voice from beside the Holy Ark, thanking the Holy One Blessed Be He for bringing him safely home.

As she left the synagogue she absentmindedly touched her head and felt something stuck in her hair. It was particles of ash from the burning school. For days she combed through her hair and still she couldn't get rid of them. But the blows of the soldiers left no scar, and Fanny's skin would remain clear and unblemished to the end of her days.

14

Larissa didn't tell Gabriel that she loved him. The phrase "I love you" wasn't as overused as it is today, and lovers in the past rarely spoke of their love, if at all. A declaration of love was made in writing, which leads to regret at the disappearance of letters from the vista of human communication, not to mention the superstitions that abounded about love letters. If the hand of the lover shook during the writing of the letter, it was a sign that the love was mutual. An ink stain on the paper meant that the beloved also yearned for the letter-writer. And since relationships involved prolonged periods characterized by the agonizing torture of waiting, the phrase "I love" had tremendous power and everlasting potency.

But Larissa never penned a single line to Gabriel, and never expressed her feelings explicitly in words. She revealed that she was in love with him when she told him that she wanted to convert.

One Friday night, when the temperature plummeted below zero and the snow was piled high in the fields, she lit two candles to the delight of Kostya, who wanted to blow them out and make a wish. Gabriel was sure that her intention was to add some heat to the freezing house, and didn't think anything of it. Later, pork vanished from Larissa's menu, and he overheard her explaining to the boy that it wasn't fitting to eat the flesh of an animal that rummages in the garbage. A fleeting whim, Gabriel thought to himself, but what really hinted at the seriousness of her intentions was the fact that she forewent her nightly portion of pleasure for two whole weeks and went to wash in the river, because she had heard that Jewish women abstained when they were menstruating and immersed themselves in water before intercourse.

Gabriel naively thought that her surprising abstinence stemmed from some women's ailment, something beyond his understanding, so he didn't pry. Larissa discreetly threaded her actions into the intimate weave of their lives, making no declarations, only asking seemingly innocent questions from time to time.

"Tell me, Gabriel, is a Jew only someone who is born a Jew?"

"No."

"How does a non-Jew become a Jew?"

"It's not simple to become a Jew. The Jews don't accept everyone. There are tests to be passed."

"Why? The Jews don't want there to be more Jews in the world?"

"I don't know."

"And someone who's born a Jew is always a Jew?"

Gabriel chose to remain silent, but the question continued to nag at him at night following another passionate encounter with Larissa. Would he still be considered a Jew after attending church regularly and making the sign of the crucifix countless times? And what would happen when he entered a synagogue again and stood before the Holy Ark? Even if the Merciful and Benevolent One in heaven forgave him, would he be forgiven by human beings?

At night he dreamed that he was in a dark, dense forest, searching fruitlessly on all fours for something, but he didn't know what. Suddenly a yawning chasm appears, emanating flickering sparks of light. As he crawls toward it, to his horror he sees that it's shrapnel, falling in silence like an upward rain of meteors. Instead of a uniform he finds himself wrapped in the prayer shawl that he wore at his bar mitzvah. He runs the fringes through his fingers as he searches for his phylacteries. To stay or to go? Either way, death awaits him.

A hand pulls grabs him, prevents him from moving away.

"You are stuck with me, Jew! We will remain together for all eternity." Von-Hoffenberg's voice echoes from the gaping cut in the earth as he holds onto Gabriel with all his might.

Better to die under an expanse of sky than to be buried with someone whose eyes are always staring open.

In the dream he punches, strikes out, and struggles, but Von-Hoffenberg won't relent. Then from nowhere an axe appears and Gabriel throws himself at the major and lops off his arm with one blow. A hot liquid sprays over his body and soaks into his prayer shawl. The fringes are dripping.

Silence reigns in the pit in the shadow of death, and only the tremors disclose the thunderous noise outside. As the two men struggle, the opening to the trench is sealed.

"I cry out before You," he screams in the dream.

Even in his half-asleep, half-awake state, he continued to feel the hot liquid crawling on his flesh like slimy worms. Suddenly another hand was on his body. He lashed out at it wildly and searched for the axe. He must rid himself of Von-Hoffenberg once and for all.

Larissa's voice penetrated the fog of his senses, hushing him as if he were Kostya.

"Enough Gabril. Enough my love."

She drew him into her embrace, trying to erase the nightmare with her caresses. When he opened his eyes he saw that it wasn't his bar mitzvah prayer shawl that covered him, but a sheet that had once been stretched taut on a Russian clothesline.

"I will stay with you. We will always be together," whispered Larissa, and his blood froze in his veins.

She immediately wanted to make love, licking his nipples and rubbing her breasts against his chest, but he remained flaccid. In the morning she pulled the sheet down to expose his body, kissing his member as she told him that she had decided to become a Jewess.

15

In the third year of the war the circus returned to Siret. Although the concept was somewhat beyond the magnitude of the modest fair that passed through the towns and villages of Bukovina each year, for the spectators it was a festive break from the troubles and a symbol of stability in a fragile and faltering world.

Fanny always loved the agile monkeys, the bear that danced to the strains of the harmonica and the wolf that ate chocolate straight from the hand of its gaunt trainer, who looked like he might be a candidate for prey himself. Lizzie, on the other hand, loathed them, and especially the three clowns in white makeup, with the red balls affixed to their noses, who amused the crowds with their pranks and deliberately tripped and fell into the puddle in the empty lot beside the market.

But there was no dispute about the jewel in the crown of the circus – the pair of acrobats who were two "of ours," as Abraham Katz proudly declared. The first was Molnar, who would walk a tightrope suspended between two houses on opposite sides of the main street. He held a long pole to keep his balance, his feet encased in soft slippers, while his energetic assistant extended a hat to the spectators, entreating them to drop more and more coins into it.

But the star whose fame extended even beyond Bukovina was "The Man with Iron Muscles," Zishe Breitbart, a Pole, or as he was commonly known, "Samson the Great." He bent iron bars with his bare hands, pulled the reins of horses with his teeth, and for his most famous trick, he would lie in the road underneath a pile of planks over which a heavy truck would roll. Fanny would see him again in the future, emerging unscathed, with her son Yitzhak – my father – by her side. After the dramatic escapade underneath the truck "The Man with Iron Muscles" would show off his bulging muscles for the children and the day when he encouraged Yitzhak to pinch them, was a memory that would stay with him for the rest of his life.

Kalman-Zelig Hirsch claimed that it was just a trick from the days of the great Houdini and that the pile of planks was really a concave structure set in place in advance underneath the truck, into which the man with the iron muscles squeezed himself until the danger passed, but who cared. The main thing was that the trickster survived, unlike so many of the children who watched the show with Yitzhak, and perished in the next world war.

But Yitzhak had yet to be born, and on that day the cries of different children could be heard in the street, "The circus is back!" they shouted, and Fanny became aware of the rush of feet moving toward the market. Ever since the nightmare evening when she had almost been raped, she had shut herself in the house, bottling beer from morning to night. She stopped reading romantic novels and even neglected Penelope the weaver and her nightly unpicking of her shroud. Anxious Abraham Katz was at a loss to respond to the gloom that had taken hold of his daughter. All the efforts of her sisters to reignite her spark met with failure. Paula shared her plans to have a child, and Lizzie told her about the struggles of the suffragettes in England to win the right for women to vote in public elections. None of it made any difference. The fact that Fanny no longer mentioned Gabriel increased the sisters' worry, and they sought the advice of a doctor who was expert in the new theories of Sigmund Freud from Vienna, only to discover that he had been sent to the front in France.

It was the children's cries of joy that cracked the shell of Fanny's withdrawal. They were a reminder that outside, a world still existed. Maybe the circus was an indication that order would also be restored in her life. At the same time, the thought of once again encountering men in pursuit of a victim horrified her. But in the end, the possibility of learning something about

Gabriel won out. Perhaps one of the clowns, or the trainer of the wolf or the dancing bear, had run into him somewhere in their travels.

Fanny covered her face with a scarf and crossed the threshold, inhaling the outside air as if re-discovering it. Despite her fondness for the darting monkeys and the waltzing bear, she chose to visit the fortuneteller. She had never been one to believe in sorcery and divination, but influenced by the figure of Cassandra, the blind prophetess who foretold the fall of Troy, she approached the tent of the gypsy woman. It was propped up against a house that had only two walls still standing, and to spruce up the ruin a screen of colorful rags had been strung across to form a makeshift entrance.

A single oil lamp burned in the tent, and the gypsy asked her customer to reveal her face. Fanny removed her scarf and leaned into the circle of light. The gypsy observed her for a while. "You have experienced great suffering," she said, before reaching for her pack of cards.

She was a young woman with nut-brown skin, bright green eyes that shone beneath her flowered kerchief and two black braids that flowed around her neck, threaded with colorful bits of cloth. Two huge gold hoops hung from her ears and she wore a gaudy bead necklace and a chain of perforated coins. Her red skirt had a pattern of tiny flowers. Fanny had never seen so much color concentrated in one woman. When she smiled, a gold tooth shone in the gypsy's mouth.

The fortuneteller extended her deck of cards like a bouquet she had gathered from the folds of her skirt.

The card Fanny chose had a picture of tiny wings spaced some distance apart.

"Fly away bird," whispered the gypsy woman.

Fanny nudged the card with a hesitant finger and acknowledged that her Yiddish name was "Faigie," which means bird.

She deliberated at length over the next card. She touched one, changed her mind, and after several false starts she closed her eyes and withdrew a card from the deck with a sharp movement. Surprisingly, this card also bore a pair of wings, only this time they were large and joined together with a hoop such as a trapeze artist might use.

The gypsy took her time examining the card, and now she kept silent. Fanny placed a pile of coins before her and urged her to prophesy.

"Your angel is delayed," the gypsy muttered, and Fanny had the impression that she was hiding something.

"Angel?"

"In the place where he is, they think he's an angel."

Fanny shoved the card away. "He was killed," she murmured in agony, "Gabriel is in heaven."

The gypsy turned over the card. The large wings and the hoop vanished. She leaned toward Fanny and the coins on her necklace jangled.

"In the place where he is, they search for his wings."

"Where is he?"

The gypsy said that only partial prophecies are received. A portion always remains secret, since the future is flexible and susceptible to change.

"Is he a prisoner?"

"He isn't free."

"Is his life in danger?"

"It's his soul that is in danger."

The answers sounded obtuse, just like those of the Oracle at Delphi in Greek mythology.

The gypsy held Fanny's wrist, opening her hand to reveal the palm. Her dark fingers flitted over the lines that traversed it.

"You will have a long life, bird," she said, attempting to infuse her voice with mirth.

"And marriage?"

"You will marry twice."

Fanny pushed the pile of coins toward the gypsy and burst out laughing. It was the first time she had laughed since the night of the flames, and her laughter was bitter. The gypsy was no Cassandra, but a fraud. The future wasn't giving up its secrets, much less so for a woman dressed in red with a gold tooth. How she had allowed herself to be deceived? How pathetic. To waste her hard-earned money on baseless nonsense. Two marriages? Even one was in doubt.

The sounds of a harmonica could be heard from outside the tent, followed by the roars of the crowd. The bear was dancing.

The gypsy leaned closer to Fanny, raising her voice to be heard over the commotion outside.

"A soldier attacked me as well," she said.

Fanny was struck dumb.

"And who saved you?" she finally asked.

"Saved me?"

Now it was the other woman's turn to laugh, and hers was a more bitter sound than her client's had been. From beneath her flowered skirt she suddenly pulled out a dagger. The light of the oil lamp was reflected in its blade.

"I cut the bastard's face. From his eye to his mouth. He bled like a stuck pig. I deliberately left him alive. That way he'll never forget me. No woman in the world will lie with him now!"

The gypsy proffered the dagger to Fanny.

"Take it bird, you'll need it. The war isn't over, and there will be another war. No less terrible."

Fanny wavered, almost tripped as made to rise. The voice of the next customer could be heard, clamoring for his turn, "Madam, move on already! There are more people waiting in line for the future."

Fanny pushed away the dagger and shoved the coins into the gypsy's hand. She bent and hid the weapon in her stocking again, under her floral skirt.

"The future doesn't only belong to you, madam!" The voice called again from outside the tent.

The fortuneteller placed the coins in a cloth purse affixed to her belt. Fanny couldn't take her eyes off it. It was the most amazing object she had ever seen, decorated with glittering gems and metal plates worked to resemble lace. A precious object that belonged in a museum.

"I wouldn't give you that for any price, bird. It was a gift."

"A gift?" The tone of Fanny's voice betrayed her skepticism.

"You think I stole this wallet, don't you? Because we gypsies are thieves. They hate us no less than they hate you Jews. But this was a gift."

"Who from?"

"From the only man who loved me."

"How do you know that he loved you?"

"He always came back to me."

"And is that proof of love?" Fanny took a step back and bumped into the lamp. The light went out.

"I will give you something else, bird."

"I have no way to pay you."

"It's free. But in return you must promise me something."

Fanny didn't reply. She didn't want to make a promise to a strange woman that she couldn't keep.

"That you won't clip your angel's wings."

Fanny groped her way to the screen of rags, guided by the strains of the harmonica playing for the dancing bear, the tattered curtain wrapping itself around her as she stepped outside. The impatient customer had already left. The gypsy's whisper seared the darkness. It was an ancient gypsy blessing, a valuable gift bestowed upon Fanny by a red Cassandra with a golden tooth.

> Our lives are short, one day only,
> We shouldn't live in darkness, alone and lonely,
> To the lives of those who come and go,
> Until the withering of all the flowers that grow,
> Until the end of all the stories has come
> And the writing of all the songs is done,
> Until the end of pain has come to light,
> Until the stars blink out in blackest night.

Fanny would recall the ancient blessing, especially during the Second World War, so accurately predicted by the gypsy.

16

Gabriel didn't believe in superstitions. If his sister Anna spat when she encountered a black cat, he chuckled. At night, when she shook in fear of monsters in the dark, he tried to persuade her that there was no such thing as dybbuks or demons.

Ever since the war he had viewed only rulers and generals as representatives of the forces of darkness on Earth.

But when it came to Larissa, Gabriel chose to keep his opinions to himself. One winter day she hung a slaughtered goose upside down, explaining that if the head pointed downward, the evil spirits would fall out. Gabriel ignored her request that for good measure he knock on the wooden table.

"It's like Jesus' cross," she said.

"Knocking won't protect us," he responded, and her face filled with sorrow.

"Who will protect us, Gabril, the Jewish or the Christian God?"

In order to placate her, he knocked on the table with his fist.

In the evening Larissa cut the goose in pieces, and Kostya joined her enthusiastically. First he licked his fingers, which were coated in fat, and then he tossed the bones in the air, laughing merrily all the time.

Larissa instructed him to wash the bones in a tub and then spread them on the table, like a deck of cards. First she rummaged through them, sniffed at them, and then began to organize them, ceaselessly creating different patterns. At first Gabriel thought that she wanted to entertain the child, but she looked serious, completely absorbed in her task.

"What are you doing, Matushka?"

"I am predicting the future."

If the bones were thick and light-colored, it would be a snowy winter, she explained. And if they were short and dark, it would be cloudy and rainy.

Gabriel did not tell her who it is who receives the gift of prophecy. To each his own belief. Who was she hurting? For Larissa, the geese were more than a source of income. She was devoted to the geese, even serenading them as she fattened them up, but when the time for slaughter arrived she never hesitated to wield the knife. That is the way of the world, she said. Animals were meant to be food for people. Wasn't it written in the holy books?

Larissa's superstitions were focused on geese. One day she heard the honking of a goose before dawn and shot out of bed in a panic. It's a warning sign, she told Gabriel. She began to frantically spread crucifixes around the house and hang garlic necklaces above the front door. Against his will he was caught up in her anxiety and spent the day looking nervously over his shoulder, expecting to see the military police with a warrant for his arrest.

Another time Larissa found a goose egg that was brownish-grey and immediately threw it into the fire, since that color meant bad luck.

At supper, when he protested, "You see, nothing happened," she replied, "That's only because I dealt with it right away."

And most important of all – the flight of the geese. Larissa scrutinized it like a lookout in the trenches, since if a goose flies in circles above the house it means that death lies in wait for its inhabitants.

Death is always lurking, Gabriel thought to himself. With or without the geese.

Kostya arranged the bones in a circle on the table, and Larissa immediately rearranged them. He clenched the bones in his fist and arranged them in the shape of a cross.

"Is this all right, Matushka?"

She knocked on the table.

"Gabril, what do the Jews do to protect themselves?"

It was the first time she had mentioned Jews in the presence of the child.

Kostya scrambled to his feet. "They don't deserve protection. They crucified our Lord the Messiah."

"No Kostya. The Romans crucified him."

There was silence in the room.

"We all make mistakes sometimes, Kostya," Gabriel finally murmured.

The boy struck the table. The bones clattered and bounced.

"That's not right, Matushka! The Jews are bad. The Jews are dangerous. Our teacher says so too!"

Gabriel bent over the child.

"Have you ever seen a Jew, Kostya?"

Kostya crossed himself in terror.

"Once upon a time there was a Jewish boy," said Gabriel, "Do you know what his name was?"

"No."

"Jesus."

The child looked at his mother.

"Is it true, Matushka? Jesus was once a Jewish boy?"

Larissa nodded. She swept up the goose bones from the table as if they were a bunch of flowers.

"It will be rainy," she declared, and she went out to the yard to throw the bones to the dog.

Kostya and Gabriel were left by themselves, the boy trying to make sense of what he had just heard.

"If our Lord the Messiah was a Jewish boy, then am I also a bit of a Jewish boy?"

Suddenly Gabriel was overwhelmed with longing. Kostya reminded him of Anna. They were both gripped by anxiety about the perils of the world. He hugged the child, trying in vain to soothe him, and his heart ached with yearning.

The next day the neighbor Abilov told them that the Austrians had again suffered a defeat, and Bukovina had fallen to the Russian army. Towns and villages had been burned and destroyed. People were turned out of their homes and scattered everywhere.

The jubilation of the farmers was more than Gabriel could bear. Feigning fatigue he declined the invitation to celebrate at the tavern. Bukovina destroyed. And maybe everything he had known was erased, gone forever? What had happened to his mother and his sister? He felt a stab of pain. He didn't give a thought to Fanny.

He raised his eyes to the trickling sky, murmuring the Song of Ascent, Psalm 130, "For with the Lord is unfailing love and with Him is full redemption. He Himself will redeem Israel from all their sins."

Larissa leaned on the windowsill and listened to his soft murmuring. The man she had fallen in love with believed in evil spirits, she told herself with satisfaction, but like all men he was ashamed to admit it, lest he be suspected of weakness. From the jumble of foreign words she caught only one, "Israel."

The next time she went to church she paid two kopeks for a candle, knelt before Mary holding the baby Jesus and poured out her heart to them. So what if her beloved was a Jew? Better a good Jew than a drunk, abusive Christian. Larissa swore to the Holy Mother and her son that she would never abandon them, even when she became a Jewess. They would understand. After all, they too once observed the Jewish commandments. By the time she returned to the farm she had made up her mind. She would travel to Odessa to find a rabbi.

It was the third year of the war.

17

By the time the Russians conquered Bukovina for the third time it was already a battered place that had been passed from hand to hand like an old whore, its pastoral views bisected, its people on the verge of collapse. Even its Slavic namesake, the maple or "buk" trees, were charred, their foliage late to bloom.

When Abraham Katz became ill it fell to Fanny to provide for the family. Now she sold their bottles of beer at the side of the road, from a small cart. Lizzie helped her to push it, complaining ceaselessly about the price that women pay for the mad wars waged by men.

Every time some drunk annoyed them Fanny regretted not having accepted the dagger from the gypsy.

She thought often about that gold-toothed Cassandra. Had she too been cursed so that no one believed her prophecies? Fanny secretly interrogated the rabbi who told her about the three angels that watch over man, Senoi, Sensenoi, and Semangelof. She memorized the strange names and would mumble them at every sign of threat they encountered on the road.

"I don't believe in angels," Lizzie announced.

The rabbi said that they are similar to people, Fanny explained. Like them, they have knowledge and understanding, and they even walk upright and speak in the holy tongue. "Only in one way are they different from us: the angels are destined for eternal life, while we are destined for death," she quoted the rabbi.

Lizzie insisted, "You must believe in them, or else you wouldn't ask for the help of Senoi, Sensenoi, and Semangelof."

Their names were already familiar to her. Had she known that the three were meant to defend against Lilith, Adam's first wife, they would have been disqualified on the spot. The day would come when the exiled woman from the Bible would become a role model, and Lizzie would wield her example as she demanded equality.

Wasn't it better to believe in angels than in people? Fanny asked herself, thinking again about the Russian colonel who had saved her life. A man reeking of sweat, filth, and blood, far from the embodiment of an angel.

"Why are there no female angels?" Lizzie demanded, and Fanny thought about the gypsy.

"Do you think he will come back?"

He.

Lizzie didn't have to say his name.

Fanny told no one about the gypsy's prophecy that she would marry twice.

To her horror, she discovered that Gabriel's face was fading from her memory. Was he as tall and handsome as she imagined, or would she not even recognize him when he returned?

If he returned.

For the first time she entertained a doubt.

On that day the sisters didn't manage to sell anything, as though there were no longer any despairing souls who required the solace of alcohol. Toward evening they managed to trade two bottles of beer for half a loaf of bread. They pulled the cart along the riverbank, staying out of sight of the Russian soldiers. Darkness fell swiftly, and the roads to town were blocked.

Fanny had no choice but to steer her sister toward the graveyard. Lizzie resisted. From there they could jump over the fence, Fanny tried to convince her. The place frightened her as well, especially at night. Not to mention that she had vowed never to set foot there until her betrothed was safely returned. But they had no other choice.

She led the way, feigning bravery, even though the creaking of the wagon, which sounded like a signal from the world to come, set her trembling. The bottles of beer knocked against each other, but they were unwilling to part with their precious merchandise.

Darkness swallowed the engravings on the tombstones – masterpieces that had made the cemetery one of the most famous in Europe. The lions, stags, and bears grasping their crowns vanished. The lights and candlesticks and priestly blessings disappeared as if they had never been.

The crooked stones looked like outstretched fingers, waiting to catch the two women and drag them deep into the earth.

"There's no reason to fear the dead," Lizzie whispered, but it seemed that she was trying to convince herself. Both had already learned that there was much more to fear from the living.

A shadow flitted among the tombstones and the sisters crouched down, pressing themselves against the cart that sheltered them.

The barking revealed that it was just a stray dog that had found refuge in the cemetery from the bullets and shells. Or perhaps it was the mythical Cerberus with three heads, who guards the gates to the Underworld, Fanny wondered.

The dog advanced, snarling at the two women.

The bite of a stray dog was fatal, and where would they find an antidote for rabies in those terrible days?

His jaw gaped and his fangs were exposed as he growled threateningly. If only she had the gypsy's dagger. Why hadn't she taken it? How stupid of her.

Fanny pushed Lizzie behind her and began to mumble, "Senoi, Sensenoi, and Semangelof." The dog's barking subsided, but it stayed where it was, a tense silhouette. "For He will command His angels concerning you to guard you in all your ways," Lizzie whispered the verse from the Book of Psalms, but neither did this cause the dog to leave. Saliva dripped from his mouth and his foul smell made them gag.

Fanny reached into the cart and extracted one of the bottles, then smashed it against a nearby headstone. Drops of beer sprayed in every direction. She brandished the broken bottle that glinted in the dark like the blade of a dagger. She was about to pounce on the dog when suddenly it shook its coat, climbed onto the nearest grave and began to greedily lap up the remains of the beer. Seizing the opportunity she hurriedly pulled along Lizzie and the cart, and they broke into a run, stepping on graves, stumbling into headstones, flattening the wild grass. An eternity passed before they reached the edge of the cemetery. The lights of the town were already twinkling in the distance. They jumped the fence, handing over the cart from one to the other, as the barking of the dog that had resumed the chase faded in the distance.

On the other side of the fence Fanny tripped and fell into an open pit. It was gaping in the earth, dry and desolate, as though it had been prepared many days before.

A grave beyond the fence was meant for one who had abandoned life by taking his own, or abandoned his people by converting to another religion. Which Jew had become a gentile and would be buried in it?

Grasping Lizzie's outstretched arms Fanny climbed out of the pit. Lizzie's laughter sounded like sobs, "You'll always be able to tell your children that you rose from the grave."

18

Larissa perched in the wagon that was harnessed to the oxen owned by the farmer Abilov, wearing her best blouse, embroidered with star-thistles, her honey braids coiled atop her head. The neighbor had agreed to drive her to the train station, after she explained that she had to reach distant Odessa urgently to visit her sick aunt.

"I didn't know you had relatives in Odessa."

"On my mother's side."

"You left the farm in the care of the laborer?"

Larissa was silent.

"You trust him?" the farmer continued, "What do you know about him? Maybe he's one of those troublemakers the Secret Police are looking for."

Larissa declared that she had complete faith in Gabriel.

Abilov insisted that there was something suspicious about the stranger. Too well-educated, too polite, always trying to please the few men who remained in the village. Maybe he was a spy in the service of the enemy? Once he had overheard him mumbling in some strange language.

"He's one of us," Larissa said firmly.

"There's no doubt that he's a devoted Christian who never misses mass in church," Abilov said. Even the priest had remarked on his piety. But who knew? Maybe he belonged to those Bolshevik firebrands who are so captivated by the theories of Vladimir Ilyich Ulyanov, that upstart they call Lenin.

Larissa swore that her laborer was a staunch supporter of the Czar's regime, and even admired the Czarina, who ruled in his absence with the aid of his advisor, the mystic and holy man Rasputin.

"The Czarina isn't one of ours either," declared Abilov. "She was born in Germany. And Rasputin is a conman who has her hypnotized." When he stopped at the train station he advised her to beware of defeatists who secretly negotiated the conditions of Mother Russia's surrender. The motherland was in danger not only from enemies without, but also from traitors at home.

"Your worker will cause you trouble one day, Larissa Yefimovna," he hissed as she climbed down. And as he snapped the reins it occurred to him that he should marry Larissa and combine the two farms.

Through the window of the moving train she surveyed the ravages of the war. Scorched fields, charred tree trunks, horse carcasses from which the flesh had been peeled off for food, the skeletons of houses like teeth half-pulled, and by the sides of the road tattered clothing, rags, rusty teapots, cooking pots and chamber pots, painful signs that people had abandoned their homes in panic.

As she gazed at the devastation she held tightly to the crucifix hanging at her neck and her heart contracted with guilt. So absorbed had she been in her tiny world, with the potatoes and the turnips, the geese, Kostya and her Jewish lover, that she had suppressed the war that continued to sow destruction around them. She hadn't visited her husband's grave in a long time. Larissa couldn't know that he was one of two million dead. Like so many other women she was clinging to life with her fingernails and her teeth, just as Fanny was doing in Siret, although so many miles separated them and Larissa would never meet her.

In Odessa she was like a girl in Wonderland. For the first time in her life she saw a streetcar and window displays in stores. She crossed the crowded street, dizzy with the comings and goings and the cars traveling on the main boulevard. At every corner someone offered her alcohol from a teapot, to circumvent the new law that prohibited the sale of hard liquor. But too quickly the delightful sights disappeared. Beggars loitered on the platforms, and legless men extended their hands to her at street corners. Amputees held out their stumps, bandaged in rags, and begged for her kopeks. Three deserters approached her. They were drunk, smashing every window they passed, and one soldier in a ragged uniform had lacerated a rat with his rusty bayonet and waved the still-twitching animal in her face.

"Buy it!" he pushed the carcass of the bleeding rat toward the silver cross at her throat. When she refused, he tried to tear it from her. She barely managed to get away, haunted by the thought that this could easily have been the fate of Gabril, if he hadn't found shelter with her.

As she searched for the Jewish quarter children tugged at her dress and begged for a piece of bread, and she thanked Jesus and Mary that Kostya had been spared such a fate. And now she was about to betray the Holy Mother and her son for the sake of love. And why should Gabril not convert for her? After all, he attended church regularly, received Holy Communion and recited all the prayers. His circumcised member would be seen by her alone.

What was Odessa to him? He could tell his relatives – whoever they might be – that he had joined his life to that of the woman who had saved him. But she knew that for the rest of his days he would hold it against her that she had forced him to abandon his faith. There was no other way. She would make the concession for him. She wanted to have his children. A little sister for Kostya. A warmth spread between her thighs, as she played with her naked ring finger. She had removed it the day before, in preparation for her journey. She doubted that Gabriel had noticed.

She found the synagogue – the Jews called it the *shtiebel* – after wandering for a long time in the Jewish area. It was a narrow nook, its windows covered in thick layers of dust, the lock for its broken door a plank of wood. In the line of people waiting to see the rabbi she heard that anti-Semites were in an uproar in the region, and had recently even attempted to set fire to the place.

Jew-haters. Like the farmer Abilov. Had he known the true purpose of her journey to Odessa he would have ordered his oxen to trample her under their hooves and then left her corpse by the side of the road.

Prayer books were scattered everywhere, their binding printed with foreign letters. Faded skullcaps lay on the seats. Poverty clutched at everything, as if the Jewish God was impoverished and would soon be reaching out his palm like the wretched people in the street.

The line extended from the *shtiebel*'s doorway, as more people joined to seek the rabbi's advice, mostly wrinkled elderly people who sighed ceaselessly. She was careful to hide her crucifix deep under her collar, as she observed her lover's people – the first she had ever seen – and they were no different from the other miserable people in the streets, except for the skullcaps on their heads and the Jewish language that they spoke. It sounded like German. Maybe one of them was his relative?

Larissa pulled her kerchief tight, copying the movements of the Jewish women she had seen at the entrance, and went in to the rabbi. She poured out her burning love before him as if he was a priest. And to convince him of the seriousness of her intentions she had come armed with a verse from the Song of Songs from a copy of the Old Testament that she had found in an ancient trunk that had belonged to her mother, "But I found him whom my soul loveth, I held him, and would not let him go."

Love is not reason enough for conversion, said the rabbi. Judaism receives only those who want to enter the fold for the sake of heaven.

"And is love not from heaven?" Larissa questioned.

What is it about you Jews, who are so reluctant to accept more people, and the few who ask to join you, you spurn? The exact opposite of the Christians who always seek to expand the circle of believers in Jesus, and even just a sprinkling more would be welcomed.

"I will believe in the God who brought my love to me," Larissa pledged. If He had chosen to send her a Jew, it was a sign that the ways of love were not foreign to him.

"Because love is from God, and everyone who loves has been born from God and gains the knowledge of God," Larissa quoted passionately from the First Epistle of John in the New Testament. The rabbi, who did not recognize the source, was impressed by her debating skills. However, he still decreed that love and faith were separate. One could believe without loving and love without believing.

The line grew longer, but no one disturbed the woman with the tight kerchief and the tightly coiled wheat-colored braids who argued with the rabbi. With his white beard and penetrating eyes he looked like the incarnation of that Jewish God, with his fill of bitter problems. How was it within the old man's power to make the Virgin Mary conceive? Perhaps his years fell away when he transformed himself into the Christian God?

Since Larissa's knowledge of the Old Testament was limited, she did not recognize the verse from the Song of Songs that was the rabbi's rejoinder, "For love is strong as death," and in fact the connection between death and love elicited a harsh response from her.

"For love is strong as life," she retorted, and he thought that could be an interesting addition to the work composed by King Solomon, who had had a thousand wives.

Perhaps some Jewish blood flowed in the veins of the woman who wielded arguments so well? The rabbi began to interrogate her about her mother. After all, the Bible had been found in an old trunk of hers.

It was possible that she was one of the Anusim, and he would find a justification in Jewish law for returning her to her people. However, he discovered no Jewish roots in her answers to his questions. She was a Russian down through the generations.

"What is the name of your man?"

"Gabril."

She described him. Tall, handsome, educated, literate, doesn't drink too much, doesn't beat a woman or curse. She said he was a soldier and by the skin of his teeth escaped death. Was raised in Odessa.

The rabbi said that he didn't know of any Gabril.

"Many waters cannot quench love; rivers cannot sweep it away," the rabbi nodded in agreement, and when she asked where in holy writ the things could be found, he sent her back to the Old Testament.

"What is 'Shema Yisrael?'"

Larissa asked this when she was just about to leave.

The rabbi stood, his trembling hand clutching at his beard.

"Where did you get those words?"

"Gabril says them every night. What do they mean?"

"Every night?"

"In bed."

Larissa looked down. The kerchief moved and her braids peeked out.

"It is a prayer recited before sleep, or before death," the rabbi said.

She raised her hand to her neck and held tightly to the hidden crucifix.

Could it be that after she and Gabril had licked each other all over, as his member trickled onto her and she still burned beneath him, he was thinking about death, of all things?

"Shema Yisrael," she whispered the phrase that was so familiar to her. "I too am also willing to say that every night. Help me, Father."

"Father," as if he was a priest.

Someone waiting in line seemed to sob, or maybe it was a sigh escaping from the rabbi. What to do with this Moabite Ruth, who was trying to convince him that his people were her people, and his God was her God? It was lucky that the rules of the Bible were once less strict than they were now. Otherwise Ruth would never have been accepted as a convert, and David and Solomon would never have been born. Then who would have written the Song of Songs?

"What is your name, woman?"

"Larissa Yefimovna."

As her fingers fumbled for something under her collar, he understood what was hidden there. Only because of the danger that this Gabril might convert for her sake and another soul of Israel might be lost did he suggest that she return, next time with him. Until then he would think about a solution to bridge between love and faith.

The meeting between the couple and the rabbi would never take place, for just around the corner the wind of the Bolshevik revolution was already blowing, and like a huge wave it was about to wash away the old world.

19

Why did the Baal Shem Tov say that the truth could be found all over the world? Because it is always an outcast, condemned to wander. Of all the

Chassidic tales Fanny had heard from her father, that was the one she remembered. Although the truth was slippery and impossible to grasp, she never ceased to search for it.

The truth was revealed to her in bullet casings, in empty, rusting tin cans, in torn German and Austrian uniforms and in mounds of dried human excrement. The truth was coils of bandages and tufts of blood-soaked cotton wool. Maybe Gabriel was one of the injured, trudging back home from the front?

Faced with the testimony from the battlefront Fanny created an alternate truth. For her he had survived. He was out there somewhere, in some temporary shelter, isolated from other people, until the fury subsided. He had written her dozens of letters, and all had been lost. He had written her name on the envelopes, but as a result of all the hardships the words had been rubbed out. She kneaded each detail in her brain until they coalesced into pictures imbued with reason and logic. An entire album of possible truths. More and more Fanny thought that he had amnesia and couldn't remember the way home. In her imagination, honed by so much activity, she discovers Gabriel wandering in a green grove. He is bare-chested like the man on the cover of the *Odyssey*. She calls his name, rushes to him, caresses his skin with her lips, and his memory is immediately restored.

"This is my woman," says her beloved as he falls into her arms.

On a spring day – clear skies and a bright sun unmoved by the ugliness and filth below – Fanny was poised to cross some tracks with her cartload of beer. A train had arrived from the front and come to a stop although there was no station in sight. Fanny abandoned her cart for a moment and hurried toward the car carrying the wounded. There weren't any windows, just a narrow slit. Unexpectedly there were no sounds of groaning or screams of pain. The men in the car were silent.

The medical officer, who had already jumped down to the tracks, tried to move her along.

"You are in the way, Fräulein."

The train idled, softly clattering, and the officer craned his head to see the engine, trying to understand what was causing the delay. The door to the car opened and an amputee was visible on the threshold, his two stumps hanging down like sacks, as he tried to hobble out with his crutches. When the officer offered to help him he swatted him away with a crutch.

He ignored Fanny as though she didn't exist.

Suddenly there was another woman at her side. Where had she come from? She was painfully thin, her hair pulled severely from her face and covered with a tight black kerchief, and she wore mourning dress.

She demanded of the medical officer that he give her the list of names of the wounded in the train car.

What did the widow want with the wounded? Her husband was no longer among the living. Why was she still searching for him? Poor woman. She must have lost her mind.

"I'm sorry for your loss," said the officer and he tried to push her away.

The woman insisted on seeing the list.

"Maybe we didn't bury the right man," she shouted at the officer. Her husband's face had been hacked to pieces and the identification wasn't certain. No one could be sure that the military authorities hadn't made a mistake. The body in the coffin – perhaps it was a strange man and not her husband. She had come all the way from Transylvania, and already been to every hospital in Bukovina in her search for her truth.

"Bury him, Madam," the amputee waved his crutch at her, "anyway, I am already dead." His laughter rolled out along the tracks. Unknown to those assembled there, the number of dead from the Austro-Hungarian Empire had already reached a million.

Fanny took a step forward. The woman's mourning scarf fluttered in the wind, partially obstructing her view, but she absorbed the sight within the car like a punch to her stomach. In the sooty light of an oil lamp she could see the field stretchers wedged together side by side. Ignoring the stench of feces and disinfectant she took another step.

"Maybe you've heard of Gabriel Herzig?"

"Another luckless moron?" the amputee bellowed again. "Why bother? Find another man, if there are any whole men left on the face of this pocked earth. Maybe you want me? I don't have any legs and my hands aren't up to much, but the mouth, Fräulein, with it I can still work wonders."

And he stuck out his tongue, licking at the air.

Fanny was undeterred as she felt for the knife hidden in her belt. She had taken it from the butcher, just in case. The amputee noticed her movements.

"What will you do to me? Cut off my member? The enemy didn't manage to destroy it. Want to feel how it stands to attention for you?"

And before he could go any further, another of the wounded presented himself at the door. A bandage was wrapped around his head, and there was a bump above the place where his ear had once been attached. He held a harmonica to his lips.

"Go back inside, soldiers," barked the officer, "Your bandages are likely to tear. That's all I need, for you to bleed on my shift."

"Then you'll be able to add two more corpses to your list," the amputee positioned his crutch in a salute.

The man with the bandaged ear began to play his harmonica. As the first strains of music filled the air the widow crossed herself and turned to Fanny, expecting her to do the same.

"You are a Jew," she hurled the words at her.

Then she spat in her direction, but Fanny managed to dodge her spray of spittle.

"You are our disaster, traitors to the homeland, dirty Jews. Cutting off part of the member. Disgusting. At lease we'll get rid of you in this war.

With one swift motion the widow overturned Fanny's cartload of beer, and the bottles rolled out, rattling as they fell. Not one of them broke. The officer leapt up, then crouched down fearlessly and crawled underneath the wheels of the train, grabbed a bottle that was lodged in the tracks, pulled off the cap with his teeth and swigged down the beer. The amputee dug his crutch into the officer's back and he obeyed, climbing under the wheels once more, gathering up bottles and handing them into the car.

A roar of joy rose from inside and the car shook.

The amputee toasted Fanny with his beer. "Long live the man with the shortened member. I hope that you find him above ground, woman, because underneath it we are all the same man. This type of member, that type. There's no difference."

The widow turned, covered her face with her mourning scarf and walked away.

One by one, more voices joined in from within the car, which now rocked to the rhythm of a song, as though buffeted by a powerful wind. The train slowly began to move and despite the increasing clatter of the wheels Fanny could make out the words.

Where oh where are the amputees?
I now have stumps just like the trees
Where did everybody go?
They're wandering the world like so.
Did I tell you, did you know?
I had a perfect body some time ago.

My stumps are not at hand,
Spread on fields of battle across the land,
One stump then another, searching for its brother,
If only one I could save, from its spot above the grave.

My leg was once right here you see
Once it was attached to me.
I took a step and tripped
From my body it was ripped
Cracked off from my bone, now it's all alone.

Long live those who come and go
Searching for those they used to know
Find another cripple,
It won't make a ripple
If the generals are right and our bones do set
We'll be cannon fodder for another battle yet…

20

Like Fanny, Larissa also searched for the truth. How can you love someone without knowing anything about him? Where did Gabril grow up? Who was his mother? Did he have siblings? He was and remained a mystery, and that intensified her attachment to him. He always made love to her with his eyes open, as if observing in wonder a luscious secret that would never be unlocked. Sometimes she thought that he feared to discover that the woman writhing passionately beneath him had been transformed into a babushka with poison dripping from her nipples. She became more and more convinced that he was one of the children who had been kidnapped by the Czar's army, who she had heard about when waiting in line at the *shtiebel.*

She had left there with her head spinning with quotations from the holy books and her wish unanswered. Why did the Jews keep to themselves and not accept others in their midst? It was that very self-segregation that made people hate them.

The street was overflowing. Larissa was caught up in the human stream. Someone stuck a red flag into her hand.

"Join the women's protest, farm woman."

The demonstrator had a delightful voice, and she fairly sang her words about the strikes breaking out across Russia and the unemployed laborers who were demanding a revolution.

"Don't pay rent to your land owner," she urged her in her melodious voice. "Soon we will be rid of all the bloodsuckers and all the lands of Mother Russia will be ours."

The idea of being free of the hold of the landowner was foreign to Larissa, and she was ashamed to reveal how limited her knowledge was of the Bolshevik Party that already controlled the duma, the Russian parliament.

The demonstrator was stocky and energetic, square-bodied, and almost without a neck, but she had perfect cherry lips and a multitude of curls that compensated for the unappealing aspects of her appearance. Buoyed by the steady stream of people there was no end to her enthusiasm. Even the deserters aren't afraid to openly express their protest, she proclaimed.

And what about my deserter? Larissa wondered. The meeting suggested by the rabbi was fraught with danger, for if Gabriel returned to Odessa it might stir up nostalgia for his former life, and who could guarantee that he wouldn't want to reunite with his relatives? Actually, why had he not tried to go secretly to the city to visit them? Perhaps he feared that someone would turn him in to the military authorities, or discover that he lived with a Christian woman.

More and more women joined the demonstration. They shouted the names of the men they had lost to the war. Larissa added the name of her dead husband, and the squat woman inclined her head in commiseration. She stayed by Larissa's side, urging her to add her voice to the growing cries of "Down with the war!"

"Where was your husband killed?"

"On the Balkan front."

"When?"

"Right at the start of the war."

The crowd advanced. Larissa noticed the members of the Red Guard, wearing the peaked worker's caps, with red ribbons on their arms. Wave upon wave of people rolled toward the main boulevard. The woman demonstrator also took hold of the red flag in Larissa's hand, and they waved it in unison above their heads. She spoke into Larissa's ear.

"And you have already found yourself a new man."

She didn't ask. She stated a fact.

"I don't blame you," she hastened to add, "We all need comfort. Why didn't you take a woman into your bed? You didn't think of that?"

Larissa hurriedly crossed herself. She had never heard such heresy before. A hundred Hail Marys couldn't make up for something that contradicted the laws of nature. But the lilting voice of the woman held no accusation or shame.

"It is also possible to love a woman. It's not a sin."

Larissa didn't say a word.

"Anyway, the men will wipe each other out," she said, "and only we will remain. A world of women."

She raised the flag higher toward the cloudy sky.

"Maybe on the other side of the border there are women like us, Serbs, Austrians, Germans, Frenchwomen, and they will also march in the streets and shout 'Down with War,' in their own languages."

She had participated in the Bloody Sunday protest in January 1905. That was when workers and their families had set out in a peaceful procession toward the Winter Palace in St. Petersburg and asked to present the Czar with a list of reforms. The army opened fire and shot them at close range. Hundreds of dead and wounded were left in the streets that day. She had survived, it wasn't clear how.

As she told the story she produced a bottle of vodka, took a long pull and began to sing. She had learned the song from wounded soldiers who had returned from the front. Recently, new words had been added.

"Repeat after me," she told Larissa.

To women to women to what they can do,
We'll find ourselves our own powers too.
We'll change the world, no guns will we wield,
But cover with flowers the whole battlefield.
Sisters, say no to those who would send us,
Like fodder for cannons to a war that would end us.

The wave of people became more and more dense, and her words were swallowed in the din as Larissa heard "fodder for cannons," a word combination with which she wasn't familiar.

"What does that mean? Explain it to me," she demanded as she took a swig of the vodka. A new world was opening before her, both frightening and wonderful. To make love to a woman. Actually, why not?

But before the other woman could reply she was savagely punched and she sagged like a rag doll. Blood dripped from her forehead.

The police bore down.

Larissa managed to drag her to the Potemkin Stairs, where she stretched out above her trying to stem the flow of blood with the palm of her hand. The woman's head drooped on her shoulders and what little neck she had disappeared. The flag was trampled under the thundering feet.

"Help will come soon," Larissa comforted her. The blood dried on the woman's face like a colorful decoration. The screams gathered volume around them. Women scattered in all directions with the police in pursuit. They even reached the Potemkin Stairs. Larissa shielded the woman with her body, pulling her face toward her. Her head was in a pool of blood that had started to trickle down the stairs. From her curls arose the smell of lilacs diluted in vodka.

"What's your name?" asked Larissa. "Tell me your name," but the cherry lips didn't move.

The expression on her face was of someone who had been disappointed. Like Kostya's when he discovered that there aren't really any angels. The pressure of the throng caused the corpse to slip down the stairs, but Larissa wouldn't let it go, even when the Red Guard took it out of her hands. Before she was finally separated from her she did something that it would never have occurred to her to do before. She kissed the cherry lips of the woman whose body was already beginning to stiffen.

"We'll change the world, no guns will we wield, but cover with flowers the whole battlefield." The words sang in Larissa all the way home, as if passed on to her in a vodka kiss from the next world.

21

That same morning, after Larissa had climbed onto the farmer Abilov's cart, a goose flew in circles above the house. Had it happened before she left it's unlikely that she would have traveled to Odessa. It was the last remaining goose from her splendid flock, for she had been forced to slaughter all the others.

The turnip harvest had also been dismal. The frost-singed fields yielded no crops, and the meadows were crushed under the wheels of the supply convoys that rolled to the front. The hard times worsened for the tenant farmers, while the landlord's agent robbed them of what remained. Even the forest was overcome by the war, and the mushrooms and wild blueberries vanished.

Gabriel had noticed that Larissa had removed her wedding ring prior to her journey and suspected that the visit to the sick aunt was a pretext, and that due to the privations she was going to try to sell her ring. If only he had had something to give her. His only possession that was worth anything was the rifle hidden in the barn, and he didn't dare to touch it.

The flight of the goose recalled Larissa's superstition. What was he becoming? Was anything left of the man he had been? Maybe it was too late and he had been completely swallowed up by his new identity, a farmer steeped in foolishness whose Jewishness was steadily vanishing. The previous Sunday he had almost confessed his secret to the priest, only managing to stop himself at the last moment. Someone in the village was yet likely to accuse him of plotting to murder Kostya to prepare Passover matzah with his blood. That's what had happened to Menachem-Mendel Beilis in Kiev five years before. Blood libel in the twentieth century. Who would have believed it?

And who would have believed that a single shot in Sarajevo would transform a hundred years of peace in Europe into the War to End All Wars?

One should fly in circles above the entire world.

Kostya stamped his feet at the goose.

"Fly away, goose!" he cried, "It's dangerous for you here!"

The boy was prepared to starve so that the last of the flock would survive, thought Gabriel, and his heart contracted. Over the years that had passed Kostya had matured and become more serious. He didn't mention angels anymore, and he had stopped singing *Farewell to Slavianka*.

"Tell him to run away, Papa. I don't want something bad to happen to him."

He called him "Papa."

"Where can he fly to?" Kostya asked, "Where can our goose find a place without war?"

What should he say to the boy? Europe was totally devastated. The Balkans were also in flames, and the campaign at the Gallipoli peninsula in Turkey, the attempt to break through the blockade to Russia, had also cost more than a hundred thousand lives.

"Is there any place in the world without war, Papa?"

The touch of the small hand pulling at his trousers. Anna. Where was she now? He probably wouldn't recognize her. Three years is such a long time for a child. Who knew what had happened to his sister? The rumors about the recurring conquests of Bukovina had even reached this remote village. Abilov proudly recounted how the Cossacks, astride their horses, had raided the houses of the Jews, raping women and pulling off the old men's beards.

Gabriel had to summon all his strength to preserve his disguise as the stories of the atrocities were told. Were his sister and his mother still among the living? Perhaps the circling of the goose was a sign that his entire family had been slaughtered?

He had to sit shiva, tear his clothing, recite the mourner's Kaddish.

The goose made its final circuit above the house and turned toward the nearby scrub, as Kostya chased after it. It seemed an eternity had passed since he had squatted before the boy, joining in the patriotic marching song among the clean sheets.

If a miracle hadn't happened and he hadn't found refuge in Kostya's mother's heart he wouldn't have survived. To die without the Kaddish. To disappear from the face of the earth as if he had never been. He wanted someone to remember him. His real name, the identity he was born into. Soon he himself wouldn't know who he was.

Kostya – quick and elusive – was swallowed up in the thick grove, and Gabriel had to navigate by the wings beating above the treetops. Heaven forfend he should lose the boy. He found him by the small pond in which floated pieces of ice like glass, watching the goose swim.

"Fly away goose, get away from here fast," begged the boy, shattering the shiny surface with his small hands.

Finally the goose reacted, and with a marvelous movement of its wings it took off, spraying them with a sprinkling of ice. Startled by the sudden movement, the frogs were roused and now their croaking filled the air.

Gabriel held tightly to the slippery boy, as he pushed at the pieces of floating ice that were soaking his clothes in the freezing water, and pulled him out at a run. When he bumped into the lump of metal at the foot of the tree Gabriel almost collapsed. His leg was bruised but the boy was unscathed. It was an unexploded shell. The war was encroaching on them. It was impossible to escape.

"Maybe the frogs also want to run away, Papa?" the boy asked through chattering teeth.

"No, Kostya."

"So what are they doing?"

Suddenly Gabriel remembered a story he had heard as a boy. Every morning, the holy man of Miedzyrzec liked to go for a walk to the lakes where the croaking of the frogs could be heard. When his students requested an explanation for his strange habit, he told them that he wanted to learn the songs that the frogs sang to the Creator.

In a thicket on gentile land, holding in his arms a child who wasn't his, the wandering truth was revealed to Gabriel – the truth that the Baal Shem Tov called "the outcast." This boy, no matter how fond of him he was, would never recite Kaddish for him.

"The frogs are singing," he whispered in Kostya's ear, which was a frozen seashell.

"Sing to me, too," the boy asked, burying his face in Gabriel's shoulder.

Three words emerged haltingly from his mouth, clothed in their melody.

"Exalted and sanctified…"

Suddenly he was struck dumb. Gabriel couldn't recite the rest of the prayer. His brain froze, while his body continued to operate like a mechanized puppet. He traversed the distance to the farm, the boy's legs knocking against him, and the only irritating words that conceded to fill his head were "Our Father who art in heaven…"

With the last of his strength he went into the house, feeling emptier with each passing moment, as if his life force had been sucked out of him. He peeled the clothes off the child – the shirt was already frozen and he had to crack the fabric – next he filled a basin with hot water and bathed him. A cloud of steam enveloped the kitchen, and only Larissa's butcher knife gleamed through the mist on the opposite wall.

Exalted and sanctified…

And what were the next words?

His great name.

Thank God. He remembered.

And what came next?

Silence.

God in heaven, he couldn't even say Kaddish for himself.

When she came back from Odessa Larissa was quiet, although her cheeks were flushed red. She washed her clothes quickly, with no explanation as to when or how they had become so soiled. When he asked how things were in Odessa, she simply said that her aunt was doing better. He couldn't know whether or not she had managed to sell her wedding ring, since she didn't scatter coins or groceries across the table. Perhaps she was ashamed of her failure.

Neither did Gabriel share with her the events of his day, and anyway, Kostya was already fast asleep beneath the warm blanket.

When they got into bed – her feet were cold as ice – she asked Gabriel to make love to her. This seemed strange to him, since she always initiated without wasting time on unnecessary words.

Although he felt no desire, he went through the motions for her sake. He still felt hollow, as if only his shell was in the bed, while his essence circled above like the goose and flew away from her.

The more Gabriel emptied out, the more Larissa filled up. She asked him to warm her feet with his lips. Then she buried her head between his legs and cried words that he couldn't understand. He thought that she was singing something. "We'll change the world, no guns will we wield." Her tears tasted like vodka and lilacs. Why was the scent familiar to him? Like the words of the Kaddish prayer, he couldn't remember that either.

In the morning they awoke to the voice of Kostya calling from the yard.

"He's back! He's back!"

Larissa pulled Gabriel out of bed and he barely had time to cover himself with the sheet. The goose was again soaring above the house, but this time flying in a straight line.

Although Kostya should have been sad that his goose hadn't found a safe haven, he was glowing.

"You see Papa, he can't leave me."

For the first time he called him "Papa" in Larissa's presence.

"You'll never leave me, right?" he called out to the goose.

Then he turned to the two of them and declared passionately, "Matushka, you won't hurt him!"

She followed the straight line of its flight and her face shone. At that very moment all the words of the Kaddish prayer came back to Gabriel, except that they were accompanied by the croaking of frogs.

22

Fanny hadn't seen a live goose since the war broke out. The Russian snipers on the riverbank used them for target practice, and those that survived were slaughtered by the starving Austrian soldiers on the other side of the river. The only reminders of geese were the abandoned feather quilts from her dowry, which Fanny had traded for a sack of potatoes and two bags of grain. She parted from them sorrowfully, wondering whose head would rest on them in place of Gabriel's. When he returned, she told herself, she would get hold of new ones.

She was somewhat encouraged by the new winds blowing through Russia. According to Lizzie's reports, Rasputin had been murdered by conspirators led by Prince Yusupov. Who would have believed that one of the richest people in the world, who filled his coffers with diamonds and pearls, would become a political assassin? The dramatic arrest of Czar Nicholas II and the members of his family excited her far less than did the women's anti-war protests in Russia.

In solidarity, Lizzie decided to organize her own demonstration, but first she added the name "Bertha" to her own, in honor of the esteemed writer

Bertha von Suttner. To everyone who was willing to listen, and also to those who weren't, Lizzie enthusiastically described the woman who had written the novel *Down with Weapons!* and dedicated her life to preventing war. It is also believed that she was one of the major influences on Alfred Nobel, the inventor of dynamite, who decided to include a peace prize among those prizes provided for in his will, to encourage peace and fraternity among nations.

From then on Lizzie-Bertha turned her back on anyone who called her only "Lizzie." The demonstration took place not far from the river, so that the voices of the women would also be heard on the other side of the border. There were only three participants – Fanny among them – but despite the paucity of protestors, Lizzie-Bertha was hopeful that the new wind was blowing just around the corner. If all the women in the world would raise their voices together, like the women in Lysistrata in ancient Greece, then maybe there was a real chance for a revolution. She discovered the play by Aristophanes through her sister's interest in mythology, and included in her speech at the demonstration was a demand to remove the sentence, "Blessed are You our God for not making me a woman," from the Morning Prayer blessings.

The third participant was a young man who requested permission to make a speech about the rights of women workers and quoted from *Capital* by Karl Marx.

"How is it that you aren't in the army?" Fanny asked.

The man responded that he had managed to escape conscription with the help of Kalman-Zelig Hirsch and his limp. He would be a soldier in the new Workers Army, he declared, and burst out singing *The International.*

"It will be our last battle, a decisive battle. Enough of the will of tyrants and kings to drug us with the smoke of war. We will build a new world of our own."

He had a reedy voice, as though it hadn't broken yet, and there was a film on the lenses of his round glasses.

He was the first Bolshevik Fanny had ever met. Although she believed that an appropriate suitor had finally surfaced for her younger sister, it was Fanny he chose as the recipient of his seductive smiles.

"I am not a revolutionary," she announced.

"I'll teach you." He removed his glasses so she would see the blue of his eyes which somewhat compensated for his acne-pocked skin.

"Go home, boy."

Although Fanny wasn't much older than he was, she felt old. Tired out from selling beer on the roadside, from the horrors of the war, and the hopelessness of her life.

The expectation that Gabriel would return – that actually exhausted her more than anything else. After more than three years she was empty, as if only the dregs of beer foam still bubbled within her. Why did she continue to chase a ghost? Maybe just to hold onto the last vestiges of her self-respect she insisted on creating a slice of a dream.

If that was love, maybe it was better not to love at all.

No, no. She wouldn't give up and she wouldn't let go. The day would come when she would hear Gabriel declare, "This is my woman."

Lizzie-Bertha intervened.

"Bring more people to the next demonstration, comrade. Especially women. Don't forget to recruit them for the cause."

The young man asked them if they knew how he could cross the border. It was said that comrade Lenin was making his way from exile in Switzerland in a special railway car and he wanted to be there at the historic moment.

"Fellow comrades, maybe you would like to cross over to Russia with me? You would have a place of honor in the revolution."

"Are you sure?" asked Lizzie-Bertha. Does Lenin's wife have a place in her own right? The little Bolshevik was impressed that Lizzie already knew her name, Nadezhda Krupskaya.

"If you join me, you'll even have an advantage. Two women to one man."

His thin voice rose in laughter. He pulled out a pair of binoculars, pressed them to his glasses and scanned the riverbank for the best place to cross. The body of a goose floated on the water. Bits of leaves and branches stuck to its feathers and it turned in the current.

"Maybe two men to one woman!" Fanny challenged.

"I have no problem with sharing you, comrade. Are you married?" he asked, testing the water with a foot to measure its depth.

"She's engaged," Lizzie-Bertha told him, "her man is missing."

"Too bad he didn't rent Kalman-Zelig Hirsch's disability." Had they heard that his trick had failed when he was called up himself? He hadn't managed to convince the committee that he was unfit for battle, and had been sent to the Balkan front. No one knew what had become of him either.

"It seems that there are no men left in the world, except for me. Take me, comrades. I'm your last chance."

The young man stepped into the water, which reached to his waist. His movements caused the floating corpse of the goose to surge forward. The trembling foliage and spots of light disguised his sores, transforming them into the stubble of a beard. For a moment he looked like a man.

He removed his glasses and handed them to Fanny.

"And how will you see?"

"Don't worry. There..." and he gestured toward the Russian side, "I will have new eyes."

She warned him of becoming a live target for the snipers. Russians, Austrians you couldn't tell one from the other.

"They are more short-sighted than I. To free love in the new world!" He forged ahead and began to make swimming motions. Then he dove and disappeared. There was no movement visible on the surface of the water, and Fanny held her breath until his head emerged at a distance, spraying bubbles.

Free love? she thought to herself, why that was a contradiction in terms. Like saying a "beautiful ugliness." Love is nothing but a millstone round your neck, like Samson's bonds in the Philistine temple. And had she chosen to love? For a moment she heard the gypsy's prophecy, "You will marry twice." She would have two? She hadn't even managed to liberate herself from one. She was her own jailer.

The diametrically opposite thought ran through Lizzie-Bertha's head. Free love is the freedom to love whoever you want. No match arranged by your father and no pairing that some superior tyranny in the sky has ordained.

To love a man. To love two, or even more. To love a woman. Why not? Lizzie would often reflect on the phrase "free love" over the course of her life and reach the conclusion that one could love everyone and one could also not love anyone.

The youth swam closer to the opposite riverbank. Again a tuft of his hair emerged from the smooth sheet of water, and no shot was fired. A strange silence hung over the other side of the border. More and more people joined the two sisters. Abraham Katz also reached them at a run. They jostled each other for the best view. Maybe the demonstration had managed to attract supporters after all, Fanny thought. But it was neither the protest nor the swimming Bolshevik that had attracted the attention of the assembled crowd. The Russian forces had begun their retreat. It was to be their final one.

With all the pushing and shoving Fanny lost her footing and slipped in the mud. The dead goose bumped against her until it came apart in a gush of clumped feathers. Abraham Katz didn't notice, as he was joining his hands in gratitude and murmuring the prayer of thanksgiving, while from the other side of the river a thin voice could be heard singing, "We shall build a new world of our own." Others joined in.

As the choir of voices swelled on both sides of the border, Fanny's father told his mud-spattered daughter that the widow Herzig, her intended future mother-in-law, had passed away.

Who will say the Kaddish prayer for her? He asked, wiping tears from his eyes.

23

Was Lenin a Jew? The suspicions about his dubious origins didn't prevent the farmer Abilov from transforming him into the living spirit that ecstatically hoisted the flag of the October Revolution. He talked incessantly about the fateful night when the sailors and soldiers stormed the Czar's Winter Palace and waged a heroic war to conquer it.

Abilov's descriptions were so realistic that Kostya was convinced that he had been there himself.

"Land, bread, peace," the boy echoed the cry that was sweeping across Russia.

"What's so bad about a Jew?" Larissa railed. After all, Lenin was also demanding that anti-Semitism be deemed illegal. She recited a quote of his for Abilov, "The pogromic incitement against Jews is a tool in the hands of the landlords and the rich to blind the poor and divert their attention from the class struggle."

Ever since her trip to Odessa Gabriel had noticed the change in her. The previously quiet, introverted woman had started to express political opinions in public. Who knew she had opinions at all, and such opinions? Sometimes it seemed to him that she was trying to expose his true identity and to enable them to live together openly, under the patronage of the new world.

However, Abilov was not about to renounce his old views so easily. If a Jew were to fall into his clutches he wouldn't obey Lenin's order. The Jews had made a fortune from the war. And even if Lenin wasn't a Jew himself, the blood of abomination flowed in his veins, since his grandfather was born a Jew, and only later did he convert and change his name.

"Jesus was also born a Jew," Larissa produced Gabriel's old argument.

"If our Lord the Messiah was once a Jewish boy, then maybe you too were once a bit of a Jewish boy," Kostya chimed in with the sentence he had offered up at the family table.

"What kind of education have you provided to your boy, Larissa Yefimovna? You should be ashamed. If his father were alive, this wouldn't have happened. No one would have dared to put such heretical thoughts into his small head."

Abilov shot a furious glance at Gabriel who stood by in silence.

Larissa approached the farmer, her eyes spitting fire.

"Religion is the opium of the people, so says Karl Marx," she declared, but this only further incensed Abilov. Farmers and workers to the government – yes. A blow to the sanctity of religion – absolutely not.

He shouted so much that he lost his voice and his next words were uttered hoarsely. Leon Trotsky was also a Jew, whose real name was Lev Davidovich Bronshtein, and you couldn't trust a Jew to conduct fair negotiations to extricate Russia from the war.

The word "peace" was never mentioned.

The argument heated up as they stood on the estate that had previously belonged to the landlord, and had now become the property of the farmers. The manor on the estate had been completely plundered. Luxury furniture, candlesticks, silver, porcelain plates, embroidered sheets, lace curtains, tablecloths, chamber pots, had all found their way into the houses in the village. The clock with its gilt decorations that had always fascinated Larissa when she went to the house to pay her rent was appropriated by Abilov. He hoped that she would continue to be fascinated by it on his farm.

Larissa refused to be a party to the looting. Maybe because during his holiday every summer the landlord would remove his hat and bow to her as though she were a duchess, and not a simple tenant farmer. Deep in her heart she felt compassion for the upper classes, which had been persecuted and despised ever since the revolution.

Gabriel, who had followed the argument between Larissa and Abilov, finally managed to define what it was that had changed in her personality. Larissa had begun to identify with the persecuted and with minorities. Something had happened on the day she went to Odessa, but what could it have been? The mystery remained unsolved, since she resisted his every effort to find out who she had met and where she had been. Her wedding ring was gone from her finger for good, and she wouldn't reveal whether she had sold it, and if so, in return for what.

This change only intensified the internal voice that urged him to remain by her side forever. The end of his travails. Tranquility. A place he could finally call "home." In the new Russia he had a chance to build a good and safe life even as a Jew.

Like Larissa, he was also shocked by the wreckage of the manor house. "But did not lay their hands on the plunder," the verse from the Scroll of Esther flickered in his memory. Despite his unwillingness to be complicit in the wrongdoing, he took a book that was a remnant of the nobleman's library. He discovered it lying abandoned among the splinters of glass and dog excrement, and realized it was written by Lev Tolstoy, his mother's favorite author. He remembered how she had said that despite his prestigious status as a nobleman, he supported the simple people and was a sworn pacifist.

The cover and spine of the book had been ripped off, so he couldn't identify it at first. When he opened it randomly his eyes traveled over the words, "women and mothers… in whose hands, more than in those of any one else, lies the salvation…"

Had Gabriel been a mystic, he would have seen Tolstoy's words as a lighthouse, illuminating the direction he should take. His salvation was with Larissa and his place was by her side. Still it wasn't the cogitations of the Russian author that moved him, but his yearning for his mother. Grasping the pages as he stood by the window of the wreckage of the estate, he heard his mother's voice from his childhood, reading aloud sections of *War and Peace*. He had once asked her what Natasha would decide, as she deliberated which of the two men to choose. Torn as he was between women – Larissa, his mother, and his sister – he gave no thought to Fanny.

That split, betwixt and between, the choice between what was right for him but not necessarily for others, was already determined then. What awaited him in Bukovina? To return there after nearly four years of absence was to take a risk. Who knew whether anyone or anything was left there for him? And yet...

At night he sat by Kostya, who was lying in his bed, and told him a story. He had to prepare him for what was to come.

Once upon a time there was a prince, he told the boy, whose name was Stefan the Great. He fought in many wars and defeated his enemies. In his twilight years, when he felt death approaching, he ordered his servants to build a large wooden chest and to prepare an iron lock.

Then he sat down beside it and sketched a map of Europe, adding the names of the countries and the fates of all the people who lived in them. Who would have freedom and who would be enslaved, who would rule and who would be ruled over by others. Whose fate would be a happy one and who could expect troubles. The prince foresaw it all.

When Stefan the Great had finished he locked the chest with the iron lock. Then he threw away the key, and ordered that the chest be buried in the city of Suceava.

"Do you know that city, Gabril?"

"Yes. I was born not far from there."

"Where is it?"

"In Bukovina."

"Is that in Russia?"

"No Kostya. It's another place."

"What does that mean?"

"Not here."

Kostya digested the words, and then asked Gabriel to tell him the rest of the story.

The people of all the nations know about the existence of the chest, Gabriel ended his story, but they are afraid to open it.

Kostya nodded, as if he understood everything.

"And you want to go back to 'not here,' right?"

"Yes."

The boy sat up in bed as if he had seen a vision.

"Of course, someone has to open the chest," he waved his hands in excitement as if searching for it in his bed.

Gabriel leaned over the child and kissed his forehead. Then he tucked the blanket snugly around him. He hoped that in the future there would be someone who would take care of him and be a father to him. It was doubtful whether the boy would remember the strange man who he once believed was an angel.

Kostya raised his head again when he asked, "And are you afraid to go back, Gabril?"

On that same freezing night in February 1918 Larissa's spirits were high. When Gabriel asked if this time he could be the one to tell Kostya a bedtime story, she interpreted the gesture as a declaration of intent. Now she was certain that her beloved would stay with her forever. His Jewishness would be no obstacle, for under the Bolsheviks even anti-Semites like Abilov would be convinced that all men are equal. She even did without her nightly pleasure and stretched across the bed, trying to overhear the story that Gabriel was telling Kostya in such a quiet voice on the other side of the wall. And although she couldn't make out a single word, she closed her eyes, happy. The war was over.

Earlier that day the entire village had listened to the dramatic announcement about the ceasefire and the end of the hostilities, although unlike the title of Tolstoy's famous book, Trotsky described the new reality as "not war – not peace."

And it was that same announcement that so gladdened Larissa, which hastened the decision made by Gabriel that would break her heart. She didn't know that he had chosen to tell Kostya a farewell story.

He chose not to reply to the boy's last question, although he had no doubt as to the answer. He was very frightened of going back. Who knew what he would discover when the chest was opened.

24

The first to return to Bukovina was Kalman Zelig-Hirsch, decorated with medals for bravery on the battlefield. Not only limping now, but stone deaf.

In the synagogue he was favored as the third man to be called to read from the Torah, an honor that was usually purchased for a high price, which only the richest of the townspeople could afford. To his daughters, who sat behind the partition in the women's section and didn't see a thing, Abraham Katz recounted that Hirsch couldn't stop crying, his tears flowing onto the Torah scroll. The *gabbai* of the synagogue was sent to the neighbor's house for a towel, and only after the rabbi had decreed that it was not a desecration of the Sabbath was the sacred book wiped down and left to dry before being returned to the Holy Ark.

Bukovina after the ceasefire resembled the goose carcass that Fanny had seen in the river. A government twilight zone. A local council was established with an independent militia and voices inciting to banish the Jews were heard everywhere. The welfare and security that had been their lot during the years of the rule of Emperor Franz Joseph had vanished. The elderly ruler was dead, embittered by the destruction that he himself had helped to bring upon his country. At least he was spared the attacks on the homes of his Jewish subjects, where the rioters confiscated anything of value as they searched for flour and tobacco. Now it was the Romanian army's turn to go in and seize abandoned territory.

Grab and take whatever you can.

"Every man will do what he sees fit," lamented Abraham Katz. Where could they go? Even in Russia after the revolution chaos reigned, and the civil war between the Bolsheviks, the "reds," and the Mensheviks, the "whites," was tearing the county apart. For the first time it occurred to him to travel to distant Palestine, of which he had heard in Czernowitz before the war, from an impassioned Zionist who seemed to him to be insane.

For fear of the looting attacks Fanny brought the few ceremonial objects they still had up to the storage space under the roof – the wine goblet for the Kiddush prayer, the Havdalah spice holder and the Sabbath candlesticks – and buried them inside the remaining comforters that were used to block the cracks around the windows in winter. There she came upon her engagement ring, with its sapphire gem, that the widow Herzig had given her four years earlier. She couldn't restrain herself and slipped it on, discovering to her dismay that it was too big for her finger that had grown so thin. "You will marry twice," the gypsy had prophesied. Why, she wouldn't have even one husband.

The looters turned the house upside down, broke all the dishes, hurled the pots and pans at the ceiling, and were especially excited about the piano. Their wild bashing of the keys only ceased when they discovered the beer cellar and forgot about searching the roof. Fanny crouched among the quilts, listening to the drunken frenzy accompanied by curses and abuse in Romanian. "*Zidani murdari*" (dirty Jews). Those were the first words she would learn in the language of the new masters of Bukovina.

She replaced the engagement ring in the depths of the quilt, her hand caressed by the goose down. What was she supposed to do with it? If she gave it to Anna, it would be an admission that her brother was dead. During the shiva for her mother the girl had looked so lost. The only one who had managed to cheer her was Lizzie-Bertha, who urged her to recite the mourner's Kaddish, for nowhere is it written that women are forbidden to do so.

On the thirtieth day following the death of her mother, the two stood by the simple headstone that was hastily erected and began to say *Mechayei hameitim*, the blessing for the resurrection of the dead, pointedly ignoring the protest from the minyan, the men's quorum of ten.

"And Who in the future will revive and keep you alive in justice... Blessed are You, the Lord, Who resurrects the dead," their voices carried through the cemetery.

Fanny stood off to the side, her eyes fixed on the words engraved in the stone. "Herzig" – that was also supposed to have been her name – and then they wandered to the adjacent empty plot.

Maybe Kalman-Zelig knew something about Gabriel. The morning after the looting she hurried to the blacksmith's shop.

She repeated her question over and over, but it wasn't only that Kalman-Zelig's deaf ears didn't hear anything, he also wouldn't read her lips.

In the end she wrote a note, "Is Gabriel about to return?"

The noise at the blacksmith shop deafened hearing ears as well, but it seemed as though the limping deaf man had also been struck dumb. Even when she pushed the note into his hand, he continued to strike the anvil on which his medal lay with mallet and blade.

Fanny stretched out her hand toward the tools, risking harm, if only she could make him stop. Finally silence descended on the shop. Kalman-Zelig raised his eyes to hers, whispering out his words like tiny pebbles.

"Even he who returns, hasn't returned."

Fanny grabbed back the note, crunching it into a paper ball with her shaking hand.

In place of the weeping in the synagogue, now Kalman Zelig-Hirsch laughed uncontrollably, and the sound that came out of his mouth – grunts and wails that shook his entire body – frightened her. He threw the smashed medal into the air as if it was a feather. He was steady on his feet, his famous limp suddenly impossible to detect.

At that very moment the church bells began to ring. It was eleven o'clock on the eleventh day of the eleventh month, in 1918. World War I was officially over.

The ringing of the bells that was heard all across Europe deafened Fanny and only the blacksmith couldn't hear them. He turned his back on her decisively, sat at the anvil, and the blows of the sledgehammer and the chisel intensified. Iron struck iron, drowning out the sounds of the bells.

In a village in Russia Gabriel listened to the chimes and counted each one. As the last echo faded away, he went to the barn and began to undress. The blouse of white silk, decorated with sheaves of wheat that Larissa had embroidered, the wide black velvet trousers, the raspberry-colored belt. The best of his wardrobe, that he had worn that festive morning when he accompanied her to church. He folded it all meticulously and slid it into a quilt cover from the bedroom as though it was the bag that contained his phylacteries.

Only the boots remained. Gabriel stood naked, shivering in the autumn chill, inhaling the scent of the hay that had become so familiar to him, and gazing at the haystacks with the light dancing upon them. The flickering sunbeams blurred his vision and he lost his balance. Dizzy, he steadied himself on the wooden ladder that rested against the golden bundles. Then his vision cleared and he climbed up to retrieve the Austrian rifle hidden atop the highest beam.

The photograph of the *liebling* that was curled around the rifle butt brought back the staring eyes of Von-Hoffenberg. Gabriel bowed his head before the image of the unattractive woman and mumbled a verse from Jeremiah, "Do not weep for the dead or mourn his loss; rather, weep bitterly for him who is exiled, because he will never return nor see his native land again."

He had barely managed to step into Larissa's husband's old trousers –the ones she had altered to fit him three years before in that very barn – when he suddenly felt the touch of her fingers on his skin, and couldn't discern whether it was a pinch or a caress. He hadn't realized that she was there. He briefly caught her silhouette, still wearing her best clothes, but not her kerchief. Her wheat-colored hair was loose and shone like another haystack.

The hand of the woman whose name was "fortress" caressed every inch of his skin. Mapping it like an explorer, she navigated her way in circles until she reached his bare chest. Then she moved down to his hips. Gabriel groaned and tried to pull away from her, but Larissa wouldn't stop, stroking him rhythmically until he was hard, and then sliding down and taking him in her mouth. The crucifix hanging around her neck knocked against him gently.

Every movement of her tongue expressed the words left unsaid. "Don't go." It was Larissa's last effort to stave off the inevitable. Maybe she wanted to make sure that her false angel would never forget her, and so she left her imprint on the one place on the body that has no boundaries, that bows to no sovereignty. Either way, it was a generous parting gift. Larissa couldn't know that with the movements of her lips and her tongue she was shaping the way Gabriel would relate to women. They would shower him with their goodness and grace, and he would withdraw and shrink away. He would always obey the command of his member, but not the command of his heart, until no command at all would remain.

After his sperm burst forth – a thick, whitish syrup, with a scent reminiscent of flowering carob trees – Gabriel pulled up the dead husband's trousers and strapped on the gun that was beginning to rust. He still hadn't said a word. Meanwhile, Larissa stared at the photograph of the *liebling* that had been wrapped around the butt of the gun.

She extracted it like a card from a deck, her eyes widening at the sight of the woman she presumed was her rival. Her expression changed. Perhaps it was in surprise at the luck of that woman, who despite her ugly features had such a faithful lover.

"That's not my woman," Gabriel said softly, but it was clear that she didn't believe him. Those were his last words to Larissa Yefimovna.

"That's not my woman" – the motto for the rest of his life.

Making no attempt to hide his delight, the farmer Abilov volunteered to drive Gabriel to the train station. He was finally rid of his rival, and had a clear path to propose marriage to his neighbor and merge their farms into a kolkhoz. As the wagon moved beyond the boundaries of the village, Gabriel glanced back. There was no movement at the farm, expect for a black spot hovering above.

Ten days later he set foot in Bukovina.

A Continuation

"How can you write about them like that? They're your grandmother and grandfather," protests my daughter. But the attempt to make me squirm or to feel guilty doesn't succeed.

The very decision to move Fanny and Gabriel to the territory of fiction gave me permission to scrutinize every corner of their existence, including their sex lives, something which lies at the heart of every love story. The invasion of their privacy is my freedom. Otherwise, what's the point of writing at all?

My conscience is clear. If I had cut corners for them and censored the intimate parts of their lives just because they're my relatives, I would be a deserter, like Grandfather. At the kangaroo court convened by my daughter, I declare that I will relate to Fanny and Gabriel according to the same criterion that I use for the characters in all my books.

Like the innkeeper in the Hasidic tale, I too concoct a stew from materials at hand and pray that the movements of my spoon will enhance the flavor.

A match is made. A couple is about to marry. The war separates them. She waits for him. He moves on. Finds another woman. That is the bare bones of the truth, and everything else follows from that.

My daughter gloats that I won't have a choice but to treat Fanny and Gabriel with some measure of compassion, not because they are relatives who deserve preferential treatment, but because I am required to be faithful to the storyline dictated by reality. The comfort is, as far as my daughter is concerned, that Fanny and Gabriel will survive to the end of the story, which can't be said about some of the characters in my other books.

My existence is the guarantee of theirs.

"And what about Larissa and Kostya?" my daughter demands, "Will you abandon them like he did?"

Since their fate is entirely in my hands, I can make it up to them and create their futures after they exit Gabriel's life, or more precisely, after he walks out on them.

I send another man into Larissa's arms, one who will never leave her, and it isn't the farmer Abilov. Since she is fond of strong, muscular men, her new lover as well, who she will encounter at a Party meeting in Odessa, will be younger than she is. Less attractive than Gabriel, but more lively and with a sense of humor that he will be forced to restrain during the period of Stalin's witch hunts. It was his blue eyes that first dazzled her and she would always remove his glasses before they made love so that she could dive into them and dream of the angel she once had. The pock marks on his skin will disappear over time, as her spectacular hair will be shorn into a short cut with a parting on the side, in the best communist style. Comrade Yefimovna will be the life force of the kolkhoz, an expert with geese and supporter of equal rights for women, while the Bolshevik youth will be an outstanding commissar in the service of the Soviet Union.

As for his fantasy about two women per man, he will have no choice but to forego that, and take solace in Lenin's words about how he who tries to sit on two chairs will find himself stuck in the space between them.

Kostya, like millions of young Soviets, will be conscripted into the Red Army during the next world war and fight in the terrible Stalingrad campaign, which, while it will bring an end to the string of Nazi conquests on the Eastern Front, will also cost the Russian side about a half a million lives.

My daughter begs me not to let him fall in battle.

If only I could save Kostya from the fate of the other soldiers on all the fronts. "Eternal rest grant unto them, oh Lord, and let perpetual light shine upon them" – not the Jewish mourner's Kaddish, but the Catholic requiem. I pray for the souls of the good people whose existence in the book does not contradict the fact that they have already departed our world.

PART TWO

Permitted to Us Those Lawfully Married to Us

1

Bukovina was awash in rumors about Gabriel's return – that could have been a good opening sentence, but it's not how it was. No one recognized him at the railway station in Czernowitz.

The platform was teeming with people – demobilized soldiers back from Siberia, farm women with colorful kerchiefs carrying goods to sell at market in sacks and baskets, and nuns singing religious songs, one of whom squinted at him from beneath her wimple. A cluster of bearded Jews chanted the evening prayer at the side of the platform and he recognized the lumber merchant who had competed with his mother, the butcher from Siret, and the dairyman from Suceava. But he was swallowed up, completely anonymous, searching for someone to drive him to Mihova.

In the end he hired the services of a wagon driver, who insisted on speaking Romanian and would only accept Russian rubles. He rejected the Austro-Hungarian money in disgust as if it was contaminated.

"Burn it," he spat, "finally we are rid of all the foreign masters who shat on us. Long live Romania the great."

All the way to Mihova the man spoke with great admiration about General Iacob Zadik, who passed through the gates of Czernowitz as a conqueror, and about the General Assembly headed by Ianco Flondor, that determined that Bukovina should be annexed to Romania. And about how good it was that other territories were annexed to Romania from Bulgaria, Russia, and the defeated Austro-Hungary. Finally the Romanian people could hold their heads high.

Gabriel barely listened. He curled up inside the old coat he had exchanged for a handful of salt in Russia, and the non-stop jabbering of the wagon driver seemed to hang somewhere above his head. The journey wound on excruciatingly slowly, while rather than urge on his horses, the driver kept busy calculating the benefits that the liberated subjects of the great Romania could expect to receive, and cursing the Bolsheviks in Russia, all of them traitors born of Jews.

The view began to improve. There were flashes of green among the scorched fields and new growth could be seen sprouting from the trunks of the trees that had been hit by shells, branches like crooked fingers groping upward, to ascertain whether the sky had cleared. As they passed by the river Gabriel noticed the spray from the geese taking wing and turned away. He couldn't allow himself to think about Larissa or Kostya. That chapter of his life was closed.

At the top of a maple tree he saw an abandoned stork's nest, awaiting the birds' annual return, and Gabriel thought about the male who always came back early, tapping his beak and stretching his wings – his agreed-upon signal to the female that he was ready to mate.

"Have you compensated yourself for your time as a prisoner of war?" winked the wagon driver. "Why didn't you stay in Czernowitz a little longer? I could have recommended a woman who would spend the whole night with you for half-price. Do you want me to turn back?"

Gabriel didn't reply.

"She is a great patriot, just like her tits. You really should try her."

Gabriel looked down, and the driver gave him an alternative option – a male whore. Perhaps the liberated prisoner, who had been forced to live for years in a camp with men, now preferred a slightly different kind of pleasure.

"It's nothing to be ashamed of," he said and offered to organize the deal for a few more Russian rubles. After all, he too was a patriot, inclined to contribute to the rehabilitation of prisoners of war.

As they continued on their way the drops of rain that had begun to fall turned to snow, dampening Gabriel's coarse stubble. Since leaving Russia he hadn't shaved.

"Winter is early this year," the driver pronounced, "It's eager to clean away all the shit we've eaten."

He pulled a bottle from under his seat and offered Gabriel some high-quality beer to warm his bones.

"Alcohol will also clean away all your shit."

He had bought the beer from a young woman who pulled her cart full of bottles along the side of the road. Stupid. She endangered herself and drove all the passersby crazy asking about some missing soldier. Once he almost took the opportunity to lie with her – she wasn't at all bad-looking – but then he changed his mind because he didn't want to infect himself with a Jewess.

"We'll get rid of our Yids too pretty soon." He took one of his hands off the reins and gave Gabriel a resounding slap on the back, promising him that the whores he was recommending – whether female or male – were all good Christians.

Gabriel sipped slowly from the bottle. The beer really was good and warmed him a little. Strange that the driver didn't suspect that he was Jewish. Had he been so swallowed up in his borrowed identity that nothing of his true self remained? He was in urgent need of some nicotine, but he couldn't manage to light the cheap Russian makhorka tobacco, maybe because of the snowflakes alighting upon it, or maybe it was his fingers that failed him.

The houses of Mihova were visible on the horizon. The slanted roofs, covered with grey tiles. The outer walls made of plain or green-painted wooden planks. The church with its twin spires. His stomach churned, but the rest of his body was frozen, as though all his thoughts, his fears, his hopes, had turned to stone inside him. In a weak voice he asked the driver to stop on the outskirts of the village, near the graveyard. From there he would make his way on foot.

But he didn't dare to enter the cemetery. In the end he managed to light the damp tobacco. Leaning against the fence, his back to the headstones, Gabriel smoked cigarette after cigarette. The few people who walked by didn't pay any attention to him. He knew them all. They were part of the scenery of his childhood. Popescu the Romanian stonemason with a headstone wobbling on the back of his ox. The grouchy lumber merchant Korlenko, his wagon loaded with lengths of wood, waving to Miklós Nagy, the Hungarian clerk from the village council – nicknamed the man with "magically filling pockets" – who was crossing the road in the opposite direction, carrying a bulging bag.

Gentiles all.

Where were the Jews? Was anyone left?

He had no nostalgia for the village where he was born and raised. In his eyes, all of Europe was cursed ground. The war that had just come to its end wouldn't be the last one, he told himself. The new borders portended only troubles and disasters. Why had he returned? It wasn't only the worry about his mother or because he missed his sister, but something else. He had answered the internal biological call like the migrating birds. He had to return to his place of origin only so that he could break away from it again.

A dog pounced on him. A pitiful, emaciated creature that thrust its muzzle into his thighs searching for a morsel of food. He gave him the bit of bread that he had in his pocket, and the dog swallowed it in one gulp. Then it fixed him with its miserable gaze and began to howl.

"After whom dost thou pursue? After a dead dog…" Gabriel mumbled the verse from the Book of Samuel, although the dog was alive, and at his back was the fence behind which lay the dead. "Dwellers of the underworld," he blurted out. Had he known that his mother was among them and that her final resting place was so close by, he would have stayed to recite the Kaddish.

More time passed. A small eternity for him. It stopped snowing and the sky cleared somewhat. The dog moved its bowels at Gabriel's feet and then resumed barking, louder now, as if urging him to go. It seemed to Gabriel that it was the only one who recognized him. Finally he pulled tight his tattered Russian coat and walked into the village, on feet of lead, with the skinny dog following behind.

The first thing he heard was the voice of a young girl. It was Luminicia Mirodan, the daughter of the neighbors, at the entrance to their house – which stood with its roof half-destroyed – and cried out, "Anna Herzig, come outside."

That's how he learned that his sister was alive.

2

How enticing it is to wrap the reunion with Fanny in a soft pink light, even in the black-and-white of an old movie. The Penelope from Bukovina finally embraces her Ulysses and tilts her head upward for a kiss.

But even Anna didn't fall into Gabriel's arms. She stood opposite him paralyzed, barely believing that the bearded stranger dressed in rags was her brother. And even when she was convinced, she didn't dare to hug him, postponing the moment when she would have to tell him that they were now orphans.

To tell the truth, he wasn't surprised to hear that his mother had died, as if deep in his heart he had already known.

"Blessed are You, the True Judge," were the first words he uttered, and then he tore his coat in a sign of mourning.

It was also hard for him to recognize Anna. The girl he had left stood before him as a young woman, long-limbed, her childhood innocence gone. They faced each other, hesitant, until Anna took the first step and stroked the bristles on his cheek.

It was Luminicia who announced Gabriel's return, her cries sounding in all the alleyways and even in the fields adjacent to the village. Quickly both Jews and non-Jews congregated, surrounding her with exclamations of praise and thanksgiving. The young girl whose name meant "small light," recited the Pater Nostra prayer – "Our Father Who Art in Heaven" – as the rabbi declaimed a verse from Psalms, "I will praise thy name, O Lord; for it is good. For he hath delivered me out of all trouble" and only Gabriel thought that thanks weren't due to any supreme being but rather to those of flesh and blood.

The only person who wasn't affected by the dramatic return was Luminicia's father, who grumbled beneath his moustache, "Just what we need. Another Yid to take care of."

In Siret, Fanny was informed about what had occurred on the other side of the river by Kalman-Zelig Hirsch, who was in Mihova that day, supplying horseshoes to the local stable master. Although his deaf ears didn't hear Luminicia's screams, the sight of all the residents abandoning their work and rushing pell mell to the Herzig house to witness the return of the ghost from the devastation did not escape him.

He found Fanny in the cellar, crouched on all fours in front of the gigantic new barrel that had just arrived from the brewery. With a finger she tasted the beer and considered its quality. Kalman-Zelig's leg dragged across the floor of the cellar, a trail of snowflakes in its wake. Lizzie-Bertha could barely suppress her giggles at his crude efforts to speak.

"He who returned has returned."

It was the deafness that had transformed the smith, against his will, into a poet of few words, but Fanny immediately understood who he was referring to. Foam dripped from her finger as she slowly rose from the floor, and Lizzie-Bertha looked back and forth between them.

"Go to him!" she screamed, pulling at the hem of Fanny's dress that had soaked up the beer. "Go, now!"

But Fanny didn't react and didn't move. She leaned against the barrel, staring at the bubbling foam, and to her sister and the blacksmith she looked like someone who was shrinking from within. She neither weighed her next steps nor planned a clever move, just tried to remember the chapter that concludes the *Odyssey* to learn something from the precedent of the meeting between Penelope and Ulysses.

A palace in Ithaca, not a remote town in Bukovina. A man and a woman finally stand before one another. His face has wrinkled over the course of time and his hair has thinned and whitened, and she is worn out, her youth faded. Penelope doesn't fall into his arms and Ulysses doesn't kneel before her and declare everlasting fidelity. An atmosphere of suspicion fills the room. To ensure that he isn't an imposter she sets him a test and commands him to move her bed into the room they share. He does not obey, since only he knows the secret. One of the legs of the bed is made of live wood, rooted to the earth – which cannot be dislodged.

But Fanny and Gabriel had no private secret, neither a son in common like Telemachus, and they had never shared a bed. There was only a sapphire-studded engagement ring, buried in a quilt under the roof, and by now it didn't obligate them to anything at all.

The last time Fanny had seen Gabriel was on her sister's Paula's wedding night – in a dream.

"Don't you remember me? I am your fiancée Fanny," she had said and he denied it.

In her imagination the tree from the bed of the reunited couple blossomed, like Aharon's orchard in Numbers: "was budded, and put forth buds, and bloomed blossoms, and bore ripe almonds." She soon came to her senses. Her demand of Gabriel to remember her, which was valid in the dream, wouldn't necessarily hold up in the real world. Not only because he wasn't obliged to remember her, but it was possible that forgetting was the preferred option in the current circumstances. Only it would allow for a renewed beginning.

In the damp beer cellar, her foam-soaked dress clinging to her body, Fanny felt again the dagger in her chest, the same pain from the dream.

Despite all her efforts, she couldn't remember who had pierced whom.

Kalman-Zelig Hirsch was ready to take her to Mihova on the spot, but she refused. She felt that the wise decision was to take the time to digest the news, but Lizzie-Bertha accused her of cowardice.

"You should be ashamed. What's happened to you? How have you lost your courage?"

Fanny didn't resent her sister's criticism, for her young age and her feminist views, which hadn't been tested yet in reality, prevented her from understanding how great the fear of discovering the ugly sides of love.

Perhaps her heart foretold that in this story no one was going to fall into anyone's arms.

3

In the end, it was Abraham Katz who journeyed to Mihova. He had to ensure that the man who had returned was still worthy of the match, and not a helpless victim of the war who would be a millstone around his daughter's neck. Besides, the right of refusal belonged to the bride.

They met at the Herzig home, where the roof had been repaired, and Anna poured tea from a cracked teapot. First the father checked Gabriel's gait and his posture. His limbs seemed whole, there were no scars on his hands or his face, and his demeanor indicated that he was in command of all his senses. Abraham Katz attributed his gloom to the death of his mother.

Gabriel rolled a cigarette and thanked the father politely when he expressed gratitude for his safe homecoming. His history during the years of his absence was not alluded to in any manner. Sipping numerous cups of tea they discussed this and that, mainly what the future held for the Jews under Romanian rule, as they skirted the sensitive subject that was the reason for the meeting. It was quite a while before Gabriel was asked whether he intended to honor his promise of marriage.

Abraham Katz cleared his throat in the smoky room and waited.

Until Anna revealed that Fanny had remained loyal to him, it had never occurred to Gabriel that his engagement was still valid. Nothing in his memory indicated that his betrothed was endowed with unusual faith and determination. To be honest, all the efforts he made during the conversation with her father to picture her only irritatingly conjured the image of another woman.

When Gabriel crushed his cigarette, Abraham Katz suggested that they cancel the deal. He stressed that all would be handled without resentment or recrimination. Each would go his and her own way.

He even offered to return the engagement ring, although he had no idea where it was or if it even still existed.

Anna assumed that before coming to a decision Gabriel would ask to see the bride from the match made in other days and circumstances that were no longer binding, so that he would make up his mind in a prudent and responsible manner. Since he had not confided in her about what he had experienced, she thought that caution should be exercised. After all, her brother was no longer the innocent youth who blindly obeyed his mother's instructions. Had she been alive, even she would have accepted the vicissitudes of fate with understanding and agreed that all vows were null and void.

The right to retreat – not to mention desert – was vouchsafed to Gabriel, but to Abraham Katz's surprise he announced that he would honor his promise.

Was it the influence of Anna's descriptions of Fanny's qualities that so impressed him, even without seeing her again? Even though they still hadn't met? Could it be that her devotion flattered him and inflated his male ego? Or perhaps he desired to respect his mother's wishes as though they were her last will and testament.

And there was another reason that only Gabriel was privy to. So soon after leaving Larissa, he didn't have it in him to disappoint another woman. Had Fanny known that it was pangs of conscience that were driving him into her arms, it is doubtful that she would have married him. Yes. He still experienced guilt feelings then, although over time his conscience would cease to trouble him, and when it came to women and leaving he would have resounding success in suppressing any sense of remorse, but let's not get ahead of ourselves. On that day Gabriel behaved like a perfect gentleman. He asked Anna to bring a bottle of cognac from the neighbor's, and with a toast and a handshake he confirmed the engagement. True, he wasn't beaming with joy, but Anna also credited his grief over his mother for his muted reaction. She would not lead her son to the marriage canopy. At least the plaque in his memory at the synagogue had been removed and as the rabbi draped the prayer shawl over his shoulders he explained that it was actually the public announcement of his death that had protected him. "It granted you longevity," he declared when Gabriel was called to read from the Torah on the Sabbath, and the community was apprised of the impending nuptials.

Anna didn't conceal her joy. For a while now she had felt close to Fanny, and viewed her as her sister-in-law. In her innocence she imagined pleasant, serene lives for all the members of her family and those to come, God-willing. Lizzie-Bertha would teach her to play the piano, and she and Fanny would read Greek mythology together.

At the urging of Luminicia Mirodan, who insisted that it was a celebratory occasion, seventeen-year-old Anna tasted alcohol for the first time in her life, but the liquid burned her throat. Why was everyone so crazy about it?

"To life!" declared Abraham Katz, "And good luck to all of us. The Master of the Universe knows how dearly we need luck."

Had he been able to, he would have poured a cold beer for the Lord Above, the perfect antidote to raging winds. It couldn't be helped that the official conclusion of the war had not brought an end to hatred, vengeance and the settling of scores among nations, which had only just stopped slaughtering each other. Who knew when the rotting abscess called Europe would burst open again? They said that in America everything was different.

That was the first time that America was mentioned. To Anna it sounded like some place beyond the hills of darkness.

When she suggested to Gabriel that she accompany him to his meeting with Fanny – she thought that her presence might prevent awkwardness – he rejected her gently. An intermediary was unnecessary he said, and besides there were things that had to be said just between the two of them.

On the morning of the meeting the temperature plummeted further. The winter really had arrived early. Gabriel stood before the mirror covered with a film of frost and finally shaved off his beard. To see his reflection he had to wipe the slippery surface again and again, and each time he realized how much he had changed. His face was now a mask. A stiff, impenetrable membrane that repelled anyone who tried to come near. He looked down at his reflection in the rippling water in the basin and there as well he encountered a stranger.

"Don't touch me," he whispered as he shook off the razor.

"*Noli me tangere*" (Don't touch me), said Jesus to Mary Magdalena after he was resurrected. Larissa told Kostya the story when she returned from Odessa.

"Who did she think he was, Matushka?"

"The caretaker of the garden."

"What garden?"

"The one where he was buried."

"So how do you come back to life?"

Gabriel remembered Larissa's response, which doesn't appear in the New Testament. In her version, the woman did not obey the man's order, but touched him and touched him some more until he surrendered completely.

"Love," she had whispered to the boy, was the only thing that death couldn't overcome, and only because of love did Jesus come back to life.

As he scrubbed his body before his meeting with Fanny, Gabriel could sense all the places – those visible and those concealed – where Larissa's hands and mouth had dallied.

Although he was naked, he didn't feel the winter cold at all, as though during his years in Russia he had stored up heat that would continue to burn secretly like a savings account gathering interest. He was an attractive man and he knew it. When Fanny would see him naked, the reservoir of heat that had been building up inside her would erupt and overflow.

Yet at their first meeting after the war, the two were dressed from tip to toe, not the tiniest bit of skin exposed.

4

The same house, the same room where they sat in the summer of 1914, although now the marks of the rioters were evident. The wall was peeling and stained with alcohol. There was a crack in the ceiling. The mantelpiece was empty and the piano was missing several keys.

Fanny and Gabriel sat facing each other in exactly the same places where they had sat then. She tense in her chair, hands clasped in her lap, in a pose that would become familiar to him. He was attired in the same suit that had hung in his mother's closet as a memory of her lost son. A slight smell of mothballs wafted from it. The only difference was that there was no audience this time. Abraham Katz and Lizzie-Bertha descended from the parlor to the beer cellar to give the couple some privacy.

Finally.

And despite the temptation to have them fall into each other's arms, the chill in the room has nothing to do with the weather.

Still, underneath the restrained exterior and the hands clenched into fists, Fanny is burning with fire. If Gabriel had made the slightest move toward her, she would have stripped herself bare and wrapped herself around him. In a parallel universe he would press her against the stained and peeling wall and their wild coupling would shake the house to its foundations until the father and sister in the cellar could have no doubt as to what was taking place above their heads and would look at each other, blush, and look away. In fact, his manners were impeccable. He asked how she was, inquired about the beer business, and even expressed the hope that her sister Paula would be pregnant soon and that Lizzie would find a suitable match. About himself he said nothing.

It was more silence than conversation.

There were so many things that she wanted to tell him, but even his name was swallowed up and never spoken. Then Gabriel rolled a cigarette and offered her one. Surprisingly, Fanny accepted it. She inhaled the smoke deeply into her lungs and the sight of her breasts rising inside the dress, unrestrained by a corset this time, didn't escape him. She choked, coughed, but didn't put out the cigarette. When she blew the smoke directly into his eyes he didn't blink. The same determination that he had recognized in her four years before, pleased him once again. And there was a faint scent of lilacs that mingled with the smell of burning tobacco.

"I will be a good wife to you," Fanny said.

The response, "I will be a good husband to you," failed to arrive.

Fanny extinguished the butt and to his surprise he saw that an ashtray had been sitting on the table all along, as though she had prepared in advance for his bad habits. Gabriel uncurled the ball of her fist and shook her hand – the first physical contact between them. He noticed that she was wearing the sapphire ring that his late mother had given to her. Why did it seem to him that there was goose down stuck to it?

"There's something that you must promise me."

"What?"

"That you will never ask me about what happened."

Fanny nodded, but did not make an explicit promise.

Gabriel donned his hat and left without giving her another glance. Outside he and Abraham Katz decided when the ceremony would be held. Lizzie-Bertha, back from the cellar, hugged her sister excitedly. For her this was a sign that the world was being repaired.

Fanny once again clasped her hands together – the one cold the other burning – and said to herself, "After the wedding everything will be different."

5

On the eve of his wedding, Gabriel paid a visit to the Siret brothel.

The renowned institution was established before the Great War by a Jewish entrepreneur with vision named Feivel. To acquire a license for a "guesthouse" that in those days only a woman was permitted to operate, he had married Ida the Catholic, daughter of the pig merchant. The father of the bride, whose support for the initiative was stronger than his loathing for the Jewish people, was promised a commission from the income in addition to bonuses in return for a regular supply of customers from both sides of the border.

"Ida's House" was established on an isolated patch of forest on the outskirts of Siret, so as not to inconvenience the residents, and on what was then the seam line between two countries. From its inception it touted fraternity between peoples, and the wall that faced the Romanian side was painted in the hues of that country's flag, while the side facing Austria-Hungary sported that nation's colors.

"Open 24 hours a day," read the sign, "Eve will receive you at the gates to our Paradise." After the communist revolution Ida changed the sign to read: "Clients of the World Unite," and during the years of conquests not a few Russians joined the ranks of the clientele.

The captivating hostesses also came from all nations. At "Ida's House" there were no quarrels, nor any friction about religion or nationality, and the only god was money, including the dollars generously scattered by the American businessman Ralph Smith, who came specially from Buffalo to dig in the ground of Siret. Unbelievably, he was sure that he would strike oil there.

Ida received Gabriel warmly. In contrast to her father the pig farmer's anti-Semitism, for her, Jews were always preferred customers. They never bargained about the price, paid promptly, weren't violent and were extremely hygienic.

Not to mention that there was already a halo hovering over the head of the good-looking Jewish soldier who had returned home unexpectedly. As far as she was concerned, the riddle of his absence only intensified the mystery that surrounded him. Alongside the rumor that he had risked his life as an Austrian spy, and was soon to be decorated, there were those who claimed that he had been held in an especially cruel POW camp in Siberia, isolated from the rest of the world.

Ida announced that she was honored to host a national hero and compensate him for the terrible torture he had endured. Kalman-Zelig had received a similar discount upon his return, although his less than compelling appearance made the mission somewhat less enticing. Ida informed the staff of hostesses that the guest was soon to assume the burden of matrimony so that it was a privilege to sweeten his last free night. When Ida heard that it was Fanny who was to be his bride she felt it was the perfect match. Maybe that consummate heavenly coupling that Feivel, her husband, so believed in, really did exist. Ida had become acquainted with Fanny at the beginning of the war, when she started to sell beer on a regular basis. A short woman who stood tall, with such marvelous eyelashes they were like a piece of jewelry. She always treated Ida and her princesses with courtesy, and her lips never uttered the epithets *hureh* in German, *blaat* in Russian, *kurva* in Romanian and Hungarian, *putana* in Italian, or *kurveh* or *pritzeh* in Yiddish.

Ida remembered how once Fanny had refused to sell beer to a thug who hit a bespectacled Bolshevik youth only because he dared to quote Lenin "There cannot be, nor is there nor will there ever be real 'freedom' as long as there is no freedom for women from the privileges which the law grants to men."

When the hooligan began to rain blows down on the boy, Fanny set upon him with a bottle, broke it over his head, pouring the beer directly into his eyes. The thug recoiled, screamed, and then ran, while the sweet princesses looked on from the windows and in a medley of languages cheered the small and courageous woman.

Ida described to Gabriel the array of options and delights as she paraded her sweet princesses before him, proudly listing the skills of each one. He would learn to pleasure Fanny she told herself, and that would be the perfect wedding present for the couple.

They were all enchanting to Gabriel, but it was Ildiko who caught his eye, the Hungarian jewel in the crown, not necessarily because of her firm breasts or plump buttocks, but because she made him laugh, which no one else had managed to do for years.

First she explained to him the meaning of her name "the fearless warrior," and then she lay him down in her bed, leaned over him so he could enjoy the sight of the whole of her lovely body and told him a joke. It had been told to her by the businessman Ralph Smith, who was a regular customer of hers, and he had heard it from a comedian in America.

Is sex on the Sabbath a sin, since it might be considered work?

The protagonist in the joke presents the conundrum to a Catholic priest. After a careful study of the holy writ the priest comes to the conclusion that sex is indeed work, and therefore it is strictly prohibited on Sundays.

But what does someone who has had to take a vow of celibacy understand about sex? He dismisses the priest's opinion and consults a rabbi with his urgent question. The rabbi reads through the Torah with utmost seriousness and rules that sex is not work and therefore not a desecration of the Sabbath.

"But if so many claim that it is work, how can you be sure?"

The rabbi replies, "If sex was work, my wife would get someone else to do it for her."

The laughter that burst from Gabriel's throat was completely foreign to him. He even rested his hand on his stomach, surprised that his body remembered. Ildiko buried her head in his lap. When he grabbed a handful of her golden hair, his laughter stopped abruptly.

"Congratulations, groom," she spoke into his loins, "I hope that your new bride won't ask another woman to take her place."

She unzipped his trousers, and her laughter increased as the sight of his erection. Her addition to the joke amused her as well, for if her hope was realized, she would be out of a job.

On the morning after, Gabriel smoked his cigarette while he stroked the blonde head of the fearless warrior. When he was about to leave, Ildiko gave him a wedding present – an ingenious gold lighter that worked on kerosene, that she had received as a memento from Ralph Smith before he returned home. With a practiced finger she spun the wheel that rubbed against the iron and ignited the longed-for spark, and they both gazed at the flame.

"It's from America," Ildiko said – she wasn't laughing now – "I dream of living there. Ralph Smith promised to send me a ticket. In America I'll start over."

6

What a catastrophe, Pearl the seamstress could not get hold of suitable fabric for the wedding dress. Even the smugglers on the other side of the border couldn't find any, although Abraham Katz was ready to pay for it with the last of his savings.

The person who came through for Fanny was Ida, who decided to contribute a silk sheet and an embroidered lace tablecloth from her establishment, to the chagrin of Feivel who considered it a total waste.

She and Ildiko took the sheet and the tablecloth and washed them vigorously, after first leaving them to soak in bleach until they were blindingly white. Fit even for Queen Sissi, if only she were still alive.

In normal times a wedding was entertainment for the entire town. Work stopped, and the boys didn't attend their studies at the heder. The men would show off in their best suits and ties and hats and the women wore their holiday dresses, competing to see whose was the finest.

The klezmer wagon, operated by a family in which all the members were musicians and singers, waited by the side of the road. On a raised platform of wooden planks stood a chair upholstered in carpets, where the star of the show would sit, flanked by her bridesmaids.

Her friends would enter the hall to the sounds of the orchestra and help her down from her chair to join them in the last dance of maidenhood, before she became a man's wife.

The young men would decorate the groom's cart. They would adorn the horses with colored paper ribbons and hang bells on their harnesses. Underneath the seat covered in a brightly-colored carpet was a bottle of Slivovitz – plum brandy – and slices of *leykeh*, the traditional honey-flavored sponge cake found at every Jewish wedding. With that ransom the groom would be released.

They would park the wagon crosswise on the road at the entrance to the town, and when the convoy of the wedding party arrived the young men would block its way, while demanding that the groom be handed over to them.

The traditional dialogue between the two camps, handed down from generation to generation, included phrases of extortion that might have been uttered by the Sicilian mafia.

"Only if you hand over the groom will we clear the road."

"Why should we hand him over to you? He grew up with us. He is flesh of our flesh."

"We, and only we, will hand over the groom to his bride."

"No. He is one of us."

"If so, we won't let you pass."

"If you don't let us, we will use force."

"Let's see you try."

"Just wait."

"Force will be met with force."

The tough negotiations about the release of the hostage were the best show in town, and the spectators were also wont to declaim the lines and even improvise new ones.

Once the groom was ransomed and the loot shared from hand to hand, a signal was given to begin the celebrations. Wearing a white kittel or robe beneath a black silk coat and a *shtreimel* on his head, surrounded by singing and dancing friends, the groom was led into the bridal hall, while from both sides of the procession the excited crowd showered him with colorful confetti. Following the ceremony the reception table was set with glowing candles in silver candlesticks and there were spectacular flower arrangements. The trays were loaded with the best of everything and the alcohol ran like water as everyone laughed uproariously at the rhymes composed for all of the guests by the local entertainer. The allusions to the challenges facing the couple on their wedding night were always met with the loudest laughter.

None of this took place at Fanny and Gabriel's wedding.

The ceremony was held in the synagogue courtyard, under a leaden winter sky. It was short and to the point. First the marriage contract was read out and then there was a quick ceremony in which Fanny extended her finger to Gabriel and he encircled it with the wedding ring. She didn't wear her engagement ring, since brides must not wear any jewelry. With lowered head he directed his foot to the glass and broke it, and against a background chorus of "mazel tov" Fanny saw tears rolling down her father's cheeks into his beard.

After the ceremony the bride and groom were brought to the "seclusion room," where they remained in absolute silence for several minutes, eating a spoonful or two of the food waiting there, since both had been fasting since the day before. When they emerged Paula was waiting for them, holding two challah breads that she touched to the couple's cheeks for luck. Then they were led to the meal of "the golden soup," to partake of the soup almonds in the shape of golden coins prepared specially for weddings, although instead of treasure a handful of over salted noodles floated in the broth. Gabriel ate his meal in silence beside Fanny at the women's table, and then the men came to take him to sit with them.

Everything was forlorn, even the Grace after Meals and the Seven Blessings recited for the bride and groom were declaimed through the tears of the guests, who were remembering the joyful weddings of old. Even the comedian, whose job it was to amuse people with his rhymes was unable to stem the flood of his tears, since both his brothers had been killed in the war, and he would never accompany them to their wedding canopies. The klezmer family was scattered to the winds, and the guests had to make do with the raspy playing of a mediocre fiddler.

The usual public announcement of gifts didn't take place either, so as not to embarrass those whose straitened circumstances meant that they were attending the wedding as if it were a soup kitchen. The only firm anchor was the dance with the bride. Every guest in turn took hold of a corner of the silk handkerchief she held and danced a few turns with her before she returned to her seat.

The last of the partners was the bride's father, who was permitted to grasp his daughter's hands directly. Little by little the others gathered round. Paula and her husband Emil Stein, Lizzie-Bertha who held hands with Anna and the younger brother Srul-Leib who had come especially from Vienna. The custom of "The Family Dance" had been considered improper by the rabbi because of the physical proximity between men and women, but at this modest wedding, the first to be held in Siret after the war, he said nothing and refrained from censuring the dancers.

The wedding dress, which Pearl had labored over for a week, looked as if it had been imported from an exclusive store in Vienna. The silk sheet was tailored to Fanny's measurements, but despite her diminutive height the fabric was barely sufficient. The resourceful seamstress added an inset to the edges of the dress cut from a shroud that she begged from the Burial Society. Only those in the know could discern the patch, and despite the grafting the dress fell perfectly. The embroidered silk tablecloth from Ida's house posed a special challenge for the seamstress, so she transformed it into a veil that Anna would also wear one day. She sewed the last stitch right before the ceremony to deflect bad luck. She was very cautious with her needle, since even one tiny drop of blood that stained the bride was enough to endanger the marriage.

Ida and Feivel were also invited to the wedding. Abraham Katz had objected, but Fanny insisted. Ida came dressed like a Viennese lady, attired in black with a pearl-studded cap on her head, and when she wished Gabriel "mazel tov" in Yiddish – Feivel had taught her the words – she arranged her features in a formal expression, and there wasn't the slightest hint that she had met him before. Although he was surprised to see her among the guests, he also kept his expression blank, touching his hat as a sign of respect. Ida's spirits were high. A great mitzvah had fallen to her. Not so much as the supplier of the fabric for the wedding gown, but because it was she who was responsible for the instruction of the groom in the secrets of the flesh and the doctrine of pleasing a woman. After all, wasn't it better that he approach his wedding night with some experience, rather than practice clumsily on an innocent virgin?

And wasn't it better that he had found some relief after years of enforced celibacy, and now could relax with his wife and prolong their coupling, without the risk of premature release. She hoped that Gabriel, who had been inducted by Ildiko, would behave from now on with utmost consideration and that Fanny's pleasure would be his primary concern. Contrary to the founding principle of her establishment, Ida believed that the needs of a woman should have priority over those of a man. She hoped that someday she would fulfil a dream and open a house of pleasure that would also offer its services to women.

If Lizzie-Bertha had known what a feminist was present in their midst she would have recruited her to the cause on the spot.

Ida extended her hand to the bride. A virgin perhaps, but no innocent. The terrors of the time had left their marks on her face, although only an experienced eye such as Ida's could discern them. A seemingly young and smooth portrait, polished skin, a blank page, everything still possible, but at the same time the corners of the mouth had toughened, a thin line of caution was etched in her forehead and beneath the long eyelashes was an expression that concealed an explosive charge. The bride would have to unbend, or else her husband might be disappointed. It still wasn't too late to instruct her in advance of her wedding night.

"Do you love him?"

"Yes."

"But you don't know him yet."

"What I know is enough for me to love him."

"And what you don't know?"

Fanny didn't reply.

"Love is blind. Only marriage restores sight," said Ida, her black-gloved hand stroking Fanny's pale cheek.

So she said, with no inkling that she was prophesying the future.

The surrounding clamor drowned out Fanny's laughter. Ida sounded like the gypsy at the fair. The tablecloth veil swirled around her and reminded her of the colorful rag partition that had separated her from the dancing bear outside.

In lieu of an ancient gypsy blessing, the vastly experienced Ida bestowed advice, "Don't close your eyes when he enters you. Even when it hurts – and it will hurt – keep them open."

7

Fanny had thought about pain when she was immersed in the ritual bath on the previous night.

First she soaped her body vigorously under the scrutiny of the mikveh attendant. Her fingernails and toenails were cut to the flesh. Next the attendant immersed her in the bath, ensuring that the water penetrated to the roots of her hair. Fanny wouldn't give up her beautiful hair and it wasn't shorn. Luckily her groom didn't insist that she wear a wig, and her father supported her as well. Times had changed.

"Blessed are You, our God, Ruler of the Universe, Who has sanctified us with His mitzvot and commanded us concerning immersion."

Seven times Fanny descended and rose. And the men she had met during her life floated there with her. Yanush with the hook who had kissed her hand, the mutilated man from the train who serenaded her with the song of the amputees, the rabbi who had proposed to her, the Bolshevik youth who dreamed of two women for every man, the Russian soldiers who attacked her, and the colonel in whose arms she had found rescue. Unknowing, each one had transferred to her some of his pain.

They rose and dipped with her in the mikveh, a part of her now.

On the last time she dived down to the bottom and tarried there. The surface above her rippled and the light flickered around her. She recalled the touch of Yanush's lips on her skin and the heat of the Russian colonel's body, and gave herself over to the water that penetrated her seven orifices, one more than a man has.

Her lungs nearly burst. The echo of the attendant's voice reached her from above, muted and shrill as her hands groped in the water to pull Fanny out of the mikveh.

"You've gone completely mad, bride!"

She emerged calm and serene, allowing the drops to drip slowly off her naked body, making no move to cover herself.

"Blessed are You, our God, Ruler of the Universe, Who has sanctified us with His mitzvot and commanded us concerning pain."

She whispered the same words when she lay in her wedding bed in the room at the top of the house. Gabriel had brought over his things that morning. There was a faint smell of tobacco in the air, surrounded by the essence of lilac with which Fanny had perfumed herself before slipping into bed. She carefully rubbed some on her breasts and especially between her legs.

Paula, who had offered to prepare her for her marriage responsibilities and had been her guide in matters of the Laws of Matrimony claimed that it was forbidden to look at that place, and forbidden to kiss that place.

Place, said Fanny to herself, like the name for the Almighty.

She believed that a man was permitted to kiss his wife in every place, including that place.

She didn't remove her nightgown. She would leave that to Gabriel. Would his touch be hesitant and cautious, or tough and decisive? And his lips – would their touch be cursory or hungry? All this she would discover four years late.

She hadn't seen him since the ceremony. Perhaps he had drunk himself into a stupor and slumped unconscious under one of the tables? That happened to more than a few grooms who were then out of commission. Had his nerves betrayed him on his wedding night? Gabriel didn't seem like someone who would be anxious about fulfilling the commandment to be fruitful and multiply. On the contrary. Fanny had no doubt that an attractive man such as he had had more than one intimate experience with a woman. Was the rumor true that he had spent time in a cruel camp for prisoners of war and undergone indescribable torture? What would she do if heaven forfend his sexual potency had been affected?

Could that be the reason why he had demanded that she promise never to ask about his experiences?

She would kiss him in precisely that place that everyone was so threatened by, and spread her legs in such a way that he would find her place with no trouble. And if necessary, she would seek advice from Ida about to how to make his member stand to attention.

Fanny pushed off the blanket. The sheet was stiff from being starched so many times and rejected the contours of her body. The bed looked as if no one had ever slept in it.

Barefoot, she glided over to the window from which she had first set eyes on Gabriel in the summer of 1914 when he and the matchmaker had arrived at the house. The street was empty. The gaunt frostbitten trees stirred under the murky sky. A colored ribbon was caught on a branch, a remnant of the wedding decorations that the wind had plucked away. Fanny turned to the back window, and when she opened it the freezing night rushed in at her. A glimmer of red faded and glowed at the back of the yard. There was also a silhouette with its back turned toward her, looking out over the remote horizon.

Quietly Fanny left the house, wearing only her nightgown, and the cold withdrew from her, as though she was bundled in a concealed protective layer.

"Gabriel," for the first time she called him by his name. He remained still for a long moment and only then did he turn, staring at her as though he had been expecting someone else.

The colored ribbon extricated itself from the tree and floated down to the yard. Then the wind lifted it again and pushed it beyond the house. Was it a sign? But the thought was quickly forgotten as suddenly the cold penetrated all her orifices. Every pain she felt was now another icicle.

She extended her arms toward Gabriel's silhouette and led him into the house, as if leading the blind.

8

Atypically, this marriage was consummated in the afternoon. Following a sleepless night the two slept for hours. Gabriel awoke first, and his hand travelling underneath her nightgown brought Fanny to her senses. Although daylight flooded the room, she didn't close her eyes even once. It was Gabriel who buried his face in her neck and all her efforts to pull back his head and "dive into the ocean of his eyes" – in the language of the romantic novels – were to no avail. They didn't share even one real kiss, unless you count a brush of his lips on her cheek or a hasty peck at the side of her mouth.

It wasn't possible that Gabriel hid his face due to shyness or embarrassment, she thought. His skill made it plain that a woman's body was not foreign to him. When Paula asked for details about her first time, Fanny told her that he treated her with respect, but omitted his words that he would have to hurt her, and therefore he would keep the "procedure" as short as possible.

"Procedure" – that's what he called the meeting between his place and her place, as if referring to a medical process. Perhaps words weren't his strong side, or during the war he had become accustomed to the vocabulary of soldiers.

The good news was that not only did he have no problem with an erection, but that she felt him throbbing with full force between her legs. At least they had not disfigured him in any way in that cruel POW camp in Russia.

True, it wasn't the experience that Fanny had dreamed of – Homer wouldn't have used it for the chapter about the reunion of Penelope and Ulysses – but it was only the beginning and they had their whole lives ahead of them. Even the pain was less than she had anticipated, and she already had a few creative ideas, cards she would reveal later on. Had she been born a few decades later she would have been considered a liberated woman, but at this stage of her life she was simply overflowing with passion and optimism.

On the surface she had many reasons to feel that way.

The house in Mihova was sold to the neighbor Mirodan, and Anna moved in with Fanny's family. The two became friends. Abraham Katz realized that his son-in-law had business acumen and brought him into the family enterprise. After studying the books Gabriel made suggestions to improve efficiency. He cut expenses and increased the amount of beer they bought from the brewery. With the annexation of the territory to Romania came more clients, and Gabriel suggested opening a pub at the front of the house. Now in addition to beer Fanny also sold high-quality Țuică a Romanian spirit made from plums, and Vilmos Pálinka, a Hungarian drink made of pears.

"There are two vocations which will always be in demand, in times of peace and in times of war – bartender and undertaker," Gabriel said to his father-in-law. Of the two he preferred bartender, because he, unlike the undertaker, staves off not only the end, but also the fear of the end.

It seemed like the groom spoke more to her father than to his wife. During the day he was preoccupied with the expanding business, and Fanny hardly saw him. At night he fulfilled his responsibility to her, but no more than that. Perhaps that is the true nature of married life, she told herself. From the start it is purposeful and directed solely toward procreation, proceeding along a deliberate path, with no unnecessary disruptions. "Desire" is nothing more than a fantasy peddled by romantic novels, to retain their readers.

It may be that people exaggerate the importance of that connection between male and female, Fanny continued her musings. In the Book of Genesis, no mention is made of Adam's love for Eve. "And is united to his wife, and they become one flesh." Like the operating instructions for a machine.

One night, she dared to twist her tongue around one of Gabriel's nipples. She hoped that he would reciprocate. And despite the low moan that emanated from his throat, he squeezed her breasts in a perfunctory way that wasn't intended to stoke her passion.

It seemed he was saving her from herself.

In fact, Gabriel was only concerned with himself. He neutralized the minefield of longing for what he had left behind through calculated alienation. His physical proximity to Fanny – her skin was now familiar to him, he was fond of her taste and smell – didn't lead to any intimacy of spirit.

The balance began to waver. The more he burrowed into his separateness, the stronger grew Fanny's determination – the very characteristic that he admired. She had to make him love her, no matter what.

Even when he turned his back on her in bed, she fitted herself to him and wrapped her arms around him, encouraged by the fact that he didn't shake her off. One night she heard him mumble a foreign name in his sleep.

"Who is Kostya?" she asked in the morning.

This time as well, the room was bathed in light, which allowed her to look straight into Gabriel's eyes. There was no ocean there, only something so bitter and dark that her eyes closed rather than face it. When she opened them a fraction of a second later, he was no longer there.

9

Can one make herself beloved, can love be forced? And perhaps the perfect love is the one that is never realized, never scorched by the harsh light of reality. These were the questions that consumed Fanny.

The romantic novels supplied her with numerous examples of challenged lovers. From the spurned lover who succeeds through an abundance of coaxing and infinite patience to make the love he desires materialize, to he who overwhelms the object of his desire, gradually forcing it into a state of non-love. It is doubtful whether the Creator of the Universe had any idea that his humble creation would come up with such a plethora of options on the basis of Adam created from dust and Eve from a rib.

And then there was Penelope of course, who came to terms with Ulysses' betrayals, although Fanny doubted that in the depths of her heart she really forgave him. She perused the list of his lovers in agitated resentment as if it was she who had been betrayed. She especially wanted to hold Calypso the nymph to account, she who rescued Ulysses after his ships went down in a storm, and for seven years tried to suppress his longings for Penelope. The one who tries to transform herself into the beloved – a failed model to be sure.

But of all the different types, Fanny pitied those who only realized that they had held true love in their hands once it was lost, and spent the rest of their lives in anguished regret, torturing themselves. Why hadn't they recognized true love when they had the chance, rather than allow it to slip through their hands?

Kostya.

Was it the name of a man, short for Constantine? Based on her experience, she didn't believe it possible that he had fallen in love with another man, not to mention that in those days it was a complicated matter, conducted in secret and held to be a crime. She suspected that it was a cover. If Sasha in Russia could be either a man or a woman, perhaps the name was really Constantina?

In devious ways she tried to nudge Gabriel to talk about Russia.

The Bolshevik revolution gave her ample pretexts, for the civil war that raged across the border cast its shadow over those living in Romania as well. In the pub, the arguments often escalated to fist fights, especially following the order that required the transfer of all food to the state, which caused considerable bitterness among the farmers.

As darkness fell the place filled up, with customers consuming prodigious amounts of alcohol and herring in cream sauce with peppercorns and bay leaves – Fanny's famous recipe – which more than one later vomited after combining with too much drinking.

One night a drunken communist tried to put up a hand-painted poster in the pub that depicted Lenin making a speech against a background of factory chimneys and a red flag. After the patrons were done beating him up he escaped by the skin of his teeth, clutching the remains of his forward-facing Lenin, his arms and eyes straining toward the future.

Fanny had no choice but to call her husband to get rid of the dominant troublemaker, who erupted in a torrent of screams denouncing Lenin and the Jews who had taken control of Russia and were now attempting to conquer the entire world. Gabriel dumped a bucket of ice over his head.

"Did you ever meet any Bolsheviks, Gabriel?" she asked as they collected the dirty glasses.

"No."

"Did you meet any Jews?"

"No."

"Do you think the lives of the Jews in Russia will improve?"

"No."

Always the same "no," that blocked any attempt at conversation.

Maybe she would recruit the Russian colonel again to help her, she thought as she washed the glasses and left them to dry. He would induce Gabriel to talk about the mysterious name he had blurted out in his sleep. When they locked up for the night, she told him about the night of terror she had experienced, and mostly about the knight who had rescued her.

"Maybe you ran into him, Gabriel?" she asked, feigning innocence. "He was born in Odessa and kidnapped by the Czar's soldiers. He hid his Jewish origin for years."

The spark that appeared in Gabriel's eyes gave her hope. Was it possible that she had managed to arouse his jealousy? The romantic novels said that was one of the best ways to make someone fall in love.

"The colonel's name was Kostya," she said.

"It's a common name," he muttered and then he turned away. That night he refused to lie with her.

In her despair Fanny turned to irregular means to spur love – quack remedies gleaned from the village women in the market and from the women who came to collect their inebriated husbands from the pub.

Gather sand from the sole of Gabriel's foot and stir it in a cooking pot with seeds of marigold. Carry a live toad in her pocket, until Gabriel swoons at her feet and declares his undying love. Mix drops of her perspiration in a glass of wine and hold it to his lips right before bed.

In the end, she chose the spell with the greatest chances of success, that she received from Ida. She claimed that it had reached her directly from Eve, who longed to erase Adam's first wife, Lilith, from his memory, along with her daring behavior in bed. The efficacy of the potion had already been proven by two of her princesses who had wanted to secure for themselves a regular, steady income by weaving strong bonds with their customers. The woman who had shared the spell with them, in return for a certain percentage from each encounter, was a gypsy from Transylvania who claimed that she had received it from Count Dracula himself. But Ida gave it to Fanny free of charge, because like her, she was a romantic at heart.

Fanny recorded the instructions precisely.

Take a red candle and engrave both names along its length. Next, spread on it what the witches refer to as "woman's sauce." On the night of a full moon light the candle and repeat three times with utmost intent:

You the candle, be as a torch
Master of fire and lord of the blaze
Ignite my beloved
With the flame of desire.

Close your eyes and imagine the two of you climaxing at the same moment. Do this over and over until the candle burns down and the flame is extinguished.

Ida added a stern warning about fires. There had been accidents in the past, and women who didn't follow the instructions suffered burns which marred their beauty, diminishing their power to attract the opposite sex and sabotaging the spell.

Fanny ordered a red candle from the local candle maker, at an inflated price. The names were engraved with the butcher knife that accompanied her on her wanderings. It was Kalman-Zelig Hirsch who sharpened it for her.

Before sundown, doing what a woman was required to do to ensure that her monthly menses had ended, Fanny inserted her finger into that place deep in her body. Why do the men in the Talmud refer to it as "weakness?" Do they feel vulnerable before that source of woman's power? As she pleasured herself with her finger, the thought came to her that she had not menstruated for some time.

Despite the full moon, Fanny decided to postpone the enchantment and she brought the red candle up to the attic for safekeeping, pushing it deep into the quilt that had once served as the hiding place for her engagement ring. She had no inkling that the photograph of the *liebling* was also hidden inside. On the morning of the wedding, when Gabriel brought his possessions to the house, he had buried it there. He had already heard that it was the safest place. Before the ceremony, he threw the rusted Austrian gun into the river.

When she slipped into bed that night, Fanny informed him that they were expecting a child.

10

Abraham Katz was beside himself with joy. At the conclusion of the Shacharit Morning Prayer service on the Sabbath he opened a bottle of wine, handed out slices of *leykeh* cake, and in a voice choked with tears announced that he was going to be a grandfather. It was the first pregnancy in Siret since the war, and all present said the Prayer of Thanksgiving not only for him, but for themselves as well. Gabriel absorbed scores of slaps on the back in recognition of his crucial contribution to the perpetuation of the Jewish people. Kalman-Zelig Hirsch waited patiently for his turn to shake his hand and for once opened his mouth and wasn't stingy with his words.

"You have a faithful wife, Corporal Herzig. Loyalty is the most important virtue of all."

Gabriel detected the envy, but the fact that another man was attracted to his wife did not make him value her more. Fanny's pregnancy had caught him off guard, as though he had repressed the thought that intercourse leads to procreation, and that offspring are the sole purpose of the Jewish family. Perhaps he wished to believe that a new life could only be born of mutual love.

But we have to be fair. Gabriel treated Fanny with respect, and sleeping with her was no punishment or hardship assignment for him. Still, the pregnancy did not fill the gaping void in his soul.

He was showered with a downpour of congratulatory words while he attempted to conceal the extent to which the pregnancy unsettled him.

He would have a child of his own. But it was Kostya who filled his thoughts.

Fanny, on the other hand, was radiant. The spell had delivered beyond expectation and with a force of its own, without her ever speaking the incantation. She had a feeling that after the birth the enchantment would be even stronger. The child would erase the memory of her mysterious rival "Kostya," and Gabriel would fall at her feet as if she had been carrying a live toad in her pocket, and not a fetus in her womb. All matches start at zero, and love is ignited slowly. Love is unavoidable the matchmaker would declare as he presented his wares.

The best example of a successful match was Emil and Paula, her sister. He was completely smitten with her and she gazed at him with puppy-dog eyes.

They were always at the top of the list, when the matchmaker recounted his successes. At synagogue Emil congratulated Gabriel for his achievement, saying he was sure it was a sign of things to come. Fanny's pregnancy would also bring blessings and luck to his and Paula's union.

Her body rounded out. Her breasts swelled and her nipples darkened, and Gabriel was aroused. Such a paradox. During the months of pregnancy they came together more frequently, and Fanny basked in the illusion that his ardor was proof of his love. She couldn't know that for Gabriel sex was always the way to fill the gaping emptiness inside him, an anaesthetizing alternative to commitment and devotion.

Outwardly, idyllic. In their spare time Ida and her sweet princesses knitted socks for the first baby after the war. Kalman-Zelig Hirsch rejected every suggestion from the matchmaker, since he compared every woman to Fanny. Lizzie-Bertha made Anna's dream come true and taught her to play the piano, and the matchmaker started to suggest prospective grooms for the two of them.

But no peace and no serenity. At night a tempest of desire, during the day, a chilling indifference.

The keenly observant Abraham Katz was aware of his son-in-law's discomfort. Siret is too small for him, he thought to himself. He needs new horizons and challenges. If he were to travel to a big city, he could utilize his talents and that might compensate for his suffering in his marriage. He proposed to Gabriel that they expand the family business and that he travel to Bucharest. "Why don't you sign some distribution contracts for our beer? Perhaps you and Fanny and the child will move there to live?

A new place, a new life.

However, Gabriel didn't like Bucharest in the slightest. For him its streets, its plazas, even the main boulevard with the Victory Gate represented just another rotten place in sinking Europe. It seemed to him that the ghosts of dead soldiers still wandered the streets.

"Why are you alive, deserter? How could you abandon us?"

In a cheap hostel that catered to refugees and fleas Gabriel surveyed the fading lights of "the Paris of the East" and felt as though he was suffocating. At last he managed to sink into a fitful sleep with a coarse wool blanket pulled over his head, to protect him from the shells that had returned to shriek in his head.

He would have no rest. Europe was a gutter that couldn't be washed clean.

In his dream he found himself in the barn in Russia. The smell of the straw and the haystacks was so powerful that he sneezed in his sleep. Small hands pulled him up, inviting him to swing dizzily in a dance.

"Kostya," he shouted in the dream, "you came back to me."

But it was a strange boy who sang to him in a strange tongue.

And when the Rebbe dances
All the Chassidim dance
Ya ba ba ba bum
All the Chassidim dance

He wore short khaki pants and a white undershirt edged in blue lines, and didn't look like anyone Gabriel knew.

"Who are you?"

The boy continued to sing.

"I don't know you."

The boy forced him to move to the Chassidic rhythm, as he danced wildly and stamped his feet. After the last "ya ba bum" Gabriel found himself hanging the rusted Hungarian rifle across the strange boy's shoulders.

"This is for the next war," he told him.

11

Fanny was pampered for her entire pregnancy. Paula cooked her favorite foods and kept the herring that made her nauseous at a safe distance. Anna and Lizzie-Bertha played four-handed tunes and Ida sent advice and talismans, to Abraham Katz's displeasure. It was one thing to invite her to wedding, but now to be friendly with her during the pregnancy? Why, it was known that the tendencies of the child were influenced by the behavior of the mother, he scolded Fanny. Rather than visit that dubious place she should go walking along near the *beit midrash* where Torah was studied, as did the mother of Rabbi Yehoshua Ben Hanania. She made sure that the child in her womb heard twenty eight different portions of the Gemara, and that's why he grew to be such a wise man.

Once again Fanny's stubbornness was put to the test, and she did not turn her back on Ida or on her advice. If it was a son she wanted, she should strew poppy seeds along her windowsill, but if it was a daughter she preferred, then she should scatter sugar cubes around the house.

"I don't mind whether it's a boy or a girl, it should only be healthy." She was always nagged by the fear that the scars of the war would be transferred to the child.

"You've already paid your dues," Ida comforted her. "The world is tired. It doesn't have the strength for another war."

Ildiko, who was present during the conversation, knitting a hat for the baby, warned Fanny not to look straight at the moon.

"If you do the child will be a sleepwalker."

"How can you tell?"

"They walk in their sleep with their eyes open."

"And what's dangerous about that?"

"You mustn't wake them. They're liable to react aggressively."

And so Fanny didn't look up at the sky once during her pregnancy. It was there anyway.

"When a woman is with child her head is heavy, her limbs are heavy and her blood stays within her." Abraham Katz looked to the Talmud, but his daughter seemed as light as a bird. During the months when her son grew in her belly, the horrors of the war, the time spent pushing the cart of beer with the butcher knife always close at hand and the apprehension about her missing fiancé were all driven away.

If only the story could end here.

It could have been the closing image: Fanny's arms resting protectively on her swollen belly, every kick sending a message from a promising future. She takes hold of Gabriel's hand and places it over the movement under her skin. He sheds an emotional tear that wets her navel, and whispers to her a verse from the Song of Songs, "When I found him whom my soul loveth: I held him, and would not let him go…"

But that scene would never take place. The gate to that garden was locked.

Only for Kalman-Zelig Hirsch did the garden gates swing open. When it became known that he had handed over his shop to his nephew Meirke and bought a ticket to America, people couldn't talk about anything else. The decision of a man who couldn't walk, hear, or speak properly to start over in a foreign world seemed like an especially crazy gamble. All the more so when in Siret everyone knew him, his livelihood was secured, and with minimal effort and patience they would find him a worthy match.

On the day when he was packing up his belongings Gabriel suddenly appeared at the blacksmith's shop. It was Meirke Hirsch who opened the door to him.

"You've come to say goodbye to my uncle?"

"I want to ask him something." He turned to face the deaf man, so that he would be able to read his lips.

"How much does the ticket cost?"

Kalman-Zelig held up his fingers to indicate the amount.

"Where did you buy it?"

Kalman-Zelig wrote on a piece of paper: "The White Star Shipping Company."

"Who helped you?"

Meirke answered for him. One of those who had availed himself of his "proxy" services to avoid conscription worked there and had cut short the waiting period for him.

"Where are you traveling to?"

Kalman-Zelig drew a car. And then another car, and another one.

Gabriel stared at the drawing in wonder.

Kalman-Zelig completed a line that looked like a crooked train track. Above it, he wrote "Ford."

"Is that in New York?"

This time Kalman-Zelig Hirsch spoke. "Michigan." And he covered his ears with his hands to show that the deafening noise at Henry Ford's factory wouldn't cause him any problem. It was a perfect job for him.

"Soon the whole world will travel in automobiles," said Meirke.

Gabriel shook hands with Kalman-Zelig Hirsch and wished him luck. The blacksmith seemed to be in no hurry. He took a firm hold of Gabriel's shoulder with his strong hand and blurted out four words, "Take care of her."

Then he placed a small object in Gabriel's hand, wrapped in newsprint, saying it was a gift for Fanny.

In that moment Gabriel understood the truth. Kalman-Zelig wasn't leaving due to financial hardship, or because he was fed up with rotten Europe, but because of his unrequited love for Fanny.

How that matchmaker in the sky does trifle with us, thought Gabriel as he walked home, carrying the gift in his hand. Wasn't the failed match between Adam and Eve enough for the Creator, when it ended with the sorrow of the birth and the loss of the son?

He tried to discern the contours of the wrapped object that he carried. It was heavy. A lucky horseshoe? A decorative item for the front door? In his presence Kalman-Zelig had transferred the sledgehammer and the anvil to his successor Meirke and asked him to demonstrate his proficiency with them. Meirke said that he wasn't finished learning and still had some practicing to do. The matchmaker in the sky also practices non-stop, but his failures simply multiply.

He loves she who doesn't love him.

She loves only when he has stopped loving her and his affections are now for another.

He or she is trapped in a love for his or her own kind that must be hidden away.

She loves he who is unable to love her in return.

Gabriel handed Fanny the gift from Kalman-Zelig Hirsch without checking to see what it was.

"What's this?"

"A farewell gift for you,"

She slipped away to the kitchen, and there she removed the layers of newsprint. It was his medal, pounded to a thin sheet of metal. Everything that had been engraved upon it was gone.

12

In the battle for love, Fanny was not about to surrender.

In her seventh month of pregnancy she seduced Gabriel to perform a spectacular erotic trick. She thrust away her anxieties that sex could damage the growing fetus, and this time she didn't consult with Ida. She "listened to her heart's command," or more precisely, to the hormones raging within her. Long live the perfect arrangement of bodies, the one that allows the parents and the fetus to celebrate together, she said to herself and thought of Lilith who was banished in shame because she refused to be satisfied with the missionary position.

For her creative idea she needed a quilt. At Fanny's request, Lizzie-Bertha climbed up to the crawl space under the roof to bring it down.

"If you roll it up, it will be the perfect support for your swollen ankles," enthused Lizzie-Bertha.

If she had only known what her sister was scheming.

"There's something inside," she announced. But before she could fish it out, Fanny had grabbed the quilt and was hugging it against her belly.

"No there can't be," she replied dismissively. She remembered well the red candle she had buried inside it on the night she realized that she was pregnant. She was glad it was there. Rather than conjure up a passionate interlude in her imagination, according to the instructions of the spell, the flame would burn in the presence of the act itself.

Everything was carefully prepared. First she made the bed with the lace-edged sheets from their wedding night. She perfumed them with lilac flowers and spread a cream made from their essence on the feet of the bed, so it wouldn't be rooted to the floor like Penelope and Ulysses' was.

She also prepared herself for her seduction campaign. She waxed her legs with strips of cloth dipped in honey. She anointed her enlarged breasts with a tincture of milk and water, and then gazed at her reflection in the mirror. Her skin gleamed and her eyelashes, her most precious feature, seemed longer than ever.

When she plumped up the quilt something rustled inside it. She had decided to light the red candle at the last minute, at the time of the act itself.

On that of all evenings Gabriel was late coming home. He said he had gone to see Meirke Hirsch to find out if there was any news from Kalman-Zelig across the sea.

"As if America is waiting just for him," groused Abraham Katz. "The streets there aren't paved with gold, and the dollars don't grow on trees. That is all nothing but tall tales."

"At the entrance to America stands a giant statue of a woman dressed in a Roman robe," Anna said.

"How do you know?"

"That's what they say. And on the head of the statue is a crown with the pointed rays of the sun, and her outstretched hand holds a torch aloft."

"A woman welcomes people to America?" Lizzie-Bertha jumped up.

Anna added that her feet are set on a broken iron chain, a symbol of her liberation from the shackles of subjugation.

"Women are liberated in America!" Lizzie-Bertha exclaimed, ready to leave then and there to follow in Kalman-Zelig Hirsch's footsteps.

Abraham Katz said firmly, "It's a statue," as if accusing the Americans of idol worship.

"Anna, don't let Lizzie go putting ideas into your head." He was the only one who refused to add the "Bertha" to his younger daughter's name. And he was adamant. The name given to a person at birth is the 249th commandment – following the first 248 active commandments about what a Jew should do – and a name that was not bestowed by one's parents was an extraneous adornment, other than "Chayim," which means "life" and was only added to someone, heaven forfend, who was lying on his deathbed.

"Over in America a woman is a lighthouse," Lizzie-Bertha pronounced with envy. "Who knows, maybe they will also grant women the right to vote."

"Really, and a Jew will be president one day? Or a black man?" chuckled Abraham Katz.

Fanny wasn't paying attention to the conversation. What did she care about women's rights and a statue in America? The only woman of interest to her was Fanny, and when it came to shackles, only those that would chain Gabriel to her.

Lately he seemed preoccupied and morose. And the hobbling blacksmith had not been a close friend of his, so why was he suddenly so interested in how he was faring? It would not be easy to seduce her husband this night, but she was primed for the challenge. From here things could only improve. She would make his member rise for her, the one some referred to as the "peacemaker."

When Gabriel went to get ready for bed, Fanny slipped into their room, pressed herself against the side of the clothes closet with the quilt in her hands and waited. The fetus kicked energetically. Boy or girl? Whichever it was, it was as restless as she. When she heard Gabriel's footsteps she threw down the quilt, stepped out of her underwear and stood only in her top. That place of hers, the one that so intimidates the men in the Talmud was breathing and waiting.

She had a newer, updated version of the Laws of Forbidden Intercourse, Chapter 28, than that authored by the Rambam in the *Book of Holiness*: "A Woman's Husband Is Allowed To," according to which, whatever a woman desires to do with her husband – he must do.

To have intercourse whenever she wants to, to kiss any part of him she wants to, and to come to him as she usually does, or in a different way.

13

Gabriel was startled when she burst out of the darkness and began to undress him from behind, and although he was unprepared for the ambush he didn't resist and didn't utter a sound. The pregnant stomach trembled behind his back and he could feel the kicking. As though someone was sending him messages from inside a trench.

Fanny's tongue traveled along his spine, and he felt his skin respond in goosebumps. Then she cupped his buttocks. His breathing grew heavier in rhythm with the kisses that inched their way along his back.

Even when her breasts squeezed his penis between them, Gabriel didn't turn. He accepted her desire to grant him a gift anonymously. Her anonymity excited him, as she chose to be "every woman," she who erases his secrets and creates him anew.

The kisses, the caresses, the touching and licking – all these took place in silence. Everything imaginable took place there, in secret, so that the others wouldn't hear the sounds.

Fanny decided that she didn't need the help of the quilt, and chose "Lilith's position." She lay Gabriel down on the bed, pushed her top off her shoulders, grasped his arms and mounted him. Her black hair fell upon her gleaming breasts that would soon fill with milk, and it was she who determined the rhythm of the rise and fall. There was no more hiding. He had to look straight at all of her. It was she and none other. Now even if he tried he wouldn't be able to forget her.

"I am with you and will watch over you wherever you go, and I will bring you back to this land. I will not leave you..."

This was her non-missionary way to say to her man, "Love you forever." The romantic declaration would be put to the test within a reality that would demand of her precisely the opposite.

"Why did the first man banish Lilith?" Anna asked Lizzie-Bertha in a whisper down in the cellar where they had gone to talk.

"She wanted them to switch positions."

"What do you mean? There's only one position, isn't there?"

"She wanted to be on top."

Anna was appalled.

"They were both made of the same stuff, equal like one body," Lizzie-Bertha defended the first woman.

In the mock court where she was tried in the sky, Adam claimed that Lilith was rebellious and wouldn't succumb to authority.

"She was the only woman in an all-male world, so she was fighting a losing battle," Lizzie-Bertha explained. Not only was the Creator a male, but he sent three angels – a tough team, like the thugs who collect for the mafia – to bring her back to her husband. "They found her standing in torrential waters," she quoted from the Midrash to Anna, who hung on her every word. Despite the fact that Lilith knew she would pay a heavy price, she refused to return to someone who had tried to dominate her.

Anna said sadly, "See how the woman who was created to diminish the loneliness of the only man in the world became herself the loneliest person in the world."

The room upstairs still held the rocking bodies of Fanny and Gabriel. The scent of lilacs wafted from the feet of the bed that moved a little from its usual place. His skin was hot and tingling, and the beads of perspiration dripping from her were reminiscent of the churning water where they found Lilith. Fanny rested her pregnant stomach on her man's rib. He turned and their eyes met for a moment, and then he hurried to close his. Afterwards he touched his cheek to the vibrating ball and listened to the heartbeat of the fetus who would be my father.

14

It was a perfect night. Better to postpone the return to reality to the morning after. Even if there is no possibility of changing the course of events, we can delay them and milk every pinch of joy from that bubble of time.

Dawn rose over the house. Fanny could feel Gabriel's sleeping breaths on her bare shoulder. After watching him for the whole night, too aroused to fall asleep, she now looked over at the brightening window. The tree across the way was in bloom, and rather than count sheep she counted the number of shy new buds. Everyone was saying that spring and summer would arrive late. That's the way it is after wartime, nature needs time to recover. They spoke less about what human beings might need.

But Fanny was snug in her shell. No worries about past or future, just the intoxicating present. She spread her fingers over the taut skin of her belly. The baby was quiet, asleep like his father. Maybe envisioning his future life, hand in hand with the angel who would accompany him from station to station. Even had she tried her hardest to imagine it, nothing would correspond to what was to come. Only the angel itself would know that her son – by now she was sure that it was a boy – would live most of his life in another country, in a different language, in the guise of a new kind of Jewishness.

Gabriel shifted. His face was so close to hers. Sleep softened his tough demeanor and for a moment she could imagine what he had looked like as a child. Would the child in her womb look like him? Fanny passed her hand over his closed eyelids, feeling the stubble of his beard under her fingertips, touching his nostrils and lingering over the small dimple between nose and mouth. He was painfully handsome. Had he exhibited the tiniest sign of wakefulness she would have climbed on top of him and made love to him again. There will be more Lilith nights she told herself, trying to gather him in her arms gently and press him to her without his turning away. What a shame that her belly separated them and prevented a full hug. In that position, her arms trying unsuccessfully to hold him close, she finally fell asleep. She always complained that arms were too short.

When she finally awoke the place beside her was empty. Gabriel's pillow had been straightened and the sheet was smooth, as if he had ironed it with his own hands. Outside the window a gray light shimmered and a handful of sunbeams danced on the rumpled blanket. The fetus was also awake, and his movements made tiny dimples in her belly. Was he in a hurry? No, child. Wait. It isn't time to come out. You have a few more stages to pass through with the angel who keeps you company on behalf of the Creator. It seemed to her as though someone was laughing there inside.

Maybe it was the laughter of the angel of pregnancy, who according to the Midrash was not called Gabriel, but rather "Night." However, now it was fully day time. Fanny remembered how her father had told her that the angel places a candle at the infant's head and that it burns until the day he enters the world.

Candle.

The memory shot through her. Fanny leapt out of bed and made for the quilt that was rolled up on the floor by the closet. When she shook it out to fold it so it could be replaced in the attic she thought that the candle inside had broken. She pushed her hand deep into the feathers but in addition to the red rod of wax, which was intact, there was also a photograph. A faint whiff of tobacco clung to it. And also the remnants of gunpowder, but Fanny didn't recognize those.

A woman looked out at her, with a pointed nose, fleshy cheeks, small sunken eyes. Above a string of pearls that adorned the high collar of her elegant dress, her thin lips were stretched into a grimace of a smile.

It stabbed her like a dagger.

Kostya. His woman.

15

The blow caught her by surprise. A sharp thrust accompanied by a twist of the blade that burned her stomach, but she kept her discovery of the photograph to herself, and didn't make a scene. In her wisdom she understood that only supreme restraint had the power to prevent a rending of the relationship and a final separation, and not for a moment did she consider giving up her beloved.

Oozing pain, she held the photograph of her rival, and rather than shred it into tiny pieces or burn it she investigated it. She even ran her fingers over the wrinkles and the stains trying to solve the mystery of the magic of the woman with the masculine name who had won her husband's heart. How could it be that of all women he had chosen this unattractive creature to love? As if love was something that one chose. For the second time in her life Fanny reached the conclusion that there is no logic to love. She even felt a speck of guilt at judging the exterior without giving a fair chance to what might be inside it.

It didn't make sense that her rival, whose photograph Gabriel had held onto during all the years of the war, was such a poor and wretched specimen. She must have something.

There was no detail of the portrait that escaped her. Even if, on the surface, the thin lips didn't invite kisses, they must know how to inflame the flesh. Perhaps the fault lay with the photographer, who didn't position her correctly before the camera. It was possible that a different pose would also reflect her more agreeable characteristics, which were hidden from the lens.

Fanny had no doubt – some quality in this woman caused Gabriel to yearn for her and to cling to her memory even after destiny had separated them.

She didn't say a word about the photograph and didn't alter her behavior. She had learned from him how to fold her emotions inside an envelope of distant politeness, and maybe her romantic outlook led her to nurture the illusion that the birth would turn everything upside down and his love for the child would awaken his love for its mother as well.

It could be said that she lost herself in self-deception. It could be suggested that she didn't want to see. But again she leaned on the Penelope precedent, since she too did not delude herself that Ulysses was abstinent for all of the years they were apart. And would Penelope have made a scene if she had discovered the portrait of the witch Circe among her missing husband's possessions? Don't men have special needs, and unlike women, only weak control of their impulses? That was the prevailing view and it tempered Fanny's reaction with a measure of tolerance.

And what had she expected? That Gabriel would confess to her about his previous loves? As far as she knew few men – if any – came to a relationship like an open book. A man's past is his to keep.

In the end she reached the conclusion that a person is entitled to his secrets, just as King David hid his encounter with Batsheva from her husband Uriah, and then added insult to injury when he cold-bloodedly sent him into battle, Gabriel was also permitted his previous adventures. In any case, what was permitted to men was also permitted to women. Her conscience was clear. Had she confessed to Gabriel how close she had come to giving herself to that Russian colonel in shining armor? No, she had not.

What would have happened if…? Fanny would contemplate this wrenching question during later stages of her life, when more men would appear seeking her love. For now, she hid the photograph in the emptied jewelry box. All that remained in it was the bundle of letters that she had sent to Corporal Herzig in the Imperial Army, all of which had returned to her stamped "Address Unknown." Kostya joined them, but only for a short time. Fanny was so anxious about coming upon the photograph that she returned it to its hiding place in the far corner of the attic.

Far from the eye, far from the heart. She mobilized every fiber of her being for the mission to increase his love. The time would come, she convinced herself, when Gabriel would tell her about the mysterious Kostya, and then she would give him the photograph.

Despite her somewhat optimistic approach, the stabbing pain continued for the next few days. Sometimes it seemed to her that the fetus felt it too. He kicked more frequently as if he was protesting the hurt to his mother and demanding amends. What explanation would the angel provide about the next life station he would encounter? There exist an abundance of excuses for why a man may not love a woman, but not for a father's abandonment of his son.

Had the angel told my father about the dagger blow that awaited him, it is doubtful that he would have wanted to be born. Thankfully, he kept that revelation to himself, otherwise I would never have come into the world.

16

On a particularly cold day in the month of November Fanny's contractions seized her. Now people were saying that a tempestuous winter that came early was the result of the war. Nature, like a soldier returning from the front, had gone wrong and couldn't reinstate itself.

Due to the fierce winds Fanny didn't realize that the birth had begun, since the wild weather outside coincided with the raging feelings within her, and only when the amniotic fluid was flowing down her legs – it happened when she was peeling potatoes in the kitchen – did she ask that the midwife be called. It was Lizzie-Bertha who volunteered to go out, imagining herself as the raven that set out from Noah's Ark, and not the dove, maybe because there was some honor attached to him, the brave one who endangered his life to find a safe haven for all.

Lizzie-Bertha snuggled into her father's fur coat – heavy and wonderfully warm, but much too big for her – and rushed out to the house of the midwife on the edge of town. But the house was locked and empty for she had stayed overnight in the neighboring village following the birth of twins. Heavy snow began to fall and blurred Lizzie-Bertha's vision. The only dwelling she could discern within walking distance in the ever-whitening landscape was Ida's establishment. Without a moment's hesitation she set out in the direction of her Ararat.

"My sister is giving birth!" she cried, as if at a demonstration, and her words echoed in the reception room that was empty of customers. Ida thought that the white apparition was a ghost and immediately crossed herself.

Abraham Katz was horrified when he saw the Madam and Ildiko rushing through his front door, trailed by a snowstorm. They carried piles of sheets – who knew who had rolled around on them and what stories they could tell – as Ida shouted instructions, "Boil water. Build a fire. Bring clean towels. Spread the sheets on the bed."

Fanny was leaning against the kitchen table, her face twisted in pain, but she didn't make a sound. Partially peeled potatoes were scattered around her, and she was still holding the knife. Ida extricated it gently from her grasp, and scrutinized it.

"Is this knife made of iron?" she asked.

"What does it matter? And who needs a knife now anyway?" asked a frightened Lizzie-Bertha. Did the gentile woman mean to slice open her sister's stomach to release the baby?

"We must conceal the knife under the mother's pillow," Ida explained. "That's what my husband Feivel says."

Abraham Katz intervened, "The four letters of the Hebrew word for 'iron' are the first letters of the names of Jacob's four wives: Bilha, Rachel, Zilpha, and Leah."

The lesson in Judaism surprised Ida the Catholic, and she listened intently to the bearded Jewish man. He put away the potato knife, which was made of tin, and dumped out the entire cutlery drawer. From the heaps of silverware he extracted a large iron knife, used to cut poultry. Later, Ida would tell Feivel that he reminded her of our forefather Abraham from the story of the sacrifice, in the Old Testament.

What was the name of the boy who was almost slaughtered?

Lizzie-Bertha was still bewildered. "Why do you need a knife?" she asked her father.

"To protect the mother."

"From whom?"

Ida barely restrained herself from making the sign of the crucifix. Did the same evil spirits that hurt Christians also harm the Jews? To be on the safe side she began to open the windows, a well-known way to get rid of evil obstacles that might block the path of the infant. The snow and cold burst into the house, but Lizzie-Bertha ignored her chattering teeth. Better a cold wind than an invasion of evil spirits. She put another log on the fire and wondered how the infant could be protected from his fellow humans.

Fanny was completely unaware of all the measures being taken to safeguard the birth, as she was focusing exclusively on her contractions, which were coming faster now, and she was immune to the cold. Ildiko was busy helping her up the stairs to the second floor, making progress in the space between contractions.

"'Birth,' in Hebrew the letters may be broken up to mean 'nearby the Lord,'" Abraham Katz told the two women as he passed them on the stairs. He placed an open Book of Psalms next to the pillow and hid the iron knife beneath it before he was sent out of the room.

"Birth is not a matter for men," Ida declared.

"And thank the Lord for that," he thought to himself. One might assume that He Who resides above was not present at the birth of Cain after he informed Eve "In pain you will bear children." Was this because of His masculine nature? For there is no hint of any female presence in Him. Maybe He hadn't had a chance to delve into the special systems within those created in His image, from the man's rib, and so didn't fully consider the severity of his curse.

The first mother in the world had no choice but to manage the delivery herself, thought Lizzie-Bertha. It was unlikely that the first man, the snake, or even the angel with the flaming sword – males all – rushed to her assistance.

Like them, her father also ran for his life when the suffering of his eldest daughter filled the room.

"Breathe during the contraction and then relax," Ildiko instructed as she spread Fanny's legs and inserted her fist to measure the opening.

"She's dilating well," she announced. Then she rolled Fanny onto her left side to ease the flow of blood to the heart. Lizzie-Bertha watched her in astonishment. Ildiko seemed more skillful than the midwife.

"She has eight siblings in Transylvania. She helped to bring five of them into the world herself," Ida explained. "She's the one who pays for the food that goes into those hungry mouths. Without the money that she makes sure to send them every week they would starve."

Now Ildiko was demonstrating to Fanny how she should breathe, and Fanny followed her instructions. She still hadn't made a sound.

"Scream," whispered Ildiko. "You don't have to keep the pain to yourself."

On the rippling stomach her bright red nails gleamed like rose petals – that's how Lizzie-Bertha chose to see them. Absolutely not like drops of blood. At Ildiko's direction she moistened her sister's lips with a little water, while Ida pushed the towels under the ever-widening opening in Fanny's body.

A spray of snowflakes flew in through the open window and melted away. Lizzie-Bertha climbed onto a chair and brought down the quilt, tucking it underneath Fanny's writhing body and then covered her shoulders with another blanket.

"So the baby won't catch cold," she said, and spat three times.

"The baby will have to get used to things. He must know what kind of a world he is coming into."

Ida said that. And from the other side of the door came the voice of Abraham Katz reading Psalm 121, considered the ultimate assistance for a woman in difficult labor.

"By day, the sun will not smite you, nor will the moon at night."

The wind pounded the walls and the roof, and its howling surrounded the room.

Ildiko leaned in between Fanny's legs and Ida pushed the quilt underneath her.

"I see the head!"

"Push, push!"

And only Lizzie-Bertha closed her eyes. She didn't want to look straight at the torn flesh or the flowing blood. She heard her sister scream. Her voice was suffused with her man.

"Gabriel!" his name was swallowed up in the first cries of the child.

At that very moment the wind peeled off the tin roof and tossed it above the house.

It happened. It really happened. Despite the fact that a snowstorm is the perfect literary device, this is no affectation to enhance the drama. The flying roof is taken from the autobiography *Zionist to the End*, that my father wrote in his twilight years.

But no one remembers what happened on the day he was born, I thought at the time, until my father explained that it was such an unusual occurrence that there wasn't a person in the town who didn't find an opportunity to mention that at the moment of his birth he managed to blow the roof off.

What would have happened if he had come into the world on a different day? With the opposite kind of weather? Would a birth on a sundrenched summer's day have changed anything?

The detached roof – that's what Gabriel saw as he was about to enter the house. As if a mysterious being had torn it off to satisfy some voyeuristic urge and peek in at the people inside. Later Ida would boast that not only did she open the windows to chase away the evil spirits, but also the gates of heaven. Did the newborn really manage to inure himself to the conditions of the world? Never would my father take for granted a roof above his head and he would live out the phrase in the Book of Proverbs: "For the goodman is not at home, he is gone a long journey."

The same verse would hold for Gabriel as well. It wasn't the birth that had brought him back home, since no one had informed him, but the raging wind and snowstorm, thanks to which he hadn't sold a single bottle of beer.

At the sight of Ida coming down the stairs holding a piece of bleeding flesh in her hands, he was sure that the fetus hadn't survived.

"It's just the placenta," she apprized him, under the roof of sky. "Mazel tov, Daddy."

17

Gabriel saw his son for the first time in a roomful of overturned cooking utensils and half-peeled potatoes. A tiny creature with a dark head, stark against his mother's white breast. He still hadn't seen his face.

Fanny was comfortably ensconced in the armchair that had been moved into the kitchen, the warmest place in the roofless house, while Meirke Hirsch was busy sealing the gaping opening where the roof had been. Even after the storm had subsided the blows of the sledgehammer could be heard, echoing the roar of the thunder. The temporary roof would become permanent and would serve as the covering for the sukkah or booth during Sukkot, the Feast of Tabernacles.

Fanny was restored to herself, the signs of the birth erased. When she turned the baby to face his father there was a tiny sound of protest at his being separated from his food. Although Gabriel didn't have the slightest doubt that the creature was of his seed, nothing about him looked familiar.

A miniature stranger from another world.

He froze on the spot and didn't make a move toward mother and baby. Only after she signaled to him explicitly did he dare to place his hand on the tiny head in a mandatory caress. The first time he would hold him in his arms would be at the circumcision ceremony a week later.

His palm was damp and the baby shivered at his touch retreating to the swollen breast. The smell of breastmilk mingled with a whiff of lilac reached Gabriel's nostrils. With his foot he pushed away the potatoes that had rolled onto the floor so that she wouldn't trip over them, and regarded her head bent over the child. She whispered something to him, as though already the two were sharing a conversation in which he had no part.

Is the love of a parent for his child built-in from the start? Something imprinted in everyone? Fanny, like many parents, was awed at the marvel of the sublime being that had emerged from her body, while Gabriel belonged to those for whom love can never be taken for granted and which both sides must secure.

Fanny returned to the Bible, "I have purchased a male child with the help of the Lord," said Eve after her first birth – in the language of ownership.

What was said by the first father in the world was not reported in the Book of Genesis. Only the voice of she who gave birth in sorrow is heard, while when it comes to him we learn only of violence. It was also the woman who chose the name Cain for their elder son, as already in that kitchen Fanny called her baby Yitzhak.

Since that was not a name already found in the family, she created a fact on the ground, following in the footsteps of the Almighty, who chose the name for Abraham's son, who was the first child to be circumcised. Perhaps it was a nod to her father who also carried the name Abraham, or maybe deep in her heart she already sensed that the grandfather would be compelled to stand in for the father.

Whichever it was, at the time it was her way to convey optimism.

The Hebrew name for Isaac is *Yitzhak*, which also means "to laugh," and her Yitzhak wouldn't cry.

She didn't even consult with Gabriel. In days to come he would tell himself that even when he was an infant, Fanny behaved as though their son was her property, and his father would be forced to acquire something of his love only by the sweat of his brow.

At the synagogue she asked to speak. She couldn't stop thinking about the family unit comprised of Abraham and Sarah. She told the congregation that in the Bible only the woman's reaction is mentioned, "God has made laughter for me."

Unlike other mothers, who escape to another room rather than witness the cut into the new flesh, the spurt of blood, and in order not to hear the plaintive cries of the baby, Fanny insisted on standing close to the mohel and didn't miss a thing: the removal of the foreskin, the damage and the sucking.

Even Abraham Katz, who had the honor of being Godfather and sat in Elijah's Chair wrapped in his prayer shawl, was beset with trembling, and the mohel asked him to press his knees together as he held the infant, since even the tiniest movement could upset the delicate procedure and cause irreparable damage.

And Lizzie-Bertha took refuge in the adjacent room and found herself pondering the question: If the Lord really wanted his people to be circumcised, why did he not create them that way in the first place and spare them the pain?

Ida the Catholic, who stood outside the synagogue holding a cake she had baked especially for the celebration after the circumcision – no one would touch it since it wasn't kosher – whispered similar sentiments to Feivel, "You Jews cause yourselves pain so that you will be prepared for the pain to come."

Her point wasn't well-received, since Ida had no reason to complain about the performance of the circumcised member or about the contribution of others like it to her flourishing establishment. In the competition between circumcised members and those with foreskins the former always took first place, Feivel retorted.

Ida apologized. Her words reflected her deep identification with the pain of the Jewish people. On the spot she expressed the wish to convert.

According to the order of the prayers that could be heard through the open window Feivel described to her what was taking place within the synagogue walls. First the blessing "Who has created the fruit of the vine," followed by "Who has created the perfumed trees" – he didn't know which perfumed plant was brought especially for this blessing, maybe myrtle. He joined in, reciting with passion the words of the blessing "Who sanctified this friend from the womb," that concludes with "Blessed are You, Lord, who enacts the covenant," and he even asked Ida to repeat the words after him.

When the prayer for the welfare of the child was recited, Meirke couldn't restrain himself and demanded that the wording of the prayer be updated. The people should also pray for the welfare of the father, since those who return from the war are those who are truly in need of heavenly mercy. Who knew what had happened to Kalman-Zelig who had been swallowed up somewhere in enormous America. No sign of life had been received from him.

At that very moment Fanny announced the baby's name in public for the first time and her father asked to speak and noted that when a child was born to Abraham and Sarah not only was his name chosen at the circumcision ceremony, but the original names of his parents were changed. Abram became Abraham and Sarai became Sarah. The day is no less important for the parents than it is for their offspring, was the interpretation of the proud grandfather, and since the letter *heh* – also the first name of the Almighty – was added to the names of the ancient father and mother, so would the Lord adhere to his growing family. If they had survived the Great War, in His grace He would also protect them in the times to come.

Abraham Katz directed his optimistic words especially at Gabriel. The man's reticence and aloofness worried him. He knew that there were new fathers who were terrified of parenthood, but was it only the weight of the new responsibility that had caused him to withdraw into himself since the birth? Could it be a refusal to share the love of his wife with a new rival? And what a powerful rival he had, who already at the age of eight days had captured all the attention and was endangering their relationship.

He had to help his son-in-law to understand just how much his luck had improved. Instead of a bitter rival he now had an ally. Abraham Katz adjusted the prayer shawl around his shoulders and embraced him outright while Fanny separated herself from the baby and placed him ceremoniously in the circle of his father's arms.

When the verse "and I said to you, 'In your blood you shall live'" was heard from within the synagogue Ida and Feivel peeked through the window to get a better view of the mohel dipping his finger in wine and twice letting the drops fall into the baby's mouth.

"*L'chayim*," said Ida in Hebrew, and Feivel was overjoyed. He withdrew a bottle of vodka from his pocket and offered her some, although what she wanted was to watch the ceremony to the end. Who knew, maybe like the biblical Sarah she too would still be like a young woman after her menopause.

The baby in Gabriel's arms was hidden from sight, because Anna blocked their view as she fussed over the bonnet he was wearing. They could just see the tips of his tiny fingers being stroked by Lizzie-Bertha.

"You see my wife," declared Feival as the two approached the door to partake of the meal, "now the little Jew is prepared for pain."

And in fact, Yitzhak didn't cry anymore. There was nothing on his cheeks and that's how Gabriel discovered that at birth man cries without tears, like the animals. Fanny erased the remnants of pain with a soft kiss. And Gabriel, surrounded by the women, didn't dare to make a move of any kind, and his arms turned to stone.

His eyes were fixed on the baby who had quieted. Although all the residents of Siret claimed that he was an exact copy of him – "like two drops of wine"– Gabriel saw no resemblance at all.

Other than the pain. He felt it move from him to the child like the echo of a distant shell. After the ceremony he buried the infant's foreskin in the dirt. He would do that again in another nearly thirty years.

18

All the life of the house revolved around "the dear child." Yitzhak nursed, slept, urinated, moved his bowels, burped. The burps were the only activity in which Gabriel was an active participant.

The women followed him like the three grim goddesses of destiny – a metaphor that would never have occurred to him since he was utterly unfamiliar with Greek mythology – as he walked through the house with the baby on his shoulder. Around and around again, all the while waiting in anticipation for the coveted sound, something between a gurgle and a sigh, that was always accompanied by the spitting up of warm milk. While he became accustomed to changing his shirt a few times a day he felt that the sour smell clung to him.

And still he grew fond of the baby. A resourceful creature, who had already managed to fit himself into the comfortable hollow between shoulder and chest. The soft exhalations into his neck were pleasant. It seemed that he had found an ally after all, in the world that was policed by women. Fanny even decided when they would next lie together. Six weeks after the birth she went to the ritual bath. That night she showered him with kisses as she removed his nightshirt. For his part he was cautious, almost as hesitant as the first time. Suddenly he felt the terror of penetrating the place in a woman that is one big contradiction. How could it be that in the Song of Songs it was referred to as a "garden," while in the Talmud, in tractate *Nedarim* it was called "the place of filth?" Confusing enough to drive you crazy. And now, after all the chaos that had taken place there, who knew what he could expect? Could he be swallowed up in it like in a mantrap?

The fear of hurting her was also there after the "in pain you will bear children" that she had undergone. In conversations at the tavern the men lamented the state of affairs in which, after a woman had completed her mission to become a mother, her desire seemed to wane. Meirke, twice-divorced, prepared him for the new era to come which would be rife with excuses such as, "I have a headache," "I'm tired," and "maybe tomorrow." At least until the time when his wife would begin to think about a second child.

However, Gabriel was surprised to discover that not only had Fanny's enthusiasm not abated, but even the presence of the baby in his crib beside the bed didn't stop her from expressing her pleasure loud and clear. He even placed his fingers over her mouth to hush her.

"Shh… the baby can hear."

"So what? He is like a witness at the blessing to come to a woman," Fanny chortled.

Why did she need another confirmation of the marriage? How could Gabriel know that her erotic advances were intended to erase his memories of her rival? Even though the quilt had been a part of the birth process, somehow not a speck of blood had stained it. Lizzie-Bertha suggested that they rest the baby on it during the circumcision ceremony, but Fanny had reacted with incomprehensible fury. So be it, the younger sister dropped the subject. It was known that some women suffered from strange phenomenon after giving birth, such as the wives of the unlucky Meirke.

Fanny never ceased to lavish kisses on the baby, which was a proven way to ensure good luck. As one of the first to be born after the Great War – a real darling of fate – he was fussed over by the women in every possible way. Anna washed his head in honey, on the advice of a vendor at the market, who said she had it on good faith from someone in faraway Ireland. Luminicia Mirodan asked if she could pour out his bathwater under a verdant tree, but the only tree that was covered in leaves during that season was a fir tree, and Anna objected. "It's a Christmas tree." However, Fanny decreed, "A tree is a tree and it doesn't belong to any religion."

Red threads were hung on Yitzhak's crib, bearing the names of the three angels Senoi, Sensenoi, and Semangelof, next to a special amulet shaped like a hand that was a gift from the rabbi. Before the war he had traveled to Casablanca to visit the Jewish community there, and the head of the community had given it to him, "a powerful treasure that can repel Ashmedai, king of the demons, who the Muslims also believe in."

When Fanny was nursing they tiptoed around her, and Anna explained that no one should upset her, lest heaven forefend she lose her milk. Ida, who came to visit with beautiful knitwear lovingly crafted by Ildiko and her friends, had more practical advice: Always begin with the left breast, and remove onions from the menu because they dilute the milk. She seemed to be vastly experienced and no one would have guessed that she had never been a mother.

Gabriel felt shunted aside. If it hadn't been for the interludes initiated by Fanny at night, he would have thought that his job was done. More than once he felt like excess baggage, an irrelevance necessary only for the making of children and his contribution to their livelihood. And yet, in the tumult of caring for the baby he occasionally met Fanny's eyes and the burning longing he saw there reminded him of Larissa Yefimovna. Once he leaned over the baby in the crib and whispered, "Kostya."

He began to spend the evenings that concluded his work days in the company of Meirke Hirsch, listening to his chatter – he was the complete opposite of his taciturn uncle – and in return for the jokes he told Gabriel supplied him with a free bottle of beer. Despite his two divorces Meirke had never stopped searching for his true love. Unfortunately, the woman who would agree to be his third wife couldn't be found. The facts that his first wife had suffered from post-partum depression and that the baby born prematurely during his second marriage – a tiny thing weighing only 750 grams – didn't survive, brought down his chances to zero. He was considered a "lethal husband." In the end, the matchmaker gave up on finding him a spouse and told him to "dress in black and go to another town," which is what the Talmud suggests for a man with uncontrollable urges.

Meirke took umbrage at the perceived insult. How dare the matchmaker compare his search for pure love to those dubious characters who seek to satisfy their lust in secret?

"Lust is not love," he argued heatedly.

He told Gabriel the latest Bolshevik joke from across the border.

Marx, Engels, and Lenin were sitting and arguing in a tavern. What's better, a wife or a mistress? Marx voted for wife, Engels wanted only a mistress, while Lenin – the greedy one – wanted both. His friends said, "But you're so busy with the revolution, where would you find time for two?"

Gabriel didn't laugh.

"Which of your two wives did you love more?" he asked.

Meirke mulled over the question for a long time, swallowed the last of his beer and replied with a question.

"If someone had two wives during his lifetime, which of them will be his wife when the dead are resurrected?"

Gabriel remained silent. The staring eyes of Von-Hoffenberg flickered in his memory.

"Of course you don't have an answer, because it's a stupid question," Meirke laughed at his own joke, "In any case, someone who had two wives won't be resurrected."

"And someone who had three wives?"

"His place in hell is assured."

Meirke had another secret that he confided to Gabriel after numerous nights of beer. His difficulty in finding a mate was also related to a certain condition that he had set for the matchmaker – it had to be a woman who would agree to travel with him to Palestine. As a youth he had happened upon a lecture in Vienna given by the legendary Theodor Herzl. He has been overcome by the beard as thick as a prophet's, the burning eyes, and the dramatic delivery. Meirke had even kept the copy of the pamphlet *The Jewish State*, that had been distributed.

"Maybe you'd like to read it, Gabriel?"

"What do I have to do with Palestine? To live in the Levant? We're Europeans."

"Herzl says we'll speak German there. In Palestine we will feel at home."

Gabriel advised Meirke not to be deceived by another false prophet. Was there any shortage of crazed lunatics who had brought their people to the edge of the abyss? That Herzl was like Shabtai Zvi, who had converted to Islam, and Jacob Frank, who had converted to Christianity. But not only would Meirke not back down, he was even more convinced that his place was in Palestine at Herzl's side, and that it was there where his "perfect Zionist wife" awaited him.

Gabriel hurriedly escaped to the bedroom and found Fanny fast asleep. No chance of sex tonight, he thought in disappointment. The baby's eyes glowed in the darkness, wide open and looking straight at him. It seemed to the father that his son was following him with those eyes. He scooped him up and held him in his arms, then noticed the smell emanating from the full diaper. He was about to put him down again and wake Fanny, since as far as he was concerned the changing of diapers was exclusively a woman's job. Just then a whispered question escaped him.

"Do you want to go to Palestine, little man?"

The baby's lips twitched. It wasn't a twinge caused by gas or an involuntary hiccough.

The baby smiled.

If I had been present at that moment, I would have shaken Gabriel – yanked him roughly from side to side like only a ghost from the past or the future can do. The baby's smile must be frozen in time for as long as possible and held up like a mirror to his father. Maybe then he would recognize that the tiny being – a lump of flesh whose entire existence ranged only from crying to sucking to relieving himself, round and round – would one day be a person.

Like Cassandra who was blind but saw all, I would have forced him to say his name with extra emphasis: Yitzhak. My father, who I loved.

Love him.

19

By the time winter came Yitzhak was laughing. This phase of his development had the adults gurgling back at him and making strange faces and funny sounds – mostly like those made by various animals. Ildiko bleated, Ida barked, Feivel honked, Luminicia Mirodan meowed, and the rabbi, unbelievable as it seemed, chirped.

The members of the household joined the leaping and cavorting choir before the baby, as though he was the Ark of the Covenant. To Gabriel they seemed like the demented King David, and he, like Michal daughter of Saul, regarded them critically. Not only because he found the efforts of adults intent on causing a baby to laugh ridiculous, but their pride when they achieved their goal was even more pathetic to him. They behaved as though they had unraveled the mystery of creation. It's easy to make a person laugh, and even easier to make him cry he grumbled.

More than once, when he listened to the baby, he couldn't tell whether what he was hearing was laughter or tears.

For Fanny the winter of 1921 was like a bubble of happiness. She thought that she had found the way to her husband's heart, and the invasive thoughts about the mysterious Kostya were pushed aside. Why disturb the demons in their lair? At the same time, the civil war that raged between the Reds and the Whites in Russia was the focus of every conversation. During the Sabbath meal, when the family gathered round the supper table at Paula and Emil Stein's house, Lizzie-Bertha spoke longingly about Katerina Breshkovskaya, "The Grandmother of the Revolution." She described in detail the military orchestra that had played for the political prisoner, and it seemed as though she herself had marched in the procession of honor that accompanied her on her return home from exile.

Lizzie-Bertha's passion for her role model was so fierce that Abraham Katz was in a frenzy of worry that in the future she might cross the border and join her.

"The revolution has no grandparents, my daughter," he admonished her. "Neither does it have a father or mother. The revolution is always an orphan."

Paula chimed in, "It has already created many bereaved families, right Gabriel? After all, you were there."

There was complete silence. It was the first time that Gabriel had been asked about his experiences in Russia.

"I want to forget what happened," he barked, and brought an end to the subject.

Meirke Hirsch, who was also invited to the meal, took the opportunity to try to convince Lizzie-Bertha that in Zion the second sex was treated with respect, and there she would have the same designation as a man. And hadn't she heard of the female pioneers who had just set sail on the ship *Roselyn* from Odessa – Rosa Cohen "The Red" and Rachel Bluwstein – who some said was a brilliant poet?

"We will return to the days of Deborah the Prophetess in our old-new land!" he declared, and the mention of the title of the Zionist fantasy novel written by his idol Herzl filled him with pride. Later Fanny would say that he was actually making an attempt at a proposal of marriage that unfortunately evaded Lizzie-Bertha. He recommended to Paula and Emil the excellent air in Zion that with God's help would bring them offspring.

"Why, the four matriarchs were all barren, so how exactly does the excellent air work?" mumbled Paula wistfully. Emil tried to cheer her up saying that in the end the Good Lord responded to the supplications of Sarah, Rivka, Rachel, and Leah and unsealed their wombs. Pregnancy, he said, is not dependent on the quality of air, but the quality of prayer.

Zion and no other, insisted the impassioned Meirke, and just then an envelope with foreign stamps dropped out of his pocket.

"What's that? A call from Zion?" mocked Gabriel.

The embarrassed Meirke tried to tuck the letter back inside his pocket, but under pressure from those present he admitted that a sign of life had arrived from America. Anna cheered and urged him to reveal the news from his uncle in the distant land.

Meirke hesitated. The girl grabbed the letter and began to read aloud. Kalman-Zelig Hirsch had been very successful, and soon he would be a millionaire. Come and see how a simple blacksmith from a remote town in Bukovina had advanced so quickly at the automobile factory in the "*goldeneh medineh*" (land of gold) and saved one dollar after another, a bill that didn't lose its value like the dying European currencies. Why, in Austria the price of bread had now reached a billion crowns, and an egg cost as much as a car. Who would want to return to a rotten, disintegrating continent, where people still traveled in horse-drawn carriages? Those were the words of Kalman-Zelig. He wrote better than he spoke. He had also found a modern hearing aid in Detroit, and even a partner – on his own, without the help of a matchmaker.

"The future is in America," he signed his letter, "Follow me."

Anna was thrilled and said she was ready to set off immediately, without even packing a suitcase. She wouldn't even have to change her first name. Anna was Anna everywhere.

But Mierke hurried to throw cold water on her plans. His uncle's tendency to hyperbole was well known from his days as the proxy who helped men to escape conscription, and one could assume that he had seasoned his words with some exaggerations. And although the envelope contained a dollar bill, the Zionists cautioned about the continent that enchants one with promises of fame and fortune, and after swallowing up our people, robs them of their identity. Here's the proof – he waved the letter in the air, drawing their attention to the last line. Kalman-Zelig had already changed his name and signed the letter "Peter Lincoln."

"Have you ever heard of such a name for a Jew?"

"Abraham Lincoln freed all the slaves. He is the Moses of America," Anna passionately defended Kalman-Zelig's choice.

Meirke almost overturned the Sabbath table. He had to tell them about Max Nordau's call from London to immediately evacuate the 600,000 Jews from Eastern Europe to the Land of Israel. "In the dimness of sunless houses our eyes begin to blink shyly.... Let us take up our oldest traditions; let us once more become deep-chested, sturdy, sharp-eyed men."

The loud voices disturbed the baby and Fanny hurriedly attached him to her breast, while whispering a Yiddish song, "Perhaps you have seen the days of yesterday?" – the question asked by the golden peacock in the ballad by Itzik Manger.

Meirke declared that he was only interested in searching for the days of tomorrow, and that to the children who, God-willing would be born to him in Israel he would sing only in Hebrew, the language of the re-born nation in Zion. He moved his head close to the baby's and in a strange accent began to sing him a song composed by a poet named Haim Nahman Bialik. "Sing to me, my bird, of the wonders of that land where springtime ever dwells," he expressed the hope that soon the poet would write a special song for children about birds. With great ceremony he told Fanny that in Zion they would change her name to Zipora, a Hebrew name which had the same meaning as her name in Yiddish – "bird."

Fanny didn't bother to respond. Perhaps she was too busy making sure the baby was properly latched on. The sounds of his nursing, heard across the table, were joined by sudden laughter. The laugh came from the baby's father.

When she heard her husband's laughter – the first Fanny had ever heard from him – she allowed herself to really be happy.

I can still hear the voice of my father singing the *Ballad of the Golden Peacock* to me as I fall asleep. The Yiddish was repulsive to me as a child. I was ashamed of it, as it stained my pure Israeliness, but secretly I was addicted to the songs of the poet Itzik Manger, native of Czernowitz, a certified prankster who liked his liquor and joined a group of traveling thespians.

In his later years he left New York and moved to Israel so he could die there.

"Daddy," I once asked before he turned out the light, "Maybe you have seen the days of yesterday?" and Yitzhak wiped away a tear.

20

The Czernowitz branch of The White Star Shipping Company was teeming with people. Gabriel walked by it on his way to a meeting with a liquor merchant from Moldova. What attracted his attention wasn't the lengthy line that snaked along the street, but a figure that stood out with its golden hair. His heart skipped a beat. Only the hair wasn't pinned up underneath a Russian peasant's kerchief, but was loose and flowed from beneath a fashionable fur hat. It was Ildiko.

"Ralph Smith didn't forget his promise," she told him, her face shining. "He sent me the money for a ticket to America."

Next to the sidewalk on a mound of snow lay a beggar, curled inside his torn uniform. He straightened up and pointed at her with his filthy hand.

"Don't they have enough whores, why should they import them from Europe?"

"Watch your mouth," warned Gabriel, "That's no way to talk to a lady."

"Lady? What lady?" the man brayed through his toothless mouth. More people gathered round and made obscene gestures.

Ildiko placed her gloved hand on Gabriel's arm to calm him. The last thing she wanted was a brawl. She didn't want any trouble that might hurt her chances of obtaining permission to travel. She retreated to the edge of the line, clutching her pearl-studded purse. But the beggar wasn't done and now he started on Gabriel.

"You should join her. Whores and Jews, get out of here! Go pollute America."

The line moved forward. People turned away, unseeing, unhearing.

When the beggar tried to grab Ildiko's hat Gabriel stepped into his path, her body trembling behind him. Still, the beggar managed to catch hold of it as a stream of curses poured from his mouth in a variety of languages. He concluded his tirade with the scream, "Jewish pimp, you are responsible for the war. You wanted to make money off our misery!"

Then he crushed the hat under his rotting boots. Flakes of snow that flew up from the sidewalk froze in the air. Ildiko pulled Gabriel away from the line, but he tried to go after the beggar. This time he wouldn't let the insults pass. His restraint dissolved and his fury was unleashed. He stood ready to pummel the man.

"It's not worth it," Ildiko said. "These people are finished. Ralph Smith is right."

Gabriel was still furious, breathing heavily. Ildiko removed her glove and dug her frozen fingers into his arm. When he returned home he would find their imprints on his skin.

They stood on the corner of renowned Herrengasse Street, shaking with anger and cold while the workers spread sawdust on the road to prevent the snow from melting and turning to ice.

Gabriel insisted that they return to the White Star office. Ildiko's hat was lying next to a frozen yellow puddle that shone on the white snow. The beggar stood above it, closing his trousers and dripping urine.

"I piss on you!" he screamed.

Gabriel retrieved the misshapen hat. The wisps of fabric turned to ice.

"It can be cleaned," he said as he offered it to Ildiko.

"In America I'll buy myself a new hat." She shook her mane of blonde hair and rejoined the line, at the end.

Gabriel decided to wait for her. People detoured around him, pushed, urged him to move forward. The wishes and longings gathered there could have encircled the globe several times. The people standing in line wanted to move on, to distance themselves from the continent that offered only suffering and despair. He watched those going in, anxiously gripping whatever funds they had, and those exiting, clutching the coveted ticket to their chests, glowing with joy. Ildiko was also beaming. She kicked her ruined fur hat in the direction of the beggar.

"Use it to wipe your shit."

The beggar was so shocked that he didn't respond. He backed away and slipped on the frozen surface with a resounding boom. There was no sign of the yellow stain in the snow.

Gabriel waved at her. Ildiko was surprised to find him waiting there.

"I wanted to be sure that no one would harass you," he explained.

"I know how to take care of myself."

She opened her embroidered pearl purse. To his amazement a silver pistol nestled there.

"And I will protect others as well." On the spot she vowed that once she was settled in America she would make sure to bring over her younger siblings from Transylvania.

A little later, when Gabriel went to seal the deal with the Moldavian merchant, her words rang in his ears. "You have a wife and child. Save them." The money from Ralph Smith bought her a first class passage.

How surprising are people's acts of generosity, Gabriel reflected as he walked home. And they tend to come from the very people of whom you would least expect help. A veteran customer who remains loyal to a service provider, or a woman with wheat-colored hair in a tiny village in Russia. Gabriel squashed the yellow stain inside him as if it was Ildiko's fur hat.

He endured a sleepless night. In the soft hour of dawn, when the sky began to lighten and illuminated the peacefully-sleeping Fanny and the baby at her breast, he left the bed and lit a cigarette with the lighter he had received from Ildiko on his wedding night.

In the middle of summer, on a muggy day, the complete opposite of the day when Gabriel met the Moldavian merchant, he would sell it for a hundred and twenty crowns, the price of a third-class ticket to America.

21

As the snow melted tremendous currents cascaded down the Carpathian Mountains and washed over the woods on the banks of the Siret River. Fanny had been going for walks along the "Lunka" – which was the locals' name for that body of water – since childhood. She had always been fascinated by the path of the water, more than 300 miles to the Danube, which carried along an abundance of branches, animal carcasses and refuse. It functioned like a huge rake invented by the Creator to clear away the surplus and rotting matter, she explained to her sisters. That's how space was created for new growth.

On a day when a hesitant sun deigned to emerge Fanny wrapped the baby well and went out with him for a walk. She was concerned because he hadn't yet rolled over, and the women's attempts to calm her with remarks such as, "every baby has his own rhythm," didn't help at all.

"And what if he doesn't roll over?"

"People can't stay put for long. He's got to roll over." said Ida.

Fanny's previous walks around the house or in the yard hadn't made any difference. The baby remained on his back, looking upward as though only from above would salvation arrive. In the end she decided to go out to the Lunka. The wealth of stimulants provided by nature would be sure to engage him and then he would turn over.

"You will get to know the world," she told him. From the day he was born she talked to the him, and to Gabriel who listened in, it seemed that the baby responded.

To be honest, the walk was as much for her as it was for the baby. She was hoping to detect signs of healing in the battered natural world, to find some encouragement there as the economic situation worsened, inflation raged, and the voices raised against the Jews gathered strength. Abraham Katz sighed as he quoted the answer to Wilhelm Filderman, leader of the Romanian Jews, when he asked the government to grant citizenship to the Jews: "It's impossible. We all know that our country is anti-Semitic."

The deteriorating situation didn't prevent Feivel – an indefatigable entrepreneur – from planning the expansion of his establishment. With Ildiko's departure he would have to do some re-organizing. He wanted to add a room with mirrors and peepholes, and had already invested in a collection of costumes that would not have been out of place in a theater; nuns' habits, ballet tutus, schoolgirl and nurses' uniforms as well as accessories such as whips and harnesses. He even ordered handcuffs from Meirke Hirsch, although of course the blacksmith had no idea what uses they might be put to.

Meirke was also crossing the Lunka on his way to Ida's House, carrying his elaborate handiwork. Although it was a detour, he wanted to gaze one last time at the verdant view before going to live in the barren desert. True, his idol Herzl had prophesied that the Jews would find creative ways to transform it into an irrigated vegetable garden, but even an impassioned Zionist like Meirke knew the difference between fact and fantasy.

When he recognized Fanny on the other side of the river he shook his handcuffs at her, which caused her to turn sharply and shield the baby.

"Sorry. I didn't mean to frighten you."

The baby gave a piercing shriek. At six months he had developed a fear of strangers.

"Did you change your mind Meirke? Have you decided to cross the river to the Promised Land in the other direction?"

"Don't go putting ideas in the baby's head. He's the one who will want to live across the river in the end..."

"This is our home," she cut him off.

And Meirke finished his sentence, "...or across the sea."

The current raged around the bridge. For a moment it seemed that the wooden supports were about to collapse. The water overflowed the riverbank and began to flood the surrounding area. Fanny moved back. This wasn't the world she had wanted to show to her son. Even the spring seemed to harbor evil. The baby squirmed in her arms, his screams competing with the din. This is not the time to roll over child, she whispered, bouncing him up and down as she walked. He wouldn't be soothed and continued to scream. Meirke walked with them as they fled the surging Lunka. When they were finally out of danger he clattered the handcuffs at the baby as though they were a toy, but he didn't manage to coax even the shadow of a smile.

"What's this?" Fanny was surprised. "Handcuffs in the Land of Israel?"

Meirke stopped his clattering and the baby stopped crying.

"A special order from Feivel," his voice was full of pride. "A defense against lawbreakers."

The thought of Feivel in the guise of a policeman seemed utterly ridiculous to her, but Fanny was impressed by anyone who thought to be extra cautious in those times. Unlike her. How irresponsible could she be? How could she endanger her child with a walk to the Lunka? How had she come up with such a crazy idea? As if nature so easily pardoned those who desecrated it. The spring was no guarantee of any good tidings. She vowed never to take her eyes off the child. She would stay by him wherever he went. Even when he grew up she wouldn't break her vow. She would stick to him like glue.

Meirke Hirsch took in the green fields saturated with water. He would never cease to miss that view, although some say that even in the desert there are floods after the rain.

He pointed to a flock of wild geese in the sky.

"Look Fanny, they're coming home," he sounded surprised.

"It's the opposite direction to the one you will take," she pointed out. Despite everything, they had come back of their own free will.

When the two turned into the town, covered with sticky mud and spattered with leaves, Meirke told Fanny that he had made an additional pair of handcuffs that he intended to bring to his new homeland.

"Are you planning to be a Zionist policeman there?"

Meirke handcuffed himself and slipped a key to her fingers. When he asked her to unlock him she said that the key didn't fit the lock. Let's see you, Meirke Hirsch, get yourself out of this like the great Houdini. Did you know that he's a Hungarian Jew, whose real name is Erik Weisz?

Meirke made a clinking sound with the handcuffs for the baby and this time Yitzhak laughed, and his tearstained face was illuminated by the feeble rays of the sun.

For a moment the blacksmith looked like a bound Prometheus. Since Gabriel's return Fanny hadn't opened her book of Greek mythology. Perhaps at the advent of spring she would tell him about Ulysses and Penelope and his heart would open to her a little.

To her surprise, Meirke extricated himself with ease, since he had created a special hidden bolt that he could release at any time to open the handcuffs.

They stood on the outskirts of the town, Ida's House on one side and the synagogue on the other, and he recited another of his favorite quotes, "When in the Land of Israel there will be a Zionist thief and a Zionist whore we will be like all the nations."

Fanny picked up a fallen goose feather which she later used to decorate the baby's crib. He too, like Meirke, would yet long for the contours of his childhood and in his final years he would recall the Lunka.

That night Yitzhak rolled over for the first time.

22

Like the powerful currents of the Lunka, new ideologies were washing over Europe. Gabriel followed the news of the communist parties that were founded in Italy, in Czechoslovakia, in Spain and in Portugal. The Soviet army took over Georgia and imposed its regime, and in Siret the First National Congress of the Chinese Communist Party was marked with excursions to the middle of the lake. Two streams joined that current, but Gabriel didn't attach much importance to them. The National Fascist Party was created in Italy and in Germany Adolf Hitler was declared the "führer" of the small National Socialist German Workers' Party. Looking back with full knowledge of the bitter results – in hindsight – had Gabriel read the writing on the wall and reached the conclusion that the seeds of madness were being sown?

Almost certainly not.

America wasn't an ideology for him. On the contrary. It represented normal life, simple and basic. A roof over your head and an opportunity for comfort and advancement, far from the degeneration of the war and the hatred of the Jews. Although Kalman-Zelig's report seemed to him like a fabrication, and no sign of life had arrived from Ildiko to indicate that she had realized the American Dream, his anxiety about impending immigration restrictions hastened his decision.

That same summer, when the United States formally declared the end of the Great War, he suggested the idea to Fanny. "First I'll get settled, and then I'll send tickets for you and the boy."

A similar promise was uttered by thousands of men at that time. On the surface it sounded romantic. They would be the advance guard, and after them the gates would open. But Fanny clung to what she had, the familiar and the routine, and rejected an adventure into the unknown. To leave Europe and her father's home seemed to her like an insane idea. She would always believe that her husband deserted her.

In the heat wave that Europe sweltered under that summer – 38 degrees in Czernowitz – Gabriel stood in line outside The White Star Shipping Company for three consecutive days.

He lied to Fanny. He told her that he had to travel to Bucharest for meetings with prospective customers. Who wasn't with him in that line? The very same routine and familiar world that Fanny clung to. Farmers, laborers, poor women alongside the well-groomed, demobilized soldiers, rabbis, Chassidic men, and even the Anti-Semitic beggar who tried to sneak in and was sent away by the clerks.

And there was also a gypsy who exploited the long wait to earn a few coins. She advanced along the line telling fortunes.

Gabriel's clothes stuck to his skin. The rivulets of perspiration made him itch, and his nostrils rebelled at the sour smell of bodies pressed together in front of and behind him, no small matter for a fastidious man like himself. However, he was prepared to make any sacrifice in the realm of hygiene if it meant he would acquire the desired piece of paper. When he reached the counter he discovered that the rate had gone up, and Ralph Smith's gold lighter just barely financed a ticket for him in the miserable bowels of the ship.

The symbol of the shipping company emblazoned on the ticket and the permit provided Gabriel with a tailwind; a red pennant with two tapered points and a five-pointed white star in the center. Even the rumor about a fire that had broken out on the *Cedric* and quickly spread to the cargo hold packed with mattresses and flour didn't diminish his sense of achievement. After all, the six sailors who lost consciousness were miraculously saved.

As he left the White Star office the gypsy rushed up to him. Young, with smooth brown skin, her green eyes sparkled under her flowered kerchief. Her thick black braid hung down over her shoulder and rested on her chest. He was taken aback to discover that she smelled like fresh leaves. She pulled a deck of cards from the sleeve of her dress.

"Don't you want to know what the future holds in store for you, sir?"

He showed her his empty pockets.

"I don't have any money."

She smiled at him and her gold tooth shone.

"For a handsome man like you I'm prepared to tell you for free." She raised the fanned deck to his face, and reluctantly he chose a card that jutted out a little. It showed a pair of wings connected by a hoop that resembled handcuffs.

"Nonsense," he murmured as he thrust away the card.

"What's your name, Mister Angel?"

He didn't answer, as he tried unsuccessfully to evade her grasp. Soothsayers and fortunetellers were charlatans who made money from people's anxieties. And yet the gypsy wouldn't relent and clung to his arm.

"Your face is familiar. Have you been to see me?"

"No."

She narrowed her eyes and observed him closely.

Are you sure I've never told your fortune?"

"I'm sure."

"What's your name?"

"What does it matter?"

"The future seeks a name."

In the end he gave in, "Gabriel."

She gazed at the image of the interlocked wings.

"Freedom," she said, "That's what you want. But you won't get it."

"America is the land of the free," he replied. With his free hand he waved the ticket at her – his trump card.

"Freedom is not a place," laughed the gypsy.

She grabbed his palm and ran her brown fingers over the horizontal and vertical lines, caressing them lightly until he shivered.

"This is your last chance. It's a revolving door Mister Angel. You can still change your mind."

Gabriel finally managed to pull his hand away and hide it behind his back.

"Maybe you'll take me with you to America, Mister Angel?"

"You're the fortuneteller. You already know what my answer will be."

"I'm not allowed to tell my own fortune." He was about to leave when she tugged at his clothes once again and asked for something in return for her prophesy.

"You told me it was free," he retorted.

"Free also has its price."

"I don't have any money. I already told you."

"I don't want money."

"So what do you want?"

"I want you to tell my fortune."

The coming of evening only slightly cooled the air, but it dried the perspiration on Gabriel's skin. The people who had been waiting in line dispersed, except for a handful who opted to sleep outside the White Star office to be first in line in the morning. Under the street lights which had yet to be lit there glowed in Gabriel another woman, with hair as light as the gypsy's was dark.

As one by one the lights were lit he took the brown hand that was shaking like a trapped bird and lowering his face toward it he traced her lifeline with a kiss.

23

That night he also bestowed a kiss, if a perfunctory one, upon his wife.

"How did it go in Bucharest?" she asked drowsily.

"I bought, I sold."

Gabriel felt that he stank not only of sweat, but also of deceit. Luckily, Fanny wasn't aroused by the kiss. She mumbled sleepily that Yitzhak had crawled from one end of the house to the other and then she turned onto her other side.

Gabriel stealthily placed the ticket in the inside pocket of his best suit, the one he wore on the Sabbath and on special occasions. As he washed his face in the washbasin the baby was woken by the sounds and stretched out his hand between the bars of the crib. This time his father didn't react, but the baby – persistent as ever – didn't give up. He rolled onto his belly and raised his head, shaking the crib energetically and setting it squeaking.

"Shhh..."

The baby kicked with his legs.

"What do you want? Are you hungry?"

The baby's fingers grabbed onto Gabriel's nightshirt and pulled. What power this creature has, and it isn't even a year old, he thought. If he has demands now, who knows what he'll claim in the future?

"Do you also want me to tell your fortune?"

Yitzhak gurgled which made Fanny stir again. Just don't let her wake up and start asking questions about the trip to Bucharest. With no other choice Gabriel leaned over and plucked the baby from the crib. Although his limbs were heavy with fatigue and his entire body screamed for sleep, he went out into the yard, pacing back and forth under the trees in the hope that the movement would lull Yitzhak to sleep. But the baby was completely alert, and humming an annoying non-stop stream of sound. How did Fanny understand what he was saying? Did only mothers possess the talents of King Solomon, or was it a personal failing on his part? For the first time he wondered if he was a flawed father. "And Adam knew his wife," it says in the Book of Genesis, but it doesn't say anything about his knowing his sons. Cain, Abel and Seth – all remained mysterious to him and inaccessible.

His distant seed.

The dawn air was a little cool and the baby shivered. Gabriel took off his nightshirt and wrapped the sleeves around the tiny body like a pair of folded wings. The baby's eyes – clear and sharp as an adult's – followed his every move, although his eyelids began to droop. As he drowsed against him, Gabriel began to talk. It was his first conversation with the baby. And of all things he chose to tell him about the fate of Cain. "You have made me a homeless wanderer. Anyone who finds me will kill me."

Stop!

The ghost from the future tries to steer the conversation in a different direction. Why are you talking to an innocent babe about murder? And isn't it too early to reveal to him the destiny of a wanderer with no place of refuge? Why not sing a pleasant and harmless song to young Yitzhak? *A Nest for a Bird*, for example. With Bialik there are no broken eggs, and the chick sleeps peacefully within its shell. But the poem, what can you do, hasn't yet been composed.

What is it Gabriel? Did you decide to take seriously the "angel" nickname that the gypsy gave you and jump into the role of the heavenly guide, who leads the baby on a preliminary tour of the stations of his life? Wouldn't it be better to spare him the blood, and the horrors and the exile and the wandering, and the other abuses that will fill his resume? But voices from the future didn't reach Gabriel. What drew his attention before he collapsed into a garden chair and sank into a deep sleep himself was the tiny impression between nose and mouth on the face of his infant son. He lightly caressed that indentation, proof that the angel had erased the preordained curriculum vitae so that the baby could leave the womb unburdened by what was to come.

It was the shrieking that woke Gabriel. For a moment he was convinced that he was in a trench and under attack. Where was the commander? Where was the person entrusted with warning them to take cover?

It wasn't Von-Hoffenberg, but Fanny, in a frenzy. When she awoke to feed the baby she discovered to her horror that he wasn't in his crib.

"They've taken him from me! My child! My Yitzhak, where are you?"

She stood under the murmuring spruce trees clad only in her nightgown, and the terror had distorted her face until all that remained was the gaping hole of her mouth.

The baby also began to wail, and his sobs intensified as he was snatched from Gabriel's arms. Fanny pounded on his chest with her fists. He stood mute and endured. Finally he regained his composure and took hold of her wrist.

"Listen… I want to tell you something…"

But she shook him off and stormed inside holding the screaming baby. She didn't only rouse the household, but she woke up the entire street. Her fury didn't abate for days, and she didn't let her son out of her sight.

And the impending journey remained a secret.

24

Every time he approached the closet Gabriel felt the ticket signaling to him from inside his suit pocket, drilling a hole in his soul. The departure date was approaching and still he hadn't said a word to a soul.

Fanny had already forgiven him and explained to everyone that he was an exemplary father and a wonderful husband who had only been concerned about her welfare on the night when he took the baby out for a dawn walk, so that she could get some rest.

The world went on as usual. September passed, and October as well, and Gabriel still hadn't mentioned his plans. Later, Abraham Katz would say that his son-in-law's further withdrawal into himself had worried him, but at the time he never said a word either.

The baby – he was their chief delight. At Rosh Hashanah – the New Year he already sat at the table without any support, and at the words, "Because of our sins we were exiled from our lands, and distanced from our lands…" he sat up even straighter, and during the singing of "Our Father our King" he banged two spoons together in perfect time.

At Sukkot – the Feast of the Tabernacles, as they sat under the opening in the roof – where the piece had blown off during the storm the previous year – he held a bottle and drank from it himself during the blessings of the four species. Lizzie-Bertha was impressed, but worried that he might grow overly fond of bottles. Anna's retort, that "the bottles are our livelihood," was swallowed up in the energetic rustling of the lulav, as the baby's attention shifted to the date palm frond.

"Just look at our wonder boy waving the lulav eastward," beamed Abraham Katz.

On November 14, 1921, there was a party for Yitzhak's first birthday. He was already standing and walking around holding on to the furniture, encouraged by the shouts and exclamations of the guests. Gabriel wore his best suit for the occasion, and the ticket in his pocket burned like a hot coal. Lizzie-Bertha played the piano, and Anna brought in the Sachertorte she had baked, a dense chocolate cake topped with a layer of apricot jam and coated with dark chocolate icing into which Paula inserted two candles. The chocolate, a precious commodity in those days, was a gift from Ida and Feivel. Fanny blew out the candles for the baby, and Gabriel watched in silence, like a stranger who had happened upon someone else's celebration.

"What do you wish for your son, Gabriel?" Meirke tried to prompt him to speak. He was in high spirits since he was about to leave for Palestine and the party was also a farewell event for him.

Gabriel remained silent. Not blessings but the question of Avner Ben-Ner, the military leader in the Bible, was what he thought of, but he chose to keep it to himself. "Must the sword devour forever?"

He wasn't surprised that this cry of despair came from a military man.

The sword devours the people – not the land.

And the man knew war – and not only his wife.

There is no peace under the sun and there is not a season to everything, nor a time to every purpose.

Another verse from Ecclesiastes came to mind, that for him was the unshakeable truth, "He that increaseth knowledge increaseth sorrow."

If the first man didn't manage to prevent the murder of his younger son by the elder, how could someone who was but a simple soldier and not a commander prevent the curse of the double-edged sword?

America. Maybe there he could find a life devoid of peril and war. Economic wellbeing. A Ford Model T. He would promise Fanny that he would send tickets for her and the boy once he'd worked things out.

He had to tell them.

His refusal to participate in the birthday celebration troubled those sitting around the table. What could be said about a father who didn't rush to shower blessings upon his son, wondered the concerned father-in-law, as Fanny took a step toward her husband and touched his chest trying to draw him into the family circle. Later she would say that she had felt his body recoil, but at the time she believed it was an embarrassed response to the public gesture of intimacy. She couldn't know how dangerously close she was to the ticket.

In the end, with scant enthusiasm, he recited the blessing, may he be "… as the dew of Hermon, and as the dew that descended upon the mountains of Zion," and Meirke hastened to raise his glass in a toast to himself, for the words were also his Traveler's Prayer as he embarked on his journey to Palestine.

"God-willing you will all come as well and I will be there waiting for you," he declared. It would be many years before his wish would be fulfilled.

"Increase knowledge, increase sorrow." Did Gabriel choose not to make his announcement so as to spare the family undue suffering, or was it pure cowardice? To the very last moment he held his cards right up against his chest, and only on the morning of the journey, as he packed his meagre possessions, did he prepare to reveal the truth at last. A final night of sex, initiated by him, had preceded the hasty packing of his suitcase. It's possible that he wanted to soften her up before delivering the blow, or that he wanted to carry some erotic cargo along to see him through the coming rainy days, for who knew when he might next share his bed with a woman.

A man flees from love. Like the concluding line in the Song of Songs, "Come away, my beloved! Be like a gazelle or a young stag on the mountains of spices." Her body and her fragrance, so familiar to his nose and tongue, were rediscovered for them both that night. He gave her a consolation prize as he drew upon all the amorous skills he possessed. The prostitute in Czernowitz, who had once foreseen great things for him, would have been proud. He showered pleasure upon those parts of the body described in the Song of Songs as the "crescent of the moon," and the "twins of a roe."

For Fanny, sex with her husband was her great comfort and promise. Before others he concealed his emotions, but when he came to her in the confines of their room the floodgates opened. His passion led her to hope that all that was needed was some patience on her part and then everything would be perfect. One day he would be the husband she had dreamed of.

Just before she climaxed, and Gabriel deliberately prolonged her passion, she asked him to give her another child, and was disappointed when he pulled out of her and his seed settled in a warm pool on her stomach. So be it, she thought to herself when her moans had subsided. I have all the time in the world.

Time – it was the one thing she didn't have.

Morning had broken by the time Gabriel closed the lock on his suitcase. He snapped it shut smartly, hoping that the noise would wake her, and when she didn't move, he touched her bare shoulder. Smooth, shining skin. Like the first time he had seen her, when they were joined by the matchmaker the summer before the war. She wasn't a beauty, but she was far from ugly. Her long eyelashes that lay softly above the blanket left a faint shadow. Her silky hair was spread across the pillow. He gently moved it aside and when she opened her eyes she knew. He was leaving.

Gabriel expected recriminations and argument. He drew a breath, about to launch into a reasoned explanation, but in fact he never managed to say a word. To his astonishment she didn't burst into tears, but stood up and walked purposefully toward the closet, dragging a chair behind her. What was she doing? Would she prove to be one of those hysterical women who tried to harm their husbands? He held the suitcase to his chest like a shield as she climbed onto the chair and reached for the crawl space above, where she rummaged for something and then climbed down holding the quilt, into which she inserted her arm. At first he didn't realize what she was waving at him.

"Are you going back to Kostya?"

In her hand he saw Von-Hoffenberg's *liebling*. Creased, squashed, reeking now of mothballs instead of gunpowder and the stench of corpses.

She repeated the name. "Kostya" – firing it at him at point blank range.

"Are you leaving us for her?"

Gabriel pushed the photograph away. He didn't even remember hiding it there.

"That's not my woman," he said, but it was clear that she didn't believe him. He repeated his promise, "First I'll get organized, and then I'll send tickets for you and the boy." It seemed to him that she did believe what he was saying now, as would her sister-in-law and her sisters who would continue to encourage her to believe in his promise. But not Abraham Katz, who understood immediately that it would fall to him to raise the child and to be more than a grandfather.

Fanny shoved the photograph into Gabriel's pocket before he left.

And now for the most difficult parting of all – from the boy. The inclination is to paint an emotional picture: the father holds the child tightly in his arms, inhales the scent of him, rains down a flood of tears on his tiny head and swears by everything that he holds dear that the day will come when they will be reunited. But that's not what happened. Gabriel gave him a quick pat on the head and then he left.

He wouldn't be present for all the developmental phases to come. He wouldn't see him take his first steps, or watch him lope through the grain fields near Siret, or hear him laughing in the ancient cemetery which would become his playground. He wouldn't walk with him along the surging Lunka after the snow melted, and he wouldn't hear his first words.

For my father "daddy" – "*tateh*" in Yiddish – would always be a foreign word. Only when my brother and I would utter it, in pure unblemished Hebrew without the trace of a diaspora accent, would a glimmer appear in his eyes behind his glasses.

His ever-present tear.

"*Tateh*," I called him just hours before he died, and he cried.

At the Czernowitz train station Gabriel bumped into Meirke Hirsch. The two took the train to Vienna and there they parted ways. The impassioned Zionist continued southward to Bucharest and traveled from there to the port at Constanta, while my grandfather made his way west to the port at Liverpool, where he bought an English-language textbook and boarded the *Cedric* to set sail for America.

On December 19, 1921, Gabriel Herzig filled in the entry form at Ellis Island – the immigrant island opposite the shores of Manhattan. I have a copy of that very document. In the space marked "race" he entered the word "Hebrew." When he was required to provide the name of a relative he had left behind in his country of origin he entered only Fanny's name.

My father didn't exist. He made him disappear.

And despite the fact that nearly a hundred years have passed since then the pain hasn't disappeared.

"Fuck you" – those are the first English words that I would teach him.

Another Thing

Go from your country, your people and your father's household to the America that I will show you.

I tell my daughter how for years the family considered Grandpa the personification of everything negative. "The deserter," "the egoist," "the son of a bitch," what didn't they say about him. But I can't dismiss his actions as desertion for its own sake. Those who flee from love – they are in a category of their own.

To gamble on a new chapter in your life with no idea where it will lead calls for a certain kind of character and Gabriel was an adventurer, a gambler – or both of those. He would scorn Zionism – the ideology to which his son would dedicate his life – and foresee disaster for the war-torn Middle East.

When I met him, at the age of five, he was already a tough old man bitter in spirit, a complainer who spoke loudly and barked at people threateningly, although I was never once afraid of him. His denouncers will say that like the other women in his life I also fell victim to his charms. Good for them. Let them say what they will.

Twenty-eight years would pass before Fanny and Gabriel met again. I stand before this inconceivable period of time and am overcome by despair. How can I encompass it? How can I bridge that ocean when she is on one continent and he on another? It seems that my writing itself will be the single connecting thread.

Before they meet again in 1949 the world will turn upside down, and they will be separated by something much deeper and wider than an ocean. The question that my father will ask, "Why didn't he come to save us?" will haunt him to the day he dies.

Rotting Europe and the Romanian Holocaust, in which Fanny and her son were trapped, were preceded by other events, whose stories also deserve to be told, which influenced the crazy relationship that is the focus of my tale.

I would have liked to be present at the moment when Fanny admitted to herself that she was an agunah. Married and not married at one and the same time.

She has a husband, and he's not there.

She is not released from her marriage and permitted to marry another.

Even if another handsome Russian colonel should appear and kindle her emotions, she wouldn't be able to follow him, as she would be chained to her estranged husband.

"Would you therefore, refrain from marrying?" Naomi asks her daughters-in-law Ruth and Orpah, and that is the origin of the concept in Jewish religious law. And here am I, actually fond of the word "anchor," which sounds positive to me. It is a weight that rests at the bottom of the sea that prevents the ship from going down and keeps it safe from storms and dangerous undercurrents. But when a woman becomes "an anchor" the meaning is turned inside out. She who bears this dubious title is robbed of the freedom to sail on to another love – until she acquires a divorce certificate.

My daughter remarks, "Apparently Fanny didn't want another love."

Even in Gabriel's absence she held on to him, as though she had swallowed him up. Missing in action, yet present. Perhaps she was already branded with unshakeable faithfulness. How is it possible that she didn't understand that the second waiting period, unlike the first, was pointless? She was here and he was there, by choice, and not due to the vicissitudes of fate. And yet they were fettered to one another until someone cut the cord.

In the coming twenty-eight years they would have plenty of opportunities to go their separate ways. After all, by now divorce wasn't considered a disgrace that ruined one's chances of ever finding a new partner, and it was no longer such a stain on a woman's character. I tell my daughter, "Neither Fanny nor Gabriel wanted to separate completely from one another. They were together even when they were apart."

But still, there had to be a moment when she said to herself, "He doesn't love me."

Had to be? Who wants to flay herself and force from her mouth the most poisonous words in existence?

My father said them to himself in response to the question that tormented him, "Why didn't he come to save us?" and the venom seeped into the family. If only I could shake off that germ of rejection that has infected me as well, and embrace illusion as my grandmother did. For how long would she recite the mantra, "He'll find his feet, and soon he will send tickets for me and the boy?"

PART THREE

And She Is Found There, an Anchored Woman

– The Jerusalem Talmud

1

For the first time in his life Gabriel saw the ocean. He had heard so much about it, but every description was dwarfed by the gigantic, endless expanse shimmering and flickering before him in a rainbow of blues and greys. Each time the spray brushed his face he felt that he was on Noah's Ark, with the flood yet to come. Maybe on that first refugee ship the creatures suffered from seasickness and vomited two by two. On the *Cedric* it didn't differentiate between nationalities. Tartars, Russians, Irish, Italians, Jews – they all puked their guts out. But not him.

For Gabriel, the most difficult part of the voyage was the poor sanitary conditions. There were only five toilets and one shower for the men and they were on the other side of the ship. Unlike most of the passengers who eschewed washing for the duration, he stubbornly and determinedly cleared a path toward them. Even the smell of the herring in the barrels placed by the door to the corridor – the main nourishment for the passengers in Third Class – didn't diminish his sense of freedom. The tension that had preceded the journey faded away. Every time his eye was caught by the foaming wake of the ship he swore to do whatever it took to ensure that the American immigration official wouldn't send him back.

Terror of the authorities weighed heavily on all the emigrants, and they were especially anxious about the doctors on Ellis Island who would arbitrarily determine their fate. The word trachoma was heard over and over again – anyone with the misfortune to suffer from the contagious bacterial infection of the eyes was promptly turned away. Although crossed-eyes, a mole, or a hunched back could also disqualify an emigrant from entry into the Promised Land. How had Kalman-Zelig Hirsch with his two handicaps persuaded them that neither his limp nor his deafness would sully the perfection of America? Maybe they were in need of hundreds of blacksmiths for the automotive industry and Gabriel should claim that that was his vocation? How did one say "blacksmith" in English? On the ship he studied the English textbook purchased in Liverpool as diligently as a page of the Talmud, and practiced the correct responses that would grant him access to the Isle of Tears.

"Are you healthy?"

"Who paid for your passage?"

"Do you know anyone in America?"

"Can someone vouch for you?"

"Are you an anarchist?"

"What will you do in America?"

To this last question Gabriel had a ready answer, "Anything. Give me any job at all."

"Job" – that was one word he didn't have to practice. It floated in the air from First Class to Third Class like spray from the waves, alongside the Yiddish word "*parnuseh*."

God Bless America, instead of "Bless my Lord the Blessed One."

The *Cedric* swayed like a madman. Its white-painted chimneys swung from side to side, poking up through the banks of clouds. A storm broke out and torrents of water surged over the metal hull that had started to emit creaks and groans. But a different, competing sound reached Gabriel's ears, despite the din of the sea and the noise of the engines. Through the curtain of drops he discerned the notes played by a musician who was directing his clarinet straight toward the roiling water. A huge jet gushed toward the oblivious player, and only at the last minute did Gabriel manage to pull him out of harm's way.

"Idiot, what are you doing!?"

"I am appeasing the Holy One Blessed Be He."

They slipped across the deck together, clinging to one another. The musician didn't budge from his clarinet. His lips were pressed to its aperture like a man trying desperately to kiss an unattainable woman.

"And you think He will listen to you?"

"Even when a man prays in a whisper the Holy One Blessed Be He hears him," the musician quoted from *Berachot* in the Mishnah.

The Creator doesn't limp, thought Gabriel, but his deafness is well-known. He wouldn't pass the entrance requirements for Ellis Island.

The two men huddled together and Gabriel tried to direct the musician toward the steps leading to Third Class. When they reached the stinking pails of vomit at the entrance to the cabins, the notes burst forth from the instrument again.

"The Holy One Blessed Be He will consider it as the blowing of the ram's horn." The musician grabbed onto the lapel of his savior's jacket. Gabriel immediately checked the inside pocket for his ticket and entry permit. There were also fifty dollars hidden there, his entire fortune, in case he had to bribe the official.

"I'm not a thief," the insulted musician blurted out before heaving his insides into the bucket.

And why not, actually? thought Gabriel. If America represented normal existence, then a Jewish thief would also have a future there, just like in the Zionist Palestine of Meirke Hirsch.

Grasping the wooden post of the lower berth the musician told Gabriel about his dream of joining a jazz band. True, he was white and Jewish, and all his experience was comprised of playing klezmer music at weddings, but in the land of liberty he would be judged on the basis of talent alone, and not be excluded because of his religion or the color of his skin he declared, as he played an improvised version of the American national anthem.

"So which of the two of us is the idiot?" he laughed, "The Jewish people have been improvising from the womb, from birth. You'll see how well we will do in the jazz world."

Gabriel was swept up in the music, and he wasn't the only one. Before he knew it the clarinet player had become the star of Third Class. An audience of fans surrounded him, and the list of requests – mostly nostalgic songs from home – grew longer and longer. He played during the day and he played at night, and even the retching public lurched to his clarinet.

An unexpected audience member from First Class joined the music lovers. She was a woman named Mrs. Jackson, who claimed to possess perfect pitch, a New Yorker on her way back from honeymooning in England with her third husband, who had made a fortune from the sales of Ford Model Ts in Europe. Not a breathtaking beauty, but the dress she wore – black lace threaded with tiny gems, and the sparkling ribbon on her forehead – elevated her to the status of a celebrity. Mrs. Jackson was the first American Gabriel had ever met. She introduced herself as a patron of the arts and she planned to spend her husband's fortune supporting Broadway plays. Her introduction to the new American music came with the sophisticated gramophone that her husband had presented to her as a wedding gift.

The sounds emanating from Third Class had been good enough for her to overcome her nausea and descend to their source. Among the pails of vomit and the herring barrels she taught the musician and his audience a new hit song in English. Whoever sang it to the immigration officer would be sure to get in.

I've been away from you a long time
I never thought I'd miss ya so
Somehow I feel, your love is real
Near you I wanna be...

The woman with perfect pitch sang off-key. She'd be better off not bursting into song at Ellis Island thought Gabriel, for if he was the immigration official he would forbid her entry, and even classify her as a public hazard. Still, he memorized the words as if they were his lessons from the heder. He despised emotional love songs, but if "near you I wanna be" would bring him even one step closer to the object of his desire, so be it.

Only later would Mrs. Jackson – "Call me Jaqueline" – reveal to him that it wasn't a tear-jerker of a song of longing for a love left behind, but rather a yearning for a distant childhood along the banks of the Swanee River, which he, of course, had never heard of. And she also told him – as she deposited a slip of paper into his pocket on which she had jotted down her address on Fifth Avenue facing Central Park – that the composer of the song was a twenty-year-old Jew named George Gershwin. The singer who transformed it into a hit was also a Jew who was born in Lithuania with the name Asa Yoelson, whose stage name was Al Jolson. Like the gypsy in Bukovina, she predicted a glorious future for him as a world famous entertainer. One day Gabriel would buy a ticket to stand and watch him perform, his face covered with shoe polish as he performed in black face. They would call him "The Jazz Singer."

Neither Gabriel nor "Call me Jaqueline" knew that Asa Yoelson from Lithuania would battle racial discrimination on Broadway.

And the nameless clarinet player? What about him? His dream must be realized, so a frenetic future jazz session can be organized for him with Charlie Parker on sax and Dizzy Gillespie on trumpet.

In a book, anything is possible.

Just like in jazz.

Gabriel didn't sing any songs for the immigration official. His well-tended appearance – he poured several buckets of sea water over his head before the ship dropped anchor – and the fact that he could pronounce the words "How do you do?" in a perfect New York accent, thanks to the patient coaching of "Call me Jacqueline," granted him the coveted entry permit. Gabriel wouldn't only fall in love with the song *Swanee*, but with the entire repertoire of Gershwin's compositions, and in his honor he would change his name to "George."

2

The second American woman Gabriel met was Lady Liberty, better known as the Statue of Liberty. He first saw her in the early light of dawn, when the *Cedric* directed its bow toward the New York Bay. It was the captain who roused the passengers from their slumber with loud blasts of the ship's horn. He was a man with historical sensibilities who wanted to engrave the defining moment in their memories.

Still half-asleep, Gabriel was pushed to the railing by the mass of people. At first he couldn't discern a thing in the dense fog, and the repetitive sound of the horn sounded to him like a lament. This wasn't the welcome that he had imagined. The *Cedric* maintained its slow progress until a woman's hand holding aloft a torch flickered in the soupy vapor followed by the crown affixed to her head. As the chorus of cheers from the excited spectators swelled in volume she was finally revealed in all her glory, riveted to her impressive base, and not far away they could see Ellis Island, whose sole purpose was to serve as a waystation.

Gabriel even managed to make out the Roman robe wrapped around the body of Lady Liberty, but not the broken chain beneath her sandals. Fanny lingered over that detail of the statue when she received the illustrated postcard he sent. The symbol of liberation from bondage did not escape the mythology enthusiast. She read the few words inscribed on the back over and over to Yitzhak: "I arrived safely. I hope you are well. Gabriel." This would remain the unchanging style of the letters he would send over the first few years, always around the time of his son's birthday. And he consistently included the same gift – a one-dollar bill. Fanny used a hairpin to keep the bills together and tucked them into her empty jewelry box, as if it was a piggybank.

"At least he remembers us," she said to herself, pushing away the superstition about how the hairpin that falls off is a sign of separation.

Perhaps the next letter would contain a fifty dollar bill. For her that would be proof that he was a man who wouldn't give up until he had tried everything, and that with his salary – whatever it might be – he would find a way to finance the promised tickets.

No one knew about the rope that Gabriel had tied around his waist, and how at first he had earned his livelihood as a porter at the docks. Intense back pain led him to seek easier work, and for a time he plucked chickens at an illegal slaughterhouse – a job he actually excelled at thanks to the experience he had gained with Larissa's geese.

When Fanny extracted his next dollar bill a tiny feather floated out of the envelope, and she placed it alongside the dollars in the jewelry box. In her romantic imaginings it was a sign that Gabriel hadn't forgotten his little bird waiting for him in Europe.

She was spared his miserable living conditions in the dank cellar he rented, with a tiny window that looked straight out onto a Lower East Side gutter. "The sidewalks of New York aren't paved with gold but with shit." The comments he made at the gatherings of the ex-pats from Bukovina were not infused with bitterness or disappointment. Gabriel did not for a second regret that he had moved to America and never lost his belief that he would find his fortune there. Even when he spent his days surrounded by piles of bleeding chicken corpses, he held fast to his optimism. Fanny divined his determination to succeed from his letters.

In secret she caressed the words he penned, and in the dark of night aroused herself, reliving their lovemaking in her imagination to the smallest details. Their short-lived relationship became the reservoir from which she derived her optimism during the early years after his departure. After all, he wasn't the first to leave in search of a better future for his family.

"He did it for us," she took pains to tell everyone as she assumed the role of his sole advocate. Lizzie-Bertha was the first to come out openly against her brother-in-law. If during the war years she had encouraged Fanny to believe that in the future he would return, she now did her best to convince her "to get rid of the bastard."

And the first postcard did nothing to soften her opinion. On the contrary. The fact that a woman was pictured as the symbol of freedom was sheer hypocrisy, she declared, since until women received the right to vote, Lady Liberty should extinguish her torch and re-chain her legs to her shackles.

"It's the men who cause all the suffering in the world," Lizzie-Bertha quoted her sisters in arms.

"Not all the men," a sigh escaped from within the beard of Abraham Katz, "only this man." He was filled with remorse for granting Gabriel his daughter's hand. Why had he given in to her romantic whims? His only comfort was his infant grandson, the joy of his life. At the age of two Yitzhak spoke excellent Yiddish and German – he had inherited Gabriel's gift for languages – and his curiosity was unbounded. He investigated everything, from the flight of the birds over the river to the tombstones in the ancient cemetery. That same enthusiasm would later embrace Zionism. At twelve he would demonstratively cut off his sidelocks and announce that from then on he had only one goal – to move to Israel and establish a kibbutz. The question, "When will my father come back?" was never uttered. On his ninth birthday, when the annual letter from America didn't arrive, he said to one of his friends, "Maybe my father is dead. If only."

Fanny heard about it. In a place as small as Siret it was impossible to keep secrets. She never said a word to her son, absorbing the blow in silence and once again removing the first postcard from the jewelry box. She sat staring at the features engraved in the marble of Lady Liberty's face, the straight nose and the full, unsmiling lips. A modern goddess she said to herself, who governs the new Olympus and seduces men to leave their families, just like Helen of Troy. Anna said that the sculptor had engraved her with the face of his mother.

Fanny's eyes filled with tears, and the photograph became the creased and wrinkled portrait of the anonymous woman that she had shoved into Gabriel's pocket on the day he left.

It didn't matter whether he had left for her or if the mysterious woman had followed him. What was important was that now the two of them were walking hand in hand along the gold-paved streets of New York, and climbing the stairs up to the torch in the woman's hand – Anna said that could be done – and celebrating their freedom. As opposed to his legal wife who wasn't even worth a one-dollar bill.

And the most disturbing thought of all was that maybe he already had a child there. In her imagination, fed by so many romantic novels, Fanny pictured Gabriel beaming down at his new offspring, raising him with a devotion that he had never displayed for her son, showering him with goodness and love – and all this in English, a foreign language. Her tears that fell on the message inscribed on the back of the postcard blurred the ink, and the ink stained her hands.

The double-edged sword began to turn. From love to hate, from hate to love, and back again.

And still, never once did the words of her son to his friend occur to her, "if only he was dead."

3

With Gabriel's disappearance Fanny inherited some of his traits, and now she too was glum and withdrawn. What remained untouched was her ability to love with absolute devotion, a quality that human nature apparently doesn't easily surrender. The burning streams of lava within her were now directed toward her son, who unwittingly became a substitute for the man she had lost.

She would never let go of the boy who had grown into a youth before her eyes, and wherever he went, she would follow.

A rumor circulated among the family that in one of his letters Gabriel had asked Fanny and her son to join him in America, but there was no proof of this. It is likely that Abraham Katz started it himself to preserve some vestige of his daughter's dignity. And there was another reason, much more important. The grandfather chose to lie to his beloved grandson to somewhat ease the pain of rejection.

"Unloved" – what torment to live with that knowledge, especially when the context is the closest relative of all.

My father has not been in our world for many years, and I still dream that I hold him and tell him in Hebrew how much I love him, except that in the dream I am the adult and he is the child. "My soul is weary with sorrow," the verse from the Psalms always comes back to me.

One way or the other, the facts speak for themselves. The tickets weren't sent, and you can't finance a transcontinental journey with a one-dollar bill.

Of all people it was Anna who joined her brother in America, but not at his invitation and he didn't pay for her crossing. The immigration authorities' entrance requirements became more stringent and slowly the gates closed. Following her marriage to Abraham Zimmer, her new husband's relatives, who had already established themselves in America, promised to be their sponsors. They sent them Second Class tickets, which facilitated a fast-track selection process with no strict medical examination. The forms also mentioned that the emigrant was guaranteed a job in the sponsor's brush factory. He hurried to change his name to Abe Zimmer.

For us, Anna and Abe would always be the "(aunt and) uncle from America." Long live the cliché.

It can't be avoided. I must be a "kangaroo author," leaping backward and forward over the hurdles of time, since it's impossible to include every event, and in any case it is to Fanny and Gabriel that I set my compass. I am but the Rottweiler at their heels.

His women. Their scents are easy to identify. Mrs. Jackson, for example. Chanel No. 5, the latest perfume from Paris that had captivated the women of New York. The note she tucked into his pocket on the boat went missing, but he encountered her on one of his walks in Washington Square Park, a square of green breathing space between the lower city where he lived and the upper city where she resided. Opposites in social status, they were identical in their aspirations for escape, she from her golden cage on Fifth Avenue, and he from his moldy basement on the Lower East Side.

She recognized him immediately. She may not have possessed the perfect pitch she boasted of, but "Call me Jacqueline" had perfected her talent to identify an attractive man even beneath a shabby exterior. Not only did she remove all of Gabriel's clothing to verify her instinct, but she even bought him a three-piece suit and a silk tie at the renowned "Barneys." Her gift would launch the impressive tie collection that he would later own.

"You look like a million dollars," she declared, stark naked and fully liberated on the satin sheets in her bedroom, while Gabriel practiced knotting his new tie in front of the gigantic mirror. She observed his appealing reflection with satisfaction and told him how the store had been opened by Barney Pressman, a Jew, of course, who had pawned his wife's engagement ring in exchange for the five hundred dollars required to take over the lease.

"You see, George, behind every successful man there always stands a concealed woman." George – she rolled his new name around on her tongue, the same tongue that was already intimately familiar with his body. Did he also have a woman back where he came from?

He tightened the tie and replied, "She forgot about me a long time ago."

He didn't understand her laughter. Was it because a man like him wasn't easily forgotten? Or perhaps the justifications of men, who always blamed the woman, were well-known to her.

"You'd be surprised at how well memory can improvise," she said as she switched on the gramophone. Was there still time to undress Gabriel for one more round before her husband came home? After a quick glance at her watch she hurried to remove the new silk tie, and the rest Gabriel took care of himself. When they were done he asked her the meaning of the word "jazz."

"It's the word the blacks use for sex," and she laughed again.

In an enormous bed, redolent of French perfume, by a window that looked out onto Central Park, with Charlie Parker and Dizzy Gillespie jamming in the background, Mrs. Jackson worked diligently on Operation Gabriel. She was his English-language textbook, and once he was skilled in the language and its etiquette she rescued him from the stench of the chicken carcasses and found him a job as an insurance salesman at one of her husband's companies. Although Gabriel didn't have the slightest idea about insurance policies, and the intricacies of the fine print in the clauses and sub-clauses were completely foreign to him, she taught him the entire business in one sentence, "Everyone is afraid to die; promise them that at least something will remain after they're gone."

Armed with her advice Gabriel amassed a seemingly inexhaustible supply of customers, as he honed his proven ability to dispense promises. He offered his patroness a commission from every policy he sold, but she wasn't interested. She had more than enough money and no fear of death. "When it comes, it will come, until then we'd better live it up."

She also added the expression "making love" to his growing vocabulary, as she explained that it wasn't merely a euphemism, but a worldview. Just like "making money."

When he opened a bank account at The Manhattan Company she signed as his guarantor, while informing the bank manager that she believed in George's financial genius, and adding that he was the personification of the American Dream.

After the signing they dined on Wall Street, as she threaded her arm possessively through his. She relished the glances of the women who turned to watch him as they passed by.

"This is your future, George," she said, and it wasn't clear whether she meant the business world or the women.

He felt so alive in the presence of the frenetic energy and the storm of humanity in the American bastion of capitalism. He felt reborn. Everything that came before was erased. The trenches, the hunger, the terror of death, the staring eyes of Von-Hoffenberg. With his savings he bought an apartment on Delancey Street, although he had no money left over for furniture. Being too proud to ask Mrs. Jackson for a loan he preferred to spread a blanket on the floor. Under those field conditions he actually slept a dreamless sleep, and never suffered from nightmares.

Gabriel found his true self on Wall Street. He began to buy and sell stocks and his bank account soon swelled.

When Anna reached New York in the summer of 1929, she barely recognized him. The person waiting for them on the pier when they disembarked after the trip from Ellis Island looked like a movie star. He wore a designer suit, a gold pocket watch across his chest, with the folds of a perfectly ironed handkerchief poking out of his pocket.

Could it be that the man who said "Welcome to America" in flawless English was the brother she hadn't seen for almost eight years? Smelling of expensive cologne mixed with Chesterfield tobacco, formally shaking Abe's hand and murmuring, "Nice to meet you," and then leaning over to kiss her on both cheeks. Only after that did he ask about Fanny and the boy.

Anna told Abe that the delay wasn't due to forgetfulness, but rather to guilt feelings, although it's possible that Mrs. Jackson with her lust for life and lack of any fear of death had succeeded in helping Gabriel to rid himself of those.

Anna was also convinced that there was another woman – a shiksa no less – and that that was why he avoided any discussion about his private life.

She sent Fanny a postcard that she bought for a penny at a stand on the Lower East Side. This one didn't display Lady Liberty, but showed the exterior of an imposing edifice with a balcony jutting from the roof. It was chosen at random, and Anna didn't know that it was a unique design for coastal houses and that the seamen's wives used to stand on the balcony portrayed to watch the incoming vessels and see if their husbands were returning to them.

However, the words written on the other side of the postcard were not selected at random and Anna chose them with great care. Fanny read them again and again, searching in vain for a hint that her husband was still her man. The words of her sister-in-law were meticulously measured and weighed, by someone who was fully aware that she was maneuvering through a minefield. Anna wrote that America was very different from her expectations, and that it would take years until she became accustomed to it, if she ever did.

New York was too crowded a city she wrote, and the haggling was deafening. The streets were filthy and the smells of horse manure and gasoline constantly hung in the air. And still, there was a feeling that anything was possible. She mentioned her meeting with Gabriel only at the end of her message: "He is well." Fanny immediately took in the perfunctory final sentence, "He sends you his regards."

In bitter disappointment she turned the postcard over again and tried to tear the picture of the house with its balcony on the roof. Perhaps Gabriel lived in a fancy house like that. She imagined her rival sprawled naked before him, while on the balcony, facing the expansive horizon of the sea, a child played.

There was no one to tell Fanny that that particular architectural structure had been nicknamed "the widow's walk." Perhaps if there had been, she would have finally recognized that there was absolutely no hope of his return.

As for the postcard, it was too thick and she didn't manage to rip it in two.

4

And so it seemed that there was no way to maintain the relationship. The little of it that remained with Gabriel was overcome by his frenzied business dealings and the dollars that were piling up, his regular meetings with Mrs. Jackson and the casual sex he had with others, mostly married women who wouldn't make demands and didn't jeopardize his freedom.

But for Fanny there was nothing to dilute the shared memories, and the small cluster she possessed remained fresh for her. The existence of Yitzhak fanned the flames and breathed life into the imaginary relationship. His physical similarity to his father – there was no one who didn't comment on it – made it impossible for her to forget him completely. And then Fanny found herself a substitute in an entirely different place – at the cinema.

A backward kangaroo leap is required.

Several months after Gabriel's departure, Lizzie-Bertha bought tickets to the silent film, *The Sheik*. From what she read in the newspaper it was clear that the plot would not be in line with her progressive views about relationships between men and women, but she was ready to make a sacrifice for her sister, if only she would be somewhat comforted.

Fanny was completely overcome by the experience. To truly understand this, we have to try to imagine that we aren't so inextricably bound up with moving pictures that it is as if we were born with screens embedded in our bodies.

It's a huge black box. Fanny is squashed on a bench in a hall in Czernowitz, wedged together with dozens of women she doesn't know, who are inhaling and exhaling beside her, in front of her, and behind her. There isn't a single man in the hall, except for the one up on the screen in supernatural size, enormous and sublime – the actor Rudolph Valentino.

Despite the fact that he opened his mouth like a fish and had no voice, Fanny, like the rest of the women in the hall and across the world, was smitten. She dived headfirst into the alternative reality, while hers retreated and shrank. The refuge she had once found in romantic novels was as nothing compared to what happened to her when she gazed at the screen. It was like walking in a dream, and she was both dreamer and the dreamed. In the film she could be the beloved Lady Diana from the moment when Ahmed Ben Hassan – savage, noble and handsome – serenades her soundlessly and nimbly leaps over the balustrade while she stands on her balcony. For an hour and twenty six minutes Fanny merged with Lady Diana, who wages a fierce war against men because "marriage is captivity – the end of independence."

Lizzie-Bertha read out the titles on the screen and some of the other spectators joined her, although one grouchy old woman on a bench toward the back hushed them. How dare they disturb the star as he tried to win over his love?

Lizzie-Bertha's preconceptions about *The Sheik* as a banal representation of the relations between men and women are overturned. At the end of the film, when Lady Diana is completely disarmed by a man, she finds infinite excuses and justifications for her, since even a feminist like she couldn't withstand the charms of Rudolph Valentino. The idol leapt out in black and white from the scratched film, a seducer in all his glory. The roguish eyes, the carefully drawn eyebrows, the devastating smile that revealed perfect teeth, the ever-present cigarette in his hand, and the smoke that curled nonchalantly around him.

When the lights went up Fanny was in a daze. She refused to leave and bought a ticket for the next screening. And she wasn't the only one. She knew the film off by heart and often recited the lines for Ida and her princesses. For her they were not only a precise description of her situation, but also a ray of hope.

"I've caused her so much suffering," the sheik admits, and his good friend remarks, "It's only because you love her."

If Rudolph Valentino had known how much consolation an abandoned woman in Bukovina derived from the scripted dialogue in the Sahara Desert, he would have made a sequel immediately and not waited four years. "Maybe all the torment I am going through is proof of Gabriel's love," Fanny poured out her heart to Ida.

Over the years there were many private screenings of the film in her head and Fanny told herself the same fiction with slight variations, but the ending was always the same. She leans over Gabriel and with infinite tenderness caresses his limp hand, until he opens his eyes, overflowing with love, and thanks her for restoring him to life. Like Lady Diana in the film, she also lays her head gently on her beloved's chest.

The perfect union.

The End.

When Rudolf Valentino died before his time in the year 1926, Fanny was beside herself. She mourned him like a close relative. People laughed at her, especially the men. They scorned the celebrated movie star with his hair pulled back from his forehead, and there were those who gossiped that the woman's idol actually harbored a preference for men. Lizzie-Bertha alone stood by Fanny's side. Rudolf Valentino was the only man for whom she would have been willing to compromise some of her principles. And she sensed that her sister's mourning was really for her true loss, and the death of the sex symbol was an opportunity to give vent to her hidden emotions. If Fanny had lived in New York, she would have joined the hundred thousand women who walked behind his coffin, crying their eyes out.

5

Gabriel was stuck at the corner of Forty Ninth Street West and Broadway among the thousands of people in the funeral procession. Not because he was among the movie star's fans, but because he had just come out of a meeting with a client who he had convinced to buy an insurance policy for cases of sudden death.

"Who knows what the future has in store," he said, "See how even the great Valentino went, just like that, at age thirty-one."

He hadn't imagined that he would find himself jostled by policemen on horseback and women tearing their hair out and trying to throw themselves, screaming, onto the coffin draped with a flowered carpet. The deceased was carried by his friends in a majestic procession befitting someone who had been sacrificed on the altar of the nation.

Gabriel was carried along by the crowd as far as St. Malachy's Church, better known as The Actors' Chapel, where out of the corner of his eye he saw the actress Pola Negri, her face obscured by a mourning veil, supported by her companions. He didn't hear her cries of, "I am his fiancée!" which were swallowed up in the wails of the other women, each of whom imagined that it was she who had been meant for him.

Public expressions of emotion were anathema to the self-restrained Gabriel, and what took place on the streets of New York that day seemed to him nothing but a performance. Every participant played a part, and every person was an audience for another, as they inflated each other's ego. He didn't lack for ego himself, but was contemptuous of dramatic declarations, and the indiscriminate showering of compliments only increased his cynicism.

The thoughts he had while trapped in that intimidating crush which paralyzed Broadway had to do with how he could leverage Rudolph Valentino's unexpected death to drum up more business and how to play on the heartstrings of, "Thou knowest not what a day will bring." The deceased's final tour, in his coffin, that crossed the United States from coast to coast by train accompanied by thousands more distraught mourners, helped to persuade future clients that it was a good idea to prepare for a rainy day.

And although the young woman weeping loudly in front of the theater where Gabriel found himself stranded in the crowd didn't look like a potential client, she was too sweet to pass up.

"What will I do without him?"

Gabriel withdrew his perfectly pressed handkerchief from his suit pocket.

"How will I live without my Valentino?"

He smoothed out the folds and handed it to her with a gallant flourish.

"What is my life worth without him? I want to kill myself."

He gently dried her tears.

Her name was Olympia and she was an immigrant from a little village near Naples who dreamed of a career in Hollywood. She lived in Little Italy, a neighborhood Gabriel was fond of for the *O sole mio* that spilled out of every window and the Chianti that flowed so freely in its streets.

It took him less than four hours to prove to Olympia that life was worth living after all, and after focusing all his attention on soothing and cheering her in her tiny, windowless room, followed by a meal of excellent pasta which she polished off and he paid for, the suicide option was off the table as well.

"Whoever saves a single life is considered to have saved the whole world," Gabriel explained the noble Jewish precept to Mrs. Jackson the following day. He chose not to elaborate on the practical measures undertaken to dissuade the grief-stricken young girl from taking her own life. Why hurt someone unnecessarily? Did King David reveal to Michal that he was lying with Batsheva? Not to mention our forefather Jacob. He certainly didn't confess to Leah that he loved only Rachel.

Everyone tries to spare others sorrow, he convinced himself as he relied on the examples of his betters to absolve himself and proceeded to divide his attention between two lovers.

The good days came to an end in one fell swoop in 1929, when the stock market crashed. Then, too, he found himself squashed among the masses, trapped in the street, although this time it was in a crowd of men.

On that same Black Tuesday in October he was joined by others like him who, overnight, had lost everything in the economic collapse. The stocks he had bought on cheap credit were wiped out and he was left with nothing.

It was goodbye to his apartment. Goodbye to his furniture. Goodbye to his benefactress.

Mister Jackson – who was also impoverished – was forced to leave Fifth Avenue and went in search of oil in Texas. The only possession that "Call me Jacqueline" managed to salvage from the collapse was her gramophone, so that during those rainy days Charlie Parker and Dizzy Gillespie were her comforters. Now and again she called up memories of her Jewish lover, "George."

Sweet Olympia gave up on her dream of Hollywood and returned to her village near Naples. Under the fascist regime there during the following years, when the Jews were stripped of their jobs in the public sector due to the new race laws, she would tell her children about a Jew named George who once saved her life – without going into detail.

Less than a year after Anna and Abe arrived in America Gabriel moved in with them in their sparse apartment in Brooklyn. Nothing remained of his previous life except for the silk tie that he regularly wore to synagogue on the Sabbath and holidays.

"The work that is done under the sun was grievous to me. All of it is meaningless, a chasing after the wind." He mumbled the words from Ecclesiastes as in a frenzy he ran the thirty-four blocks from Wall Street to the Empire State Building on the day when America plummeted to depression. He hoped to find at least one branch of a bank that hadn't gone under. What he witnessed dissolved his tough exterior. This was no performance, but a horrifying reality: people whose worlds had collapsed, in desperation jumping to their deaths from the windows of the tallest tower in the world.

He would tell me this, years later. To a five-year-old girl who believed that an eight-storey building in Tel Aviv was a tremendous Zionist achievement, he would describe the terrifying spectacle he had seen, just to prove to her that a hundred-storey tower wasn't a figment of his imagination, but actually existed. Not under Zionism which in his opinion was doomed to failure, but in America –

forever the Promised Land. I remember him explaining to me the concept of a "skyscraper."

"Only in New York can you scrape the sky," he boasted.

Except that I was focused on the fatal collision with the ground. For years I was haunted by nightmares that the people I loved were smashed to pieces. I would wake up, paralyzed with fear, and grope for the wall to make sure that I wasn't falling too.

The nightmare returned to me on my television screen on September 11, 2001, when the Twin Towers fell.

The same horror. People jumping out of windows again.

I burst into tears. Grandpa, I pleaded with his ghost, why did you have to tell me that bedtime story? Couldn't you have spared me?

6

Ripples from the tsunami of the depression in America hit the rest of the world hard. In Romania a law was enacted that forgave the farmers' debts, and Abraham Katz, whose entire business was based on credit, was wiped out overnight. Along with Fanny he checked and re-checked the account books, where they recorded the names of all the people who owed them money. All of them were now exempt from paying what they owed.

"And I am poor and needy," he quoted from the Book of Psalms, and he told Fanny to throw the account book into the fire. She tried to cheer him with a quotation of her own, "You hear of my poverty, my Lord," but she herself didn't believe it anymore. It was true that during the war years He had heard her prayers and sent her beloved back to her, but a miracle doesn't happen twice. She had apparently expended her allotment of His attentiveness to her. And besides, how would she have the strength to drag the wagon of bottles through the streets as she had done when she was younger?

Fanny was rescued from her dilemma when the permit for the sale of beer was transferred to Mirodan, Anna and Gabriel's old neighbor from Mihova. He didn't hide his delight at their misfortune.

"The time has come to teach a lesson to those Jews who have sucked our blood for all these years," he informed his daughter Luminicia, "Now they'll see who's really in charge."

She begged him to show some compassion and asked that he at least might allow Fanny to work as a simple laborer, and load the crates, but he refused. "Why are you worrying about them? The Jewess probably has a fortune in dollars hidden away that her husband sent her from America."

"Ask your husband for help," she pleaded with Fanny.

Even Lizzie-Bertha was in favor, although it contradicted her outlook that held that a woman shouldn't be dependent on a man. Women in Romania had received the right to vote, but only in local elections, and thus Lizzie-Bertha had moved to Bucharest where she gave piano lessons and contributed to the struggle for full equal rights.

A rumor circulated that a letter was sent to Gabriel asking for help, but it's unlikely that Fanny sent it. Not only because of her pride, but even more than that she had no desire to confront the bitter truth. If Gabriel ignored her request it would be positive proof that he was her husband only on paper.

Ida, now a respectable convert to Judaism who had closed down her old business, offered to write to Gabriel for her, but even if she had sent a letter, it would have arrived at the wrong address, since he was already living in Brooklyn.

In her generosity Ida allowed them to live rent-free in a narrow structure that stood on the path to the old graveyard. It's possible that it was the proximity to the cemetery that nudged Abraham Katz into his deep depression. He spent his days, from morning to night, at the Vizhnitz Chassidic synagogue, praying for heavenly mercy. Fanny now had to support two men – her elderly father and her teenage son. To finance her son's studies in the high school in Czernowitz she didn't balk at any job. She went from house to house among the gentiles, seeking work as a seamstress. She washed floors and scoured pots, sewed burial shrouds, embroidered tablecloths, and became an expert at darning socks.

I remember her in her old age, securing a sock on a wooden toadstool and patiently pulling together the threads that matched its color, until the darn could hardly be discerned. She also decorated my first lunch box for nursery school, embroidering it with stiches in a rainbow of colors to make it easier for me to recognize it hanging on the hook at the entrance, so that I wouldn't be delayed coming home.

Her purpose in life – to make sure that whoever was meant to come home really arrived.

She waited for Yitzhak at the railway station when he returned home for vacations from his studies, and the sight of Sisera's Mother seated like a statue on the bench with a basket in her hand and a scarf to wrap around him and protect him from the cold, became routine. Yitzhak himself refused to be a millstone around his mother's neck and struggled to be financially independent. He supported himself by giving private lessons and proved that the apple really doesn't fall far from the tree. Despite not knowing his father or being raised by him, it seemed that the attraction to the opposite sex was hereditary.

In his later years he would tell me about a student who studied Hebrew with him. During one of the lessons he felt the sole of her foot slowing climbing up his thigh, and in no time the student became the teacher.

The more Abraham Katz saw his daughter struggling to earn their living, returning home late at night exhausted and defeated, the more despondent he grew. What would become of her when he was gone? Who would protect her? The news from Germany about the Nazi regime that was so hostile to Jews upset him more and more. Fanny had to marry again. She was still relatively young, in her mid-thirties, her figure was pleasing and her face hadn't aged beyond recognition. She still had a chance to find a man who would take her on, or at least share her burden. He requested a meeting with the Admor, Boruch Hager, the founder of Chassidism in Seret-Vishnitz, whose father, Rabbi Israel had been his own much-admired rabbi. He had always hosted the elder Admor at his home, clearing out the entire top floor for him. He no longer had a house in which to host anyone, when he turned to the new Admor for help with a halachic solution as to how to release Fanny from her marriage.

"Where is the husband?"

"He lives in America."

"Where?"

"His exact whereabouts are unknown."

No effort must be spared to locate him, decreed the rabbi, and if he is not persuaded and insists on refusing, it is permitted to offer him a bribe.

What would he bribe him with? They had nothing left. "For I am poor and needy, and my heart is wounded within me," the words escaped Abraham Katz with a sigh.

"But He lifted the needy out of their affliction and increased their families like flocks," the rabbi replied.

The verses from the Psalms were uplifting, but they contained no practical advice.

"And if there has been no word of him for such a long time, perhaps he is no longer among the living?"

You must secure proof that the husband is dead, the rabbi ruled, and for that one witness is sufficient, and not two, as is usually required.

The search will take years, lamented Abraham Katz, and by then his daughter would have no chance of finding a new match.

Finally the rabbi made a decision. The last resort was to find a flaw in the marriage ceremony and to declare it null and void. The validity of the witnesses would be examined. Abraham Katz could rest assured that a creative argument would be found to show that one of them was not valid.

It seemed as though a solution had been found, but Abraham Katz rejected it outright. The price his grandson would have to pay, once he was branded a child born out of wedlock, was too much to bear. And he was not a man who would be dishonest with himself. The witnesses were valid, and there was no defect in the ceremony.

The rabbi stood firm. If the wellbeing of his daughter was the issue, there was no choice but for Fanny to appear before the rabbinical court, to testify that she had not expressed her unequivocal agreement to marry at the time of the ceremony.

And if Yitzhak was declared a child born out of wedlock, what would that mean? Why, he wasn't a bastard and was still considered a member of the community. Even Yiftah the Giladi had been in the same situation and it hadn't stopped him from becoming a judge and a warrior. Who knew, perhaps a similar future awaited the boy, and in the fullness of time he would be a leader of men.

So he prophesied, unaware of the significance of his words.

Yiftah the Giladi. We have no idea what price he paid, reflected Abraham Katz as he left his meeting with the rabbi. It seemed he would have no choice but to sacrifice his daughter. However, it was the mention of the judge that caused him to resist. He did not want to surrender to this solution, and refute the vows. Preferring not to reveal to Fanny what was expected of her, he brought her to the rabbi. When presented with the suggestion that she deny her wedding vows she was furious.

Standing before the respected Torah scholar she screamed, "I agreed to marry Gabriel Herzig. With every fiber of my being I granted my permission. He is my legal husband until the end of days."

The whole of Siret heard her screams.

Should we admire her honesty or be appalled at her stupidity? When I was a child she told me, "It's better to lose to a clever person than to profit from an idiot."

If only I knew whether she regretted her insistence on holding onto her marriage at any cost.

7

Life under one roof with his sister and brother-in-law convinced Gabriel once and for all that communal living was not for him. He liked Abe, of the round baby face and the kind heart. He distributed candy to the Black and Hispanic children in the neighborhood and even gave Gabriel a job in the grocery store that he opened in Brooklyn. Anna and her husband did everything they could to make him feel comfortable in their tiny apartment, but the lack of space, the laundry draped over every available surface, the cooking smells and the shouts from the neighbors, made him even more determined to regain what he had lost. Ever since the good days when he had lived in his own apartment he had become addicted to having his own space. Abe urged him to find a full-time job. In the years of the Great Depression that was considered the ideal. A regular salary at the end of the month, and modest financial security. For a time Gabriel gave in to the pressure and worked as a clerk at the Post Office, but the boredom was excruciating. When Anna became pregnant, he already had one foot out the door. The savings he had managed to accumulate in the past sharpened his sense of initiative and he constantly followed the stock market and dreamed of returning to Wall Street.

As a little girl, I remember him glued to the enormous radio that he brought with him from New York, listening religiously to the Economics Report on the Voice of America, and my father visited him every day to read the NASDAQ index aloud. The names and numbers sounded to me like another foreign language.

"What is a stock, Grandpa?"

"A paper that has value."

"How can a paper have value. It's just a piece of paper."

"Money is also just a piece of paper."

This was followed by an exhaustive explanation about the stock as representative of a given manufacturing company, such as an airplane factory. At the time, all I knew about airplanes was the nursery rhyme "Fly Down to Us Airplane, Take Us up to the Sky" and I had never set foot in one.

Although he wasn't one of the workers who actually attached the wings to the plane, he explained, he still had rights in the factory and was a partner in both its successes and its failures.

He was so enthusiastic when he spoke, and I was so bored.

He even insisted on teaching me the English word "share." Only in retrospect did I understand how ironic it was to learn that very word from someone who had done his utmost his entire life to avoid sharing.

And the most important lesson that my private broker whispered time and again into my young ears was, "What goes down must come up."

I took his words at face value and skipped up and down the stairs, while Grandpa listened to my footsteps, and I tried to understand why this was an inexorable truth.

And now I skip through his story, up and down and back again.

Gabriel recruited his new clients from among his landsmen from Bukovina, fellow members of the organization that supplied the immigrants with a warm framework and modest refuge from the foreignness that surrounded them.

Anna and Abe regularly visited the clammy basement where the expats from Bukovina held their meetings, and where they could converse in their mother tongues. They published a newspaper in German and in Yiddish, filled each other in on the news from home and played the records of the famous Joseph Schmidt. For the Purim holiday amateur singers sang songs from *The Megillah of Itzik Manger*, and on other days poets recited odes to the landscapes of Europe, that brought the listeners to tears.

It was a bubble packed with longings and memories, which painted the world left behind in shades of idyllic pink. Occasionally they discussed the increasing persecution of the Jews in Germany, but there had always been, and would always be hateful people, and in what way was this generation's evil Haman any different from his predecessors?

Gabriel, who wasn't one for nostalgia, attended the meetings for the sole purpose of identifying business opportunities, and while he was at it met several women. Gisella Werther, a charming widow who worked in the clothing industry on Seventh Avenue and aspired to be a famous fashion designer; Vera Meisels the closet communist, who mumbled praise for Stalin, "the sun and liberator of nations…" in her sleep; and Irena Lubovich the dancer, who opened a ballet studio for girls in that very basement. Entwined with her flexible body Gabriel experimented with some imaginative acrobatic positions.

However, he didn't content himself with the women of Bukovina, and expanded his horizons to representatives of other nationalities, such as the Irish Mary McMurphy, whose husband the policeman was never home, and who treated him to smuggled whiskey; and Shi-yan Chu, the owner of the laundry, born in Shanghai, who looked like a china doll and taught him words of love in Mandarin.

He sold shares to all of them, and bestowed himself as well, as a bonus.

The fact that he was married – which he never concealed – became Gabriel's protection against unwelcome demands and pressure. The absurdity was that his marriage guaranteed his freedom.

When his lovers inquired, he would evade the question as to whether he had children.

He was a very handsome man – according to the tastes of the time – but that wasn't enough to explain the diverse women on his impressive list. So what was the secret of Gabriel "George" Herzig's charm?

Firstly, the perfect manners. He always treated women gallantly, making each one feel like a princess. They saw him as the consummate support and shoulder to cry on, who listened intently when they shared their feelings, although this was but a well-crafted pretense, since he wasn't really interested in anyone but himself.

And another important asset of Gabriel's – he never confided in one woman about another, and never boasted of his conquests. He treated each woman as though she was his one and only.

"I hope there's a lot of sex in your book," declared one esteemed man in Israel, who had just celebrated his ninetieth birthday. His wife was the sole remaining witness to my grandfather's life in New York. Let's call her M.

She had known him as a girl and was my most reliable source of Gabriel gossip and lore. I would draw her out in their home filled with books and old newspaper clippings about the Bukovina club, which were liberated from the attic in my honor. We drank tea in delicate china cups decorated with flowers, and she told me that what she remembered about Gabriel most of all was that he was a serial seducer with excellent business sense. She and her husband hoped that he had left behind a respectable inheritance.

"And the inheritance of the story, isn't that a treasure?" I ask.

I promise the distinguished husband to fulfill his wish about the sex, and M. promises that she will sift through her memories and let me know what she comes up with.

"Did my grandfather have other children?"

She claims that he didn't.

Too bad. I would have liked to discover a Chinese uncle or an Irish aunt.

8

Anna was the only one who had reservations about Gabriel's share schemes. She saw the stock market as a dangerous and irresponsible game. Hadn't he learned a bitter lesson from that disastrous Black October? He had already lost everything once when the stock market collapsed, so why make the same mistake twice? Shares were a cursed temptation. One day you're on top, the next day you hit rock bottom.

"What right do you have to gamble with the destiny of others?" she challenged him.

"I don't swindle anyone. They all know the risks in advance."

Is it possible to know everything in advance? Her laughter was bitter. If someone had foretold what an "exemplary husband" her brother would be, why, as much as she loved him she would have prevented the marriage. One word from her to Abraham Katz when Gabriel returned from the war and the match would have been called off.

After the birth of her first son, Anna became even more upset and found herself identifying deeply with her faraway sister-in-law. Every time she rocked the infant in his cradle, she was overwhelmed with thoughts of Yitzhak, left behind with his forlorn mother, who was "anchored" to a man who had abandoned her. Her guilt feelings were replaced by anger. Didn't Fanny have the right to another chance, to compensate her for the failure of her first relationship? How dare Gabriel prevent her from expanding her role as a mother, how dare he limit the number of children she could have? Anna vowed to do whatever it took to end the marriage that she had previously worked so hard to nurture. A surprising solution to the knotty problem arrived from an unexpected direction. One sunny morning, Sam, the black delivery boy who worked at the Chinese laundry adjacent to their grocery store in Brooklyn, told her an African tale about a go-between for love. It happened after she had rushed to his assistance, when he collapsed under the burden of a huge pile of pressed and ironed sheets, neatly folded and stiff as boards. The baby carriage was transformed into a delivery cart, and together the two of them pushed it toward Brooklyn Bridge.

The baby gurgled at Sam and stretched out his plump hands. Sam chuckled at the child.

"If only I could have a wife like you, Mrs. Anna."

"You're young Sam. There's no hurry."

Sam looked down.

"If I don't hurry, she'll get away."

"Who?"

The object of his love was Rose, the daughter of the Lipmans who were regular customers at the grocery store. The shy, brown-eyed girl was sent to deliver the family's linens to the Chinese laundry and that's how Sam had met her.

"Maybe you'll help me, Mrs. Anna? Convince her that I love her. Please, talk to her father."

Anna didn't reply. At that time a mixed couple was a huge scandal. She herself – hardly a romantic anymore – didn't believe that such differences could be reconciled, but Sam's eyes burning with such powerful faith reminded her of Fanny. Like her sister-in-law once did, he too stood with her in the middle of a busy street and told her a story, not about a pair of lovers from Greek mythology, but about Blacks in Africa. His forefathers had passed it on from generation to generation in the cotton fields, "because they didn't want to forget the place from where they were kidnapped into slavery."

And as Fanny had once transported her to ancient Greece, so now Sam took her back in time to an African village and a chief and his daughter Ipeh. In the ancient language of his ancestors the name meant "love."

Ipeh had three suitors, Sam recounted, and in order to discover which would be the perfect husband her father decided to put them to a test, which required the services of a messenger. He was instructed to bring each one the news that the bride-to-be had died, and that the father requested his help with the burial. The first suitor took to his heels on the spot. The second did the same, and he too declared to the messenger, "She's not my woman."

Only the third burst into bitter tears, and stood ready and willing to do whatever he could for the dead woman he loved.

"You understand Mrs. Anna, he loved her even if he couldn't have her."

Sam took the laundry into a house at the foot of Brooklyn Bridge, while Anna waited for him outside, rocking the carriage and watching the stream of cars crossing Manhattan, her thoughts swinging along with the motion. She saw her marriage as a blessing. Abe was a loyal husband and a devoted father. She was already pregnant again and they were hoping for a girl. She was lucky, unlike Fanny who hadn't been aware of the risks and had lost everything. Even if someone – definitely not her – decided to be Sam's go-between for love, his chances were slim. Some loves are ill-timed. A black man and a white woman, a raven and a dove, would have to wait several decades before they could set up house together. And the sick connection between Fanny and Gabriel had to be undone.

Divorce by messenger. That was the idea that took root in Anna after listening to the laundry boy's story.

A grateful Sam wanted to share his two-cent tip with her, but she refused, saying, "Maybe it will bring you luck."

As they strolled back Sam finished his tale. Faced with the suitor's grief, the messenger revealed to him that his beloved was really alive, and the two burst into tears of joy that were heard by the entire tribe and in the neighboring villages as well.

The baby also started to cry, but only because he was hungry. Anna brought the bottle to his lips, and Sam's "They lived happily ever after," was accompanied by the baby's smacking sounds. Sam was determined to declare his love to Rose Lipman, with or without the help of a messenger. He tossed his coin into the air. "You've got to take a chance, Mrs. Anna, don't you think?"

She thought it was too dangerous. Today you're up, tomorrow you're down, and even deeper. She asked him whether the messenger and the suitor in the story were actually the same person.

"What difference does it make? The most important thing is that the beloved is the same person."

Anna wanted to prepare Sam for what was to come, and so she explained to him that he couldn't rule out the possibility of separation. However, Sam rejected it outright, since the name of his heroine was "Love."

"Tell me, Mrs. Anna, do you have the name 'Love' in the Jewish language?"

Anna said that the name was too demanding. Why tempt the evil spirits that are always eager for some kind of trouble. A woman named "Beauty" is liable, heaven forfend, to be ugly, and "Honesty" may turn out to be a liar. Anyone saddled with the name "Love" might feel rejected and abandoned for her entire life. She didn't mention her nephew Yitzhak, whose Hebrew name meant laughter and was destined to cry more than most.

The rabbi in Brooklyn, with whom she consulted, claimed that divorce via messenger was an acceptable solution according to Jewish law for when a husband and wife lived in different countries. The special messenger would travel to Siret, and in the presence of an ad hoc rabbinical court of law that would be convened for the purpose, would deliver the divorce to Fanny in place of Gabriel. There was only one small problem. The husband and wife were required to provide their consent in advance, first and foremost the husband. To her astonishment, Gabriel rejected the proposal and refused to sign the letter of authorization for the messenger.

"But you don't love her!" Anna protested.

Gabriel reacted with a stubborn and incomprehensible refusal.

"Release her and the boy!" she snapped at him.

"I'm his father," he insisted. "There, here, everywhere."

If Gabriel had agreed to the proposed solution the story would have ended here. But the question as to whether Fanny would have agreed to accept her divorce from the hands of the messenger will remain forever unanswered. We can assume that she would have ripped it to pieces and sent the representative of the rabbinical court packing. Her voice would have reached the other side of the ocean and screeched at Gabriel: "Coward, don't hide behind a messenger. Stand before me, and just as you once asked for my hand, now ask me to take it back."

9

Many jokes were whispered behind Fanny's back about women chained to their departed husbands who sought to be disconnected from them at any price, including the woman who hired a hitman to assassinate her husband, only to have the murderer fall helplessly in love with him and find that he was incapable of pulling the trigger. Or the woman who went to talk to the rabbi and remained with him behind closed doors for a long time, only to emerge and tell the Chassidim that the pious rabbi had promised that her husband would return to her soon, "If God wills it."

The *gabbai* who managed the synagogue told the assembled Chassidim, "And I'm telling you that the husband will never come back." The Chassidim were furious. How dare he contradict the saintly rabbi? The *gabbai* declared, "Gentleman, unlike the rabbi, who didn't bother to look at the woman, I have seen her."

So what was he doing in there with her for such a long time?" they asked.

"What you do without looking," the *gabbai* replied.

Lizzie-Bertha was enraged at the rabbi's "If God wills it," the phrase which releases the man from responsibility and transfers it to the Creator. One way or another, the woman's fate was in the hands of the men. Lizzie-Bertha vowed that the day would come when women would sit on the rabbinical courts, and then there would be no more women "anchored" to their husbands.

Despite her situation, Fanny had more than one admirer during those years. The owner of a flour mill from Cluj met her when she was embroidering tablecloths for his daughter's dowry and asked her to be his mistress, promising her a furnished apartment and a new wardrobe. Her answer was a resounding slap.

The gentile who took her place bottling the beer in Mirodan's cellar pinched her thighs every time he saw her and proposed that she return to her previous position – this time as his wife – on condition that she convert, of course. Her answer to his proposal was a kick between the legs.

Her most serious suitor was Feivel, now that Ida had passed away. Fanny's marital status didn't bother him in the slightest. If the blessed Lord had seen fit to convert his previous spouse and in His grace had favored their establishment for so many years, he felt sure that He would sanction his union with Fanny even in the absence of a bridal canopy and wedding vows. Feivel was also sure that Ida, rest her soul, would approve of her successor. After all, she had always been fond of Fanny.

What worried Feivel more was where the two of them would live. The anti-Semitic Romanian National Party "Everything for the Homeland" had joined the Romanian government, and King Carol had tasked the anti-Semitic poet Octavian Goga with the formation of the government. "The Jewish problem is a Romanian tragedy. We simply have too many Jews," he said in an interview with *The New York Times* as he smoked a cigarette imprinted with a swastika.

The poet didn't publish any poetry, but he did pass a new law. Every Jew had to prove in court that he had been a Romanian citizen for generations past, and wasn't one of the thousands of infiltrators who had invaded the country to suck its milk and its blood. Although Feivel possessed the necessary funds and connections to acquire the citizenship documents, he had heard about the bold Kimberley Plan devised by the lawyer and activist Yitzhak Nachman Steinberg who wanted to buy agricultural land and resettle tens of thousands of Jews in Kimberley Australia.

"We will live far from the winds of evil that blow through Europe," he told Fanny, adding that Australia had iron ore, copper, diamonds and gold. Who knew, maybe they could embark on a new career. He would adorn her neck with jewels. Not only would they find a safe haven from danger at the other end of the world, but in that place no one would investigate too closely or care whether they were or weren't married "by the book." Feivel kindly offered to finance her son's emigration as well.

Fanny didn't even bother to tell Yitzhak about Feivel's idea. Ever since meeting the Zionist emissary at the age of twelve and cutting off his side-locks, Yitzhak dreamed only of the Land of Israel. When the broken-hearted Abraham Katz brought him to the Admor of Viznitz, the rabbi surprised him by saying, "Never mind. So he'll be a Zionist, so long as he's a good Jew."

Unlike her son, Fanny was not inspired by Zionism, and to her mind Palestine was nothing more than an adolescent fantasy. She jeered at the letters that arrived from Meirke Hirsch, who wrote in flowery phrases about how the wilderness was being made to bloom, in part due to his efforts. And now Australia? Good heavens, that was even farther away than Palestine.

Feivel didn't give up easily. First he showered her with compliments. Her figure was lovely he said, and her firm breasts inflamed his nights. She could still have children, and with her he would realize his dream of an heir. They would enjoy a glorious future together, he whispered in her ear.

When sweet words didn't do the trick, Feivel opted for slander. He denounced Gabriel for his disgraceful behavior, called him a "villain" who was contemptuous of women. If he had learned one thing from his past experience it was respect for the second sex. And the proof was his generous donations to Lizzie-Bertha's women's movement. Not to mention that he had always supported women who took their lives in their own hands and refused to be at the mercy of men.

He even recalled the story Ida had once told him about Fanny and a gypsy.

"I will be your second husband."

"I haven't divorced the first one yet."

"Our forefather Jacob had two wives."

"That was before Rabbi Gershom ben Judah banned polygamy."

When all else failed Feivel regaled her with juicy descriptions of Gabriel committing adultery with another woman, a shiksa of course. The beautiful lovers of New York. What don't they get up to there, ay yai yai! And he insinuated that he knew a thing or two that was being kept from her.

Fanny didn't budge. And instead of a harsh slap or another well-placed kick, she told Feivel a Jewish fable that was already circulating, having been inspired by her situation.

It was a story about a woman who informs the rabbi that she wants a divorce. He asks what is wrong with her husband. She replies, "Since he is my husband, I won't speak ill of him."

After the divorce, the rabbi asks what the problem had been. The divorcee responded, "As he is now a stranger, I won't shame him in public."

This was the moment when Fanny should have realized that even if the Lord willed it and she and Gabriel were to be reunited, he would be like a stranger to her. And yet she couldn't imagine such a chain of events. Still, she didn't shame Feivel, and wished him luck finding a good match in Australia. If she was forced to leave her homeland, it would only be to follow her son, and no other man.

10

"The Jewish problem is a Romanian tragedy. We simply have too many Jews."

Gabriel read the interview with the poet prime minister of Romania, Octavian Goga, in *The New York Times* in January 1938, while smoking an unfiltered Chesterfield that he had rolled using the tobacco from his silver-plated cigarette box.

Early morning on Wall Street. The blue-grey glow was reflected in the windows. The tip of Lady Liberty's torch was visible through the fog. But Gabriel was already accustomed to the view, and had long ceased to be impressed by it. With a cup of murky coffee at his elbow, the newspaper spread before him, he sat tranquilly in his office, awaiting the gong that signaled the start of the trading day on the stock market. His favorite sound in the world. In one moment the silence was transformed into a frenzy of noisy motion that he was part of. Maybe that's how the world was created, he said to himself, imagining the Blessed Creator as a broker on high. "Who will wax rich, who be made poor?" as is recited in the prayer on the Day of Atonement.

He was also waiting for his second-favorite sound, the noise emitted by the ticker, the precursor to the computer, which spat out bits of paper that bore the prices of shares that Gabriel would pluck like a nature lover collecting flowers for a bouquet.

When I was a little girl he gave me some of the ticker tape that he had saved. To me it looked like nothing more than coiled bits of paper and I even used it to make decorations for our *sukkah*.

Gabriel didn't notice the gong that day for the item in the paper shocked him. Octavian Goga had detailed his plan to expel a half million Jews from Romania. "I heard that your Jews in America have filed a motion against me. That suits me fine, it's actually perfect. I suggest that all those who will be expelled from Romania should move to other places. Let the world find a place for the Jews."

If up to that point Gabriel had dismissed the news from Europe as only German madness, now it was clear to him that the pestilence was spreading, and the cloud of poison was hanging over the heads of Jews in other places as well. Those close to him were in danger. For the first time in years he thought of his son.

On that particular day he was especially successful and his shares yielded tidy profits, although he hadn't lifted a finger. Maybe it was a sign of things to come thought the man who scorned all superstition, as he deposited the profits in a separate account.

"But divide your investments among many places, for you do not know what risks might lie ahead," the verse from Ecclesiastes came to mind as he strode the forty-two blocks to Times Square in the bitter cold.

Although the newspaper's offices had long since moved to new premises he wanted to see the streaming news headlines which still galloped across the front of the building. There was an item about the celebrations for the fifth anniversary of the ruling Nazi party and about how "Hermann Goering had announced the establishment of a war council in Germany."

There was nothing about Romania and Octavian Goga. Nothing about Jews.

But rather than feel relieved Gabriel was even more worried, as though for an instant a satanic plot had been revealed to him only to be whisked away and hidden from view. He found himself trembling, and not from the cold. A storm of hail descended. Times Square emptied out, and Gabriel ran for the shelter of the buildings. Suddenly an umbrella was above his head and he sheltered beneath it. He quickly realized that the extended arm belonged to a woman. A delicate scent reached his nostrils and it wasn't Chanel No. 5. The hailstones pelted the umbrella and pierced the fabric. The moving headlines continued to glow, but the words were obscured by the sheets of falling ice pellets.

They took refuge in a movie theater. Once the Rialto, New York's most extravagant theater, had stood on that very spot. During the years of the Depression Gabriel often found solace there, especially in the films of Charlie Chaplin. He remembered the walls of the hall, decorated with depictions of Venice, its gondolas and canals, and the ceiling strewn with stars. Nothing remained. The Rialto was sold and rebuilt. Venice was gone.

Wordlessly Gabriel bought two tickets, and they went inside, the only patrons in the hall. The woman closed her umbrella and placed it on the floor in the dark. The water puddled at his feet. He still hadn't seen her face. He didn't know whether she was young or elderly. Her dripping, windswept hair even obscured her profile.

An animated film blazed on the screen. Mickey Mouse in black and white accompanied by *Yankee Doodle* on the piano. It was *Plane Crazy*, which Walt Disney had created after being inspired by Charles Lindbergh, the first pilot to fly from America to Europe. Although in the movie the mouse is the pilot, the challenges he faces are no less daunting.

Mickey collides with a tree.

Mickey has to rebuild his plane.

Mickey receives a horseshoe for good luck from his girlfriend Minnie Mouse.

Mickey makes romantic advances throughout the flight – today his behavior would be described as sexual harassment – first tickling her neck, then trying to force himself on her in a hug. But when he tries to kiss her against her will Minnie slaps him so hard that he (and the spectators) see stars, and then bails out of the plane. Her underwear is transformed into a parachute, she survives and Mickey crashes. The lucky horseshoe which survives the impact lands around the neck of the sex offender.

And Minnie? She leaves him.

Not a happy ending.

The woman seated next to Gabriel never stopped laughing. While he sat like a stone, and didn't bother to peek at her or at the cartoon. He wasn't occupied with the ups and downs of Mickey and Minnie's relationship, but with the scheme that had been revealed in the newspaper. Octavian Goga even boasted in the interview about how he had initiated a comeback of the popular play *Bloodsucker of the Villages* and invited *The New York Times* reporter to the premiere.

Out with the Jews.

Gabriel heard the low, musical voice of the woman beside him.

"Tell me, are Mickey and Minnie married?"

He recognized a German accent.

"Maybe in real life, but not in the movies," he replied in German, in a foreshadowing of the kind of answers Walt Disney would supply to similar questions about the relationship between the two mice he had invented.

On the spot, in the darkness of the cinema, Gabriel confessed to the stranger that he was married and the father of a son. Plain and simple. So there would be no expectations. Her name was Clara Mendel. She was an immigrant from Bukovina who would be his romantic partner for many years to come. They spoke German and a little Yiddish. That is, when they were talking.

When the lights came up he looked at her closely. Round cheeks, sparkling eyes, soft curves. Bright red lipstick outlined her mouth and she laughed often, which he initially found enchanting and later drove him crazy.

When they left the movie theater the hail had turned to rain. Now it was he who held aloft the perforated umbrella, covering the hole with the palm of his hand. Wet and shivering they traveled on the subway, and he escorted her to her apartment on Norfolk Street on the Lower East Side. A short time later he rented an apartment for himself on nearby Clinton Street, and so their relationship formally began.

Since separate residences for a couple were far from the norm in those days, Gabriel can take credit for the idea. How did he convince Clara that it was the perfect arrangement? Each person retains independence and personal space. The boundaries were clear. They met for lunch – a break from the ticker tape for some homemade Viennese schnitzel – and they spent the nights at her place. And even this wasn't to be taken for granted, but something to be mutually agreed upon each time.

This comfortable arrangement allowed Gabriel to enjoy Clara while safeguarding his freedom. And in his private space he could host any number of women.

Unusual for him, he didn't sleep with Clara that night, but went through an entire packet of Chesterfield tobacco, returning over and over to the interview in *The New York Times*.

After a long silence she said, "Maybe you can still save your son."

Wall Street at dawn on the following day. The streets sparkled under a cloudless sky. It was still bitterly cold. This time Gabriel repeated a different verse from the prayers for the Day of Atonement, "Until the last day of their lives You are waiting, and if they repent You receive them at once."

Unusually for him he ignored the clatter of the stock ticker and ordered a telephone call – an expensive undertaking in those days – to the State Department, requesting the Romania section.

Before the close of that day's trading he had bought a respectable amount of stock in the Disney Company as well as a new umbrella for Clara.

On the other side of the ocean Yitzhak was surprised to receive an urgent summons to the American Embassy in Bucharest. He was informed that an immigration visa that had been sent by his father awaited him. It was for him alone.

Fanny's screams could not be contained. It was unthinkable that her son would leave her. And there was no point promising that she could follow him. Fanny didn't believe in promises anymore. Lucky for her, Yitzhak didn't even consider the proposition. His loyalty was absolute, not necessarily to his mother, but certainly to Zionism. One who was consumed with trying to immigrate to Israel would not suddenly abandon his ideals for the flesh pots of America.

It seemed that the gene for desertion had not been passed on. My father told the American Embassy in Bucharest that he was turning down the visa, and he didn't bother to attend the meeting that had been arranged.

The connection with America was severed.

11

The war years. The Holocaust in Romania that remains in the shadows.

I have already transported myself to that dark time with characters of my invention, but now I am torn as I face the members of my own family as fictional characters.

How can I convey an iota of the horrors they experienced? All I can do is cry with them in the spaces between the words. Weep over the loss of memory.

Father said, "Another generation or two and it will all disappear."

The more I write, the less I understand.

During the years of terror Fanny and Yitzhak were trapped in the maw of the Romanian Nazi-Fascist regime – the Iron Guard. Hitler designated a special area for the Jews expelled from Bukovina and Serbia beyond the Dniester River. It was he who coined the term the Transnistria Governorate. That is where Fanny's brother Srul-Leib and his three children were lost, and even their names fell into the abyss of oblivion. Paula and Emil Stein would also be sent there, along with Lizzie-Bertha, who had remained single. Mihova, where Gabriel was born, that was situated near the border with Poland, would be the arena of the first battles and the location of the collapse of the Polish army when it met the Germans.

The abominations that the gypsy had foretold, and worse, came to pass.

If during the First World War Fanny had clung to life for the sake of the man she loved, during World War II her will to survive drew its strength from her son. Had it been within her power, she would have connected him to her with a new umbilical cord and banished anything that had become a threat to his life, mainly his Zionist activities and his membership in the anti-Fascist underground. With her very body she would have stood in the path of anyone who tried to take him from her. Everything for him, only for him, the utmost for him – until she forgot herself.

Under such a barrage of love Yitzhak learned to hide large chunks of his life, and secrecy became second nature. Those who had known Gabriel claimed that despite growing up in his absence, the son had inherited one of the father's traits. They couldn't know that it was a reaction to having barely any private space. Everyone at the Hanoar Hatzioni Zionist youth movement knew the mother who accompanied her son to all their gatherings and joined them on their journeys to the agricultural training farm, where she scrubbed pots, washed clothes, and cooked for the passionate young people. They assumed that she was deeply committed to the cause, but it wasn't ideology that drove her. Having learned from experience she followed in her son's footsteps everywhere he went, near and far, never letting him out of her sight.

To make sure she wouldn't lose him.

If in New York his father had achieved the freedom he coveted, his son was near-suffocated by love. To love women – and he too was successful in that regard – Yitzhak had to evade his mother and create a parallel existence behind her back.

The more she hung onto him the more he sought to be released, and since this was physically impossible, he chose emotional escape. He didn't only censor his relationships with women, but also the most dramatic events of his life, so as to protect himself from her excessive anxieties. Fanny would never hear of his imprisonment or the interrogations he experienced. He chose not to talk to anyone about the torture and he buried the terror and the fear of death in a place beyond words. Only when he was very old did he tell me about the time when he was about to be executed and was saved thanks to a flat tire on the truck that was waiting to drive him and his comrades to the forest firing squad.

Even when he crossed the border into Transnistria with a rescue delegation to search for children who had survived and send them to the Land of Israel – most of them orphans and amputees who had lost limbs due to frostbite – Fanny had no idea where he was. He was hoping to be able to tell her that he had found her brother Srul-Leib or his children, but that miracle didn't come to pass. Over time Yitzhak barricaded himself inside his silence until it became an inseparable part of him, and perhaps this really wasn't only the result of the circumstances of his life, but also of his similarity to his estranged father.

All his life his love for his mother was bitter and aggrieved. And yet somehow, despite the restrictive situation, his independence managed to develop and flourish. Like a branch of a tree that stretches in the opposite direction to the rooted trunk. He constantly defied the love that would not slacken and became insatiable, but at the same time he was devoted to his mother, gentle with her distress, and came to terms with his permanent shadow.

Desertion was out of the question.

No one would have wanted to be in his shoes some years later, when he would face the dilemma of how to relate to his father.

Before the expulsions to Transnistria had begun Yitzhak managed to rescue Fanny from Siret. Armed with the false papers of a husband and wife the two caught the night train to Bucharest, hoping that the cover of darkness would minimize the risk of exposure during inspection. Since he was already being followed by secret agents, who suspected him of spying for the Soviet Union, Fanny wound a thick wool scarf around his face. "Pretend that you have a toothache," she instructed.

The policeman barked for their papers.

"This is your husband?"

"Yes."

The policeman tried to pull off the scarf, but before his face was revealed Yitzhak cried out in feigned pain.

"Don't you touch him!" Fanny took a step toward the policeman.

"What will you do to me?"

"You don't want to know."

The officer turned to Yitzhak. "You've got a hot-blooded wife, haven't you? A little old for you, no? Maybe she's the one who landed the punch that broke your teeth?"

And he laughed at his own joke. Only after Fanny had slipped a gold chain with a crucifix into his palm did he return their false papers. Ida had left it to her. "I'm already a Jewess and you can sell it and save whoever you want to save."

As the policeman tested the purity of the cross with his teeth, he advised Yitzhak to take a good bite out of his spouse when he was feeling better.

"Taking a good chomp out of a woman is what keeps your teeth strong."

Had Lizzie-Bertha been with them on the train it's possible that they wouldn't have reached their destination safely, because unlike Fanny, she would never have managed to restrain herself.

They traveled the rest of the journey in silence, Fanny holding Abraham Katz's gold watch in her hands. It was all she had left of her father. On his way to synagogue one day he had lurched forward in the street and died of a heart attack. At least he was spared the Second World War.

At first they stayed at the Floriaska training farm in the most primitive quarter of Bucharest. Fanny was the only adult there. In blackened pots she cooked potatoes and corn that she stole from the market, and listened as they sang songs of yearning for the homeland where they had never set foot. After they were driven out of the farm and the area was declared *judenrein*, the young people descended on the offices of the Zionist Organization, although there they were the victims of surprise searches and arrests. When Yitzhak disappeared on one of his missions, Fanny was arrested. For three days she was interrogated.

"Where is your son?"

"He's with his lover."

"Which lover?"

"He has several."

The policemen hit her, pulled out her hair, kicked her, but she withstood it all.

When she was released, she dismissed her arrest as a triviality and kept it from her son. The desire to spare the other was mutual.

They needed a new hiding place and Yitzhak told them that he had made a connection with a woman who was a fervent anti-fascist. It was Sorina Negresku, known as "Black Sorina," the madam of a Bucharest whorehouse with whom he had made a deal.

When I asked how he had come to know her, he laughed and said, "Use your imagination."

Black Sorina promised to hide the Zionist young men in her establishment, and they were moved from room to room according to the schedules of the women. She wove creative cover stories for each of them. This one was a maintenance man and the other was a cleaner, while the third was a salesman who dealt in sanitary products. The conspiracy was concocted under the noses of the senior officials of the Romanian regime and the Nazi officers, who visited the house on a regular basis.

When Yitzhak brought Fanny the madam refused to shelter her. The presence of a woman who was no longer young was likely to arouse suspicion. Fanny offered to assist her. She was familiar with her kind of business and knew how it was run. The fact that she didn't sit in judgment on Black Sorina, and didn't look down her nose at the women who circumstances had forced to live unfortunate lives, convinced the madam not only to take her in, but to ensconce her in her own room.

The other tenants, all of whom held the same anti-fascist views, saw a surprising resemblance between Fanny and Sorina. They both wore a permanent scowl and were tough women with remarkable posture and skin like polished ivory. Sorina was delighted by Fanny's long eyelashes, which she discovered when she taught her how to use makeup, important camouflage in her establishment. She introduced Fanny as her cousin, a refugee who had fled the communists in the north. She hung a carved wooden crucifix about her neck, and took advantage of her presence to leave the house and trade on the black market. The women were especially fond of Fanny's cooking. She managed to wring a creative menu from the handful of products that were available, with the addition of ingredients brought by some of the customers as a gift. The only thing she refused to cook was pork.

For the women who worked there, her meals and her motherly presence were a ray of light in the gloom. Fanny and Sorina spent the nights confiding in one another, and Fanny found herself telling Sorina the story of her suspended marriage and the husband she had lost.

"You haven't stopped loving him."

"It's beyond my control."

"You have to try."

"How? How do you bury love when it's still alive?"

Sorina sighed.

"If only we could, it would make us rich."

"If only we could, you would lose your livelihood," Fanny replied, and they both laughed.

On the evening when Obersturmbannführer Rolf Beck, a senior advisor to the Iron Guard for improving the efficiency of the expulsions to Transnistria, arrived at the house, Sorina was away, and Fanny was the acting madam. Not a muscle twitched in her face as she faced the Nazi on the doorstep in his black dress uniform, with the skull insignia shining on his lapels. Only her insides trembled. In broken Romanian he asked to see the catalogue of women as he waved a thick wad of German marks at her.

When Fanny responded in fluent German, his demeanor changed. His face lit up and he doffed his hat and gave a polite bow, clicking his heels together. He even kissed her hand gallantly before settling himself in an armchair and asking for a glass of brandy.

"Are you also from the Fatherland, Madam?"

Fanny welcomed him with exaggerated politeness. If he suspected that she was a Jewess every member of the household would be in danger. She poured him some brandy, and flashed a sweet smile, stalling for time so that the women and boys in the back rooms could do what they had to do.

"Among all these sub-humans it's pleasant to see one of us."

Rolf Beck stretched out his legs and made himself comfortable. "The boots pinch a little," he apologized, describing how very hard it was for him to be far from home, and so far away from his mother, to whom he was especially close. But what isn't one prepared to do for the fatherland.

"Perhaps you would like to work for us? I can help."

He lit a cigarette and extracted another from the silver case embossed with a swastika. He would be the second man with whom she would share a cigarette. He couldn't know how much time had elapsed since her first. She didn't even choke. The smell reminded her of Gabriel. As she sat with the Nazi, she found herself imagining sharing a cigarette with her husband.

"I know a concentration camp commander who needs a manager for a brothel. Are you interested?"

She poured him another glass of brandy.

Rolf Beck allowed his head to fall back, and with half-closed eyes began to declaim a poem in German.

> They've tortured me and left me in miserable state,
> Some of them with their loving, the others with their hate.
> The wine I drank they poisoned, poisoned the bread I ate,
> Some of them with their loving, the others with their hate.

He had finished the last drop of brandy when he asked, "You didn't pour poison into my glass, did you, madam?"

Just then the women came out of the rooms and stood before him. Fanny loathed this part of the proceedings. It was a meat market in which her friends – to the end of her days she would remember them with warmth and compassion – were compelled to display their bodies and describe their specialties. She was relieved that not a sound could be heard from the back rooms.

She postponed the show for a moment longer and completed the lines written by Heinrich Heine, "But she, who more than any, tortured me, gave me gall, she never even hated, nor ever loved at all."

The minute she finished, she regretted what she had done.

Why had the Nazi chosen to quote a Jewish poet, when all his books had been burned and it was forbidden to read his works? Had he set a trap for her? With her own mouth she would bring devastation down upon the house. But he didn't reach for his gun, as he surveyed the procession of women and then dismissed them with a wave of his hand.

"There aren't any Jews among them, correct?"

"They are all pure Aryans."

He rose and threw down his empty glass. He was tall, and he stooped slightly toward her, gazing deep into her eyes.

"And you madam? What are you? Are you sure that you aren't also a sub-human?"

"I am who I am," she replied.

Her daring appealed to him and he declared that he had chosen her to be his partner for the night. He offered to pay double. For too long now he had been yearning for sex in German. And he started to push her toward the corridor that led to the rooms, tugging at her wooden crucifix. His gun bumped against her ribs. At that moment Black Sorina came home. Despite not understanding a word of German, she couldn't miss his hand moving down Fanny's neck toward her breast.

"Take two for the price of one," she proposed in Romanian, "and leave her alone."

Despite not understanding a word that she uttered, he couldn't misunderstand the way Black Sorina shoved Fanny aside.

"She'll cry all night long. This frau can't seem to stop mourning her dead husband."

Obersturmbannführer Rolf Beck turned to Fanny, who translated the words into German. And then she added a few more lines of a different poem by the apostate Heinrich Heine.

I can't forget I had you, dear woman, sweet to hold,
That I once possessed you, your body, and your soul…
They can bury your soul, love, I've soul enough for two.

"Your husband isn't dead," Black Sorina said to Fanny the next day. "Maybe he's worried about you. Why should he think that his wife isn't among the living? It would be a shame for him to mourn you in vain." And she implored her to send him a sign.

Her rich experience had taught her that there are men for whom a reminder of love that stays true regardless of the blows that it suffers can be the purest of aphrodisiacs. According to Sorina, words had the power to awaken and rekindle desire. However, Fanny refused to put the theory to the test so the madam took matters into her own hands and unknown to Fanny she wrote a letter to Gabriel in her name. It opened with a quotation from Heine, that she had asked Fanny to translate into Romanian for her: "I can't forget… that I once possessed you."

One of her veteran customers, the political attaché at the Swedish embassy, promised to send the letter to the United States in the diplomatic pouch, in exchange for an entire night at the brothel. But Black Sorina never managed to give him the letter. During the earthquake that shook Bucharest that year she was trapped in the tallest building in the city, sitting on a sofa on the eighth floor, busy selling a pair of earrings to the mistress of an official in the Iron Guard, in exchange for a sack of potatoes and preserved beans to feed her women. The building collapsed, and the letter to the live husband remained in the coat pocket of the dead woman and was buried with her.

12

"They are all dead," Clara Mendel cried bitterly in New York when the news arrived about what was happening in Europe. Not one of her relatives was left alive. She had arrived in America alone, and alone she would remain.

A memorial ceremony was being held by the organization for ex-pats from Bukovina to commemorate those who had been murdered. Gabriel and Clara sat next to each other as the prayer Merciful God was recited, accompanied by anguished cries. Her tears fell on the back of his hand, and he offered her his starched handkerchief.

Manny Greenberg, the moving spirit behind the organization who had initiated the memorial event tried to comfort her, saying that the knowledge, as bitter as it was, was preferable to uncertainty. However, had it been possible, Clara would have chosen doubt, since in that case she could at least have held on to a sliver of hope.

Gabriel refrained from joining the conversation.

For seven years the two had conducted themselves openly as a couple. He supported her financially. They went out together to public events, mostly song evenings arranged by the organization, and he bought her a seat at the synagogue for the Days of Awe. "His common law wife" – was how she was routinely described, other than by Anna, who mumbled the phrase in a critical tone directed at him, and not at Clara, who she liked. She was impressed that she bore the tainted label "mistress" without embarrassment or complaint.

And one other person insisted on remembering that Gabriel had a legal wife in Europe – Manny Greenberg, who searched tirelessly through the lists of the murdered and the survivors.

"All of Europe is filled with refugees trying to return to their homes. It's a continent of wanderers," he said in his speech at the memorial. When he combed the lists of survivors he never came across Fanny's name.

Manny was the only friend Gabriel made during those years, and he was his diametric opposite. A loyal husband and model father, Manny was always volunteering to help others.

"You find the good in everything," Gabriel told him. "That's your curse."

"And you find the bad in everything," Manny protested. "That's a blessing?"

On the surface the two had nothing in common, other than the same birthplace, and yet despite the differences they shared a true bond. Manny was like the Jiminy Cricket conscience to the lead character in the animated film *Pinocchio*, that Gabriel and Clara had gone to see some years earlier. It was their default choice for an outing, since she always preferred the theater. He agreed to see the film since as an investor in Disney shares he was willing to examine the company's latest product and calculate the profits it might yield.

Faithful Clara Mendel with her raucous laugh touched Manny's heart. After the disaster that had befallen her, he saw it as his mission to help her rid herself of the dubious status of "living in sin" and elevate it to that of a kosher wife. Unbeknownst to Gabriel he continued to search for witnesses who could reveal what had happened to Fanny.

If Gabriel was a widower, then he was free to marry, and if his wife had survived, he could finally give her a divorce and marry Clara in the eyes of the law.

This knot had to be untangled.

Clara was also interested in a respectable solution to her situation. Her motivation, however, was different and much more important to her than her honor or her reputation. Clara believed that if they formalized their union Gabriel would have a child with her. It was her last chance. Her biological clock ticked no less than his beloved ticker. And if after the birth he still insisted on maintaining separate apartments, so be it. She would manage.

The devastation in Europe strengthened her longing for a family. "With the improvement of the Jews' situation in America and the protection they received from the horrors of the Nazis, it was now their obligation to further the existence of the Jewish People." This was the ideological argument she employed when she announced to Gabriel that she longed for an heir.

The conversation took place in her apartment on Norfolk Street. She gave him plenty to drink and put in a supply of Chesterfield tobacco so that he would stay the night rather than return to his apartment on Clinton.

"I'm not built to be a father," Gabriel confessed in a rare moment of honesty. "It was a long time ago."

He sat in silence, chain-smoking. In his memory Yitzhak remained a squalling infant. His whole life he recoiled from helpless creatures that were unable to express themselves. A child was the opposite of freedom.

"Now you have the opportunity to repair things, Gabriel."

"Do you really believe that it's possible to repair anything?"

An image of Kostya glimmered in his mind, although he hadn't thought of him for years. The child would now be the same age he had been when he hid among the washing and heard him sing *Farewell to Slavianka*. Kostya had certainly forgotten about him long ago.

Clara said, "Maybe we'll have a daughter."

"That which is crooked cannot be made straight, what is lacking cannot be counted," he quoted from Ecclesiastes, and she wondered why he always recalled the gloomiest passages of the Bible.

Her hopes were fueled by the way he doted on Anna's daughter. Sweet Florence with her head full of curls reminded Gabriel of his sister as a little girl, and every week he would pamper her with cheese blintzes from Katz's

Delicatessen on the Lower East Side, located in the heart of the cluster of Yiddish theaters. What Anna and Clara didn't know was that the blintzes concluded his rendezvous with an actress, who he pampered in her dressing room before and after she appeared on stage.

More than once Clara had been tempted to throw him out – down all five flights of stairs to the basement – and end their relationship. Especially when she suspected that he was being unfaithful. More than once she had discovered traces of lipstick on the collars of the white shirts that she ironed for him. He never hid the fact that there were other women in his life.

Once she made a jealous scene, when she found out that he had traveled to Texas to visit an old lover named Jacqueline on the pretext that he was buying oil shares. She screeched and raged – they heard her on both Norfolk and Clinton. She threw flowerpots and threatened to donate his cufflink collection to a secondhand store, while he stood like a statue and weathered the attack. When it was over he shrugged, "I am who I am."

He moved the box of cufflinks to his own apartment, except for one cheap metal pair that he left at her place. Early the next morning he arrived with a bunch of flowers and pulled her toward the bed. Consolation sex always worked.

What good would it do if she was possessive? Clara sighed in bed, as he shaved in preparation for another day on Wall Street. In the end fits of jealousy would just push him away, and God knew that unlike her, he had alternatives. When she was tidying the room she was surprised to discover a theater ticket to a Yiddish play under one of the flowerpots. He always preferred the movies.

She had long ago given up hope that he would tell her he loved her in so many words, and she made do with the public nature of their relationship, no less proof of love than an intimate confession or a formal ceremony. It was true that he went to other women, but he always came back to her, and she hoped that a child would grant his life new purpose and fill the bottomless pit that gaped within him. Perhaps he would finally be rid of his relentless craving for approval.

He sucked out love.

No longer a young man, but still virile, he thought. He was at "the beginning of my strength and vigor," as is written in the Book of Genesis. He hadn't reached 1,000 women like King Solomon, but he was definitely a contender.

"Why can't you keep your what's it called in your pants?" asked Manny Jiminy Cricket Greenberg.

"And why can't you call the 'what's it called' by its name?" Gabriel laughed.

They were sitting in the bustling Katz's Deli, surrounded by the aromas of gefilte fish and knishes. It was a culinary temple that even non-Jews flocked to. Gabriel had chosen the meeting place, and for the whole of their conversation his gaze alternated between his watch and the entrance to the Yiddish theater.

"You're a shmuck," said his friend, "Your woman is in mourning and wants a child and you don't care?"

"She's not my woman."

Once again he uttered that sentence, and added, "I don't want to be a father out of pity."

"You didn't want to be a father at all, but that's what you are, whether you like it or not."

Gabriel didn't take his eyes off the building opposite. The audience was crowding around the entrance, and exclamations of "I was here first!" and "Don't push!" were loud in the street.

Manny paid the bill, eager to return home to his wife and daughter, but Gabriel had two free tickets, and although it was clear that this evening he wouldn't be pampering the actress in her dressing room, he managed to convince his friend that Abraham Goldfaden's *The Witch of Botosani* was an experience not to be missed. He had seen the play numerous times he exclaimed in an uncharacteristic outburst of enthusiasm, and knew the words to all the songs. It was a real Snow White story, in Yiddish.

A beautiful daughter, a jealous stepmother and an evil witch. And there's also a prince, but in the play he isn't really a prince like he is in the animated film by Walt Disney, but just a nice guy. Incidentally, the profitable film swelled Gabriel's bank account.

And the actress who played the beautiful Mireleh – what a talent. She would go far, maybe even to Hollywood. When she sang, "Jews, have mercy, have mercy, a kind heart beats within you," she had the entire audience in tears.

"Is there a happy ending?" asked Manny as the curtain went up.

"The bad guys get burned," whispered Gabriel as the lights dimmed.

13

Clara also wanted a happy ending, as she tried to become pregnant without telling Gabriel.

She went to a Chinese doctor in China Town who stuck pins in her belly, her thighs, and her earlobes, and to an Italian doctor who concocted a fertility potion for her from garlic cloves and gingerroot imported from Tuscany. She also went to Spanish Harlem for advice in Black Magic from a dubious Trinidadian witch doctor.

It was all for nothing. It seemed that Gabriel's lack of desire for parenthood caused the fetus to choose not to be born to such a father.

The protest of the unwanted.

Still, the witch doctor from Trinidad refused to give up. She claimed that she had one more powerful option – but it would cost the white lady an additional twenty dollars – and she asked Clara to describe the son of the man from whom she longed to be pregnant. It was the elder son who had put a curse on the womb of the second wife she pronounced. Perhaps he didn't want to share his future inheritance. Were there properties he was angling for and unwilling to split with future siblings? And did not the first firstborn son in the world murder his brother with a stone? What were their names, again? Never mind. What was important was that she needed a photograph of this elder son in order to remove the curse. She would pierce him with pins and open the blocked womb to clear the way for a new brother or sister.

Early in the morning Clara set out on her mission. First she made sure that Gabriel had left for Wall Street, and then she snuck into his apartment. She used the key she kept in case of emergency, and got down to snooping.

There was ticker tape everywhere, pressed flat as though it had been ironed, packets of tobacco in boxes, bottles of high-quality whiskey, and a few additional interesting details that the amateur detective discovered. A pair of gold cufflinks attached to a ticket to a jazz performance in Texas, a receipt from Barneys, a catalogue of Walt Disney films with pictures of Bambi, Snow White, and Dumbo the Flying Elephant, and in the fridge a half-eaten cheese blintz. What really surprised her was a Yiddish newspaper on the night table by Gabriel's bed, folded at a review of the play *The Witch of Botosani*.

Since when was he interested in the theater? There were no shares involved and theater people were always paupers. Not only did they barely make a profit, but they were usually in debt. One of Clara's annoying laughs escaped her as she carefully replaced the article where she had found it, as she did with all the other objects she touched.

Next she examined the contents of the dresser drawers, wiping away the accumulated dust while she was about it, along with her guilt feelings about desecrating the private space so cherished by her man. At the bottom of the drawer, underneath his American passport which bore the name "George," she found what she was looking for.

A photograph. As wrinkled as an old, withered face.

Clara's hand trembled as she smoothed it out. Its corners were blackened and torn and the image was faded. Not a baby, not a toddler, not even a young boy.

A woman.

A sharp nose, pinched nostrils, fleshy cheeks, tiny, deep-set eyes. Thin lips stretched in a false smile above a necklace of pearls resting on a high collar.

The other wife. She was the one responsible for her sealed womb. She and not her son.

"Why do you cling to him so tightly, Fanny?" Clara addressed the photograph, and her laughter turned to sobs. She rubbed her finger across the portrait. A woman without charm, with a furious expression on her face. And yet, wasn't it written in tractate *Avot*, "Do not look at the vessel, but rather at what it contains." What was contained in the vessel that held Gabriel hostage? What hidden power did she have over him that reached across such a great distance to block his seed?

"Release him, Fanny," she whispered again to the photograph.

Her gaze fell again on the folded newspaper, and she absentmindedly picked it up. The review of *The Witch of Botosani*. The compliments and praise didn't interest her. What caught her eye was the photograph. It was a portrait of the actress who played Miraleh. Although she was dressed in rags, this Jewish Snow White begging at an Istanbul bazaar, it was clear that this was a spectacular vessel. Strands of blonde hair flowed from beneath her head covering, and her costume did nothing to hide the beautiful body it sheathed.

This was her rival, and none other. She would take the photograph of the actress to the witch doctor from Trinidad, and that is what she would stick with pins to remove the curse of her barrenness.

Clara folded the paper carefully and replaced it on the night table. She left the apartment and hurried to the nearest newspaper stand to buy another copy to take to Spanish Harlem.

"You also like theater?" asked the vendor, and before she could reply he had burst into ear-splitting song, "Jews, have mercy, have mercy, a kind heart beats within you."

More people gathered round, applauding his performance. For a moment he was a star. Clara's tears confirmed his opinion that his was a glorious performance. If something unexpected should prevent the actress from appearing, if she were to fall ill or break a leg, then he could easily replace her. After all, there was a time when the men played the women's roles in Yiddish theater. He could be a perfect Miraleh.

A photograph. A newspaper. These two will be revealed as a fateful combination, but I have to restrain myself. At least until the next chapter.

"Watch out for spoilers," my daughter warns. There's still a long way to go.

Someone had disturbed his innermost sanctuary. Everything was in its place, but still Gabriel sensed that a ghost had wandered through his rooms and poked around in his things. The night table where the newspaper rested – although the paper lay just as he had left it – was dust-free. He opened the drawer. His American passport was there and underneath it the blackened, faded photograph of the *liebling*. Why did he bother to keep it? Hadn't the time come to get rid of it? Maybe it was her ghost that had broken through for a final accounting.

What nonsense, he immediately reproached himself. He had never believed in another world or "the other side."

Dust came and went. It wasn't evidence of an unknown entity with the power to do evil. The evil in the world originated only with those of flesh and blood, who knew better than he.

That night he dreamed that he was at the theater. Manny Greenberg was the usher and he seated him in the front row. It was the same performance, but instead of Miraleh there was a baby onstage. He wore a cloth diaper cape from underneath which ritual fringes peeped out. His features were those of an adult, while the hands that he held outstretched were chubby and dimpled. His arms were not extended in a plea for alms, like those of the heroine in Goldfaden's melodrama. The baby tried to drag Gabriel onto the stage to take a bow.

"Kostya," cried the dreamer in the dream, "I'm coming," but it wasn't anyone he knew.

14

Back on the ravaged continent Yitzhak once again took leave of Fanny to join the wanderers, a colossal wave of homeless people seeking shelter. A moment after liberation he was already fully absorbed in his next Zionist mission, and this time he revealed his destination and told Fanny that he was going to Paris.

He knew the "City of Lights" only from books and was excited about visiting its famous sites, although he wasn't travelling for pleasure, but to attend the first Zionist Youth Conference to be held after the war. He was to pave the escape routes to the ships that would carry the immigrants to Israel.

With a false travel document Yitzhak crossed the border into Budapest, continued to Vienna and then reached Frankfurt, bribing numerous policemen and officials along the way. He sent a postcard to Fanny in Bucharest so she wouldn't go out of her mind with worry. At the border crossing in Saarbrücken, between defeated Germany and France, the last of his money disappeared into the pockets of a border smuggler who didn't deliver the goods. After two weeks of wandering from country to country, filthy, unkempt, his stomach aching with hunger, he wandered the streets in search of a place where he could rest and eat a hot meal. Even if he had had money he wouldn't have been able to buy food without coupons, and he didn't have a coin for a stamp. He told himself that he would be able to send Fanny another postcard when he reached Paris, hopeful that he would overcome the final obstacle. He wandered for hours until he could hardly stand, when he saw the sign "Soldiers' Hospital."

"I'm a refugee returning home from a DP camp," he lied in French to the compassionate nurse in the doorway, and to be on the safe side he translated his words into German as well. The nurse was spooked by his command of the language of the vanquished and suspected that he wasn't what he claimed to be. How could a Frenchman speak German, and with a flawless accent?

"My mother is of German descent."

"And your father."

"I don't have a father."

It was the second sentence that convinced the nurse that he was telling the truth. Yitzhak uttered it with such conviction. Like Black Sorina, the compassionate Celine would join the list of generous women he encountered. Perhaps because she, too, no longer had a father. Hers had been a member of the French Resistance who was cruelly executed by the Vichy regime. First she gave Yitzhak bread and pickled cabbage, and then she took him in secret to a back storeroom that was crowded with buckets, brooms and other cleaning materials. She gave him a blanket and a towel and insisted on dragging over an old armchair with broken springs in which he spent the night. He didn't spend it in her arms, since the height of his pleasure at that time was the stream of running water washing the dirt off his body. This authentic detail I gleaned from my father's autobiography. He mentions it explicitly.

Fresh and clean, but with an aching back from the night spent in the broken chair, he set out for the train station to try his luck at reaching Paris. Needless to say, he didn't have a ticket, and so he stowed away in one of the carriages, slouched in a seat with his eyes on the floor as the view flowed past the windows. When he heard the ticket taker approaching he hurried through the train in search of the toilets. Just before stepping inside he was caught.

"I'm a refugee returning home," he said in a plaintive voice in French.

The ticket taker wasn't impressed and demanded his passport.

"How did you get through occupied Hungary, Austria, and Germany?" he barked.

Yitzhak proffered his documents.

"These are fake."

The ticket taker said he would put him off the train at the next stop and hand him over to the police. Yitzhak's pleas that he treat him kindly and allow him to reach Paris after all the hardships he had endured fell on deaf ears. The ticket taker demanded money – a lot of money.

"I'm sick of you, all of you. Refugees. Bah. You think you're the only ones who went through a war? I also suffered, and now it's time to earn a living."

He pushed him toward the door. Yitzhak struggled. The train swerved and he could just make out the writing on the sign that flashed past, "You are about to leave the occupied German zone."

Out of nowhere there appeared a hand with a wad of bills. American dollars.

A second glance revealed that the nails on the fingers were long and manicured, although not polished.

A strange woman had come to his aid. He was the incredibly lucky recipient of a rare act of generosity.

The ticket taker snatched the money and cursed. The Hungarians, the Russians, the Poles, the Germans, the rotten Nazis who promised a thousand-year Third Reich. He even cursed God who sat in His rotten paradise and didn't lift a finger, didn't spit in the direction of the tiny people eating shit. Maybe he also needed to be bribed.

The train slowed and then picked up speed, the sound of its wheels clacking in time with Yitzhak's heartbeat. They finally crossed the border. Now the signs were all in French.

The ticket taker shoved the bills into his pocket and disappeared. As Yitzhak voiced his gratitude in every language he knew there was a violent jolt. He lost his balance and grabbed onto the stranger so he wouldn't fall. Or maybe it was she who clung to him. That was when he noticed her high-heeled shoes. Glamorous and polished, in stark contrast to her tattered coat, below which hung the hem of a shabby dress.

It was already dark when she led him to her empty compartment at the end of the train. She locked the door, stepped out of her spike-heeled shoes and carefully placed them one beside the other. Next she removed her coat and her dress, both of which were torn. Without a word she held him in her arms and rested her head against his chest. He could barely make out her features. A single tear rolled down her cheek when she moaned – was it in pleasure or in pain – and it glittered like a diamond in the flickering light coming in through the window. She stopped, reached up and abruptly pulled down the shade so that they were enveloped in total darkness.

It was a night of demented passion suffused with profound despair, my father would tell me many years later. "It was as if the strange woman wanted to absorb some basic human warmth, and I gave it to her."

"And you didn't speak?"

"Not a single word."

"And what was her name?"

"She didn't tell me."

Yitzhak arrived at the Zionist Youth conference in Paris radiant and overflowing with energy, as though he hadn't nearly collapsed with exhaustion on his arduous journey. When his colleagues asked him about his high spirits he attributed them to his passion for the Zionist ideals. Finally the way was opening for everyone to reach the Land of Israel. He neglected to mention the night of wild rapture on the train.

On the postcard he sent to Fanny – with a picture of the Arc de Triomphe – he wrote, "I arrived safely. Paris is a dream come true."

His glowing countenance was captured by a photojournalist for a Yiddish newspaper, who had been sent from New York to cover the convention. He chose Yitzhak as the subject of his full-page feature article. In the headline he referred to him as no less than "The Fulfillment of the Zionist Dream."

15

On that particular morning Gabriel missed the newspaper vendor, a Puerto Rican youth with a voice like a trumpet who waited for him on the corner of Clinton and shouted out "George!" when he spotted him.

"The most important news in the language of the Jews," was handed over with great ceremony, and in return he always received the same ten cent tip and the greeting "buenos días."

Unusually, Gabriel had spent the night at Clara's apartment. The previous evening they had attended a concert at Carnegie Hall. It was Clara who had bought the tickets. Although Gabriel preferred jazz to classical music, that evening they were playing the score from George Gershwin's *American in Paris*, and ever since hearing *Swanee* on the ship he had felt a special affinity for the composer whose name he had adopted. They said he integrated the sound of taxi horns into his work. However, once inside the concert hall Gabriel was less interested in the music than in the parted legs of one of the musicians – the cellist, whose curved instrument rested between them.

The concert was Clara's private celebration for dealing successfully with her competition from the Yiddish actress. Her rival hadn't broken a leg, but had left for an extended countrywide tour of the play. As far as Clara was concerned, the inflated price she had paid to the witch doctor was worth the result. The enemy had been driven away, and the heart of her partner was meant to be hers and hers alone. However, to the strains of Gershwin it became apparent to her that his antennae were already sensing a new conquest. And there was no doubt in her mind that the cellist was sneaking furtive glances his way from behind her music stand.

Clara didn't wait for the cheering and the applause to subside, but fled Carnegie Hall in deep and bitter disappointment. On the subway she slouched in her seat and cried as the other passengers turned away. In Yiddish, she cursed the crooked sorceress who had banished one obstacle but not dealt with the threat to come.

When Gabriel knocked on her door a little while later, she refused to open it and cursed him in Yiddish screaming, "*paskudnyak*!" and then adding "son of a bitch!" in English. Only after he swore that his relationship with the cellist was entirely the product of her wild imaginings was she mollified. What did he care about the cello? Why, she knew full well that he had always preferred the clarinet. In the end she opened the door a crack, and when he saw her swollen, tear-stained face, he made an exception and spent the night.

He postponed his date with the cellist until after her next concert.

She would wait. They always did.

Gabriel had a hard time falling asleep in Clara's bed, not because he was troubled by his juggling of romantic partners, but having to remain in such close proximity to another human being for an entire night was suffocating to him. And yet in the past he had twice shared a bed for an extended period. How could it be that nothing remained of that experience? It was as if his previous life had faded away, as if it had taken place in a book read long ago and since dropped off at the secondhand store. Larissa and Fanny blended into one person, and if you'd asked him he wouldn't have been able to say which one had flaxen hair and which was graced with the long eyelashes. Only in his dreams did they appear separately, but the dreams were rare and quickly forgotten. Unlike Clara, whose presence was like a pair of slippers. True, they were worn, and had stretched out beyond the size of his feet, but they were still so comfortable to put on. At his not-so-young age he could appreciate the advantages of the habitual, but never at the expense of a new, thrilling adventure.

"Death will come when it comes, until then we'd better live it up." The punchline to Mrs. Jackson's life. Her motto.

The razor that Clara kept for him on the shelf in her tiny bathroom was dull and he had an unsatisfactory shave that morning. He would buy a new razor on the way to Wall Street and remove every black bristle in the washroom at his office. He was becoming a silver fox, as grey hair began to appear at his temples, and it didn't bother him at all. On the contrary, the cellist had informed him that she liked mature men. Their experience only enhanced their performance. They really knew how to tend to the needs of a woman before seeing to their own pleasure.

On another occasion he was lying beside Clara, thinking about his newest lover. In addition to her talents as a gifted musician her views were similar to those of Lizzie-Bertha, and by the side of her bed he had discovered the groundbreaking comic book starring the first female with supernatural powers – Wonder Woman.

"A woman of valor who can find?" he snorted. "What is she holding in her hand?"

"That's the Lasso of Truth."

Gabriel laughed and the cellist flicked him lightly with her cello bow.

"She hunts her victims with her lasso. Whoever she catches has to follow her orders."

Then they had made love again as Gershwin played in the background.

On the side of the bed where Clara was sprawled, emitting little annoying giggles even in her sleep, Gabriel found a skullcap. This was another thing she kept for him, in case he should need it. He recited the morning prayers, placing particular emphasis on the phrase, "Blessed are You, Lord our God, Ruler of the Universe, Who has not made me a woman."

Gabriel was in such a hurry to leave that he even neglected to buy his daily paper and on that morning the Puerto Rican boy didn't receive his usual tip. What difference did it make anyway? Every day was more or less the same as the one that had gone before.

In his apartment on Delancey, Manny Greenberg perused the headlines.

"In rainy weather, at the Foreign Ministry in Washington, The Anglo-American Committee of Inquiry opened its discussions about the Land of Israel. President Roosevelt's special envoy stressed the urgent need to grant the Jews the possibility of a life of freedom.

Next page.

"The order was to wipe out all the Jews," admitted the mass murderer at the Nuremberg Trials.

A shudder.

"We will clothe our brothers and sisters in Romania who are dressed in rags. The campaign to inspire life and hope has begun. Pack up your contributions and bring them yourselves to the offices of the newspaper."

The previous day, Manny had dropped off a parcel of used clothes. He was first in line.

Next page.

"Stalin was put forward as a candidate for election to the Supreme Soviet at a meeting of workers at an electrical appliance factory in Moscow."

Damn communists. God forbid they should ever sneak into the United States and ruin the American Dream.

Next page.

"The agreement has been signed for the American oil pipeline to extend from east to west in the Land of Israel, as far as the Mediterranean Sea."

Greedy opportunists, exploiting underdeveloped countries. What else is new?

Next page.

"Is the bagel the hole that is surrounded by the roll, or the roll that surrounds the hole?"

Manny paused. The Yiddish paper quoted the recent article in *The New York Times* that discussed the existential nature of the bagel, posing the question as to whether it is "defined by its doughy being or its holey nothingness."

Manny sipped his coffee and chewed on the fresh bagel that his wife Doris had bought early that morning at Katz's Deli. A generous layer of cream cheese covered the hole.

"Nu, what do you say, Doris? Maybe we should add the genesis of the bagel to the Book of Genesis?"

"The first man added the sesame seeds, and Eve added the poppy seeds?"

Doris draped a thin slice of pale pink smoked salmon over her bagel.

"Why isn't it mentioned in the Bible?"

"A man cannot praise what he himself is responsible for."

"Maybe the 'Mark of Cain' is the bagel above the head of the first elder son in the world?"

Manny chimed in "'So that no one who found him would kill him.' You understand Doris? That's so that he would stay alive," and then he went back to the paper.

"It says here that initially they gave the bagel as a gift to new mothers. That was three hundred years ago in Poland."

Doris was impressed by the exalted age of the bagel, but had no recollection of ever having received one in honor of her femininity. Maybe the women's rights movement would adopt the bagel as the symbol of its struggle.

"In an emergency, it could be used as a wedding ring. The rabbis will approve it," offered Manny, and they both laughed. His bagel, doughy and firm, was gone, but a dab of cream cheese remained on his plate.

"You see, Manny, the hole was filled," Doris pointed out.

As he saw it, it was the hole that was proof of the existence of the circle of dough that surrounded it. It was the "lack" that pointed to its abundant existence, and not the other way around.

Doris poured more coffee into his mug, picked up her plate and brought it to the sink. One should never start the day with depressing thoughts. That was why she never read the newspaper. It was always about what was lacking. The sound of the water running from the kitchen faucet blocked out the rustling as Manny continued to read.

Next page.

Suddenly Manny shouted. Doris started and dropped the plate she was soaping, which crashed into the sink.

"Gabriel's son is alive!"

His shouts woke their twelve-year-old daughter, who came skipping into the kitchen. The sight of her father holding the outstretched paper as if it was the doors to the Holy Ark in the synagogue and pointing at the photograph of Yitzhak, would remain etched in her memory forever.

She described the moment to me as excited as if it had taken place yesterday. M. – my last witness. It was from M. that I learned how my grandfather found out that my father had not been relegated to "nothingness," but was abundantly alive.

Still in her slippers and pajamas the girl trailed after her father as he rushed through the streets of the Lower East Side in the direction of Wall Street, informing the neighbors staring out their windows that a miracle had occurred.

"Until the last day of their lives You are waiting, and if they repent You receive them at once."

Gabriel stared at the photograph of Yitzhak, and it was as if he was looking at himself.

16

It's too good to be true. The good souls out there are shaking their heads at the dramatic coincidence and the moment when the father recognized the son. What an example of deus ex machina they must be thinking, of a contrived plot device intended to extricate an author from a sticky situation. It may also seem like the Yiddish idea of a *gemacht*, one of my father's favorite expressions for something that is overdone.

My daughter warns me. They'll think I'm overdoing it, that I am meddling with reality and staging events to suit my purposes. But in this case I must doff my cap to "He who forms the mountains and creates the wind," Who in His madness creates the defining moments, since I couldn't have come up with such a moment. It is entirely authentic. Truth usurps fiction.

And anyway, my fiction is sprinkled with blips of truth.

Clara's breath also caught in her throat when she recognized the father's expression reflected in the face of the son. And considering that there had been no contact between them since he was a baby, the similarity was even more compelling. At that moment she thanked the Lord that she hadn't discovered his photograph during her desperate search and had thus prevented any harm coming to him from the Trinidadian witch doctor. She alluded to the doctrine of ancestral sin in a conversation with Manny Greenberg, although she omitted her foray into black magic.

She also discussed with Manny whether the firstborn son might be the key to unlocking his parents' dismal marriage. In his photograph in the newspaper he seemed to glow, and that was a characteristic he certainly hadn't inherited from his tough and cranky father. She imagined that his ugly, graceless mother, as she appeared in the faded photograph hidden in Gabriel's drawer, must take comfort in the fact that her offspring was such a good looking young man.

Clara Mendel always appreciated an attractive, well-built man, and the French beret that Yitzhak worn at a rakish angle enchanted her. She was especially encouraged by the optimism of his concluding words in the article. They were in stark contrast to his descriptions at the start of the interview, of the horrors experienced by the Jews of Romania and the devastation he had witnessed on his journey through Europe. Anyone who could speak of the future with such enthusiasm could be her ally in breaking away from the past.

The interview in Paris made no lasting impression on Yitzhak, and he never even mentioned it to Fanny. For him it was a trivial occurrence when compared to the news he brought back from the conference. Their path to the Land of Israel had opened. Another person who noticed the radiance in his face was a young woman named Mimi Margalit Liquornik, who had survived the Auschwitz extermination camp and returned to Bukovina alone, after her first husband perished. The blue-eyed, fair-haired man from Transylvania, with whom she had fallen in love as a high school student, would remain with her forever, and she would never speak of their baby daughter who didn't survive. At the age of twenty-four Mimi was a widow and a bereaved mother, who found comfort in the arms of Yitzhak, who overflowed with assurance. For him she left the religious Bnei Akiva movement and joined the secular Zionist Youth. She wanted so much to start a new life and leave her bloody past behind.

Mimi would be my mother.

Clara read the article out loud to Gabriel. The more she read, the more she discerned the crack that was opening within him. Not only was his son alive, but he was now an impressive person, with solid and well-reasoned positions – although they were the opposite of his. Due to his pride in this achievement that he chose to take credit for he listened intently as she read.

For Clara, it was a glimmer of hope, and she scanned every word and nuance in the article searching for a mention of Fanny. Dead or alive, this was the opportunity to find out what had happened to her and to come to practical conclusions.

"My mother and I survived," Yitzhak asserted at the end of the article.

Finally, she saw a way out. At long last the divorce could take place. Clara urged Gabriel to do something. She even called the newspaper offices herself and made an appointment for the two of them to meet with the journalist.

"Why shouldn't I meet him alone?"

Again, the serial evader clung to any pretext to avoid making a decision.

"Only together," Clara insisted. She didn't want to miss a word, and mostly she didn't trust him to give her a reliable account. She wasn't going to allow this rare opportunity to slip through her fingers.

Like a skilled researcher she faced the journalist and milked him for every detail about the Paris encounter. He actually remembered the young Zionist interviewee with the French beret. A refugee who hadn't lost his belief in a better future was hard to forget.

"Do you have his address?"

"Do refugees have an address?" he snorted.

The vivacious woman touched his heart more than the handsome man at her side, who sat in stony silence and chain-smoked. It was odd that it was she who was so determined to locate his lost family.

For a long time the journalist searched through his notes, until he finally produced the original notebook in which he had recorded the interview in Paris. In the smoke-filled room he did his best to decipher what he had written.

"Herzig the pioneer said explicitly that they were going to Palestine."

"How can they go? Why, the British are forbidding entry."

"Illegal immigration."

"On which ship?"

"He didn't say."

"From which port?"

"He didn't say."

"What did he say?"

The journalist flipped through his notebook. It was important to him to quote things accurately.

"In spite of the opposition of the British I will reach Palestine."

The Yiddish expression he used was "*Oyf su loochus*" (to annoy or to anger), a trait considered the essence of the Jewish DNA which had slipped so easily into the Israeli version. That is something that Yitzhak undoubtedly inherited from Gabriel, Clara told the journalist.

What a juicy story had fallen into his lap. And it was due to an article that he had penned. "Emotional Reunion of Father and Son" – that would be the headline. He would describe how the two fell into each other's arms and declared that they had never stopped loving one another and longing for this day. Every copy of the paper would be snapped up and he might even get a Pulitzer. He received special permission from the editor, including reimbursement of expenses, to accompany the couple on the train to Washington, and even coordinated their meeting with the mid-level official at the Foreign Ministry.

In his notebook he described George Herzig, formerly Gabriel, as he signed the request to locate first-degree relatives, who were now the American citizens Yitzhak Herzig and his mother, Fanny nee Katz. The journalist even photographed the visas that they received on the spot, and remembered to acknowledge the contribution of the Ministry official to the dramatic search.

He transformed Gabriel's fierce expression to a "fierce yearning," and attributed "frantic tears" to Clara, ignoring her nervous laughter. A small fib never hurt a good article.

He even scribbled a caption on the photograph: "The happy father recites the *shehecheyanu* prayer. Happy ending coming soon."

We can conclude here and send our readers off, satisfied and thrilled. Only reality doesn't tend to Hollywood-style endings, but more to those found in Greek tragedy. Antigone goes to her death, Oedipus gouges out his eyes, Medea murders her children.

It's actually the heartbreaking endings that sell newspapers, and Fanny would swear to them, not necessarily because of her fondness for Greek mythology, but due to her life experience which had taught her that, "The righteous suffer and the wicked thrive." The land promised to her by her son was not her aspiration, but she didn't want to throw cold water on his dream. Why foretell a land flowing with blood and agonies? There as well they would be viewed as intruders by hostile neighbors. As she packed her meager possessions in preparation for the move to the Land of Israel, she mumbled some words from the Traveler's Prayer, "Save us from every enemy and ambush, from robbers and wild beasts on the trip, and from all kinds of punishments that rage and come to the world."

She took along a small rug, the only possession to survive from the house in Siret, rolling it up and tucking it under her arm. At least she would have comfortable bedding when the time came, and she could always cover herself with it in the cold. Fanny could never have imagined what else it would be used for.

The editor added some optimistic lines to the article, written by Eliezer Steinbarg, the renowned fable-writer from Czernowitz: "Is the world really meaningless? Is it dark, with the despair penetrating to the bone? But, friends, what would happen if the sun suddenly shone?"

Not under a radiant sun, but in the dark of night Yitzhak, his new wife and Fanny set out on their difficult journey to the fishing port of Aaker, on the coast of the Adriatic Sea, where a dubious cargo ship that had once transported its freight down the rivers in America awaited them.

They didn't know that Gabriel had begun to search for them.

The request from the American Foreign Ministry to locate relatives arrived back in Washington with the message: "Fanny and Yitzhak Herzig are no longer on Romanian soil." The journalist's hopes of winning a Pulitzer were dashed.

Perhaps it was Nemesis, goddess of retribution – often portrayed as blind –Who decided to teach Gabriel a lesson. Now it was his turn to face those two terrifying words: "Whereabouts unknown."

Nemesis laughed, and Clara cried. Her tears smudged her makeup and she looked like an actress in a failing play. Even though Gabriel suggested that they spend the night together at her apartment – a rare and generous gesture on his part – she chose to remain alone. She wasn't even interested in the comforts that he could offer her and instead tortured herself the entire night. Was he relieved that his freedom wasn't in jeopardy?

It was a shame that she couldn't see how heavyhearted he was. Perhaps it was guilt feelings, reawakened after all those years, or the result of his disappointment at not being able to discover the kind of man his son was. "Whereabouts unknown." The words continued to pulse within him.

He wandered aimlessly through the streets of the Lower East Side, found himself at Katz's Delicatessen, ordered a slice of cheesecake that he didn't touch, and later lay awake till dawn. The next day, in his office on Wall Street, his head lurched forward onto his desk, landing in a tangle of ticker tape, and he slept for long enough to have a dream.

He is surrounded by the thunder of falling shells, but far away from the trench. Out of nowhere a hand pulls him toward a giant ticker tape machine and the paper strips curl round his body. Someone, he can't tell whether it is a man or a woman, says, "Gabriel, you have a place."

In early November 1946, the illegal immigration ship *Knesset Yisrael* set sail. My parents and grandmother were among the 4,000 people packed onto its deck, most of whom were Holocaust survivors. When they weighed anchor, there was a spontaneous outburst of singing of the *Hatikvah* anthem. Only Fanny remained silent.

Yet Another Thing

How little we know about the people who are closest to us, especially when we are children.

Mother is a mother, father is a father, and a grandmother is a grandmother.

The adults were on an elevated plain, I explain to my daughter. They belonged to a mysterious territory that we had no access to. We were focused solely on our daily existence and our immediate welfare, as if the child was in the center and the adults its satellites.

There was a kind of "blindness to childhood" in that generation. Parents and grandparents were human fortresses that never shared their emotions, never opened the smallest window into what they had experienced, and all the more so when it came to the secrets, which were jealously guarded and barricaded. If these were exposed, it happened unconsciously, as a kind of accident. Besides, any random glimpse that occasionally protruded from the shadows was terrifying to me.

To write about Fanny, I have to free myself of the monolithic-grandmother figure that enveloped my childhood and invade her sealed-off spaces. I have learned that fiction has the capacity to scrape at the crust of truth. How absurd that of all people it is Fanny who on paper becomes flesh and blood.

To be honest, I love her more on paper than I did in life. I didn't really know her. It never occurred to me that she had a story. And if I sensed any story at all, simmering within her, it wasn't something I wanted to hear. Her staggering love for my father embarrassed me. Fanny was so all-encompassing that she had little left over for others. I was embarrassed, too, by her ever-present tsunami of anxiety. I heard the whispers and the mockery, "The crazy Frau Herzig." I was afraid that her madness would be passed on to me, and I did whatever I could to distance myself from her. In response, and maybe since it was in her nature, she treated me harshly, especially with respect to the eating disorder that I suffered from. As she saw it, a refusal to eat was a severe survival malfunction that had to be fearlessly assailed. "Skin-and-bones" was how she always referred to me, lamenting that it was unlikely that I would grow. There was a slight softness to her only when she embroidered or when she cooked her acclaimed dishes, especially pickled herring in cream sauce. That was when I noticed the long eyelashes, the silky white hair and the ivory skin. Looking back, there was certainly also grace and determination underneath the mad exterior, and maybe that is the choice I make today between the live Fanny and Fanny on paper. Isn't it preferable to breathe in the smell of bay leaves and allspice rather than salted fish?

"Remember with compassion," my daughter begs, and what's the point of wallowing in old grudges and bitterness and endless reckonings with the dead? I tell her that what is detrimental to memory, according to the pervading beliefs of the shtetl, is when you wear a garment inside-out. It is entirely likely that that is what I am doing now.

In my topsy-turvy memory there remain a few moments of wrinkled grace, like the collection of paper napkins I used to have, and now I array them before my daughter and iron out the creases.

PART FOUR

You Are Hereby Permitted to All Men

– Jewish Divorce Document

You Are Hereby Permitted to All Men

1

"Where's your husband?"

The question, seemingly innocently posed, was camouflage for other questions, such as, "When did he die? Where did he perish?" Onboard the ship Fanny was asked more than once to explain her situation, since in the first years after the horrors the survivors still shared what had befallen them hoping to learn about loved ones who had vanished.

They would subsequently fall utterly silent for long years and hide everything from their children.

On the *Knesset Yisrael* thousands of illegal immigrants were packed onto wooden boards in the sleeping halls on the lower decks and Yitzhak, who had been appointed Command Secretary and also representative to the *Palyam* and to the organized clandestine illegal immigration to the Land of Israel known as Aliya Bet, was occupied with his new bride and all the logistics and arrangements. The trumpet blasts of the attendants alerted the groups of passengers that they could start to take turns to go into the storeroom for their food, which consisted of surplus battle rations from the US military in Europe. The "Bucket Brigade" distributed the drinking water, and Fanny was a member. She took the pails from the containers that were used to stabilize the ship, which had previously contained salt water, and had to constantly fend off complaints about the terrible taste.

When her shift was over she retreated to her spot next to the engine room, supporting her head on the rolled-up carpet. She was drenched in perspiration, her ears assaulted by the din of the engines. She blocked her nostrils so as not to breathe in the stench of the vomit that sloshed around from the upper deck, and waited for night to fall. To avoid detection by the British reconnaissance planes that circled the skies during the day, the passengers were only allowed to move about on deck under cover of darkness.

Gabriel. Now, during the hours of waiting on the ship, she found herself thinking about him. Had the conditions of his voyage to America been any better? At least he hadn't had to crouch like a rat in the bowels of a floating, groaning iron wreck and drink seawater.

So much time had elapsed, and yet his memory remained, pickled inside her, like the food in the cans of preserves that the illegal immigrants had collected before setting sail, as "ammunition to be used in the event of an altercation with the British soldiers."

Squashed on her plank, her elbow digging into the ribs of the stranger lying next to her, she heard again the familiar question.

"Are you also alone?"

A young woman sat up next to her. Prematurely wrinkled, her black hair roughly shorn, her cheekbones prominent. Her large eyes glowed in the dim light of the lower deck.

Fanny hesitated. After all, she had a son and a daughter-in-law, and maybe in the new land there would be grandchildren. But Yitzhak's marriage hinted at loneliness to come, for as it is written, "Therefore a man shall leave his father and mother and be joined to his wife…"

The young woman rose and started to undress, until she was completely naked.

"Have you no sense of shame?"

Fanny quickly covered her with the rug. Only then did she notice the woman's protruding belly. She was in an advanced stage of pregnancy.

As the engines emitted their oppressive heat, the girl used the rug as a fan, trying to cool their bodies.

"You should also take off your clothes," she suggested. "Otherwise you and your modesty will melt together."

Fanny removed her shirt and waved it too in the stagnant air.

"Yes, I'm alone. My husband left me."

As she spoke the words, she was flooded with relief. Now she had finally truly distanced herself from him. There was much more than an ocean separating America and the Land of Israel.

"Good that you are rid of him. We can also be happy without a man."

The girl reminded Fanny of Lizzie-Bertha.

Rather than reply, Fanny took off her skirt and lay in her underwear. The air around them seemed to boil. She poured her companion some water from the bucket, apologizing for the salty taste, but the only thing she complained of was pains in her back. The young woman twisted her body, searching for a comfortable position for her belly. Fanny remembered her terrifying encounter with the drunken soldiers. Had this pregnant woman experienced something similar? Perhaps no colonel in shining armor had come to her rescue at the last moment.

She rolled up the carpet and balanced in on the bucket so the pregnant woman could lean against it. She took Fanny's hand and placed it on her belly.

"He will be a child of Palestine."

Palestine, the word sounded more like a threat than tidings of the future.

"I have no choice." The woman emphasized that she wasn't a Zionist. She had returned alone from Transnistria. Not one of her relatives had survived. All her possessions had been looted. She even saw her mother's Sabbath candlesticks set out in the neighbor's window. What did it matter where she ended up? This country or that one, it was all the same. The loneliness would be the same. In every place people would find excuses to bleed others, would detest those who were different and murder each other for less than a crust of bread.

She thrust her foot forward, revealing the part that had been frostbitten in the sub-zero temperatures of Transnistria. Who could guarantee that she would find a cure in Palestine? They said that the sun blazed there and toughened the soul. And Hebrew. What an impossible language. How would she ever get used to it? She never mentioned the father of the baby, who kicked incessantly under Fanny's palm.

"He's excited to come out. The child of Palestine is impatient. Maybe he knows something that we don't know," Fanny said, and she told her about the angel that accompanied the fetus and erased its memory before birth, so that it wouldn't fear entry into the world.

"If the angel's already at work, let it erase my memory too."

She shook out the rug and lay across it, stretching her limbs. As Fanny watched, the swollen belly became a mound beaded with radiant drops.

Fanny said, "When they ask you, tell them that your husband is dead." And then she took off all her clothes.

Night finally fell. The passengers, fully or partially dressed, rushed to the upper deck to breathe some sea air. The two women remained alone by the engine room, cradled in the rocking motion of the ship. They didn't hear the commotion above when the *Knesset Yisrael* was discovered, and two British minesweepers – the *Espiegle* and the *Octavia* – and the destroyer the *Brissenden*, embarked. They were unaware of the fluctuating searchlights and continued to sleep as peacefully as though they had already arrived at their safe haven.

In the morning the girl woke Fanny in a panic. The rug was drenched in the water that was also puddled between her legs. Her contractions had begun.

Fanny hurriedly threw on her clothes and supported her bunkmate as she pushed through the crush of bodies. In between contractions she managed to locate Yitzhak. Between them they half-carried her to the captain's cabin, which became a maternity room.

The screams of the new mother mingled with the words of the British commander that boomed over the loudspeakers: "Any attempt to reach Palestine is doomed to failure and will cause you unnecessary suffering."

The head of the infant – fair as the down on a chick and covered in blood – crowned at the same moment when on all the decks and from the water below echoed the immigrants' response. It was just one word, repeated like a chant: "Palestine, Palestine, Palestine!" The wails of the newborn mingled with the choir.

We can only wonder about the name that his mother chose for the baby. One assumes that she wanted to perpetuate the memory of one of her dead relatives. But even her name is lost. Maybe she never told Fanny who she was.

The baby's circumcision took place in the detention camp in Cyprus.

Eleven babies were born on the *Knesset Yisrael*, my father noted in the journal he kept throughout the voyage. "The day will come when it will remind me, and perhaps others as well, of the stormy days. One day it will all seem like a story or a film."

2

Gabriel was also thinking about Fanny, and not because he was suddenly overcome by a wave of nostalgia. Those around him – especially Manny Greenberg – refused to drop the subject, and Clara was in regular phone contact with the official at the Foreign Ministry, demanding updates.

"A single pubic hair of a woman has the power to drag an entire ship," said the comedian at the Catskills. Clara had dragged Gabriel there for a vacation.

It was an old joke, but Gabriel had to admit that it contained more than a grain of truth.

Ever since the meeting in Washington Clara had demonstrated her determination. Sometimes that trait seemed to remind him of Fanny, although he was unsure whether what he remembered was a real person or a faded figment of his imagination.

To spend a week alone with her in a hotel in the Borsht Belt – the favorite summer resort area for the Jews of New York – seemed like a nightmare to him at that time. He hoped she wouldn't get any ideas about living together, or, heaven forfend, marriage. After all, it was his sole heir he was searching for, and not a divorce to re-enslave him. If she hadn't taken on the mission of locating his wife and son and appointed herself the go-between with the clerk at the Foreign Ministry, he would have cut the connection long before and sent her packing.

However, Clara created facts on the ground and conspired with the Greenbergs to organize the holiday.

"Maybe he will finally understand that the specter of an ordinary relationship isn't so terrible," she rationalized to Doris. And just between the two of us, what's so bad about sex in a romantic atmosphere in the heart of nature? Except that the rented cabin with its faux-country style, wood-paneled walls, and fireplace complete with a pile of logs at its side, reminded Gabriel of the farm in Russia. He complained constantly about the hard mattress and the poor water pressure in the shower. What did he care about "going back to nature?" He vastly preferred the modern conveniences that made washing oneself pure pleasure. A bubble bath with a cigar in hand, and a partner to scrub his back.

A bath like that would yet appear in his life.

Gabriel turned up his nose at the lavish breakfast with which the holiday-makers started their day: bagels, lox and cream cheese. All he needed was coffee and a cigarette. Lately he had noticed that Clara's figure wasn't what it had been, as food had become her source of comfort ever since she had learned of the loss of her family, although that wasn't the reason that his attraction to her had faded. The relationship has run its course, he told himself, as he sat drinking his coffee and smoking a Chesterfield. It was time to move on. He already had a new target in his sights. She was the aunt of my ultimate witness, M. She was very pretty and very married, which didn't bother him at all. On the contrary.

Gabriel dodged the sporting competitions and walks along the mountain trails claiming that he had to listen to the stock market reports on the radio, but in the afternoons he was coerced into participating in the Bingo games, and he openly ridiculed Clara who won time and time again.

"Let her enjoy a moment of happiness," Doris reprimanded him, and Manny chimed in, "She's had enough sorrow."

And the gossip at that place. Oh my God. A matchmaking exchange flourished in the Catskill Mountains.

Who was widowed, who was dying, and who would soon join the list of those who were available? Who had left a generous bequest, or settled accounts with his heirs and left everything to the Society for the Prevention of Cruelty to Animals. There were also some recently widowed women who noticed Gabriel's cold treatment of Clara and started scheming. Every time he walked along the path to the dining hall he could hear them whispering behind his back.

How could people waste their time in such a way, Gabriel grumbled, especially when the Marshall Plan for economic assistance to rebuild Western Europe was about to kick in and financial opportunities beckoned.

The only ray of light on the imposed vacation was the evening performances of the comedians, although Gabriel had plenty of criticism about them as well. Their jokes were old, and predictable, and he was sick of them making fun only of Jews.

"But these are the best of our people," Manny enthused. For Manny the holiday was a fabulous opportunity to see the comedians he so admired. He followed all those whose careers took off in the Borsht Belt, and he had memorized all their jokes. David Daniel Kaminsky, better known as Danny Kaye and Joseph Levitch, whose stage name was Jerry Lewis. Samuel Joel Mostel, who achieved fame under the name "Zero." The Marx Brothers – Leonard, Adolph, Julius, Milton and Herbert, who became Chico, Harpo, Groucho, Gummo, and Zeppo."

"I put an ad in the paper that I'm looking for a wife. The next day there were dozens of replies: 'You can have mine.'"

Gabriel didn't laugh.

"My wife met a friend at a party. She said to her: 'You're wearing your wedding ring on the wrong finger.'

The friend answered: 'That's because I married the wrong man.'"

Clara laughed.

"Women worry about the future, until they find a husband. Men never worry about the future, until they find a wife."

Manny Greenberg laughed.

"When I was born, all I wanted was to get out of a woman's body. Ever since, I can't stop trying to get back into one."

Doris Greenberg laughed.

"Why are married women fatter than single women? The single women go home, see what's in the refrigerator and go to bed. The married ones see what's in the bed and go to the refrigerator."

Clara didn't bother to check Gabriel's reaction before demonstratively walking out of the performance. She suddenly realized that she was wasting her feelings on an undeserving partner, one who could sit through an entire comedy show curling his lip in condescension, completely unmoved. Even if the divorce finally came through she wouldn't marry him she cried to Doris who had hurried out after her.

"I've wasted my best years on him. The self-centered bastard. I wish he'd go back to his ugly wife. What did he ever see in her? Why has he held onto her for so many years?"

Under the canopy of rustling trees, adjacent to the illuminated performance hall, Clara told Doris about the hidden photograph she had found at the bottom of Gabriel's drawer, omitting the reason for her trespass. In her fury she hoped for Gabriel's son's sake that he would never be reunited with his father and discover what kind of a man he was.

Doris was outraged.

"Why are you so ungrateful?" hissed Manny as the comedian onstage delivered joke after joke at dizzying speed.

The jokester's practiced eye discerned what had led the woman to walk out in the middle of his act – it was the sour demeanor of the man at her side who hadn't reacted to even one of his jokes – and he immediately homed in on him.

"Tell me the secret mister, how do you get a Jewish woman to stop having sex?"

All eyes were on Gabriel. The spotlight dazzled him, but he was a tough nut. No embarrassment, no squirming in his seat, no stammering justification. Even though the answer was on the tip of his tongue, he held back and refused to deliver it to the master of punchlines. "Hey, clown, I've never had to deal with a challenge like you."

His defiant silence brought the comedian down from the stage to point a finger at him.

"You want to know how to get her to stop having sex? Marry her!"

The crowd roared with laughter. There were those who suspected that Gabriel was a plant and that their dialogue – obviously scripted – was intended to pack an even stronger punchline.

When he arrived at the cabin he found that Clara had locked him out. He didn't bother to shout or to plead with her to open the door, but retraced his steps and went back into the empty hall. He found a half-full bottle of Jack Daniels on one of the tables and decided to spend the rest of the evening in its company.

Gabriel sat up onstage sipping slowly from the bottle, thinking about how he could escape the Catskills. If he could find a taxi he could still get to New York before the start of the next day's trading. It was good that Clara was the one who had chosen to end the relationship with the slam of a door. That would at least save him the insults and accusations. There were advantages to being abandoned.

A shadow approached from behind the curtain. For a moment he thought it was Clara. That was all he needed, for her to change her mind now and start in with emotional blackmail. He hated it when they cried.

"You're the son of a bitch who didn't laugh at my jokes."

Gabriel suppressed his laughter in another swallow from the bottle.

"It can't be that I'm not funny. You don't have a sense of humor!"

Gabriel held out the bottle. The comedian hesitated a moment before accepting it.

"Are you married, mister?"

"Only on paper."

"And the woman who walked out?"

"She's not my woman."

Those words again.

The comedian drained the bottle. Then he juggled it in the air. "Do you know what it does to an actor when someone walks out on his act? You'll ruin my career."

"You'll survive."

"Show business is a killer."

What did he know about killing? But Gabriel didn't voice his thought.

"Why are all your jokes about women?"

"That's what the audience likes."

"I'm not sure you're right. The women hang on while we die out. They are your future audience. You'd better start changing your repertoire."

The comedian burst out laughing. He patted Gabriel on the shoulder and even offered him a ride to New York in his Cadillac convertible.

On the way, with the wind in his hair, Gabriel told him an old joke from Bukovina. The only one he remembered. The clown, a miserable refugee in need of a handout, had told it at a wedding.

A Jew is lying on his deathbed. With his dying breath his asks his wife, "It's true, isn't it, that I was always your first violin?"

His wife answers, "With an instrument like yours you should be thankful that you were in the orchestra at all."

The comedian incorporated it into his act, and it became his signature joke in the Borsht Belt. The audience, mostly women, would shout out the punchline in unison. For the rest of his life he would be grateful to the tough customer George who contributed to his success in show business.

And Clara? The rift lasted three days, until the fateful telephone call Gabriel received at the end of a work day. She sounded flustered, on the verge of tears, but it wasn't because of the altercation in the Catskills. The clerk from the Foreign Ministry had informed her that Fanny and Yitzhak had been located.

3

A beautiful island, Cyprus. Fanny never tired of the golden sand spread like a carpet at the foot of the sea, so different from the irascible foaming wake that accompanied the *Knesset Yisrael* on its nineteen-day voyage. She had never seen so many shades of blue, azure, and turquoise, flecked with spangles of light. And on the horizon ridges covered with olive trees and pine groves that glowed red at sunset. A picture postcard image viewed through barbed wire.

Fanny, Yitzhak and Mimi's entrance into the Karaolos internment camp near Famagusta was less of a pleasure. They were herded into the disinfection tent along with hundreds of others where they were sprayed with DDT by the British orderlies who cursed the "fucking Jews" indiscriminately.

Mimi panicked. Another camp. Her third. More watchtowers, more sentries. Her scars reopened. Fanny tried to calm her, telling her that this camp was just a waystation. Yitzhak comforted her, "It's exile deluxe, British-style." Cyprus was no Garden of Eden, but it wasn't hell.

Fanny was the first to adapt. She shook the sand off her rug and spread it at the entrance to their tent. So that the young couple could have some privacy, she spent a lot of time outside, gazing at the view beyond the fence. The carpet became the identifying feature of the "Herzig Residence," a kind of flag. Its colors had faded some, through its various uses as bolster, fan, labor mat, and a bat with which Fanny had tried to fend off the British soldier who forced her off the ship. And yet it was still up to its next tasks, the first of which was to provide a resting place for a stray dog. The scruffy creature attached itself to Fanny and followed her everywhere, perhaps because she fed it all the camel meat that was given to the camp inhabitants and that she never even considered consuming.

"He eats out of her hand," laughed one of the youngsters.

"He doesn't care whether or not it's kosher," and it wasn't clear whether she was referring to the camel or to the dog.

The mutt, covered in sand with a lolling tongue, first sniffed her out when they were ordered to identify their belongings from the huge pile next to the administration hut. They had had to wait awhile after they were moved to the camp before their possessions were transferred there. Mimi stood gazing horrified at the mountain of clothing, but Fanny took hold of her daughter-in-law and guided her away from the mob. That's when she first felt the dog's snout poking into her hand. She tried to shoo him away, but he wouldn't leave. The dog licked her and stood by her while she promised Mimi that she would outfit her with something new. Barely any of the things in the pile were wearable anyway.

And she kept her word.

The dog claimed the spot at the entrance to the tent like a sentry and stayed there, cotton threads entwined in his tangled fur. The fashion house that opened in Cyprus would have humbled Coco Chanel and Christian Dior. It is no small thing to create something out of nothing. And His Majesty's military manufacturers could never have imagined the heights of creativity that would be reached by "the simple tent dwellers" imprisoned in their camps. Whose bright idea was it to use canvas tent sheets as the raw material for clothing? That will remain a mystery. Meanwhile, Fanny and her team of seamstresses diligently peeled away the three layers that comprised each tent: the blue, the white, and the yellow. She trained them to work quickly, since a large amount of material was needed in a short time.

The jewel in the crown of the fashion line was its unisex trousers – produced before the concept existed. First they sewed by hand, using Black Sorina's sewing box that Fanny had kept as a treasure to remember her by, and later they used sewing machines smuggled into the camp by the Greek tanker drivers who supplied the drinking water.

Ioannis Angelopoulos was the spirit behind the smuggling. He was a member of the Cypriot Underground who considered the imprisoned immigrants brothers-in-arms opposing British Imperialism. Initially Fanny saw him as no more than a courier. But at second glance she was impressed by his height, his broad shoulders, and his sun-browned skin. But it was the sight and touch of his hands that made her stop and really look at him. Despite their rough appearance they were soft as silk. She felt it when she handed over the Camel cigarettes doled out by the British. Everyone received six per day. They became a sought-after commodity, and in exchange for cigarettes Ioannis smuggled in fish, fresh vegetables, and cherries from the Troodos Mountains, and notebooks and writing implements for Yitzhak, who set up the "People's University," so that those who had been sentenced to idleness could make use of their time.

"Have you never smoked, *kiriya*?" Ioannis asked Fanny, as his velvet hand fluttered over hers.

"No."

"Does the smell bother you?"

"I lived with a smoker."

He never asked, "Where's your husband?" and she didn't ask him whether he had a partner. When he requested that she sew him a pair of tent trousers, she took apart another canvas sheet and chose the blue cloth. She had to guess at the size.

Trousers for a man. For the first time in a long time she felt a sense of deep satisfaction.

Ioannis pushed aside the rug that had now been suspended to create a makeshift dressing room and stepped out two minutes later preening in his new trousers.

"You look like a consummate refugee," was her comment, "watch out, they may lock you up as well."

"Damn British. Soon we'll be rid of them. Who will do it first, *kiriya*, the Jews or the Cypriots?"

He offered to buy her small carpet, saying he had the perfect spot for it at the entrance to his house in the village of Pissouri on the west side of the island.

"No Ioannis. I can't part with it. It's the only thing left to me from my father's house."

He mumbled something in Greek that she didn't understand. Perhaps he wanted to teach her the word "house" in his native tongue.

On his next trip he brought her a gift of haloumi cheese that he had made himself, wrapped in mint leaves to keep it fresh. Once again she felt the touch of his soft hands.

"*Efcharisto*," she said – "thank you" in Greek. She even gave some haloumi to the dog and decided to name him after the cheese.

When Ioannis stroked him the dog moaned with pleasure.

From Ioannis she learned to say "*kalimera*," and "*kalispera*," and the words sounded to her like the names of Greek goddesses. "It's a great privilege to be on Aphrodite's island," he told her, "the goddess of beauty and love who inspires desire in the hearts of all creatures." But in his broken English the words lost some of their power.

"Have you heard of her, *kiriya*?"

"Yes, she was made of foam in the sea."

"A Jewess who was familiar with Greek mythology? He proudly recounted that it had happened right next to his village. A spring flowed through the rocks there and couples visit it in search of the goddess's blessing.

"You understand, *kiriya*? To be on Aphrodite's island is a blessing."

"Even as a prisoner?"

Ioannis replied, "When you are a free woman, I will take you there."

A free woman. She laughed. His skin was so tanned it was hard to tell whether he blushed.

"And among you Jews, who is responsible for love?" He chose each word with care.

"Among us, God demands all the love for Himself."

In the improvised synagogue in the camp they read the verse from Deuteronomy, "Only the Lord had a delight in thy fathers to love them..." The question as to why he didn't share that love with thy mothers she kept to herself.

"Mameh, do you have a suitor?" her son teased her.

"At my age?"

It's tempting to have him respond, "Every age is the right age for love," but my father would never utter a sentence like that, not even in a novel.

Fanny was then under fifty. Her body was firm, her figure was good, and her skin was smooth. It was her radiant skin that had first attracted Ioannis Angelopoulos and then he found himself imagining her long lashes fluttering under his fingertips.

"Be careful, you might find yourself wanting to stay in Cyprus," Yitzhak told her. But the first person to stay was the first of the immigrants to die. In the protest over the reduction in the quota of immigration permits – a punitive measure taken by the British in response to the armed struggle in the Land of Israel – hundreds of those imprisoned in the camp stormed the fences. The soldiers on guard opened fire, and Moshe Lerer was killed. It fell to Yitzhak to find him an honorable resting place. With special permission from the camp commander Ioannis drove him to Margo, southeast of the capital, Nicosia, to the home of the head of the tiny Jewish community on the island.

Yitzhak approached the man with a quote from Chayei Sarah. Years later, he would tell me that he recalled it from his days at heder. He reminded the head of the community about how the forefather Abraham had stood before the sons of Cheth and asked them for a burial property for his wife. The community leader responded with the words of the sons of Cheth to Abraham, "In the choicest of our graves bury your dead. None of us will withhold his grave from you to bury your dead."

He also remembered how he and the head of the community – he was also a Romanian refugee who had fled the Kishniev uprisings at the start of the

20th century – had stood together on the balcony gazing out at the horizon and beyond. Yitzhak re-named Margo "*Margoa,*" a Hebrew word for rest or serenity, and that is where Moshe Lerer was buried. Later the others who died in the camp joined him there. Many years afterward their bones were transferred to Israel.

Ioannis Angelopoulos waited for Yitzhak until the funeral was over. As a sign of respect he donned his cap and leaned against the side of the blazing hot tanker, listening to the lament of the Hebrew prayers. If Fanny had been permitted to leave the camp, rather than her son, he would have seized the opportunity to propose to her. He imagined the two of them bathing in Aphrodite's stream. She was a goddess who didn't demand all the love for herself. He kept the blue trousers she sewed for him to remember her by, and over the years, whenever Israel was mentioned on the news, he would sneak a glance at them, and stroke them with his hands, now roughened by age.

At dusk, as he drove Yitzhak back to the camp, he wondered whether to confess to the son the feelings he had for his mother and to ask for his help as a matchmaker. He never did, since the sun was about to set and Yitzhak was in a hurry to return.

His feet sank into the pristine sand, and he lost himself in the red glory spreading over the sea – that alluring picture-postcard scene – so that he didn't notice the British colonel waiting impatiently by their tent. He soon saw how upset his mother was. She was clutching the end of the carpet that was hanging on the tent peg as though it was the only thing preventing her from falling.

"You are not refugees without citizenship," the colonel called out to him, waving a document in the air. "We have received notification from the American Foreign Ministry in Washington that represents the citizen Gabriel George Herzig."

He read formally from the document: "His wife Fanny and his son Yitzhak are American subjects and hold valid passports of the United States of America."

Yitzhak took a step back. Fanny tore the carpet from the peg. Haloumi barked.

"His Majesty's government provides your immediate release. Sign here and be on your way. Your father is waiting for you in New York. You are free."

Yitzhak refused to sign. He sent away the dumbfounded British colonel after delivering a loud and explicit refusal. The colonel, who had anticipated that mother and son would fall all over him with tears of gratitude, was appalled at the thought of the scandal that would likely sully the good name of the British with the Americans and might even cost him his rank. After long and fruitless attempts to persuade Yitzhak he turned to Fanny, referring to her time and again as a "free woman." However, she was silent as a stone and just stood there hanging on to the tent. Haloumi barked incessantly as Yitzhak kicked the document into the sand under the carpet. He would receive his freedom only with the rest of them. The whole camp could hear him yelling, "I'm not American. I am Israeli."

4

In the life of a refugee people come and go as if through a revolving door. They are transient guests who flicker and vanish, and few remain lodged in memory. It's impossible to nurture relationships, or to make any kind of emotional investment, since a refugee like Fanny is destined to move on to the next temporary location. She had to leave behind the dog, Haloumi, who stayed in Cyprus, howling miserably at the enforced separation. If she had remained in one place, maybe Fanny would have adopted a dog or taken a chance on a new love. The war had done away with societal conventions, so it wasn't fear of scandal or of a stain on her reputation that prevented her from forming a relationship with a new man, but rather her uncompromising allegiance to her son. The remnants of her love for her husband languished in a safe whose combination was nearly forgotten.

Meanwhile, Gabriel's safe had been blasted wide open, and what had survived in there wasn't his wife, but his son. During the waiting period before he heard from the authorities he often examined the photograph of Yitzhak in the newspaper. One time he interpreted his son's expression as severe and obstinate, and then he would see the opposite in his face. He even taped it up next to his own reflection in the mirror.

As time dragged on with no news, Clara phoned the clerk in Washington again. By now he recognized her voice and her nervous laugh. The annoying

Jewess. Why didn't she give up? For her sake he was supposed to search for a needle in a haystack?

Yes, the message had been passed on to Mrs. Herzig and her son, and he had received the permit, but there was no explanation as to why they weren't on their way to New York. Perhaps the problem was the political situation in that insane region? The British were about to leave and war was expected to break out. He spared Clara what the clerk had said to his colleague as he replaced the receiver on the telephone, "Once again the Jews are dragging everyone into war."

Why was it that this miserable generation, which had endured two World Wars, was destined to live only in the brief respites, Fanny wondered, and then find itself once again next to a battlefield? Had she dared to utter those heretical thoughts aloud, Yitzhak would have responded with fury. For him, the War of Independence wasn't the first in a series. It was true that the Arabs had rejected the UN Partition Plan, but the voice of reason would prevail, and Israel and the Arabs would have to learn to live together, he often repeated.

It wasn't the war that postponed the renewal of contact between Fanny and Gabriel. Yitzhak refused to discuss the confrontation with the British colonel in Cyprus, and as far as he was concerned the words "America" and "father" were buried with the document. However, unknown to him Fanny had secretly retrieved the paper, dusted off the sand and placed it in Black Sorina's sewing box.

When the entry permits finally arrived and the family was preparing to leave Karaolos internment camp she secreted the American document in her rolled-up carpet. The address of "the citizen Gabriel Herzig" continued to dance before her eyes – Clinton Street 122, New York – at each of the subsequent stations on her way: the Shaar Aliya camp at Atlit, the Jewish Agency camp for new immigrants in Givat Shmuel, as part of the group "In Struggle" on the border between Herzliya and Kfar Shmaryahu, and at Kibbutz Alonei Abba, where Yitzhak and Mimi were founding members.

In each of them Fanny lived in a tent. At times she couldn't recall ever having lived under a roof, between walls. Would she be able to re-adapt to living in a house? Maybe she would never want to leave the tents. After all, they had their advantages. You could roll up the canvas and gaze at the sky strewn with stars, higher and brighter than those of Europe. Although unlike the enthusiastic innocents surrounding her, the sight of the sky didn't raise her spirits, but triggered unease. Still, had her son decided to move to the North Pole, she would have trudged along behind him and set up house in an igloo.

The tent in Palestine seemed far inferior to the British one, and its canvas couldn't be used as material for clothes. She was disappointed that she had been forbidden to take along even one original Cyprus fashion item as a souvenir, for the British soldiers searched through their possessions and confiscated everything.

The blue trousers she had sewn for Ioannis Angelopoulos. Did he still have them?

And another question troubled her. Did an object have the power to nourish memory? She had no souvenir of Gabriel, and to the best of her knowledge, he had nothing of hers. So why did he suddenly remember them? Although she was touched by the thought that after so many years he hadn't completely forgotten them, her resentment was stronger. "A woman can hide her love for forty years, but can't conceal her anger for even a day." While Fanny wasn't familiar with the Arab proverb, it was evidence that she had adapted to the Mediterranean region.

It was so hot in the Land of Israel. The air was always almost at boiling point, and in the evenings all one hoped for was a slight cooling breeze. Not consummate perfection after all, in contrast to the promises that had been so generously scattered. Even the Declaration of Independence on the eve of their arrival at their new settlement was received with an absence of enthusiasm. It's true that they crowded around to listen to David Ben-Gurion's historic speech on the radio, but no one burst into spontaneous dance like they did on Rothschild Boulevard by the Tel Aviv Museum. "Maybe it was the exhaustion following months of tension and difficulties attempting to adapt," my father wrote, "or anxiety about what was yet to come."

And maybe the fear of rejoicing was already in their blood?

There's no war on Clinton Street, Fanny thought when an Egyptian plane dropped a bomb on her. At the time she was working as a laborer in an orchard near Herzliya. The walls of the packing house collapsed, but she was unharmed. Who would guarantee that she would survive the next attack?

"Luck doesn't work for us," she told Lizzie-Bertha and Paula who arrived in Israel at the height of the fighting. With Emil they shared an abandoned Arab house on Stanton Street in downtown Haifa. When Lizzie-Bertha found the possessions of the previous tenants who had run for their lives, in terror of the Jews, she thought about the plight of all refugees.

Fanny's tough negotiations with luck would not have embarrassed Gabriel. When the men traveled to Emek Yizrael to build fortifications, she joined them despite the warnings. The German village Waldheim, where they intended to establish a kibbutz, was set up by a faction that had broken off from the German Templars. They had come from Germany in the previous century to hasten the arrival of the Christian messiah and to serve as a moral and economic model. Their village was ten kilometers away, as the crow flies, from Fawzi Al-Qawuqji's military headquarters in Nazareth.

"It's dangerous Mameh," Yitzhak pleaded.

"So why are you going?"

"A man can face the danger."

"Why? Is luck a woman?"

Even the lauded warrior at the head of the Arab Liberation Army wouldn't prevent her from protecting her son. She would force luck's hand – regardless of its gender – and make it work for her.

The Fargo truck lurched along the twists and turns of the gravel path, and Fanny held her breath. Not for fear of the steep curves, but at the sight of the view. It was a small island of Europe in the heart of the Middle East. Slopes planted with oak trees, cyclamen peeking out from under the rocks, and anemones staining the sides of the road red. When the crimson roofs of the German houses came into view Fanny forgot where she was. A main street lined with trees on either side. White stone houses with staircases and wooden balconies, surrounded by gardens.

After helping the men to build the fortifications she had time to wander through the back yards where there still stood barns full of feed and farm buildings for the animals. For a moment she drank in all the things that reminded her of her childhood landscape. Finally she pushed hard on the heavy wooden door of the church in the center of the village and looked up at the bell tower and its weathervane. A mirror image of the world she had left behind, yet inanimate and devoid of life. Waldheim was abandoned, after the British exiled its "fifth column" residents to Australia and all the household contents, including photographs of Hitler, the speeches of Goebbels and swastikas, were left there. In the church Fanny found a handwritten copy of a speech by Dr. Schlaninger, a representative of the Nazi Party, who came especially from Germany to explain about the racial composition of the Jewish people and to warn against their dangers.

They gathered up all these and burned them.

In another irony of fate, it was in the houses of Nazis that these Holocaust survivors found their first homes in Israel. They called the new settlement "Neve Ya'ar," Hebrew for "Forest Home," which is the meaning of the German name "Waldheim." It was also the address on the letter that made its way to New York in early 1949, written by Lizzie-Bertha.

From Stanton Street to Clinton Street.

Fanny's decision to send a letter to Gabriel crystallized when Mimi told her that she was pregnant. My mother told me that she wanted to wait until the cessation of the battles, so that her son could be born in a calm moment.

Her first husband and her baby daughter who had perished were never mentioned.

Yitzhak opened a bottle of Carmel Mizrahi wine that he had bought in the nearby town of Afula, the members of the kibbutz toasted lechayim, and one of the thick-walled buildings on the side of the hill was designated the future Children's House.

The arrival of a new child cracked the code of Fanny's hidden safe, and the sliver of an ember was reignited.

"Write to him," she told her sister, "tell him he's about to be a grandfather."

She herself wasn't capable of writing a single word, not even his name.

5

Shalom, Mr. Herzig,

I understand that your name is now "George," but to me you were, and will always be Gabriel. You probably don't remember me. I am the youngest sister of your wife, of whom you also probably have only a vague memory, if any. After all, you left the family when we were all young, and now we have experienced what we have experienced, and the marks of age and time are seared into us. I don't intend to confront you with your deeds. You'll have to settle your accounts with yourself.

Lizzie-Bertha threw away the rough copy. It was written in German.

Dear Gabriel Herzig,

I am your sister-in-law, inasmuch as you recall that concept. I was a young girl when you left. If I were to say that at times it seems like yesterday, I would be lying, because so many yesterdays have gone by since then, and your image is very vague in my memory, but not your deeds. First and foremost I would like to know whether you have any other offspring.

Lizzie-Bertha threw that page into the trash as well. It was written in Yiddish.

Shalom, Gabriel,

My name is Lizzie-Bertha Katz, and Fanny is my elder sister. We were surprised by your attempt to make contact after so many years, and we don't understand the reason. We have chosen to live in the State of Israel, including your son Yitzhak whose age you can certainly calculate. I would appreciate your letting us know, first and foremost, about your personal situation. Does your son have any siblings?

The fate of that page was the same as its predecessors. It was written in Romanian.

Gabriel "George" Herzig,

In the name of my sister, who you attempted to locate recently in Cyprus, I would like to inform you that she and her son live today on Kibbutz Alonei Abba, previously Neve Ya'ar, in the Jezreel Valley in the State of Israel.

Sincerely,

Lizzie-Bertha Katz

Shivat Zion (Stanton) Street, corner of Maale Hashichrur (The Bourge), Haifa.

P.S. Your son is expecting a child.

Lizzie-Bertha wrote this letter in English. She used stamps from the "Hebrew Post," that bore the picture of an ancient coin from the period of the Great Revolt, stamped with the words "Freedom for Zion." She licked the stamps twice.

They traveled a long way before finding themselves floating in an enamel bowl in the Greenberg family kitchen, slowly drifting apart from their envelope. The melting glue muddied the water a bit. Gabriel had contributed the stamps to Manny's impressive collection – they were his first from Israel.

"Did she also send a photograph?" Manny asked.

He fished out one of the stamps and laid it carefully on a piece of kitchen towel to dry. He had never seen a likeness of the mysterious Fanny, who had been spoken of for so many years. It couldn't be that Gabriel hadn't saved even one picture of her, for in Bukovina it was customary to photograph a couple upon their engagement. Doris had heard Fanny described by members of the organization as having beautiful skin and long eyelashes, but she never dared to question Clara about whether she had found proof.

"They didn't send anything." Gabriel spoke in the plural, although Manny insisted on the feminine singular.

"And was she happy that you made contact?"

Gabriel had no expectations, and therefore he wasn't disappointed by the spare and formal tone of the letter. If Fanny and Yitzhak had chosen to use an intermediary, he assumed that forgiveness wouldn't be part of this story. While Manny was absorbed in his stamp collection, Gabriel sank into regret about the renewed connection. What did he need with unnecessary complications that would upset his comfortable life? And the timing wasn't good either, since he had just embarked on a relationship with M.'s very lovely and very married aunt, after a long and energetic courtship. Anyhow, what was the point of reopening old wounds? They couldn't possibly expect him to apologize at this late date. It would have been better to leave things as they were and make do with dreams about offspring who had inherited his good qualities.

Manny lifted another stamp from the basin, gently shook off the droplets and held it up to the light. His next question was about something else entirely. Why had the Israelis chosen a coin, of all things, to represent their young country? Hadn't it occurred to them that the connection between Jews and money was likely to strengthen the anti-Semitic stereotype? It was hard to imagine that they would make a decision in negligence and haste, although it might be a matter of immaturity. Had he been in their shoes he would have chosen a different symbol –a mezuzah for example, or a yarmulke. After all, they had even designed their flag to look like a prayer shawl.

Despite his criticism, the young country aroused Manny's enthusiasm. For him its establishment was a miracle on a biblical scale, and he was always prepared to open his wallet for the Jewish National Fund. After each donation he would describe to Doris the new forest they had planted on a bare hill in the Zionist wilderness.

"Promise me that you'll donate all the stamps from there to my collection."

Manny Greenberg was an optimist. He was born one, and would remain one, Gabriel thought to himself. Perhaps it was their opposing natures that had cemented their friendship for so many years. How could he explain to him that there was no certainty that this was the start of an extensive correspondence? It was entirely possible that this was to be the first and the last letter. Gabriel actually did remember Lizzie, but not with the additional name, "Bertha." A nuisance of a teenager who had never stopped going on about the contribution of the suffragettes to the betterment of the world. She was more suited to America than to the Land of Israel.

He didn't share the letter's postscript with a living soul, not even his sister. "Your son is expecting a child."

At night he shoved the letter into his dresser drawer, closed his eyes and murmured the verse that comes after the Binding of Yitzhak: "Yitzhak spoke to Abraham his father and said, 'My father!' And he said, 'Here I am, my son.'"

6

There are those who claim that remembering a dream depends on the will of the dreamer, but inasmuch as it depended on him, Gabriel used every ounce of his will to repress any memory of his dreams. Clara, the person with the most seniority when it came to any investigation of his sleeping habits, asserted that although he talked in his sleep and sometimes even yelled – always only in German or Russian – he had never, in all the years they were together, told her about even one of his dreams.

He dismissed her belief in dreams with a contemptuous wave of his hand and declared that he was one of the lucky ones who didn't dream at all.

This time Clara didn't back down. "Even animals dream," she protested.

"I don't remember a thing, so why should I dream what I don't remember?"

Her belief was further strengthened after she read Freud's book, *The Interpretation of Dreams*, a gift from Doris and Manny for her fiftieth birthday. From Gabriel she received a bottle of Chanel No. 5, accompanied by the Yiddish saying, "Women remember their birthdays but forget how old they are."

Even if dreams didn't foresee the future, as the gypsies of Bukovina claim, she hoped that they might be a way to peep into the sealed, unyielding soul of the man to whom she had devoted the better part of her life. She still hadn't lost hope that one day she might break through the thick shell of separateness which had become his second skin.

When he dozed off by the radio she would spy on him and try to decipher his mumblings. Perhaps she would uncover the key to his hidden depths. Once she thought that he had blurted out a word in Russian, which made her cringe. What did he have to do with the Soviet Union? That's all they needed, to suddenly discover a communist stain in his past that would only cause trouble.

"What did your son write to you?"

Clara was convinced that it was the son who had sent the letter. When she asked to see it – after all it was she who was responsible for the renewal of contact – he claimed that he couldn't remember where he'd put it.

She stole a glance at the drawer, but didn't dare to rummage around in it. He had probably hidden it there along with the picture of his wife.

Try as she might, she couldn't forget that unattractive portrait.

"You can't possibly have lost the letter," she feigned innocence, "Maybe you left it at the office?"

"It will turn up in the end."

"What did it say?"

"What you would expect."

"What did you expect?"

"I don't expect anything."

Serial liar. He had always had expectations, mostly related to stocks and lovers. Although she suspected that he had a new lover, she had no more desire to spy on him, as she had in the earlier years of their relationship. At the age of fifty there was no chance of changing him, and "Better an ugly patch than a pretty hole," as the Yiddish proverb went.

And still, despite the fact that according to Freud happiness is an unattainable objective, wasn't the desire to get closer to the goal worth something?

Maybe it was Clara's willpower that activated Gabriel's memory mechanism for dreams. The one he had the night after their conversation about the letter haunted him.

He is walking the streets of a foreign city. The small houses are similar yet not similar to those of Siret or Mihova, except that the walls are plastered bright white. And instead of windows there are mirrors that reflect his image. In one he is a boy, in another an elderly man with a walking stick, and they keep changing. He tries to smile at the alternating images, but they always frown at him. In the distance he can make out the Arc de Triomphe, but the street is too narrow and rundown to be the Champs-Élysées, and as he approaches he discovers a gate located by an estuary that connects between a muddy greenish stream and a gray and turbulent sea.

The eddies swirl around his ankles like the wakes of innumerable ships steadily advancing. He stands on the shore, waiting to be rescued from this place that is suffocating him. It feels as though he stands there for hours. His patience runs out and he wades into the water, waving for help. Maybe one of the passing ships will notice him. Again he sees his reflection, but it is distorted by the foaming sea, and he is surprised to see that it isn't his face.

"Are you the son of my son?" Gabriel asks in the dream, but instead of a reply he is doused with seawater. The salt stings his eyes and everything goes dark.

He awoke in terror, and felt himself all over to make sure that he was there. It was some time before he could discern shapes and the light returned. It was the only night when he was sorry that there was no one by his side.

7

"Blood is thicker than water," Fanny had heard since childhood. Her mother said it, and also her grandmother and her great-grandmother, a dynasty that had whispered, screamed, hissed, and roared the words through the generations. And despite the tinge of extortion, it was still the emergency brake before the final deterioration of the roiling stew of emotions known as "family." Lizzie-Bertha used those words, which have the power to prevent an irrevocable rift or permanent separation between quarreling relatives, in an attempt to persuade Yitzhak to cool down after a heated argument.

"How dare you send him a letter behind my back?" he roared.

"Him," he said, as if referring to someone whose name shouldn't be mentioned and to whom he had absolutely no connection.

The shouts could be heard all along Shivat Zion Street (formerly Stanton Street) in Haifa, from the top of the stone staircase where Lizzie-Bertha lived with her sister and brother-in-law in an apartment that was designated abandoned property, and down to the bottom of the steps where Mimi waited for her husband to return from his courtesy call to his aunts and uncle. In her sixth month of pregnancy it was hard for her to climb all the way up, and she took advantage of the opportunity to be alone – a rare occurrence for someone living on a kibbutz – and look out at the view, which was still foreign and new to her. She was especially captivated by the piece of blue sea that she could just catch sight of from where she was leaning. It was as if a curtain had been momentarily pulled aside to reveal a brief glimpse of the beauty of the land that was so harsh and hostile to those who loved it. For a moment the view obscured the family disagreement taking place above, and Mimi breathed in the powerful smell of spices carried on the air. It was a mixture of sheep's fat, foreign spices, and Romanian kebab.

"What's in your belly?"

The boy was speaking to her in Arabic. He had thick curls and bright, laughing eyes.

She made do with a smile. She wished that she could respond to him with words but had never learned Arabic, and even the Hebrew she spoke was too polished and formal, studied far away in the diaspora.

In sign language the boy offered to help her climb the steps but she cradled her stomach and stayed where she was.

From the apartment at the top of the staircase Yitzhak could be heard shouting that no one could force on him a father he didn't want. Why should he want a connection with someone who hadn't wanted him from the start? Disinclination begets disinclination. Rejection begets rejection.

Meanwhile, Paula and Emil Stein's little daughter Sidi came dancing down the steps. She had been sent out to play while the adults argued.

"Maybe your father will help us all," Paula tried to mollify Yitzhak.

"I don't want his help! We've managed without him for almost thirty years. What does he want from us? To take what we don't have?"

Down below, the Arab boy abandoned his questioning of the strange woman about what she was carrying in her pregnant stomach as he and Sidi played a jumping game on the stairs. He jumped up, she jumped after him. He jumped down, she followed, and their laughter drowned out the shouts from above.

Mimi looked up at the house. Her husband's aunts and uncle spoiled them exquisitely. Potato pancakes with sour cream, blintzes filled with raisins and cheese, mountains of strawberries and whipped cream, and perfectly manicured and engineered watermelon slices always awaited them. And she was charmed by their home. The high ceilings, the vaulted rooms, the painted tiles even in the bathroom. There was an echo that whispered of secrets similar to her own, although she was afraid to acknowledge them and her eyes returned to the children on the stairs.

Jump up, jump down. Over and over. An Arab boy, a Jewish girl, both refugees, both now Israeli citizens, playing together on the same staircase while an Auschwitz survivor looks on, carrying a new child in her womb. How much more charged and symbolic could the picture be?

Sidi wore shiny black shoes – her party shoes. The boy wasn't wearing any shoes at all. He gestured for her to take hers off. They continued their jumping game, both barefoot now. She was a little worried about what the adults would say, but Mimi didn't seem angry.

Yitzhak was still shouting at Lizzie-Bertha.

"How could you do such a thing to my mother?"

"She's the one who asked me to write to him."

"What?"

Lizzie-Bertha insisted that she had carried out Fanny's explicit instructions. It was from Fanny that she had received Gabriel's address in New York.

Yitzhak was dumbstruck. At first he couldn't understand where his mother had found out where that man lived. But what truly bewildered him was the realization that in some part of her she still held on to him, and to the memory of her young love.

That was the moment when Lizzie-Bertha declared, "blood is thicker than water," and the two children suddenly froze on the steps.

With all due respect to Yiddish, the immortal phrase is also used by Iraqi Jews, although in the future tense, "blood doesn't become water." And among the Persian Jews it breaks all records for creativity: "Even if we eat each other's flesh, we won't throw away the bones."

And in Arabic? In honor of the barefoot boy I searched for an equivalent in his language. "Blood doesn't become water" – they have it too.

In the end it was Mimi who convinced Yitzhak to accept his father. "He's our child's grandfather," she said.

He supported her so that she wouldn't trip over the bottom step, and when the patch of blue sea disappeared she added, "Maybe your mother still remembers her first love. Even if you try very hard, it's something that's impossible to forget."

He felt that she was talking about herself.

8

"For your grandson?" asked the saleswoman at Tiffany's.

Clara paused before replying. Not in embarrassment, but because she was in awe of the exceptional color that met her eyes no matter which way she turned her head. "Tiffany Blue" – which was added to the official color catalog as number 1837, to mark the year when the renowned store was established on Fifth Avenue, corner of Fifty-Seventh Street.

The display table stood between Clara and the saleswoman and her eyes caressed the spectacular objects arrayed beneath the expanse of glass, in which the light medium robin egg blue color was also reflected. Was it inspired by the color of the sea, maybe the one along Israel's coastline, or was it the blue commanded by the Bible?

On one of their Saturday walks along Fifth Avenue, when Clara had stopped at the Tiffany display window, Gabriel had quoted a verse from Numbers, "Speak to the people of Israel, and tell them to make tassels on the corners of their garments throughout their generations, and to put a cord of blue on the tassel of each corner."

But the founder, Charles Lewis Tiffany, wasn't Jewish.

The saleswoman jangled the key and deliberated whether the customer was worth the effort of opening the case. Was this a serious buyer with an unlimited budget, or one of those nuisances who loved to ogle the items that they could never own, as if the store was a museum?

She examined Clara with a practiced eye. Well-dressed, although the garments weren't top-quality needlework. Hair dyed a reddish color and swept up at the back of her neck. Slightly clumsy shoes. Not the height of fashion, but no cheap imitations either. What convinced her to serve the customer was the scent of Chanel No. 5 that wafted from her, which signified the appropriate economic status. She couldn't know that Clara had worn the perfume in honor of her outing to the store, since for her Tiffany was the holy of holies. In the years of attempting to convince him to marry her she would drag Gabriel to the display of wedding rings in the Tiffany window. After despairing of ever being a bride she continued to visit Tiffany's alone and survey the wares like a child at a candy store. She vowed that one day she wouldn't be "just looking," and that someone else would pay the bill.

The saleswoman showed her the display. As the customer's hand rested on a miniature hairbrush shaped like a heart she noticed the absence of a wedding ring. It was too late to take back the question about the grandson.

"Boy or girl?" she asked as she withdrew a set of silver combs. One had a blue tassel attached at the end, while the other was adorned with a pink one.

"It's for a child who hasn't been born yet."

The saleswoman raised her eyebrows.

"Isn't that tempting the evil eye for you?" and she hastened to add that there wasn't anything in the store that bore a Jewish symbol, although "we have numerous clients of your sort."

"Of our sort?"

"You know… I have something that I think you'll like."

She chose a porcelain savings bank shaped like a little elephant and Clara was drawn to its Tiffany blue eyes that twinkled at her from either side of its trunk.

"Take it, take it, feel it. There's room for plenty of coins. It's just right for you people."

Clara held it in her hand and with a hesitant finger stroked the plump little elephant. It really was pleasing to the touch. For a moment she was tempted to tilt her palm downward just to watch the woman's face as the elephant crashed to pieces on the floor. But why should she pay for the damage? Clara pulled herself together. She instructed the woman to show her the other items on display and deliberately spent much longer than necessary examining each one, in private revenge.

As if there weren't clubs in New York that restricted their membership to non-Jews. Not to mention apartment buildings such as the one from which Manny and Doris had been turned away, with the explanation that they "didn't match the agreed-upon tenant profile."

Clara thoroughly enjoyed torturing the saleswoman. She spent ages examining a tiny silver-plated cup, even demanding that it be filled with tea so that she could ensure that it didn't leak, heaven forfend. She also insisted on testing the solid silver bubble maker with soapy water brought specially from the employees' kitchen, and then announced that it was a ridiculously unnecessary item in today's world. As for the picture frame, the store's best-selling children's gift – she held it up to the light the better to see the hot air balloon etched in the corner, and decreed that the artist had failed to convey a sensation of flight.

The saleswoman was on the verge of collapse. If she hadn't been worried about her job she would have thrown her customer out. When Clara was done considering the selection of silver spoons and mulling over the respective virtues of the one with the cut out stars versus the one shaped like a heart she finally chose a delicate teaspoon whose handle was carved with a father bear holding a bear cub. The saleswoman let out a relieved sigh and the cash register opened.

There was no chance that Gabriel would miss the symbolism of the father embracing the son, Clara told Anna as she showed her the gift, wrapped in a soft felt pouch, colored Tiffany Blue, of course. They were at Gabriel's apartment. She didn't mention the outrageous price she had paid.

"What will the baby do with a silver spoon on a kibbutz?" Anna asked her.

"Oatmeal can also be eaten with a silver spoon."

"You don't understand, Clara. On a kibbutz everyone has equal rights. No one has any personal possessions."

"Not even a child?"

"The teaspoon will belong to everyone," Anna insisted. "Better you should send them preserved milk or powdered eggs. At least all the little mouths will be able to enjoy those."

"So the descendants of Gabriel the capitalist are communists," Clara laughed. The irony of fate. The man from Wall Street might have to share. "Let's see him share his living quarters with total strangers and eat in a common dining hall."

Gabriel's ticket for the journey by ship from New York to Haifa with a short stop in Marseille sat waiting by the open suitcase. It already contained his best suits and a selection of ties, including the one he had bought especially for the circumcision ceremony, assuming that the grandchild would be a boy.

The ideological debate about Zionism and Communism took place between the mistress and the sister in the bedroom, while Gabriel sat smoking in the kitchen, reading through his ticker tape.

"Tell me Anna, did he ever tell you about what happened to him in Russia?"

Anna lowered her voice further as she explained to Clara that her brother refused to discuss that period. There had been rumors that he was tortured during the days of the communist revolution, but no one had dared to question him about his early experiences. And anyway, so much time had passed now. It was unlikely whether he himself remembered Russia. She then provided Clara with confused explanations about the difference between an Israeli kibbutz and a Bolshevik commune.

"So everyone shares what they don't have," Clara concluded the discussion, and Anna agreed that "there is full equality when no one has anything."

Gabriel was moving around in the kitchen. First they heard his footsteps, then they heard him switching on the radio.

Even though the sounds covered her next question, Clara asked it in a whisper.

"Do you remember her?"

Anna knew exactly who Clara was referring to. Ever since Gabriel's surprising decision to travel to Israel she had thought often of Fanny. For years she continued to refer to her as "my sister-in-law" even in the presence of Clara, who always seemed unmoved. She still remembered the day when Fanny had held her hand and told her about the faithful wife from Greek mythology who had never lost hope that her husband would return to her. But if Penelope hadn't recognized Ulysses after two decades, how would Fanny recognize Gabriel after a 28-year separation?

The question troubled Clara as well. When Anna left the bedroom she opened the dresser drawer for a second time, alert to any sound from the kitchen.

The old photograph she had come upon by chance years before was easy to find this time.

That likeness of Fanny would help Gabriel to recognize her. She ran her fingers over the features that hadn't faded. But what if the years had been kind to her and granted her a touch of beauty? He was unlikely to recognize her.

What did it matter? One way or the other she would be a stranger to him, for it is impossible to bridge the chasm of the years. The expression "blood is thicker than water," that well-known inhibitor, flashed through her mind as well. It wasn't a divorce or the formalizing of her relationship with Gabriel that were important to her now, and not even Gabriel's son who she had liked immediately, but the future grandson or granddaughter.

His would be hers.

Clara Mendel longed so deeply for family to fill the emptiness inside her.

Even if she never became his legal wife, and would forever be only his common-law partner, she would adopt his relatives. She had a feeling that Fanny wouldn't object.

She wedged the photograph underneath the white ribbon tied around the gift from Tiffany's, and when she accompanied Gabriel to the New York Port, she informed him that Fanny was also packed with his things.

His eyes glazed over. He had no idea what she was talking about.

And the silver spoon, what was its fate? Clara never found out that the kibbutz council held a serious debate about the gift. Opinions varied. There were those who held that everyone had a right to a personal possession that had sentimental value, but that was a minority opinion, and Yitzhak didn't interfere.

The result of the vote was a unanimous decision to send the spoon to a silversmith in Haifa. Father bear and his bear cub were melted down and the kibbutz used the proceeds to buy sacks of seeds to plant crops.

On November 28, 1949, the vessel *Negba* anchored at Haifa Port. My grandfather didn't know that two days previously his first grandchild was born. It was a boy, just as he had hoped.

9

Fanny refused to go to meet him. The thought of standing before the husband who had abandoned her and saying the words, "Do you remember me?" was more than she could bear. In any case, it was a trick question, which would only cause both the questioner and the respondent to be unsure of who they were. There's nothing more humiliating than to treasure the memory of someone dear to us only to discover that he or she doesn't remember us at all.

Fanny wanted to preserve her self-respect. Yitzhak would have to deal with the challenge of recognizing him. In any case he and Gabriel didn't know each other, so there was no test of memory involved. But her carpet of memories was unfurled, and she was surprised to discover that the fibers were still vibrant, and by some miracle the original colors hadn't faded over time. Even the memory of the last time they had lain together was reignited. If the others on the kibbutz had known what "kibbutz member Tzippora" was imagining at night, they would have called an emergency meeting.

An important matter, fellow members: Is a person permitted to maintain intimate assets and arouse oneself in private, set apart from the interests of the group?

Go forth and see, a woman of her age sprawled on a straw mattress in a narrow Jewish Agency-issue cot revisiting twenty-eight-year-old desires. Desire, Fanny's advocate at the kibbutz meeting will claim, is a non-perishable resource, and imagination is the ally of memory.

Her skin is still clear, her lashes long and extravagant, but in her hair are streaks of grey.

Gabriel had his anxieties as well. It wasn't memories of Fanny that assailed him, but Doris Greenberg's objection to his trip. She warned him endlessly about a settling of accounts, painting horror stories about what was waiting for him: revenge of the mother, hostility of the son, an interminable litany of accusations.

"They will be cruel to you, they'll punish you, drown you in their bitterness."

How could he travel without a companion to defuse the anger and play the part of conciliator? Had he lost his mind? Manny offered his services, and then Anna also volunteered to be his lightning rod. Abe promised to take care of the children in her absence.

But Gabriel stood firm and insisted, "I can take care of myself." Doris wouldn't let up. The people in the Zionist wasteland were wounded souls, tending to outbursts. They hadn't yet healed from the horrors of what they had experienced in Europe, not to mention the War of Independence that had barely ended. And besides, a country of Jews is a dangerous idea which will just make it easier to annihilate them. And if there must be a concentration of Jews with independent sovereignty, wouldn't it be preferable to choose a more comfortable and less disputed corner of the world? Zion could be imagined anywhere. Why this insistence on the Middle East, roiling with compulsions and accounts to settle? Israel was a country of spite, Doris bemoaned, although this in no way affected the fact that she would continue to donate to the Jewish National Fund to her dying day, so that at the very least they could enjoy a little shade over there.

At the emergency family meeting convened in New York everyone suggested to Gabriel that he postpone his trip. Sending money or a package would be sufficient to defuse the loaded atmosphere, and pave the way to a future meeting under more conciliatory circumstances. What was the rush? So many years had passed, and a little more time wouldn't make any difference.

Only Clara remained silent.

During the voyage, he often reflected on her support for his trip to Israel. For a moment he doubted her motives. Could it possibly be a plot? Perhaps she was the vengeful one who bore a grudge, a sort of Delilah tempting him into the lion's den to be rid of him after years of disappointment. Every time he opened his suitcase, that "Tiffany Blue" radiated from the wrapping of her gift. She had refused to tell him what she had bought, claiming it was a secret.

Tiffany's didn't have any knives, Gabriel reminded himself, staring out at another blue that had nothing in common with the unique shade of No. 1837. The clouds and the sky were like a grey fabric, from which an annoying rain poured down. His imagination was kindled as well, only it wasn't Fanny or Yitzhak who starred there but he himself in the role of the sandek who holds the infant boy on his lap at his circumcision ceremony. He dismissed Doris's grim prophecies as the reaction of a hysterical woman. After all, even in the family of our forefathers, rife with discord and conflict, Jacob and Esau reconciled after years of mutual loathing.

"But Esau ran to meet Jacob and embraced him; he threw his arms around his neck and kissed him. And they wept." If Esau the betrayed and the deceived was able to overcome his fury and pursuit of vengeance, there was a chance that Fanny and Yitzhak were also prepared to turn a new page, or else Lizzie-Bertha wouldn't have sent the letter.

And still, he was anxious. It could end in tears, and not necessarily of the conciliatory kind shed by the sons of the biblical Yitzhak.

It was Gabriel's second sea voyage and the opposite of his first. No deck reeking of vomit, but a spacious cabin in First Class, with a private bathroom that he was especially grateful for when they hit a storm near the Strait of Gibraltar. He missed the moment when they moved from the Atlantic Ocean to the Mediterranean Sea because this time he was seasick. He spent two full days under the shower which was the only thing that soothed his writhing gut. Once the sea had spent its fury he lay for hours on the upper deck smoking and staring out at the waves, and in the evening he dined at the captain's table, along with two enthusiastic proponents of Israel Bonds, a mother and daughter, each of whom invited him to spend the night in her company.

The man in the elegant suit with the slicked back hair and ever-present cigarette looked to them like some mysterious movie star traveling incognito. And the other person to fall under his spell was Chief Engineer Juan-Pablo, a Spaniard who was involved with the illegal immigration operations. He admired the Zionist inventiveness and for the entire duration of the voyage he kept his eye on the attractive man at the captain's table. When Gabriel gently declined the offers of seduction from first the daughter and then the mother, the engineer offered himself. Apologizing, Gabriel assured him that had he been attracted to men, the engineer would have been his first choice.

They dropped anchor at Marseille, where Gabriel transferred to the Zim liner *Negba,* since at that time there was no direct route from New York to Haifa. To his surprise, once again he saw Juan-Pablo burst out of the engine room. Now he revealed that he was a descendant of the Anusim. As a child he had come upon his grandmother lighting candles in secret, although she also frequented the church on Sundays. After Mass she would point to the crucified statue and whisper, "Jesus was a Jew. Don't forget."

"I smuggled our persecuted people to the Land of Israel. Grandmother would have been proud," Juan-Pablo told Gabriel in a voice choked with emotion.

From the time of its founding he had dreamed of visiting Israel. Maybe there he would discover his roots. He hoped to find true love in the country whose proclamation of independence declared that Israel "…will uphold the full social and political equality of all its citizens without distinction of race, creed, or sex…"

In Israel, he wouldn't be discriminated against because of his sexual preference, he said. There was no doubt that the Jews would remember that men who loved men also perished in the gas chambers, just as they did.

Gabriel remained silent. Why should he be the one to tell the naïve Spaniard about mankind's selective memory? Who could guarantee that the Jews would display fraternity toward other persecuted peoples?

"Are you also going home, Horche?" That was Juan-Pablo's version of the name "George," with which Gabriel had introduced himself.

"I'm just going for a visit."

An Israeli flag fluttered above them. For the first time, Gabriel saw it from up close. The shade of blue was different from what he had expected. Darker, more opaque, and the Star of David was somewhat off-center, perhaps it was the buffeting of the wind. He adjusted his tie as he stood before the word "Negba," painted in Hebrew letters below the previous names that had been erased: Equador, Santa Olivia, and Luxor.

Juan-Pablo was also fascinated by the foreign letters. "That is the language that Jesus spoke." And while Gabriel was explaining that the son of the carpenter from Nazareth actually spoke Aramaic, a crowd of Jews from Morocco walked up the ship's gangway. The Grand Arénas transit camp in Marseilles had been their waystation on their journey to Israel. Elderly women wearing headscarves climbed heavily aboard. Men with deeply lined faces and youth brimming with the future also surged ahead, all of them carrying bundles tied with string.

Although they didn't speak Yiddish, they reminded Gabriel of the population of Siret or Mihova.

They didn't know English, and Gabriel didn't speak a word of French or Moroccan Arabic, and yet he was able to communicate with them through prayer.

"Blessed art Thou, Lord, King of the universe, Who sets captives free. Blessed art Thou, Lord, King of the universe, Who restores sight to the blind."

Verses from the Morning Prayers in an abundance of accents merged with the announcement over the loudspeakers in virginal Hebrew, "We are nearing the Haifa coast."

It was a wintry November day, the sun concealed behind a thick blanket of cloud. A broken promise of warmth. Alternating blessings and tears swirled around Gabriel. One of the Moroccan immigrants chanted psalms with all his heart, "When the Lord restored the fortunes of Zion, we were like those who dreamed." Juan-Pablo left the engine room, pointed to the summit of the Carmel and made the sign of the cross.

"Look, Horche, how beautiful is the land of the Jews."

And yet all Gabriel could see was a veil of fog.

10

Lizzie-Bertha and Yitzhak stood on the pier, narrowing their eyes. A motley blend of humanity was jammed together on the deck of the *Negba* that had just docked. How would they recognize him?

Although it was she who was meant to have Gabriel fixed securely in her memory, Lizzie-Bertha couldn't visualize a single one of his features. Was he tall, as she seemed to recall, or had he become stooped over with the weight of the years? What kind of hair did he have? Had it turned white? Was it thinning? Perhaps he was completely bald? Men were known to develop a paunch, to grow a double chin, and to lose all trace of what they had been in their youth. Women, on the other hand, preserved their vitality and beauty, even underneath the wrinkles and flaccid skin. What still burned in her memory was her brother-in-law's withdrawn and taciturn nature. But those characteristics were no help when it came to identifying him in a crowd.

The passengers started to walk down the ramp. Yitzhak strained for the sound of Yiddish among the chorus of Moroccan Arabic and French that bombarded him from every direction. Many of the new immigrants bent to kiss the ground, or more precisely the pier, that had earned the nickname "The Platform of Tears." Yitzhak didn't bother to search for his father among them. He had no doubt that Gabriel would never be described as a sensitive soul. Instead he approached a member of the crew standing off to the side, although for some reason he seemed quite emotional himself.

"Excuse me, but was there an American on your ship?"

The response, in a thick Spanish accent, was "I met only one, Horche."

Horche. George. That wasn't him.

And suddenly Yitzhak was filled with relief. His father hadn't come. He had changed his mind at the last minute. No surprise there. Desertion was just his style. Hadn't that always been his way? It was possible that he had never boarded the ship in Marseille. If he had turned around and returned to New York it was all to the good.

He found himself saying the blessing for good riddance – the one that the father of a bar mitzvah boy recites for his son when the boy assumes the yoke of the commandments at age thirteen.

Yitzhak was dealing with a double burden of stress, since instead of traveling to the hospital in Afula to collect his wife and his two-day-old son he had had no choice but to travel to Haifa to meet his estranged father.

The sounds of weeping assailed him, but he was dry-eyed. What shook him was the realization that three years before he had been dragged off that same Platform of Tears by British soldiers who had forced him onto the ship that took him to exile in Cyprus, and now, who would believe it, he wasn't a refugee without a country anymore. His son – as yet unnamed – had been born an Israeli citizen.

Relatives of the new arrivals burst through the gate and surged ahead. People were locked in embraces, Jewish Agency officials scurried around with documents, and Lizzie-Bertha strode through the human volcano asking if anyone had seen an American tourist. She had no doubt that he was there. They just had to find him.

A girl clung to the hem of Yitzhak's coat, mumbling agitatedly in Moroccan Arabic as though she had seen a vision. Maybe it was his unkempt kibbutznik appearance. He searched his pockets, hoping to find some chocolate or candy, but all he came up with was a safety pin, a ubiquitous item. The coat was from the clothing storeroom on the kibbutz and the garments he received never fit him properly. The child was compelled to make do with a smile, as Yitzhak turned to the Jewish Agency representative.

"Excuse me, could you please give me a piece of paper and a pen?"

"Who are you sir, and to whom are you reporting on the situation?"

Winter was early, and the official was anxious about the floods at the immigrant and transit camps. The *Davar* newspaper had reported a "catastrophe." People up to their knees in water and tents and shacks overturned. Only once he was persuaded that the man in the oversized coat was not an agitator who had come to foment unrest among the new arrivals did he tear a page out of his notebook and lend him a pen.

Yitzhak hastily scrawled the name "Herzig" and used the safety pin to attach the page to his lapel.

Lizzie-Bertha was in the office, requesting the ship's manifest so she could check the names of the passengers. The pouring rain that had started to fall was breaking up the knots of emotional people. Yitzhak was practically the only one on the emptying platform. He had no umbrella, and so he took refuge under a jutting awning. The rain quickly turned to hail. Through the curtain of falling ice he could just make out a figure walking toward him as though he was out for a stroll in the park. From the hat on his head Yitzhak realized that the figure was a man. Only later did he notice the elegant coat made of top-quality British fabric, custom designed by a master tailor. A piece of paper with a name on it was affixed to the man's soggy lapel.

They hadn't coordinated in advance, and here, despite everything, a resemblance was revealed between father and son.

On the Platform of Tears they were the only two who kept their distance. They regarded each other for a long moment, and then they shook hands without exchanging a word. Gabriel was the first to extend his, although his grip was weak. Juan-Pablo, observing them through the office window, wondered who the young man was, who received Horche with such formality. He had the feeling that the American had a secret no less deep than his own.

The rain and the hail soaked both name tags and the letters bled away. Yitzhak's cheeks were coated with moisture while his father's face remained dry, protected by the wide brim of his hat.

It wasn't until Lizzie-Bertha approached them that Gabriel finally spoke. "You I remember," he said in Yiddish, and she noticed that he spoke with an American accent.

They went on foot from the port to Stanton Street. Confronted with the water cascading down the steps Gabriel hesitated. He looked questioningly at Yitzhak who nodded and then he hopped over the first step and began the climb. Lizzie-Bertha walked between them, narrowing the gap.

Halfway up Gabriel set down his suitcase on the landing, which had become a waterfall.

"Where's Fanny?"

"She's waiting for you," said Lizzie-Bertha, motioning toward the houses above.

The slightest of movements could be seen through the glass, and then it was gone.

11

A few hours previously. Dawn breaks on the kibbutz. It's a gloomy winter's day, bitter cold. In the middle of the tent, standing on the rug from Siret, is a kerosene heater that emits miminal heat and many noxious fumes. Fanny is alone. Yitzhak has gone to the office of the kibbutz secretary to get the keys for the truck he will drive to the Haifa port. Kibbutz-member Amalia has volunteered to go in his stead to collect Mimi and the baby from the hospital in Afula. His mood is dark, and he and Fanny barely speak.

On the hook above her narrow Jewish Agency-issue cot there hangs a small mirror and she examines her reflection. The air shimmering with the flames from the heater blurs her image somewhat. She runs her fingers over the web of tiny lines that have accumulated beneath her eyelids and the fine indentations in her forehead, lingering over the tracks around her lips.

"Wrinkles should merely indicate where smiles have been," said Mark Twain, an American writer, not one of whose books Fanny had ever read. But for her, wrinkles were evidence of precisely the opposite. In her case they were a map of her sorrows. And although she was still an attractive woman, she saw only the half-empty glass when she looked at herself. Her only consolation was the photograph of the woman she had found on the day when Gabriel left her. If her rival was that plain, tight-lipped woman with the sour expression, then perhaps he would overlook the changes age had wrought in her.

Aging, she sighed in despair to her mirror, why did it always come at the worst possible time?

In a special gesture agreed upon at the kibbutz general meeting in honor of the reunification of the family, Fanny was permitted to choose any dress she liked from the communal closet. However, she made do with a dark skirt and a white shirt, rubbing out the stains in a bucket of water and bleach. One particularly stubborn stain withstood the scrubbing, so she concealed it with her cross stitch embroidery.

The mirror on the hook was too small to allow her a view of her whole body. And although her active life on kibbutz and the Spartan fare had helped her to keep her figure, this was of little comfort to her as she readied herself to meet Gabriel. It was impossible to make the twenty-eight years that had passed disappear, but it was also unlikely that he was the same handsome man she had fallen in love with at first sight.

How was it possible that she had endured all those years of forlorn abandonment and still that inner trembling remained?

"Old love doesn't sour like milk" – the Yiddish saying was the explanation that Fanny gave to Mimi to explain her decision to receive Gabriel in Israel. The kibbutz secretariat supported the decision, and the members had their own motives. A person who lived in America was likely to be well-to-do and might be a source of economic assistance. Family reconciliation seasoned with some kibbutz-style hospitality might just convince him to open his wallet.

Kibbutz-member Anutza made an emotional speech. The anticipated reunion was nothing short of a miracle.

"And Elijah picked up the child and carried him down from the room into the house. He gave him to his mother and said, "Look, your son is alive!" she quoted from the Book of Kings. "If relatives rediscover one another after so many years, we mustn't give up hope. Those we thought were dead may suddenly reappear."

When Fanny recited the phrase about how old love never sours, Mimi turned her face away and Fanny knew she was crying. Like her unknown father-in-law, Mimi had also hoped for a boy child, but not because she was concerned about continuing the dynasty or preserving the family name.

She feared that a daughter would be too painful a reminder of the child she had lost.

The next in line would be me, but I wouldn't come along for a few years yet, and by that time my older brother would have managed in many ways to heal some of the pain of Mimi's loss.

Paula and Emil tiptoed around their home on Stanton Street during the hours of waiting. Even Sidi was sent to her room and told to keep quiet. To Paula the thunder was an ominous warning, but Emil laughed.

"It's just the welcome that Gabriel deserves. He's being drenched from the sky with all the tears your sister has accumulated because of him."

"I hope the sky isn't pissing on us," was Paula's only response.

Fanny ignored them. Her face was glued to the window, but she wasn't worried about wrinkles now, and in any case she could barely see her reflection due to the screen of falling rain. At the sound of footsteps on the stairs leading up to the house she felt the pounding of her heart to the same rhythm, strong as a sledgehammer in the hands of some crazy Kalman-Zelig.

I can make her regret her decision. In this fictional account I can have her banish her contemptible husband and refuse to meet him. I can make her desert him – behave just like he would. Finally she would be rid of him. She could settle that account and leave him on the other side of the door, humiliated and despised. The temptation is great to be the Goddess of Revenge, only my grandmother won't allow it.

"That's enough, granddaughter," she tells me, "You have no right to interfere. Let me fight my battles alone." And then she threatens, "If you rewrite history, you won't be born."

Fanny and none other opened that door and stood erect before him.

"Hello, Gabriel. It's me."

He removed his hat, making puddles on the floor, and bowed to her politely, as if meeting her for the first time. Who would have believed that years before this man and this woman had enjoyed nights of passion together. Well he hasn't lost his manners, was the first thought she had. You can take the Bukovinian out of Bukovina, but you can't take the Bukovina etiquette out of the man, Lizzie-Bertha would whisper to Paula as they set the table for lunch. Sidi peeked out of her room and chirped, "Can I come out now? Did the uncle from America come?"

On the doorstep Gabriel extended his hand formally to Fanny. His handshake wasn't weak. She caressed his fingers for a moment too long, he felt a pinch of pain, and then he let go.

12

What did they talk about? What do people discuss when a poisonous cloud hovers between them? Everything is directed at keeping at bay what is potentially explosive. They navigate around the words of the mundane conversation, all the while inspecting each other like strategists preparing for the decisive battle; buying time until the inevitable explosion occurs.

"How was the voyage?"

"How long have you been living on kibbutz?"

"What kind of a city is New York?"

"Do you Israelis also hold a circumcision ceremony or are you new Jews?"

A ballet of general questions and measured responses.

It is the silences around the table that a fly on the wall would try to listen in to. From the secret exchanges of glances it would glean a considerable amount of information.

Fanny watched Gabriel as he ate. He scrutinized her as she served the food. She inspected his manicured hands. He studied her figure. She watched him deal with the lakerda fish and carefully set aside its bones. He peeked at the outline of her breasts through her white shirt.

She saw that he didn't wipe his mouth with a napkin, but with a starched handkerchief that he plucked from the pocket of his elegant suit, and he noticed the stain under her needlework.

Most of all, Fanny followed his glances at Yitzhak at the end of the table. Almost in supplication. Her son ate nothing at all and didn't ask his father even one question. All he wanted was to be on his way and to see his wife and baby. She saw no resemblance between them.

The fly on the wall manages to pick up a few more details that glitter in memory's emergency storeroom. Her crumpled nightdress discarded on the floor by the wall. The trail of his kisses on her breasts. Her nipples in his mouth. Her warm hand gripping him, stroking.

And both are remembering the celebration of Yitzhak's circumcision in Siret.

The new baby – only that topic somewhat defuses the tension.

It was the period of *Tzena* or Austerity in Israel, and Paula had used up her best coupons to prepare the meal. There were no whole chickens to be had, so Emil bought some chicken breasts at an exorbitant price on the black market, and she used them to prepare *krmendale* – Bukovina-style schnitzel – served with eight grams of noodles bought with her coupons. The daily allowance of fifty-eight grams of sugar, sixty grams of flour, twenty grams of margarine, and two eggs from the Tnuva food processing cooperative, she mixed together to bake a cake that she topped with five grams of crumbled biscuits. Apart from the menu determined by Dov Yosef, Minister of Rationing and Supply, she made cutlets from mallow leaves that Emil had gathered that morning from a nearby yard.

He protested, "In Transnistria we ate garbage off the ground. Who would believe that we would have to do the same thing in Israel?"

Paula wasted time persuading him that mallow was healthy. The neighbors from Casablanca said that it was full of vitamins, a suitable substitute for meat. She asked Emil to help her to dry the leaves that had been absorbing the rainwater all morning, which actually made them easier to mix into a green paste. To enhance the mixture she used her one remaining egg from her stock of coupons.

Gabriel thanked Paula for going to so much trouble and expounded on the financial advice he would provide to Ben-Gurion and his ministers about how to solve the financial issues that plagued the young country.

"They have to set up factories. Attract foreign investment. Create a stock exchange."

He rose from the table, and extracted the gifts from his suitcase. Small vials of Chanel No. 5 for Paula and Lizzie Bertha, a colorful silk tie for Emil, a box of chocolates for Sidi. For Fanny and Yitzhak he held out an envelope bursting with dollars. Yitzhak pushed it away and his arm blocked Fanny. One bill floated down but no one stooped to retrieve it.

"We don't have private possession on kibbutz," it was the first sentence that Yitzhak had uttered to his father.

"It's for the boy. I'll open a bank account for him. Have you thought of a name yet?"

Gabriel bent down, picked up the errant bill and shoved it into the envelope.

It was a very awkward moment. Even the fly on the wall would admit that the single dollar bill was a trigger for a potentially particularly explosive memory. Luckily, just then Sidi opened her box of chocolates and her lip-smacking joy broke the silence.

The package from Tiffany's remained in the case. It was neither the time nor the place to present the gift from Clara.

He looked down at the exquisitely beautiful painted floor tiles. Paula had worked extra hard to make them shine for his visit. Then he examined the arched ceiling.

"Who did you buy the house from?"

"We didn't buy it."

"You got it for free?"

"From the government."

"A generous government you have. I wonder who paid for it."

Silence.

"Who lived here before?"

"We don't know."

"Where are they?"

"They left."

"Why did they leave?"

"Because of the war."

"And what will you do if they come back?"

It was Lizzie-Bertha who answered his questions, except for the last one, to which Fanny shot back a retort.

"Whoever leaves – leaves. We also won't be going back to what we had."

For a moment it seemed as though she had removed the pin from the grenade. But Gabriel restrained himself.

Not for a moment were the two left alone together. During the meal and afterward they were surrounded by the members of the family. It may have been deliberate, to create a buffer and postpone the explosion for as long as possible.

Yitzhak's irritability didn't bode well. He seemed like the grenade from which the pin had been extracted. They had barely tasted the cake when he began to hurry them on their way, saying that they had to get back before dark. He removed the kibbutz overcoat from its hanger and it was clear it had seen better days. The page with the washed-out name was still attached with the safety pin. Yitzhak tore it off and left the balled up paper on the plate with the cake crumbs.

Only on the threshold, as Gabriel was helping Fanny with her coat, did their eyes meet and the unasked questions hung in the air between them.

– Do you live with the woman in the photograph?

– Do you have another man?

She threaded her arms through the sleeves and he straightened her coat from behind. It was the first intimate contact between them. She thought a caress was bestowed, but she couldn't be sure.

Before they climbed into the truck there was an argument about the seating arrangements. Gabriel offered Fanny the front seat, beside Yitzhak who was driving. She insisted on sitting in the back. Not because she believed that that was a woman's place, but because at this stage she preferred to contend with only the back of his neck. To see him as a tourist who was passing through.

As he had come, so he would go.

Gabriel, striving to form some connection with his son, chose to tell him about the behavior of stocks, how they rose and fell and how important it was to identify opportunities. He spoke in praise of America, which had provided a safe haven and transformed him from a refugee into a citizen with rights and possessions. He even mentioned the society for people from Bukovina, omitting any detail about his private life. He occasionally turned around to make sure that Fanny was listening.

A faint scent arose from her, but it wasn't lilacs.

Near the town of Tivon he suggested to Yitzhak that they switch places. He was an experienced driver he said. In New York he drove a Chevrolet, the latest model, and he had never had an accident.

Yitzhak refused. "You don't know the roads. Nothing works smoothly here."

The gravel road in the Jezreel Valley was crooked and narrow, and the passengers swayed in the battered truck. Fanny held fast to the door handle as the remains of Bukovinian *krmendale* sloshed around in her stomach. Yitzhak slowed down. Thousands of droplets shone on the branches of the dense thicket of oak trees, and the wintry landscape looked totally European to Gabriel. This wasn't the desolate sunbaked Levant he had been expecting.

What expectations did he have? Fanny wondered. What did he hope to achieve with this visit? At each question the ancient fluttering was revived within her. To her joy or her sorrow, he was still an attractive man. For twenty-eight years she hadn't slept with a man, and now she was amazed to feel the dampness between her legs.

They missed the sign for Neve Ya'ar, as the early darkness cloaked the surroundings. It wasn't until Yitzhak pushed down on the gas pedal that Gabriel realized that they had entered the kibbutz. They galloped past the German cemetery, and the white gravestones pierced the night.

"So many dead you have?" asked Gabriel, a tone of mockery in his voice. The answer was on the tip of Fanny's tongue, but she didn't have a chance to respond. Yitzhak parked by the church, pulled up the handbrake with a screech and prepared to catapult himself into the nearby Children's House. Light shone from between the slats of the wooden shutters, and Mimi's silhouette could be seen behind them.

Yitzhak stopped suddenly at the open door.

"Do you have other children?"

"You are my only one," Gabriel replied.

13

When a child on kibbutz said, "I'm going home," he didn't mean to his parents' house. The two-day-old creature that lay in a bed in the Children's House on Kibbutz Neve Ya'ar didn't yet know how to talk, not to mention to espouse kibbutz ideology, every fiber of his being was concentrated in his rooting for his mother's nipple.

For the first time in years Mimi felt that she had found her place. And it was the sleeping arrangement at the Children's House, so reviled and disparaged by those who grew up with it and never ceased to lament the ordeal, which granted her a temporary respite from the nightmares of her past. Were it not for the support of the more experienced mothers it is unlikely that she would have overcome her anxieties and learned to care for her baby without sinking into a depression about the daughter she had lost.

The evidence of her deep loss touched something in Gabriel. Then there was her golden hair and round face that may have brought to mind another woman. And maybe their connection also had something to do with his special talent to awaken a woman's affection.

Whatever the reason, there was a bond between Gabriel and his daughter-in-law and it was to her that he gave the gift from Clara. Mimi apologized that her hands were full and asked him to set it down next to the pile of clean diapers that had just emerged from the kibbutz laundry.

"What a lovely shade of blue." She promised to open it after the ceremony, so as not to tempt fate. "The color of the sky," she added, "to chase away the evil spirits."

"They don't leave so easily," whispered Gabriel, and he wasn't sure whether she had heard him.

With special permission from the kibbutz secretariat he was allowed to live alone in one of the German houses that hadn't yet been requisitioned for family housing. The room at the front of the building, with its thick walls and sturdy roof, suited the guest from America. It had been thoroughly cleaned in his honor and re-plastered, and the holes made by the nails that had supported the portraits of Hitler and Goebbels had been filled in. So that he wouldn't suffer from the biting cold Yitzhak brought over the kerosene heater from the tent, and Fanny made do with a small burner.

No one dared to suggest that she move in with her husband.

Until the circumcision ceremony the two never had an opportunity to be alone together, and they bumped into each other only at the dining hall or the Children's House. However, the mutual scrutiny continued. Like two rival generals they collected intelligence with which to plan their next moves.

Fanny noticed that Gabriel's seemingly impenetrable exterior – the source of such frustration and anguish during their short married life – was still firmly in place. Underneath the mask of politeness and the American manners was the same man, barricaded within his fortress, stingy with words and expressions of warmth. At the same time, she discerned a small crack. If when Yitzhak was born he had recoiled from fatherhood and kept his distance from the baby, when it came to his grandson he was allowing himself to be drawn in.

His face lit up when he touched the tiny head covered in golden down. Are people really capable of change, or are their characteristics so permanently anchored within them that any apparent change can only be superficial? Hadn't she already learned that a trait that is like a soft roll and easily kneaded when one is young, becomes unyielding and fossilized with age, having absorbed the burns and bitterness of the years?

Fanny took precautions, but her demonstrative distancing of herself and her efforts at evasion along the pathways of the kibbutz didn't emanate from revulsion for Gabriel. It was actually the reverse. She was the first to admit that her feelings for him had been reawakened, regardless of his terrible character. It was illogical and made no sense, as though love and passion had shaken off their shrouds and were dragging her toward them against her will. And, despite the fact that old love doesn't sour like milk, there was little sweetness there.

The bris, or circumcision ceremony was but one of many, since nearly every month a new baby was added to the kibbutz. The first Jacob was born in April and the second Jacob in May, Gadi was born in June, Adam in September, and Shrulik in October. Yitzhak and Mimi's son was not the last, but his ceremony was unique since it fell on a Saturday, the Sabbath. The mohel who was to perform the ritual, Zachariah Cohen, agreed to leave his family for the weekend, and even brought along his own kosher food. A single room was also arranged for him, next to Gabriel's. Kibbutz members and a handful of relatives gathered in the German building for the first family celebration in the country after the Holocaust. "Joy and tears mingled together," my father would write in his book.

Until the last moment, no one knew who would receive the honor of being sandek and hold the child during the ceremony.

The night before the bris, Yitzhak couldn't sleep a wink.

At daybreak he stole out of the tent. The sky was clear but the bitter cold still gnawed at him. In addition to the coat that had become a shaggy rag, he was also wrapped in the rough woolen blanket that covered them while they slept. Mimi's side of the bed was empty, for she had spent the night by the baby in the Children's House, and only Fanny's breaths were audible from the other side of the blanket that bisected the tent into two crude living areas. After the bris they were to move into the room where the mohel was currently staying. Yitzhak hadn't yet informed Fanny of this kibbutz decision, for fear that she would oppose sharing a living space with Gabriel. The idea troubled him as well, but there was no choice. His mother would accept the decree, for an improvement in their living situation was for the good of the family, even at the price of daily contact with her estranged husband.

Four days had passed since he had arrived, and apart from exchanging pleasantries in German and Yiddish Yitzhak hadn't spoken to his father. It was as though his tongue turned to stone in the presence of the meticulously shaven man in the elegant suit from whom wafted a decidedly foreign scent. What did he have to do with that stranger? Had they met by chance, they would have been unaware that they shared a bond. Hidden particles are not always attracted to each other, and often they repel one another. If people were permitted to choose their parents or siblings, they wouldn't necessarily choose the very ones that biology saddled them with, Yitzhak reflected.

His legs carried him toward the church. Above the bell tower the weathervane spun on its axis, and for a moment he thought he wasn't in Israel. Maybe it was his father who had imposed this early winter. His heart was also frozen. Not a flicker, not a spark of warmth did he feel. As though his body and soul had united in their refusal to recognize that blood is thicker than water.

By one of the cypress trees that the Templars had planted as a windbreak he suddenly spied Gabriel reciting the morning prayers. He stood in a puddle formed by the water that ran off the forest paths, and the hem of his fashionable coat floated in the muddy water. For a moment, just a moment, he reminded Yitzhak of Abraham Katz, the beloved grandfather who had been like a father to him.

"Who illuminates the world and its creatures with mercy." Of all things, it was hearing those Hebrew words in Gabriel's mouth, with his American pronunciation, that melted the ice in Yitzhak. There are few of your generation who are privileged to have the chance to repair their families, an inner voice reproached him. How dare you reject your own kin, when others will never again see their loved ones? What right do you have to kick over the milk jug of your good luck?

Under the tree he saw Gabriel remove his coat and shake off the dirty water. Then he adjusted his tie, and gazed up at the cloudless sky before turning in the direction of the Children's House, mumbling as he walked.

Yitzhak wondered what he could be saying, since he had concluded the prayers. Fanny's head popped out of the entrance to the tent and was hastily withdrawn. Yitzhak pressed himself against the church wall. The blanket slipped down from his shoulders and dragged on the ground. He heard the wail of the baby and then silence. Mimi had taken him to her breast.

Even if the man in the glamorous suit was a complete stranger and nothing connected them, maybe this baby, or the next grandchild, would find the strength to make space for him and accept him as family.

Father, no. Grandfather, yes.

When Yitzhak told Fanny that he had chosen Gabriel to be sandek, she didn't object.

She had the honor of being the *kvatterin*, the one who brings the infant boy from his mother and hands him to the sandek who sits in Elijah's Chair. In this case it wasn't a luxurious piece of furniture, but a wooden folding chair from the dining hall covered with a freshly laundered, clean-smelling sheet and upholstered with two cushions from the storeroom. Fanny had spread her famous rug beneath it.

Their hands touched but their eyes didn't meet.

Fanny drew Mimi out of the room before the cut. She remembered well that at Yitzhak's bris she had insisted on standing right next to the mohel and hadn't missed a moment of the ceremony: the cutting of the foreskin, the separation of the skin that remains under the foreskin, and the mohel's symbolic sucking out of the energy of negativity that remains under the skin of the foreskin. In retrospect, she would have been happy not to witness that part of the ceremony. She explained to Mimi that it was better for the mother not to witness the cutting of her child and the sight of his blood. When the bit of cotton wool soaked in wine was placed in the baby's mouth, he calmed down. Then he was transferred from hand to hand and all present smiled at him and chorused promises that this little infant would achieve greatness.

It was Yitzhak who announced the baby's names. Gabriel was surprised by the middle one. He hadn't anticipated that the child would also bear his father's name – Haim.

For Fanny, this was a sign that the connection between them could be renewed, or perhaps Yitzhak was seeking to ensure long life and good health for his firstborn son, according to the belief about the addition of a name. A few months later, when there was an outbreak of polio and all the babies were in quarantine, he would tell Mimi and Fanny that the name was the talisman that protected his son.

Gabriel recited the blessing of the sandek, "May it be Your will, my God and the God of my fathers, that an altar of atonement be before You, to atone for all my sins, iniquities and transgressions." Fanny caught a gleam in his eye. A romantic would choose to believe that it was a tear, but it's more likely that the sun that had finally come out was reflected there.

The first family photograph with my grandfather was taken during the ceremony to bury my brother's foreskin. "Bury it in sand and dirt," says the *Shulchan Aruch*, as the Children of Israel did when they circumcised their sons in the desert.

The hole in the ground is beyond the frame of the photograph and the face of the man burying the foreskin is obscured by his wide-brimmed hat. A child held by one of the kibbutz members is passing the hoe to him. Fanny and Gabriel stand at the back. They are next to each other, but not too close. As always her hands are clasped and his face wears its characteristic sour and gloomy expression. In the photograph they both look much older than they are. To my grandfather's left is my mother, and it is surprising to see the happy expression on her round face, for she didn't often smile.

And my father, where is he? Was he the photographer? Not likely. His way of preserving significant moments was with words, not pictures. It's also unlikely that he is the one doing the burying underneath the tilted hat, since my father's shoulders didn't stoop like those of the man in the photograph. If it wasn't for the caption that explicitly states that the photograph was taken at the ceremony to bury the foreskin I would have thought that they were planting a tree.

I creep into the photo, squeeze into the space between those arranged there and say to them, "And when ye shall come into the land, and shall have planted all manner of trees for food, then ye shall count the fruit thereof as uncircumcised..."

14

Gabriel was surprised to discover that he wasn't indifferent to his family. Perhaps he had mellowed with age, or maybe it was the circumstances that allowed him to bestir his capacity to love. It pleased him to see how the members of the kibbutz regarded his son as a leader, an achievement he attributed to character traits that he had passed on. His blonde daughter-in-law and her sadness played on hidden heartstrings, and he found that he admired Fanny for her reservation and the distance she kept. The more unattainable she was, the more he was attracted to her.

But the jewel in the crown of his awakening feelings was his grandson. The only one who bore him no grudge and had no accounts to settle with him. When the infant's small hands reached for him with complete acceptance through the bars of the simple kibbutz crib he was willing to give him everything. Clara would surely be glad to visit Macy's department store on Thirty Fourth Street to buy a new crib, fit for a prince.

It seemed to be a successful renewal of the family relationships, although Gabriel was far from enamored of his relatives' Zionist ideals and he didn't conceal his dissatisfaction with the place and the lifestyle they had chosen. For him, the fact that his son, an educated, erudite man who was studying law and spoke seven languages, spent his time as a cowherd in the fallow fields of the Jezreel Valley was proof positive of the failure of the Zionist vision.

Why wasn't it every man according to his abilities like in America? If the desires of all were subjugated for the common good, how would independent initiative ever develop? How would the individual set goals and try to surpass himself? Your Israel is on the wrong path, he decreed and he never ceased to argue the point. There were kibbutz members who rose to the challenge and the American – always immaculately dressed in his suit and tie – was often seen standing at the entrance to the dining hall debating with someone or other about social class and economic theory. The world according to Gabriel, described in terms of profit and loss.

"If only you were to invest what you have in the stock market."

"We invest what we don't have."

Gabriel chose to dwell on what was lacking. There was no radio, no cinema, no ticker tape machine, no bustling streets below towering skyscrapers, no beautiful women to seduce, no Clara. When he told Mimi about her he referred to her as an "old friend."

Several of the single women on kibbutz took note of his good looks and charisma, but no one would dare to approach "Fanny's husband" and sabotage the fragile reunion. He took pains to tell Mimi that he was not committed to that particular old friend in New York, and that as far as he was concerned it would be possible to come to a respectable arrangement. After all, he had never concealed the fact that he was married.

"Did you open the present?" he asked.

Mimi asked him to thank Clara on behalf of the baby and promised to send a personal note of gratitude. What she didn't tell him was that the spoon had been handed over to the kibbutz secretariat. But she had held onto the felt bag in that beautiful shade of blue, as a keepsake. She told no one, not even Yitzhak, that she had broken a rule of the collective. She couldn't help being undone by that breathtaking color and harboring a hope that her son's eyes would have the same hue.

The woman on night duty in the Children's House found an old photograph near the wrapping paper from Clara's gift. She gave it a scornful glance and said, "That must have belonged to one of the German women who lived here. How did it survive our clean-up?" Without a second thought she crumpled it up and threw it in with the pile of soiled diapers.

After she left, Mimi rescued it. By the light of a lamp she smoothed it out and examined the photo that still clearly displayed the woman's portrait, despite the tribulations it had experienced. Someone once loved this woman, she thought. As pinched and unattractive as she seemed, she had given her likeness to someone, so he wouldn't forget her. So how could she dispose of her, as though she had never existed?

Mimi wiped the photograph, and while her hungry baby mewled in her arms, she shook scented talcum powder over it. Strangely it was the smell of gunpowder that seemed to rise from its surface.

She decided to keep the picture.

Gabriel's sensitive nostrils were also attuned to smells – an abundance of new scents so different from those he was accustomed to in New York.

Freshly-mown hay, sandstone dust, fresh oak leaves, rock cyclamen flowers, steaming laundry, and the pungent odor of cow. The latter adhered to his son.

"You stink like a Russian peasant."

"What do you know about Russia?"

"I was there once."

"When?"

Before you were born. I learned the hard way what it means to live like a primitive farmer.

Yitzhak protested. "To work the land is a noble calling. We are new Jews."

The confrontation took place in a meadow in February 1950, as the cows grazed on the grass that grew in abundance after the rains. The fresh smell covered the stink of the cow pats.

Yitzhak was dressed in worn work clothes, and tucked under his arm were two books. The German poetry of Paul Celan, a native of Czernowitz, and *The Seventh Column*, in Hebrew, by Natan Alterman.

He took the two volumes with him each morning when he went out with the cows, to help to pass the time, and he would alternately declaim, "Your golden hair, Margarete, your ashen hair, Shulamith," and "We entered the lean shack, that shook in the wind as though it were alive," and observe the reactions of the herd. He admitted to himself that his work assignment was crushingly boring, but to his father he insisted that he was proud to be responsible for the cows.

Gabriel burst out laughing, and the nearest cow rolled its grass-slicked tongue and mooed. "You travelled all the way to Israel to do the primitive work of a gentile?"

Yitzhak's pronouncements about the need for a revolution, and to exchange the work done by Jews in the diaspora for productive manual labor, further angered Gabriel and the herd scattered in fright.

"We have to root out the weak and passive *luftgescheft* in our midst," Yitzhak shouted. Now Gabriel was furious. The allusion to the way he earned his livelihood – with enterprises based on "nothing but air" – was insulting, and he pointed at the filthy rubber boots on Yitzhak's feet.

"You want to remain stuck in that shit? I'm offering you America."

"My America is here!"

"You're a dreamer."

"And you, what are you? You show up after almost thirty years and try to educate me?"

Both were keenly aware that the status quo was so fragile that any disagreement could lead to an irreparable rift. But the last word would be Fanny's. Yitzhak cut short the argument to round up the nervous animals. His books slipped out from under his arm and in a conciliatory gesture Gabriel retrieved them for him.

Dreamer or not, Mimi was the one who suggested that Yitzhak take his father to see Tel Aviv. Maybe the large developing metropolis would impress him and he would realize that there was more than one option for the realization of the Zionist vision.

She hoped that the long journey would improve the communication between the two men. To be honest, her affinity for Gabriel had deeper sources. She missed her parents who, although they had survived Transnistria, had not yet managed to immigrate to Israel, and her father-in-law was a kind of stand-in, not to mention that he showered warmth and love on her baby.

Although Fanny was invited, she refused to join them on their trip. Aware as she was of Gabriel's effect on her she was anxious about spending an entire day in his company.

When her son and her husband climbed into the truck, she watched them from the entrance to the German house, and for the first time discerned a resemblance between them.

Gabriel was not impressed by Tel Aviv. To him it was a provincial town that had absolutely nothing in common with New York. No tall buildings, no wide avenues, no lively traffic, and instead of the Atlantic Ocean, a greenish, muddy stream with pretensions of being a river. When Yitzhak prophesied that one day the city would be a bustling metropolis, and the skyscrapers wouldn't be long in coming, not to mention the first Hebrew stock market in the world, he again referred to him as a "dreamer," but it seemed that this time he used the word affectionately.

One required a lot of imagination to predict the future of Tel Aviv, and at that point Gabriel could see no more than what was in front of him. Sand and more sand and only sand. Yellow, getting into your nose, blinding you, dusting your fancy suit with its rough particles, and stinging your skin.

They stood at a building site – later it would become Arlozorov Street – and at the edge of a pit that had been dug there, as Gabriel smoked the local Matossian cigarettes, since his Chesterfields were nowhere to be found, Yitzhak tried to convince him to invest in the property. He even stuck his neck out and quoted Rabbi Moshe Ben Nahman, "We will not leave our country to any other nation, or to the wasteland."

Gabriel remained unmoved. Other than by the word "wasteland," which was just the way he would have described Israel. Under duress he obliged Yitzhak and climbed onto the scaffolding, covering his nose and mouth with a freshly-ironed handkerchief. It was evidence of the high regard in which Yitzhak was held that the women in the laundry were willing to go out of their way for Gabriel. Coughing and sneezing he presented Yitzhak with an ultimatum. They were to return with him to the United States. The purchase of property was a possibility, but only in New York, and only in his grandson's name.

"Think about his future. Your country is dangerous. You will dress him up in a uniform, and he will eat shit in the wars to come."

"He will be an Israeli soldier," Yitzhak protested.

"Don't try to sell me patriotic bullshit. They dressed me in a uniform and forced me to crawl through trenches. Listen son, all the leaders are the same. Even your Zionists. They don't love people, they love land."

He called him "son." Maybe that was why Yitzhak turned his back and began to stride along the boards that partially covered the open pit. Mounds of gravel surrounded him and towering piles of building material were stacked nearby. He bypassed the workers who were busy carrying bags of cement. They worked slowly, and Gabriel's mocking laughter, "that's no way to build a shtetl," trailed behind him. The boards swayed and he steadied himself, called out to him to be careful, but still the word "father" stuck in his throat and refused to emerge.

On the way back Yitzhak suggested to Gabriel that he drive. The enforced intimacy, the comparisons between Tel Aviv and New York, and mostly the ultimatum, had worn him out and he was worried he might fall asleep at the wheel. Gabriel could easily navigate back to Haifa, following the road signs, he thought, and once there they could switch places again.

Only Gabriel didn't stop at Haifa. At his side Yitzhak slept so deeply that he decided not to rouse him and he found his way to the Jezreel Valley by instinct. He steered the truck smoothly along the narrow, curvy gravel path between the oak trees and only when he pulled in by the church did Yitzhak wake up. Upon opening his eyes he discovered his father's hand hovering above his cheek. Gabriel moved away quickly, like someone caught red-handed. He lit himself another Matossian cigarette, the last one in the pack.

"If Mother decides to join you I won't stop her," my father said to my grandfather.

15

"It's easy to conceal hatred, but difficult to hide love." In Fanny's case the Yiddish saying worked in reverse. With great skill she succeeded in hiding her love for Gabriel from everyone, but not from herself. If people could only know which particular choice determined their fate, things would be very different. She had the opportunity to make a decision in real time.

During her shifts in the dining hall or when folding diapers in the laundry, she never ceased to wonder about the second chance that stingy life had granted her. To accept or reject? Even if there was another woman in his life – she already knew of Clara's existence – Gabriel had chosen to cross the ocean to her. It sounded romantic, like a story from the slim German romances she so wished they stocked in the kibbutz library.

To travel to New York. To start a new chapter. Both of them had amassed many experiences, not a few wrinkles, and much grief, and yet, that internal fire of desire still burned. This time it would be a different alliance, she told herself, a carefully-considered relationship, lived in material comfort, based on a sober choice and not the result of historic circumstances and outmoded rules of behavior and traditions.

She could no longer justify anything with the excuse that "my son needs me." Yitzhak had a family of his own, and was committed to an ideological framework that gave meaning to his life. He would manage just fine without her, maybe do even better. From America she could send him what he lacked. Sooner or later he would need financial support, for it was clear to her that he would not be content with a career as a cowherd, and would strive to realize his Zionist yearnings in a less-collective manner. To do so he would need a financial safety net.

She consulted no one, not even her sisters. Between themselves Paula and Emil discussed Gabriel incessantly and reminisced about Anna. How could a brother and sister be so different from one another? He was self-absorbed, vain and irritable, while she was pleasant, compassionate and always considerate of others. At least that was how she had been in her youth.

If Fanny decided to join him, Anna would be a loyal ally. "And what about his common-law wife?" asked Lizzie-Bertha? If the arrangement of one man for two women was acceptable, why not one woman for two men? If she was in Fanny's shoes, she would rush to find herself a lover.

What a shame that she never had the pleasure of even one lover, never mind two at the same time.

One shouldn't envy the difficult decision Fanny had to make. Whether she decided one way or the other, both sides of the revolving door would exact a heavy price. Even assuming she was capable of leaving her son, the grandson was another story. She saw it as a clear case of abandonment. And although a grandparent isn't a parent, and no one would have criticized her, she didn't want to be an abstract, unattainable grandmother on the other side of the world. The kind of father Gabriel had been to Yitzhak.

During the months that his father stayed on the kibbutz he never deluged him with accusations and never confronted him about the terrible thing he had done to him. When I asked him how he was able to restrain himself – something that most certainly would have been beyond me – he said that had he allowed that volcano of burning lava to erupt, it would have set off a huge blaze, and he would have been responsible for ruining his mother's last chance for a new life. He wanted her to be happy, even at the cost of separation.

The inevitable face-to-face encounter between Fanny and Gabriel happened by chance. They both went to visit their grandson at the same time and neither had a backup getaway plan. It was dusk, a favorite part of the day for Fanny for the silence and tenderness that embraced the world, and a time that Gabriel loathed because of the impending darkness. She saw him first, leaning over the crib and stroking the baby's cheek through the bars. This time she chose not to back away, leaning instead against the metal cabinet where the infants' clothing was stored.

Is that how Penelope observed the stranger who arrived at the palace in Ithaca? According to Homer, she also hesitated. "Would she call to her beloved husband from afar, or approach him, embrace him, and kiss his head and his hands?"

At which moment did Penelope unravel her doubts and concede that he was the only man for her, whether in the guise of a beggar or as an elderly man? If Gabriel had appeared clothed in rags, or as one transformed by old age, Fanny's decision would have been easier. But confronted with this good-looking gentleman, attractive as ever despite the passage of time, she had to hold herself in check, and not kiss him as her mythological sister-in-destiny had done. In contrast to Ulysses, who had kept his silence, Gabriel sang softly to his grandson. It was the ballad *The Golden Peacock* by Itzik Manger, which Fanny could recite word-for-word.

For the first three stanzas, when the golden peacock flies off to the east, to the south, and to the north in search of the days of yesterday, she remained silent. In the final stanza, in the west, the peacock meets a woman dressed in black, leaning over a grave, and he understands that he has found what he is searching for. The widow is the days of yesterday. As Gabriel sang tenderly, Fanny choked back tears. Stupid little bird just as her Yiddish name described her, she chided herself – she felt as though Itzik Manger had written her own story. In Yiddish, a peacock is a female bird.

Hearing a sound, Gabriel turned sharply and Fanny emerged from behind the metal cabinet. Its side was cold, or perhaps her body wasn't generating any heat.

The song about the golden peacock stopped abruptly. The baby started to wail. Maybe he wanted to sing too. At that moment Mimi came in. It was time to nurse the baby. To her surprise she encountered the estranged couple alone in the same place, Gabriel extending a hand to Fanny. The distance between them narrowed, then closed.

As they left the Children's House Mimi whispered to the baby, "You see, *yeingele*, sometimes in this miserable life there is also a happy ending."

It didn't make her more optimistic, or him less pessimistic.

It was the husband who held the wife and kissed her head and her hand, and it didn't happen in a palace in Ithaca, but in an abandoned German church. That was where Gabriel led Fanny, or perhaps it was she who led him there. The alcove that was once used for prayer became the cradle for their coupling. Not exactly a bed, since all that remained there was a cracked and dusty wooden bench.

The taste of his skin was familiar, as though twenty-eight years hadn't elapsed. He too, who unlike her had had so very many partners, relished her skin – just as smooth as he remembered. He first sought her lush lashes, and then all the rest.

"…you uncovered your bed, you climbed into it and opened it wide…" no one murmured that verse from Isaiah.

Age didn't matter, neither the chasm of the years, the hurts, the insults. Everything was forgotten when they touched each other. Perhaps the German ghosts heard their cries, first wild, later soft moans.

The darkness was absolute; in the church, where all of the openings had been sealed long ago, not a fissure remained through which a glimmer of light could penetrate. Fanny had to grope blindly to find her undergarments.

"Is this also kibbutz property?" Gabriel whispered, and she giggled. From outside they could hear the footsteps of the night watchman, and the two froze in perfect unison. Later, when he separated from her the bench flipped over. He kicked it away and Fanny heard the sound of wood meeting stone. Gabriel extended his hand toward her in the darkness, but she stood up by herself.

"Come with me to New York?"

As she fastened her buttons she replied, "I want a divorce."

He granted her the divorce in a short ceremony that took place at the Haifa rabbinate. "Instead of a reunification of the family there was a legal and binding separation," my father would write in his book. On February 3, 1950, the freshly divorced Gabriel boarded the ship that would return him to the United States.

That's it? End of story? Over and done with?

Not quite.

Although it sounds improbable, even impossible to believe, there is another chapter to come in the on-again, off-again relationship between my grandmother and grandfather. For them the days of yesterday continue to search for the golden peacock.

And Another Thing

If she loved him, why chase him away?

Fanny was taking preventive measures. Once she had tasted his body again, she realized that she would never possess Gabriel's soul. For her, love was absolute. For him, she would be one of many.

She couldn't withstand yet another abandonment, and so she protected herself. With head held high it was she who abandoned the ship of Gabriel, so that he would never again stab her with the dagger of "that's not my woman."

The family lines were redrawn. He was there, she was here. A separation by the book. It seemed like the end of the story. But the dramas that life creates are beyond the abilities of any playwright, says my daughter. And it's impossible to compete with one who has Shakespearian talents and can teach us all a lesson in conflict and the vicissitudes of fate. He won't abide by a predictable narrative or a meaningless tale, and so he planted a gun in Fanny and Gabriel's relationship that wouldn't go off until the fifth act. The divorce didn't tear them apart for eternity, as assumed, but simply kept their operational systems in vibrate mode. Were they veins of desire that had still to be mined to their depths, or was it some kind of sick interdependence that only a skilled therapist could ever resolve? It's unlikely that they were aware of the webbed cocoon that they spun around themselves.

The more one peels the onion of this love-hate relationship, the more Fanny and Gabriel come to represent the two poles of Jewishness. He is the "sea," she is the "land," like the children's game when the couch is the land and the carpet the sea and you jump back and forth as someone alternately calls out the words. Fanny represents Zion. The element which insists on the mysterious promise, holds fast to the fantasy and continues to pursue an ancient spirit, despite the lack of evidence of its validity. And Gabriel is the diaspora. The eternal wanderer, a serial breaker of promises, utterly self-involved who always lands in his comfort zone. In their twilight years they will merge into "sealand," straddling both.

If troubles and yearning are the building blocks of the Jewish people, in their case those materials constructed a wall, but not one that was sealed with plaster. In Fanny and Gabriel's "sealand" there are crevices through which one can peek and observe. They were their own sleeper agents.

I slip in through one of those chinks.

PART FIVE
And He Shall Take His Former Wife

1

Like Fanny, Clara too, who was supposed to finally achieve her rightful place, chose to relieve the pressure and stopped nagging Gabriel to marry her. No ring would make her leopard change his spots. The chances of his suddenly becoming a faithful lover and devoted family man were zero.

Even in the sixth decade of his life he barely slowed down, and quickly reverted to his old ways. He added more romantic scalps to his belt, starting with Martinella, the niece of his Italian lover Olympia from days gone by, who he met when she was waitressing at his favorite restaurant in Little Italy. For him she was proof that he still had what it takes, and for her he was the perfect sugar daddy. Wealthy, reasonably well-preserved, and far from a disappointment in bed, like so many other men his age. What more could she ask?

But the scandal that whipped up a storm in the ex-pat Bukovina community in New York was Gabriel's affair with the very lovely and very married M.'s aunt. Even today, as an old woman, M. remembers the details of how my grandfather was caught in her aunt's bathtub when her husband came home from work unexpectedly.

"What is Gabriel doing in my bathtub?" she quotes her uncle's query, which became part of the local folklore of those years. Her aunt's reply was, "He only has a shower at his apartment so I let him use our bathtub."

"And what were you doing while he was in the bathtub? Scrubbing his back?"

The husband's roars could be heard for miles around, so that the story couldn't be kept even from the young girl.

Gabriel became a pariah, and for an entire year he was forbidden to attend meetings of the Bukovina club – a unanimous decision taken by the men in the group.

M. is hesitant about sharing the story with me but her esteemed husband insists that it is the perfect material for a novel.

"Why are you so embarrassed?" he teases his wife. "They're all dead by now."

"It seems that they retain their vitality even in their shrouds," I suggest, and we both laugh.

M. finds it far less funny, and her conscience continues to irk her for bringing out so much dirty laundry, not to mention that she feels as if she is speaking ill of the dead.

And Clara? Although Manny and Doris tried to shield her from the scandal, some kind soul took pains to ensure that the story reached her ears, which cleared the way to her decision.

"I prefer to suffer his infidelities as his common-law companion than as his wife," she told Anna. They were not destined to be sisters-in-law. The topic of marriage to Gabriel was dropped, but an old salt of a lawyer drew up a document that ensured that one day she would receive her fair share of the inheritance.

Although Clara had never met Lizzie-Bertha, she chose a plan of action in the spirit of her worldview and set out to find herself a lover to balance the equation. The contender was Morris Schwartz, a good several years younger and the owner of a flourishing business in fur hats, most of which he sold to the ultra-Orthodox community. He left a silver fox stole on her doorstep and a card decorated with hearts. Although Gabriel was far better-looking, she almost gave in. Anna would whisper that it was her conservative nature that gave her cold feet, but what finally kept her at Gabriel's side was her commitment to the values of loyalty, if not necessarily of the sexual kind.

Over a cup of tea poured from a gleaming samovar at the Russian Tea Room at 150 West Fifty-Seventh Street Clara and Morris Schwartz conversed about transitions and the countries they traversed.

Had she met Gabriel in the Old Country? In all innocence she mentioned that in his youth Gabriel had spent time in Russia.

Morris visibly tensed. "When was that?"

"A long time ago."

"Before or after the Communist revolution?"

"He doesn't talk about it."

"Does he have connections from there?"

Clara changed the subject. It was unseemly to gossip about her partner with her potential new lover. Besides, she wanted to lose herself in the pleasure of finally being in the New York institution that oozed luxury. For years she had dreamed of feeling, for just one evening, like a movie star or a Broadway actress, but Gabriel always said that it was a waste of money and preferred to eat at simple restaurants. Everything at the Russian Tea Room was as splendid as she had anticipated. It was as if she had moved from the crowded, muggy streets of New York to a palace in Moscow. Her eyes widened at the display of glittering samovars, the dazzling paintings on the walls, the decorations shaped like Fabergé eggs and the red chandeliers above her head like crowns above a royal throne. The soft lighting created a false image of Morris Schwartz who appeared to her now like an old-world aristocrat, and even his thinning hair, combed over to disguise his imminent baldness didn't seem ridiculous to her at that moment. She would make sure that their night out would reach Gabriel's ears and those of the rest of the club.

When the waiter dressed in a red uniform served them their ceramic dishes on a silver tray, as Morris stuffed his mouth with Beluga caviar and Blini, he returned to the subject of Gabriel's past.

"Does he speak Russian?"

"Only in his sleep."

"What does he say?"

She barely managed to steer the conversation back to furs, a subject on which Morris Schwartz could hold forth ad-infinitum. Then she had to spend the rest of the evening feigning interest in the differences between Sibrian sable and chinchilla from the Andes. In the throes of his enthusiasm to snare her as his mistress, the furrier even promised her a fifty percent discount on a mink coat.

When Morris asked his nosy questions about Gabriel, Clara was reminded of a sultry summer day when a strange man had appeared at her door, brandishing a document from a law enforcement agency and announcing that he had come to ask her some questions about Gabriel Herzig's past.

It was during the days of the McCarthy witch-hunts. The Jews Ethel and Julius Rosenberg had been convicted of spying for the Soviet Union and executed by electric chair. Anyone suspected of supporting the "Reds" lost his job and was publicly denounced. Who knew, her interrogator suggested to Clara, it was possible that the red devil was active in the deep darkness of Wall Street.

Maybe Herzig was hiding a Bolshevik skeleton in his closet? After all, he was a Jew, "and we have received information that he spent time in Russia during the Revolution."

"Information? Who from?"

The man refused to elaborate.

Clara didn't fall for it. "You're talking about a first-rate American patriot," she declared, "And here's the proof: he wouldn't agree to move to Israel, even though both his wife and his son live there."

At that information the eyes of her interrogator lit up.

"Why did Herzig choose to remain in America?"

"Because he believes in capitalism."

"Where are the wife and son?"

"On a kibbutz."

"Aha! Socialists." The ultimate insult in those dark days of "cleansing." She was so incensed at the denigration of the values of the Zionist state that she didn't even offer the man a glass of water and relished the sight of him drowning in his perspiration.

"Miss Mendel, we are asking you to cooperate."

Defiant silence.

"For your own good you should report any suspicious activities by your lover. He calls himself 'George.' Maybe his real name is Grigor? On your nights together do you call him by the nickname 'Grisha'?"

"Miss Mendel, you will inform us about who he writes to, who he meets. We know everything about you."

"And if I refuse?"

Now it was his turn to maintain a thunderous silence.

"What will you do? Send me off to the electric chair as well?"

Drawing herself up to face the investigator, in a voice hoarse and quivering with rage, she treated him to the concluding words of the American national anthem, "And the star-spangled banner in triumph shall wave, O'er the land of the free and the home of the brave." When she was done, she sent the sweaty emissary from Senator McCarthy packing. She also cut contact with Morris Schwartz. She wouldn't have a snitch for a lover.

"Anyone who hands a Jew over into the hands of heathen, whether physically or financially, has no share in the world to come." Clara Mendel wasn't familiar with the Rambam's Mishne Torah, but he would certainly have been proud of her. She would never know whether it was her defense of Gabriel that was behind her second invitation to the Russian Tea Room where, perhaps as a gesture of gratitude, he belatedly proposed to make an honest woman of her.

However, just like Fanny on the other side of the world, Clara refused him.

Meanwhile, Gabriel's divorced wife also received a proposal of marriage. Her suitor was none other than Meirke Hirsch.

2

Where did he come from all of a sudden? The last we heard of him was in 1921, when he and Gabriel boarded the train from Czernowitz to Vienna, where their paths diverged. One to America, the other to the Land of Israel.

As a tiny stain on the cloak of the world, Israel is characterized by stifling proximity among its inhabitants, and the chances of bumping into someone from the past are immeasurably higher than in a country like America.

Ildiko and Mrs. Jackson disappeared without a trace in the huge continent, but Meirke Hirsch popped up in Israel. In the relevant circles he was known as the number one locksmith in the country and the chief supplier of handcuffs to the Israel Police. It was his grand handiwork that cuffed not a few Zionist thieves and whores. Israel didn't let him down when it came to earning a living and he even found a home for his political aspirations when he joined the Land of Israel Worker's Party, better known as Mapai. At every opportunity he waved his "red booklet," proof of his membership in Mapai and his entry pass to the club of "one of us." He was wont to tell anyone who was willing to listen, and mainly those who weren't, about his connections to the people at the top. Once he even exchanged two sentences with Ben-Gurion, a prime minister whose hands were never cuffed behind his back.

But Meirke never found his Zionist dream woman and remained a bachelor. And now, after thirty-five years, life once again placed Fanny Herzig from Siret in his path. He had been sure that she was living in the land where the streets were paved with gold, with her husband who had sent her a ticket once he was settled. That's what he had promised, hadn't he? Astonishingly, he recognized her right away, even though he only glimpsed her profile, leaning over the printing press in the cellar where she worked.

Two years before, the family had left the kibbutz. When a majority of the members voted to transform Alonei Abba, previously Neve Ya'ar, into a moshav – a collective settlement combining the features of a moshav and a kibbutz – the cowherd realized that he had exhausted all the possibilities that his agricultural career had to offer. His young son's cries of "Daddy-boo," the child's version of "Daddy-moo" when his father returned from the cows, fused with the other legends of the place.

Working with the cows, there was no way that Yitzhak could support himself and family as a householder on the new moshav, and the aspirations that his mother had recognized years before finally moved to the forefront. He was ready for new challenges. With no assets they moved to an immigrant neighborhood on the outskirts of Tel Aviv, and in the meantime a baby girl had joined the family. At sun-up each morning Yitzhak traveled to Jerusalem by bus to his job at the Foreign Ministry. Despite the fact that he lacked a red booklet, as a man who spoke seven languages he was able to find a job there. Since he wasn't "one of us," his salary was a pittance and he had no chance of receiving tenure. In the evenings, after a full day of work, he completed his law studies at the Hebrew University of Jerusalem and barely saw his children. The packages that arrived from America granted the family some breathing space in those years of economic austerity. It was Clara who made sure to buy tins of condensed milk and packets of powdered eggs and who was responsible for the packages that arrived regularly from New York. A warm correspondence developed between her and Yitzhak, and she always remembered to include regards from Gabriel.

"Why doesn't he marry her?" Yitzhak asked Mimi, when Fanny wasn't around.

"Do you want a stepmother in addition to the mother you already have?" was her answer.

In their tiny apartment, she took care of the two young children and her mother-in-law helped to support the family. The beer cellar was replaced by a no-less gloomy underground room where campaign posters were printed for the third elections to the Knesset.

"Fanny, is it you?"

"Meirke Hirsch, who would believe it?"

During the exclamations of mutual recognition – in German of course – he observed her wedding finger. No ring gleamed there.

"My condolences," he intoned, feeling far from unhappy.

"I'm not a widow."

Only the sound of the printing press could be heard in the background, spitting out one election poster after another.

"Gabriel and I are divorced."

Meirke Hirsch's face shone. In the half-light of the cellar she didn't look much different from what he remembered, except for the streaks of white in her hair. The fact that she was now a grandmother with two grandchildren, which she announced on the spot, didn't faze him in the slightest. Even if she was a little worn out, deep inside she was still the same woman that he and Kalman-Zelig had so admired. Destiny had returned her to him, and it was better late than never.

"You are a free woman now, Fanny Katz, and I am also available." He tried to grasp her ink-stained hand, "Let us tear out for ourselves a coupon of happiness from the ration book. No one else will give it to us."

Once a romantic, always a romantic.

When Fanny extracted the poster with the slogan, "The Mission – Southward," Ben-Gurion's call to follow him to settle the large desert region in the Negev, he saw it as a sign from above. He had found his helpmate to further the work of the party. A struggling immigrant from Bukovina, who had experienced the horrors of the Holocaust, an internment camp in Cyprus, and had helped to establish a kibbutz, could be a great asset to the pre-election propaganda campaign. With him, Fanny wouldn't work as a simple laborer. She would have a place of honor in his flourishing handcuff factory, and there would never be a lack of criminals and law-breakers in the entire world, including the land of the Zionist dream. However, what led Fanny to seriously consider his offer was his promise to help her family. No more packages from America.

"You don't have to be dependent on your ex-husband, over there in the flesh pots of the diaspora," Meirke declared.

Near the wall, on the ink-stained floor where different colors of ink from other orders had run together in a muddy mess, rested rolled-up posters smelling of fresh ink. "Wipe Out Discrimination, Vote for Equality for Everyone," from the Sephardic and Eastern Party; "Enough of the Rule of the Booklet" from the General Zionist Party; "Ben-Gurion Serves the Rich!" from the Communist Party; and "Down with the Dictatorship. Join the Freedom Ship!" from the Herut Party.

"We will win," Meirke declared. The tidings would emanate from Sde Boker, the kibbutz where Ben-Gurion had settled. Why shouldn't the two of them go southward to the Negev to receive the blessing of the leader? She didn't have a red booklet? How could that be? It was inconceivable. He would get one for her with his connections.

No, she wasn't a Mapai supporter. No one would ever tell her what to think or how to vote. With all due respect to Ben-Gurion, she was not in his pocket, nor in anyone else's.

Despite that being the moment when Meirke should have given up, Fanny's resistance raised her value in his eyes. It seemed that this character trait was the one that often made her attractive to men.

It was Mimi who encouraged her to give the suitor a second chance. Although Fanny helped out with the daily grind, Mimi would have gladly separated from her very own "Mother of Sisera" who held fast to Yitzhak's heels and adhered to the couple throughout their married life. She dreamed of the freedom of a family unit where she was the reigning female.

She helped Fanny to iron her one good dress, and even brought black henna and a brush from one of the neighbors to cover the white streaks in her hair, but Fanny would have none of it.

"I have no intention of concealing my age!"

Resistance – the exact same trait, although on the flipside of the coin it was far less appreciated.

The entertainment to which Meirke invited Fanny was the ceremony to mark the opening of the "Yarkon-Negev" water line, which was held at the pumping station in Rosh Ha'ayin, at the feet of the Antipatris Fortress built by Herod the Great. Although he had been confident that his tickets were for seats up front, as befitted a party activist who was "one of us," they found themselves seated on wooden planks balanced on Tnuva produce boxes and hemmed in on all sides in the back rows. Fanny couldn't make out anything that was happening onstage.

She missed out on the performance of *The Water Pact*, the choir's rendition of "Spring Up O Well," and as for the dancing, she caught only the tails of the young girls' cloaks. Straining her eyes she could just about discern the humps of a camel convoy that provided the stage setting. The speeches of President Yitzhak Ben Zvi and the ministers were swallowed up in the screams of the crowd, which surged angrily toward the front rows. Meirke, who was either blessed with excellent hearing or knew in advance what the dignitaries planned to say recited choice pronouncements into her ear: "The desert will surrender to the pioneer and the water," and "The Yarkon will be a bathing spot for all, a giant swimming pool extending for twenty kilometers."

In the chaos that reigned he wasn't able to steer them toward the rows where the leaders sat, and so she missed her chance to see Ben-Gurion up close.

"Don't despair Fanny. All hope isn't lost." Meirke promised to make it up to her with a festive dip in the Yarkon when it was officially opened as a beach. They would even see Ben-Gurion perform one of his famous headstands. The oxygen from the brain must be transferred to the heart, the leader declared, and everyone should stand on his head at least once a day. "Maybe we can practice together?" Meirke suggested.

The only speech Meirke ignored was the one delivered by the governor of New York, who had come especially for the ceremony. Maybe he didn't understand English. But Fanny paid attention to what he had to say. "It is the aspiration of every American to help you. Our ability to work together holds symbolic meaning."

She felt a painful twinge.

The ceremony concluded with a festive display of the prowess of the pump, as water burst forth from the arms of a seven-branched menorah erected on the stage. The shouts of grievance gave way to one roar where all voices merged in jubilation. Meirke, too, cheered the Zionist achievement, while Fanny watched silently as the jets of water were propelled upward like a circus act, and recalled the gypsy who had foretold that she would marry twice.

What nonsense those fortune-tellers spouted. She would not share the remainder of her life with a new husband. A strange smell. A strange body. A strange taste. Meirke Hirsch ignited no spark, not even the tiniest glimmer. Maybe such inclinations had been permanently extinguished in her, or desire wasn't permitted to women of her age. She said none of this when she rejected his proposal of marriage. Deciding that the phrase, "we aren't suited," would suffice, she wished him much luck with his handcuffs, and when the elections were held she did not vote for the ruling party.

All she could remember of the gypsy's ancient blessing were the words, "Until the end of pain has come to light."

That evening she set up the narrow folding bed and pushed it alongside her two sleeping grandchildren, while on the other side of the wall she could hear the rustlings of her son and daughter-in-law. She caressed the golden tresses of the boy who sang even in his sleep – he was truly her beloved one – and lightly patted the new baby girl, sucking her thumb in the crib next to him. "My son's small brain is taking in its first knowledge and beginning to decode the secrets of the universe that are slowly, slowly, being revealed to him," is how my father described my older brother at that time, in the collection of letters we recently discovered. My grandmother tried to embrace her grandchildren, the strands of her dangling hair white above their heads as she whispered, "There is no cure for pain."

The baby in the crib is me.

3

I am not the protagonist of this tale, nor is my brother. We are all background figures who must clear the stage for the lead characters. It can be a challenge to move to the side and play a supporting role. "Walk humbly" is not a stage direction that we easily accept, and so there is no choice but to take distancing measures to protect the story and to refer to Fanny's grandchildren as "the boy" and "the girl."

The closer I come to the period when I was present, and to events that I witnessed, there is a danger that reality will plot against me and garble this love-not-love story. An eternal filler-in of the gaps, that's me, at the command of my father who once told me, "If something's missing, make it up."

What happened, happened, but I also embrace what might have been. I strip away the story buried inside the story and bring it to life, laugh with those who cry and cry with those who laugh, in keeping with Bertolt Brecht.

They didn't even know that they had a grandfather. His name wasn't mentioned, and the packages from America were said to come from some "uncle."

And anyway, in families where the number of dead exceeded the living, the word "uncle" didn't necessarily imply a biological connection. The name was preserved in German for the true aunts and uncle in Haifa: Tante Paula, Tante Lizzie-Bertha, and Onkel Emil. The children went with Fanny to visit them during the holidays, and when Mimi's parents finally immigrated to Israel, the house on Stanton Street became a regular stop on the way to visit them in the Krayot neighborhood. The small family expanded, the number of living began to exceed the number of dead, and the children received a new grandmother and grandfather. Mimi's father, Berl-Dov, an observant Jew with a wonderful voice and an exceptionally pleasant demeanor, won the boy's wholehearted admiration and taught him the melodies of the prayers. Fanny was now nicknamed "The Old Grandma," and still lived with them in the neighborhood in North Tel Aviv that the family had moved to.

It was crowded there. A stew of emotions that gradually congealed. The folding beds were still opened at night and put away during the day. There were still whispers in German and Yiddish and the ever-present buffer, "Not in front of the children." This apartment had one more room, but it was as if the walls had shrunk. There was a mother whose losses in the Holocaust gnawed at her incessantly, as did her bitter disappointment at having left the kibbutz where she had finally felt at home. And there was a father who only came home on the weekends, exhausted by his work and his public pursuits, always addicted to his Zionist dreams. The boy escaped outdoors to football games and record albums, and the girl found refuge in her collection of dried flowers, all the while telling herself stories that had happy endings. She called Fanny "Grandma Snow White," for the dark color was now almost completely gone. And yet her face was still like polished ivory, and her long eyelashes continued to cast their shadows, especially when she was in a rage. The girl was afraid of her. Sometimes she looked like a witch. Only the boy could soften her permanent scowl, and she doted on him as she did on her son. The two men in her life filled her gaping void, and there wasn't room for anyone else. She had left her job at the printing press and now she took in sewing or spent her time embroidering tablecloths. Her hands flew over the fabric, creating countless intricate designs, but she was stingy with words.

What was the point of talking? Hadn't enough been said?

She never wrote to Gabriel. Not even one line, and observing Yitzhak as he diligently maintained his correspondence with Clara, she asked herself what would have happened if they hadn't divorced. Perhaps it would have been she sitting in New York, sending letters to her son. And Clara, not she, would have become the abandoned woman. Occasionally she enquired, innocently, whether the two had married, and Yitzhak always stressed that his father had remained a bachelor.

Only once did Fanny return to Greek mythology. It was in a children's book, with illustrations, that she discovered at the German bookstore on Ben Yehuda Street. Bringing it home, she skipped over the saga of Penelope and Ulysses – she already knew how that story ended. Inspired by the girl's dried flower collection, she chose to linger over the allegory about Narcissus, the beautiful young man who loved no one, until he fell in love with his own reflection. That night she told the girl a fable, a rare occurrence, since none of the adults had the time or the energy for bedtime stories, and the two children would make up their own to whisper to one another.

The harshness in Fanny's face seemed to melt away as, sitting with her wide-eyed granddaughter she gave herself over to the description of how Narcissus was so enthralled by his reflection in the water that he didn't hear the cries of the nymph Echo who pursued him. She was in love with him to the depths of her soul.

The girl asked, "Why didn't he hear her? Was he deaf?"

"He saw only himself," Fanny replied.

"Too bad he wasn't blind," said the girl.

Fanny wanted to turn off the light, but the girl was afraid of the dark. Fanny quickly turned the page, censoring the ending in which Narcissus plunges to his death upon realizing that his love will never be reciprocated, because one didn't mention death to children. To soothe the girl, Fanny placed a finger on the picture of the narcissus in the book and suggested that she find the flower and add it to her collection. But this didn't satisfy the child. She insisted on a happy ending.

Fanny said that if there was such a thing she didn't know of it, and even if she did, she wouldn't have had the first idea how to tell it.

"You're as stubborn as a dybbuk," she murmured with a sigh, and the child couldn't decide whether that was a compliment or a criticism.

Her pleading didn't help, so she had to imagine a new ending for herself. In her version, she told the boy later, the nymph Echo didn't cry, but brought her own face nose-to-nose with that of the one she loved "to the depths of her soul." The girl repeated the expression that she didn't comprehend. At the conclusion of the girl's story, the two faces were reflected side by side in the water.

"If Narcissus sees someone apart from himself do you think he will change?" he asked.

The girl said she wasn't sure, she would have to think about it, and then he switched off the light.

Ten years had passed since the divorce. In the national elections of 1959 the Mapai Party won again, and Ben-Gurion formed the government. The riots in the Wadi Salib neighborhood over the discrimination against the Oriental Jews took place not far from the home of the aunts and uncle in Haifa. Lizzie-Bertha hurried down the steps on Stanton Street and joined the protest of the oppressed. The fact that she was a European Ashkenazi Jew was no obstacle as far as she was concerned, for she believed that women were obligated to fly the banner of rebellion everywhere they found discrimination or oppression. She even struggled with the police and shouted slogans denouncing the establishment.

Another dramatic event took place that year. The emotional meeting between Paul Newman and his father in the Hollywood movie *Exodus* was filmed in a German stone house on the cooperative moshav Alonei Abba, and so the place was forever memorialized on celluloid. And meanwhile, in New York, Gabriel and Clara attended the premier of the new Disney film *Sleeping Beauty*. He had a purely business motive, since he wanted to check on the value of his stocks, while she was excited to show off her new hairstyle a la Jackie Kennedy, a true American princess, who was infinitely more regal than the one in the animated film. Like the elegant wife of the presidential candidate, Clara also wore white gloves, a flower-shaped pin on her lapel and a string of pearls around her neck, although hers were false.

During the screening Gabriel complained that the color was disappointing. Everything looked too dark, and he predicted that the film would be a flop. He would sell his stock in Disney before it plummeted. Clara started to argue with him, and the other viewers hushed them. Technicolor was the height of new technology she thundered in a whisper, a new way to split beams of light to achieve glorious color. "Everything always looks black to you."

When they exited the cinema a photographer with a Polaroid camera was plying his trade. Gabriel detoured around him, ignoring his cries of "an on-the-spot souvenir that will last forever!" It was Clara who grabbed his arm and forced him to pose for a photograph with her. It was a copy of the one of the Kennedys that had been published in all the newspapers, although Clara's contribution to the original arrangement was to position her face close to Gabriel's. Then they had to stand and wait until the final product emerged from the camera. Gabriel was impatient and fuming. He considered photographs to be a conspiracy to raise the value of the happiness stocks. It was unlikely that John and Jackie's marriage was all roses, as it appeared in the famous photograph.

Unlike Clara, who was enthusiastic about the result, he dismissed the photo of the two of them – the only one, by the way.

"Everything is too dark. You look like a black woman." First he blamed the photographer, then he blamed the camera.

The following day the Disney stocks soared on the stock exchange, but rather than celebrate, Clara scheduled an appointment for Gabriel with the eye doctor.

4

Dear Yitzhak,

Although we have never met, I am taking the liberty of writing to you in a personal manner. Through our correspondence I have learned of your virtues as a human being as well as your devotion to your family. I am especially moved by your relationship to your mother. It is not to be taken for granted that a man will care for a woman to such an extent, especially in light of the difficult circumstances of your lives. If only I had a son like you.

Who knows better than I the price paid by one whose fate is solitude and the absence of love? You'll be surprised to hear that I identify with your mother's circumstances and I feel fondness toward her. She has never done me any wrong, unlike other women who tried to steal my man from me and embittered my life. I hope that she doesn't feel resentment toward me, since it was not me who wronged her either, and my presence in her husband's life was never at her expense. It was only my love for him – I know, an illogical, even humiliating love – that kept me by his side for all these years, without the security of marriage and in the absence of any formal commitment. I managed to come to terms with those. The main difficulty was the liberties your father took when it came to other relationships he carried on at the same time, and permit me not to elaborate and to spare his honor. However, I can no longer carry the burden alone. I am also not getting any younger and I won't have the strength to contend with the blow that fate has landed on your father.

Yitzhak, we have gone from doctor to doctor in New York, and each one gives the same unequivocal diagnosis. Your father is going blind. He has glaucoma, an incurable eye disease.

For now he still sees the world in shadows, but soon he will see nothing but total darkness.

I am sorry, but I won't be able to care for him in his current state. His sister Anna and her husband Abe have generously offered to move him to their home in Brooklyn, but in addition to their apartment being too small and unsuitable for a blind man, they have recently experienced a family crisis following their daughter's love affair, and so there is no other way. The responsibility to care for Gabriel in the dark days to come falls on you.

You are his son, for better or for worse.

Yours in sorrow,

Clara Mendel

The letter was re-read in the kitchen on Stanton Street, this time aloud. Lizzie-Bertha was the mouthpiece for Clara's distress and pointed out that it is the men who are dependent on the women as their lifeline, and not the reverse.

"See how she springs into action for him."

"Springs into action? She's abandoning him!" Emil cried, pointing at Yitzhak, "It's the man who has to come to the rescue."

The conversation around the table was held in German – the language of ghosts, used for topics deemed unsuitable for the ears of children – and the girl, who was always busy trying obsessively to unravel secrets, didn't understand the meaning of the word "abandoning," although she had long ago absorbed the words "love" and "wrong."

The boy wasn't listening. Foreign languages didn't interest him, and all he wanted was to travel to the Krayot to visit his beloved grandfather and sing with him in the synagogue. His gaze was riveted to the doorway, where a large, double-locked suitcase stood waiting. His mother was next to it, and in her hand she held a small felt sack colored a glorious shade of turquoise-blue. Fanny sat at the head of the table, hands clasped in her lap, not saying a word. The plates, piled with refreshments that no one had touched, were set on the table between her and Yitzhak who kept folding and unfolding the ticket in his hand, either trying to get rid of it or to make sure it was real. The following morning he was to set sail for New York on the *Shalom*.

"Will you come back?" the boy asked.

"Yes my son, I promise you."

The boy turned his head. He was already at the age when you know that the promises of adults are almost always nothing but hollow words. The girl still believed in them, and in the months of their father's absence the boy would try to wean her off her innocence and to prepare her for the opposite eventuality. That was the job of a responsible big brother he told her and himself.

"Where is America?" she whispered as they watched the adults who continued to speak in their secret language.

"Far away."

"How far?"

"As far as you can go."

"How do you know?"

"We always go to the sea at the end of the Yarkon. Have you ever seen the end of the sea?"

"No."

"So America is beyond the end."

"And what is there, after the end?"

"That's where people get lost and are never seen again."

The girl started to shake. And she didn't stop shaking even when they said goodbye to their father at the port.

"I won't see you anymore Daddy?"

"Of course you will, bunny."

"When?"

"When you are a little bit bigger."

"When I'm old like Grandma Fanny?"

"No, bunny. You'll still be a little girl."

She forced herself not to cry – if she did her brother would call her a baby – and begged her father to take them with him to America. That way they could watch over him so that he wouldn't get lost at the end beyond the end of the world. She was afraid that there wouldn't be anyone in the world who would call her bunny. Gently her mother lifted her away from her father, and then he knelt down and embraced the boy.

"Take care of your little sister."

The boy promised, even swore that he would, because the promises of children are always uttered with pure intent, and he was also shaking.

Only their mother was fully in control, as if she was already skilled at farewells. She handed Yitzhak the felt bag in that unmistakable shade of blue, and he opened it and removed an old photograph. Mimi explained that it had accidentally gone missing from among Gabriel's things when he had visited the kibbutz a decade before. At the last moment she had managed to salvage it from oblivion. It was likely that the woman in the photograph was Clara.

"This way you may be able to identify her on the pier in New York."

The features of the woman in the photograph had faded. It was impossible to tell whether she had been hideous or beautiful. Only the string of pearls around her neck still shone, unblemished.

Fanny was the last to say goodbye to Yitzhak. As she approached him he hurriedly hid the photograph in his pocket. Why hurt her unnecessarily? At least he could conceal from her the face of her rival. In any case, the two would never meet.

The horn was already sounding. Fanny continued to hold onto her son as he advanced up the ramp, her tears pouring silently down her face. For the first time in their lives, the two children saw an adult cry. But what shocked them even more was that as their father moved farther away he suddenly looked like a child.

Yitzhak never asked Fanny what had happened on the day that she bid farewell to Gabriel in Bukovina so many years before. How far had she accompanied him when he set off for America? Or perhaps she had chosen not to accompany him at all, to spare herself the white-hot knife of parting.

Go from your country, your wife, and your children, to your father who you never loved, to the America that I will show you.

5

"Is it you?"

"Yes, it's me."

Yitzhak needed time to adjust to the touch of Gabriel's fingers on his face. At first they were light and cautious, and then they pressed harder, like someone learning the topography of a country and committing it to memory so as not to forget a single detail. The high forehead, the thick hair – always combed back from his face – the fleshy cheeks, the long eyelashes he had inherited from Fanny.

"You resemble me more every day."

Yitzhak tensed. His father's fingers traced the angry creases.

"No I don't."

The two spoke only in English. Yitzhak had chosen that language. It suited the desert island where he found himself. At the age of forty he was suddenly forced to live with a stranger who on paper was his father, and to share with him an involuntary intimacy. To inhale his smell – always some expensive cologne mingled with Chesterfields – to hear the sound of his breathing and sometimes his groans as he slept. When mumbling in Russian arose from the pillow Yitzhak always blocked his ears.

Against his will he was now adapting himself to his father's life of disrupted routine. Since going to work at the stock exchange was now out of the question, Gabriel sat for hours listening to the financial programs on the radio, and instructing his son in how to decipher the enigma of ticker tape. He taught him the basic principles, such as price fluctuations, stock indices, and dividends, simultaneously haranguing him with sermons about how capitalism was the perfect economic system.

"Even you in Israel will yet discover it and throw off the burden of socialism."

"We are building a society that will be an example to all," Yitzhak declared, adding that social solidarity was a Jewish value.

Gabriel snorted. "You Zionists always speak in slogans. No one is a 'light unto the nations.' Your theory runs counter to the competitive instinct inherent in human nature and one day it will blow up in your face.

Yitzhak restrained himself. Among all the great ideologies of the twentieth century, only Zionism was destined to survive, because there was a historical correction at its very core, and not a lust for power for its own sake or a desire to dominate.

His father snorted, "You are so naïve. The Jewish People are a success story only when they are scattered and dispersed across the world. Better the Jews shouldn't start to compete with one another."

Despite the ideological chasm, these arguments between them were like measured and subdued games of ping pong, as though they were two scholars on an academic podium, and the true animosity was hidden away.

They didn't talk about the blindness either. Gabriel kept his bitterness to himself, and only when he recited the daily Amidah did Yitzhak notice the special emphasis he placed on the eighth prayer, "Heal us, O Lord, and we will be healed; help us and we will be saved; for You are our praise. Grant complete cure and healing to all our wounds…"

With the help of his connections Manny Greenberg made an appointment for Gabriel with a specialist on the West Coast, but they would have to wait three months, and so Yitzhak's stay was extended. Despite his deteriorating condition, Gabriel was adamant that he maintain his high standards of grooming and insisted on shaving himself every morning, without help. This was a relief for Yitzhak, who did all he could to avoid physical contact with him, but at the same time examined his father's face hoping to detect a spot he had missed. To no avail. Gabriel ran his fingertips over every inch of his own face and shaved himself perfectly.

In the afternoon Yitzhak would walk him over to Clara's apartment, and in the evening he would bring him back. The same routine every day. It appeared that the regimented separation was what preserved their relationship during that turbulent time. Maybe the arrangement of two separate households wasn't such a crazy idea after all. And although he suspected that it hadn't come about at her initiative, Yitzhak was aware of Clara's willingness to adhere to the agreement.

In reality she looked completely different from the woman in the faded photograph that Mimi had pressed into his hand at the Haifa port, and when Yitzhak learned that she had lost her entire family in Europe, he chose not to ask her when and where the photograph was taken so as not to reopen old wounds. She compensated for Gabriel's silences with constant chatter. Mostly she repeated the latest gossip from Hollywood and the trials and tribulations of John and Jackie Kennedy. She refused to listen to any rumor about the senator's dubious connections to Senator McCarthy and even volunteered to help with his election campaign. When an heir was born to the Kennedys, she celebrated as though it was her next of kin. Each time she fixed her gaze on Yitzhak he felt that she was seeing the son she might have had, and in contrast to her bursts of giggles her eyes were always veiled with sadness.

With Clara he chose to speak in German.

During the hours that Gabriel spent with Clara Yitzhak walked the length and breadth of Manhattan, swallowed up in the hustle and bustle of the city. More than once he wondered what would have happened had he grown up there. It is doubtful that he would have been gripped by the Zionist ideology that had determined the course of his life. "In America a man works for his home, not for his country," he wrote in one of his letters home. Tel Aviv looked so infinitesimal when compared with the skyscrapers of booming New York City. The highest building in his city stretched eight stories and had been built not far from the immigrant neighborhood where they lived, near the Yarkon River – not too impressive – but when he stood below the Empire State Building it seemed to him that the needle at its tip pierced the sky and imbibed a non-stop infusion of ambition. He even found work as a journalist and covered the UN debates about Israel for the Hungarian daily *Új Kelet*. Still, the more New York presented him with exhilarating challenges, the more he longed for home. Through all those long months of absence he sat at night near the open kitchen window on Clinton Street – in a desperate attempt to catch a breeze in a steaming New York summer –and filled page after page. The first thing he did after bringing Gabriel over to Clara was to visit the neighborhood post office. The amount of glue he absorbed licking stamps was enough to bind together entire families, not only his.

"Why not transfer your whole family to America?" suggested the postal clerk, who had grown fond of his regular customer. "It would be cheaper than sending letters."

Despite the fact that the option of citizenship arose again, and Gabriel was even willing to consider a creative solution for his ex-wife, for Yitzhak the very idea smacked of sacrilege.

"In spite of everything, a Zionist is what I am," Yitzhak uttered the same sentiment that would inspire the autobiography he would pen many years later. But what tortured him most of all was the trauma of abandonment. Would he repeat the pattern, and be considered a father who had abandoned his children?

The boy and the girl remember the day when they were told that their father would be calling them from America. They didn't have a phone yet, so the event was to take place in the neighbor's apartment, on the top floor. For hours the two stood by the magical black machine, holding hands and waiting for the jangle that would be followed by their father's voice coming from the end beyond the end of the world.

The girl asked him, "When will you come back?" and the boy asked, "Will you really come back?"

I save like a treasure the letter that my father sent me from Clinton Street. It is a thin slip of paper, almost transparent, upon which words are written in one breath, with no crossings out or corrections.

> *My maidele, my bunny,*
>
> *The mother wrote to me that you are sad and you say that Daddy ran away. That's not true. I didn't run away. I love my bunny very much. I went to buy her a doll with hair and a pretty dress, but so far I haven't found one. Soon they will be bringing pretty dolls from Japan and I will buy you a beautiful doll, and more beautiful presents. I will take the grandfather from here and we will travel together to Tel Aviv and to the children, to Mother, and to Grandmother who are waiting for us there.*
>
> *So don't be sad. Be joyful. Play nicely, bathe in the sea, and then I will ring the doorbell. You will open up for me and we will all be at home.*
>
> *Raisins and Almonds is playing on the radio now, and I am thinking about my bunny who loves that song. How are the curls? And how are the dolls? Are they good girls?*
>
> *Lots of kisses for your cheeks, your hair, your curls, and for the whole maidele you are.*
>
> *With love, Daddy*

6

"He didn't run away," the girl insisted. "He knows that we aren't angry at him."

The boy answered, "We don't know why grownups run away. Maybe when we are grown up we will know."

The girl said, "Daddy promised that he'll come back."

"But he didn't say when," the boy replied. Later he promised, "Even when you're old I will take care of you."

The photographer who took their picture berated them for disrupting his concentration. In the photograph the boy's eyes are shut because of the glare of the flash, but his smile is flawless and he beams at those beyond the frame, as if to an anonymous audience. The girl is posing nicely, her curls tied back with a gigantic ribbon, and she is also smiling, revealing a mouth full of baby teeth. Yitzhak held tight to this display of small happiness, and described every detail to Gabriel. It was always in his pocket, and he showed it to Anna and Abe countless times. They became his family, and the weekend visits to their house in Brooklyn were rare hours of pleasure.

With them he spoke in Yiddish.

Anna, whose face was a female version of Gabriel's, was his complete opposite in character. He believed her to be gentle and overflowing with compassion, kind and welcoming. Until the moment when he discovered that brother and sister really were cut from the same cloth.

It happened when he asked why he hadn't yet met his cousin Florence and expressed his wish that she be invited to the next family gathering. Anna's face hardened and closed, and she was transformed into a duplicate of her brother. A bitterness settled on her husband as if rather than a simple request, an axe stroke had fallen on the conversation.

"She's dead."

Abe spoke. Anna was silent.

Yitzhak reflexively recited the Hebrew formula recited at such news, "May God comfort you among the other mourners of Zion and Jerusalem," and only when his gaze wandered to the framed photographs on the wall did he realize to his surprise that the daughter was missing from all the family pictures. Were they not overcome with longing for the girl who had died an untimely death? Was their sorrow so great that they weren't able to go on living with the sight of her portrait? Just the mention of her name had brought the conversation to an abrupt end, and faced with the cloud that suddenly hung over the table Yitzhak quickly sought a pretext to return to Manhattan. At the station closest to Central Park Gabriel asked to get off the train and instructed Yitzhak to lead him along the path that led to the water. They sat down on a bench by the boat house and there he told Yitzhak that Florence had fallen in love with a Catholic and chosen to follow him. Anna and Abe had observed the traditional shiva mourning period and disowned her. Gabriel referred to her as "the convert."

"How did you allow it to happen?" Yitzhak attacked him. For the first time the dangerous pain from the past, so meticulously kept under wraps, escaped its constraints.

Gabriel roared back, "As if you can control love. Nothing could have stopped that woman."

"Who's talking about love?" Yitzhak raised his voice higher. "I'm talking about death. Haven't we had enough deaths in the family? You're the elder brother. You shouldn't have allowed them to tear it apart."

Gabriel murmured the cliché about one who leaves the Jewish faith and is considered as one who has died.

"What do you know about what her man would have done for her? Maybe he would have joined her, joined us?"

Passersby turned to look at the two men quarreling on the bench by the rocks. Yitzhak was red with fury. Had he been endowed with a different nature, one less-forgiving, he would have left on the spot and boarded the first boat back to Israel. For a moment he wondered whether the blindness was a punishment from on high, befitting a man whose eyes were unable to see anyone but himself.

This time Gabriel's hand stretched out to mold his face, pinching and kneading the skin, as though trying to create him in his own image. Yitzhak pulled away and fell off the bench straight onto the rocks.

At the sound of his fall Gabriel groped in the air trying to help him up, but Yitzhak dodged his hands.

"You don't care about losing people. You rip them out without batting an eyelid and move on. For you abandonment is a way of life." He lashed out with those sentences in German, "But I won't give up. I will find Florence."

Through the tear in Yitzhak's pants a cut was visible. His thigh was bleeding. Gabriel extracted his ever-present, perfectly-pressed handkerchief from his suit pocket and held it out to his son. How did he know that he had hurt himself when he fell? Yitzhak had already reached the conclusion that Gabriel's other senses had sharpened to compensate for his failing eyesight.

Maybe he could smell the blood.

A waiter from the boat house hurried to their assistance, his black skin a stark contrast to the white handkerchief he applied to Yitzhak's leg.

"Maybe you need a tetanus shot mister," and he offered to take him to the nearest hospital.

"I have natural immunity," Yitzhak responded. After all, he had absorbed not a few knocks and injuries in his life, and never been infected.

The waiter grinned, revealing blindingly white teeth and wished him a speedy recovery. When he finished his shift he made a formal complaint about the hazard and demanded from the park authorities that it be seen to immediately.

A lame man and a blind man made their way along the path to the pond, accompanied by the rustling of the leaves. Gabriel stopped at the fountain in the middle of Central Park, his ears cocked toward the sound of the water, and described every inch of the statue at the top. It was a bronze angel in the form of a woman blessing the water below. Some claimed that she had healing powers.

"You don't look to me like a man who believes in superstitions," Yitzhak remarked.

"I've learned to respect them," and then Gabriel asked whether there were any geese flying overhead.

"Empty sky," Yitzhak replied, without bothering to look up and check. Gabriel claimed that geese could bring good or bad luck, depending on the way they flew, adding that there was a story in the Talmudic literature about how, on the day when the forefather Yitzhak was born, vision was restored to all who were blind. To this his son had no reaction at all.

Gabriel still lingered. He was convinced that he had heard the honking of geese. He approached the fountain, arms extended. When pursuing women, he had often brought them here. He would take them for a ride around the park in a horse-drawn carriage. Perhaps he was clinging to a fond memory. Yitzhak suspected that his father's memory had also sharpened. From where had he suddenly come up with this nonsense about geese?

Gabriel dipped his fingers into the water and touched them to his eyes. Then he leaned his head in the direction of the angel that was oxidizing to a greenish hue, and murmured a verse from Ecclesiastes, "For healing may lay great offences to rest."

Yitzhak demurred when Gabriel suggested that he sprinkle some water on the cut in his leg. He was thinking more about the great offences than the healing. By the time they exited the park the handkerchief he was pressing to his thigh was soaked through with blood. Knowing that for Gabriel every detail of his attire had to be impeccable, he wondered if it could ever be returned to its pristine state. When he consulted Clara she said that it was impossible to remove bloodstains and tossed it into the trash.

"But Gabriel won't see the stains," he tried to argue.

"We will see them," she replied.

When they emerged from the subway station on the Lower East Side Gabriel asked to stop again, this time at a secondhand store he knew. It was an Ali Baba cave cluttered with objects piled on top of each other, the possessions of refugees and immigrants who had parted with them for a few dollars.

To Yitzhak's surprise, Gabriel asked the owner to show him a selection of walking sticks. He handled each one slowly. The cane with a handle like a cobra, and others whose heads were carved in the shape of a frog, a horse, a dragon, an owl, and a lion. The proprietor recommended a stick with a sphinx that he said was very stable, but after a quick examination Gabriel rejected it. He lingered over the one with a small carving of Atlas, carrying the weight of the world on his shoulders, and even asked his son to check its ability to support a man.

Yitzhak rejected it out of hand. No mythological creature carried the weight of the world, but rather men of flesh and blood. The proprietor's face turned yellow. This was a precious treasure he had purchased years before from a lovely woman who spoke with a heavy Hungarian accent. Her beauty was hard to forget, not to mention her bearing and style of dress. Glamor and good taste of the highest order. No doubt an old world aristocrat, maybe even a princess. He still remembered her name – Ildiko. Who could forget such a name? All of a sudden Gabriel became more animated, but his interest was piqued less by the walking stick than by its previous owner. He even asked the shopkeeper if he had by any chance kept the woman's address.

"I'm sorry. I lost it."

Gabriel seemed disappointed. And although the man urged him to buy the Atlas stick even just as a souvenir of an illustrious past – he might make a tidy profit from it some day – in the end he chose a wooden cane made of birch with a sterling silver handle and no carvings. This time Yitzhak objected for practical reasons, claiming that Gabriel's hand might lose its grip on the slippery metal and his balance would be upset. Not to mention that he hadn't been born holding a silver handle, and preferred not to lend his hand to an unnecessarily ostentatious purchase. Perhaps it was this outburst that led the proprietor to assume that the cane was meant for the man with a limp.

"You have a generous supporter," he remarked when Gabriel paid the bill. Not for a moment did he suspect that the pair was father and son.

Although they were now the owners of the stick, neither man was eager to acknowledge his infirmity in public. They hobbled along slowly between Clinton and Norfolk streets, supporting one another, the silver handle bouncing between them. Sparks of light reflected in the silver bounced off into the eyes of the passersby, and one man shouted mockingly, "You'd be better off with a seeing eye dog!"

"Mind your own business," Gabriel barked, and then he remarked to Yitzhak that he hadn't lost all hope. The specialist on the West Coast would find a remedy for his failing eyesight. American medicine was the most advanced in the world.

They stumbled along in silence, until Gabriel finally used the cane as a support. Soon the pain in Yitzhak's leg passed, and he was able to walk normally.

"Florence isn't lost," he said as he pushed Gabriel through the door. "No matter what you say, I will find my cousin."

He spoke in a mixture of languages, uttering the first few words in Hebrew.

In the end he did locate her, in Little Italy, where she lived with her Catholic husband Jimmy DiMauro. When he introduced himself on the telephone, she burst into tears. It was the first contact from someone in her family for a very long time. However, he didn't manage to meet the lover who had crossed the lines, since the appointment with the eye specialist was scheduled for the same day.

American medicine was of no help at all. The sentence was final. Total blindness.

7

To move to Israel? Inconceivable. Yitzhak's furious prophecy, "Your America will be a world of darkness," was countered with equal fury by Gabriel, and revealed some of what was hidden between his seemingly impenetrable mask. It was a major attack as befits one who was trained by the Austrian army and fought in the First World War. Gabriel returned to the trenches. He launched volleys of insults, fired missiles of slander against the Zionist chutzpah to establish sovereignty in the bleeding Middle East of all places, and the ultimate weapon he utilized – the mustard gas as far as he was concerned – was to accuse his son, as the representative of the younger generation that dared to gamble with the destiny of the miserable nation that knew only horrors, and now "you are leading us astray and selling us an intangible bill of goods from the Bible. The land of our fathers had a safe existence in our dreams and our prayers, and you are transforming them into reality and endangering us all."

To his credit, it must be noted that this time Gabriel did not desert. Even as they boarded the *Zion*, he continued to oppose the conspiracy that had been weaved behind his back, and even told one of the ship's passengers that his son was an agent sent to encourage emigration to Israel and seduce innocent and wealthy Jews into emptying their pockets. He was sure that even the name of the ship was part of the plot, and the number of times Yitzhak explained that it was one of the very few liners that sailed the New York–Haifa route, made no difference at all. A ceasefire was declared only when Gabriel was promised the status of a Temporary Resident, and Yitzhak swore that if the experience in Israel didn't go well, he would take him back to the United States.

From the other side of the ocean Fanny also returned fire, proving that the couple may have had more in common than people suspected – and all this when they were already divorced. A veteran of struggles in her own right, she also did her utmost to abolish the evil decree, although there was no decision-maker on her end with whom she could bargain. Therefore, she was compelled to make do with the declaration that she would not allow "that man" to set foot in her house. The girl, who was a terrible coward, searched for solutions.

"Maybe we can chase him away?" she asked the boy.

"We can ignore him. As if he doesn't exist."

To the girl this sounded like the cruelest of punishments. Like that time when the boy was angry because she wasn't prepared to do what he told her. He didn't speak to her for days, even turned his back on her at night, when she begged him to tell her a story. At the time she thought she was dead. Maybe she never should have been born at all. Maybe that's what would happen to "that man," and he would run back to the end beyond the end of the world.

The girl was afraid that she would turn into her mother, or into her grandmother who insisted that she would shut out "that man."

Even before she met him she felt compassion for him, although she had yet to learn the word.

It was the same feeling her father felt.

It is important to be accurate. Yitzhak did not love Gabriel. He didn't even like him. The months spent alongside him had dispelled some of the distance, but the alienation was untouched. Truth be told he could have chosen a different solution and been rid of him, and no one would have faulted him. Clara even came to an agreement with a Jewish old age home in Riverdale and promised to visit Gabriel regularly. But Yitzhak couldn't live with the abandonment.

That mosquito of a conscience, the one that hums within the soul, what to do about it? As is well-known, there is no remedy for it.

And then there was Fanny. Yitzhak knew that she of all people wouldn't forgive him.

The voyage took two weeks. The sea was rough, which was difficult for them both. Yitzhak worked hard to prevent Gabriel from falling over. Meanwhile, Gabriel recalled his first crossing from Liverpool, rather than his trip of a decade before. The sights assailed him as if the experience was fresh. Buckets of vomit. The foul-smelling deck. Mrs. Jackson and the song *Swanee*, which was and remained his favorite American tune, that he would often hum to himself while he shaved.

"I've been away from you a long time, I never thought I'd miss ya so…"

Yitzhak covered his ears to spare himself Gabriel's tuneless rendition.

He could still distinguish between light and shadow, and sometimes make out figures, so that there were instances when he would shake off his son and grasp the ship's railing instead. In the evening they were invited to sit at the captain's table. The captain had been a member of the Palmach's naval force and respected Yitzhak for his activities on the illegal immigrant ship *Knesset Yisrael.* The preferential treatment his son received made Gabriel puff up with pride, and in public he made sure to list his accomplishments, in stark contrast to the disdain he affected when the two were alone.

He dressed up even more than usual for the meals at the captain's table. He chose one of the ties from his collection – recently added to at Barneys in New York before he sailed – and insisted on knotting it unaided. His demeanor was impeccable, and he ate whatever was on the plate that the waiter placed before him, with no one the wiser about his impending blindness. He wore sunglasses at all times, claiming that his eyes were sensitive to light.

"You'll have to adjust to that," said the captain, "We have a surplus of light in Israel. People find it blinding." Next he raised his glass in a toast to the new immigrant. "What is a Zionist? He's one Jew who begs money off a second Jew, so that a third Jew can go and settle in Israel."

Gabriel concluded the joke, "And then a fourth Jew borrows money from a fifth Jew to get out of there."

Everyone laughed except for Yitzhak. For him, Zionism and black humor would never go together.

Another diner at their table was a woman whose laugh reminded Yitzhak of Clara's. She was Gloria née Rothstein, who always wore bold-colored floral dresses and was a heavy donor traveling to Israel as a guest of the United Jewish Appeal, a widow who had been married three times. Over a glass of dry Avdat wine – only Israeli wines were served at the captain's table – she recounted that her origins were in a New York business dynasty, neglecting to mention her infamous uncle, Arnold Rothstein. Better not to be associated with the man considered to be the father of organized crime in the United States and one of the most well-known Jewish gangsters of the twentieth century.

The presence of a woman caused a total personality transformation in Gabriel. This was Yitzhak's opportunity to watch a master Romeo in action. Even at his advanced age his father could still pluck all the rabbits of seduction out of his hat. The moment Gloria learned, from his son, that Gabriel was divorced, she homed in on him, relishing his achievements on Wall Street – "I was the first Jew to break the glass ceiling of anti-Semitism there" – and when the fried potatoes were served, for the first time Yitzhak heard a reference to his early life in Russia. He provided a rendition of the marching song *Farewell to Slavianka* as he downed glasses of Carmel Mizrahi wine, and remembered every word.

"To which Slavic woman did you bid farewell?" asked his son.

"I erase all farewells," his father shot back.

If blindness leads to an improvement in memory, with respect to Clara, Gabriel undermined the tendency. He preferred to forget his last night with her. The way she had packed his things one by one, like an art curator removing works from the walls and cataloging them in the bowels of a museum. She adhered to the order he strictly observed, first shirts, then trousers, then each tie, rolled and encased in its own sack. She occasionally mentioned when a particular handkerchief, undershirt or pair of underpants had been purchased and noted what she had bought for him and what he had bought for himself.

She also packed the gifts for the two children. She paid a fortune at Schwarz's toy store on Fifth Avenue for a fire truck for the boy and a doll with hair for the girl, just like the one she had always dreamed of.

It was a relief to Gabriel that Clara didn't cry. Neither did she give him advice or predict what he might expect. The only thing she said when they embraced for the final time was, "Be happy that you have grandchildren." Only now did he notice how her body had thickened. He hadn't touched her in years.

She refused to accompany him to the port. Before handing her the keys to her apartment he uttered the cliché he had never set much stock in, "Take care of yourself," and she responded with a quote from the Wayfarer's Prayer, "… and grant us grace, kindness, and mercy in Your eyes and in the eyes of all who see us."

He wouldn't see, but there would be those who would see him. He had managed to erase this thought as well.

Even though Gloria Rothstein's laughter reminded him of Clara's, hers was more natural and didn't hint at embarrassment or lack of confidence. By the time they had finished their meal at the captain's table she had invited him to accompany her to the bingo game and the entertainments presented in the ship's Hora Hall. She never dared to participate in card games so that no one would suddenly associate her with the Rothstein who was the gambling kingpin of New York. Her greatest fear was that in Israel they would discover that her money was tainted and reject her donations. With an impressive man at her side, especially a new immigrant whose son had impeccable Zionist credentials, her image would be kosher and her unsavory family connections forgotten. They danced a tango to the strains of the on-board orchestra and Gabriel allowed Gloria to lead, which charmed her further. It seemed that even his vision was somewhat restored, but it may have been his romantic frame of mind that created the illusion of an improvement. Whichever it was, he succeeded in deceiving her, for a while.

The dance of flirtation didn't escape the attention of the captain.

"It's never too late to marry…" he remarked to Yitzhak when the two were left alone at the table, and Yitzhak didn't conclude the sentence with the other words of that saying: "or to die."

What would happen when Mrs. Rothstein realized that the charming man was going blind?

For several days Yitzhak amused himself with the fantasy that the new paramour would be revealed as a merciful nurse. She would take him back to America with her and care for him devotedly for the rest of his life, a glamorous deus ex machina for this romantic drama. However, a cheap trick like that wasn't part of the plan concocted by the most talented scriptwriter in the world. It was but a short respite before reality returned to stare them down.

On the last night aboard ship there was a farewell ball. The orchestra played Israeli songs, and Yitzhak found himself translating the words of *The Tag Song*, a Hebrew hit composed by Amitai Neema about a couple who were childhood friends who used to play Tag together. When he wanted her, she ran off to the balcony, and when he became a grown man and managed to root her out of his heart, she remained alone on the balcony, waiting in vain for the love of her youth to return and play Tag with her again.

"His grandchildren love this song," Yitzhak told Gloria, as he pointed at Gabriel.

"I have two. I've never seen the girl," Gabriel proudly withdrew a photograph that had been tucked behind his handkerchief in his breast pocket.

"See how cute they are. Fully kosher sabras."

Except that the photograph wasn't of two children, but portrayed the faded image of a woman. Gloria ran her finger over the strand of pearls around the woman's neck and touched the white oval that had once contained a face. She held the picture up close to Gabriel's face and he examined it with his fingertips.

"Is this your true love? Are you returning to her?"

Gabriel felt the creases in the photograph under his fingertips. Only he could sense the one-time presence of gunpowder. That is how he realized it was the *liebling*.

"This isn't my woman," he declared, and handed the photo to Yitzhak.

And that was how Gloria née Rothstein discovered that Gabriel was completely blind. She removed his sunglasses, folded them and placed them in his suit pocket, behind his handkerchief. What luck that she hadn't inherited the gene for revenge from her gangster uncle. He ruthlessly murdered anyone who threatened the empire of crime that he had created. With him, such fraud would have ended in the best case with a bullet to the head, and in the worst with dismemberment of limbs which would be tossed into the Hudson River. Except that Gloria, like the granddaughter who didn't appear anywhere in the photograph, felt compassion for Gabriel.

The Tag Song played on in the Hora Hall. Yitzhak hadn't told a lie. The girl really did love it. The singer Shulamit Livnat had a clear voice and a consummate Israeli accent, and the girl imitated her. But what worried her about the song was why the music was so joyful, when the words were so sad.

In the song, when he wanted her, she didn't want him, and when she wanted him, he didn't want her, and so it went on. Why wasn't it possible to bring them together on the balcony once and for all and put an end to that game of Tag?

The girl didn't understand that everything is a question of timing.

The SS *Zion* approached the Israeli coastline, with the lights of Haifa flickering in the distance. Yitzhak saw that view for the third time in his life. The first time it was as an illegal immigrant on the *Knesset Yisrael*, which was being towed by a British destroyer, the second time on the freedom ship that brought him from Cyprus with Mimi and Fanny as legal immigrants. The view of the lights had changed since then and the luminous display was scattered across the Carmel Mountain and beyond. The light was even blinding.

As he described it to his father, Yitzhak embellished the view and attributed to it a majesty that it didn't possess. Just like his little girl, who would also soon learn to use her imagination and take advantage of the fact that by that time, Gabriel couldn't see anything at all.

8

Again, it was Fanny who opened the door to him when he arrived. In some strange way he had recognized her footsteps, although it made no sense. They had lived together for only a short time, many years before, so there was no logical explanation.

"You've aged," were the words with which she greeted him.

"I can't see you so I can't tell you the same." Gabriel's response was evidence that he hadn't lost his sharp Bukovinian sense of humor along with his eyesight.

He heard her chuckle. Unlike Clara, her laughter was bitter, as though her vocal chords had been splashed with absinthe.

"How do you know, Gabriel? Maybe in Israel we go backwards. In the end I'll return to the age I was when we met."

He made no effort to feel her face, as he did to all the other members of the family.

The girl was shocked at the touch of his fingers, but wonder of wonders, they grazed her face softly, just like a butterfly's wings, and she soon stopped shaking. She never referred to him as "that man," but as *Zayde* – Yiddish for grandfather. The boy used the same name for him, but in his mouth it sounded like an insult. From the first moment he recoiled from the elegant old man with the foreign smell that seemed to embody pure diaspora, and was a blemish on the "Israeliness" that was his most fervent desire. The irony of fate. It was his eldest grandchild to whom Gabriel was particularly drawn. He reminded him that he had seen him in his crib in the Children's House on the kibbutz, that he had caressed his fair, downy head and held him at his circumcision ceremony, but the boy retreated further and never touched the fire truck. He moved to sleep next to Fanny on the balcony, and a folding bed was set up for the girl in the adjacent room with Gabriel. At night she missed her brother and held tight to the doll with hair from which she was never parted.

The prohibition against the union of a divorced couple was the ostensible reason for the separation, but in truth it was a blurred demarcation in an arena which consisted of only vengeance and compulsions. "An eye for an eye," with full recognition of the irony of that biblical expression in the current circumstances.

Every time Gabriel discerned Fanny's approaching footsteps he tried to leave the room. For her part, she deliberately came toward him and enjoyed watching him search for an escape route only to find that he was backed up against a wall. He rejected the food that was served to him, mainly if she had prepared it, and complained about a lack of salt and spices. She was ever stingier with their use, "for health reasons." He grumbled that the apartment was too small, and she pushed his bed against the wall arguing that he might fall out.

He found more and more things to criticize. The Israeli weather was the embodiment of hell. The flies and mosquitos were Zionist mutations. And the strange odor that rose from the Yarkon, as opposed to the clear Hudson, was the flatulence of the Zionist enterprise.

From the moment when the mask that he had worn for all those years finally fell, everything came tumbling out. Except for his blindness. He never mentioned the root of his current bitter circumstances and the true reason for his fury and frustration.

Those first months were a period of wounding. Unwittingly the two children were exposed to a wide spectrum of mutual abuse. It started with stinging remarks and insults, continued with comments that nullified, scorned, and belittled the other, and culminated in the cruelest treatment of all – deliberate disregard and refusal to acknowledge the other's existence. Following the exchange of verbal blows, for days Fanny and Gabriel behaved as if the other didn't exist. The girl swore that she would never make anyone else feel as though he didn't exist.

The boy said, "Grownups are much worse than children."

The girl didn't ask whether there was anything they could do about it, maybe because she could guess what the answer would be.

And yet, she was aware of the presence of something else between the grandmother and grandfather that she couldn't give a name to. A concealed effervescence humming just below the surface. A white noise that only she could hear. Since the girl didn't yet understand English, how could she know the expression "old flame?" There was no one to explain to her that an "old flame" was an earlier love. One that continues to burn like an ember from a Lag b'Omer bonfire, which is something with which she was familiar.

When she asked the boy he said it was like someone pulling on her braids.

"What kind of a game is that?"

"He's so frightened that she'll realize that he loves her, that he behaves as if he hates her more than anything." The boy was exceptionally wise for his age.

But the girl didn't understand why anyone should be afraid to love, and if they already were in love, then why would they want to hide it? She vowed never to play the games the adults played, although it was a vow that proved difficult to keep.

And yet there were moments of grace. On the Sabbath Yitzhak would lead Gabriel to the Ashkenazi synagogue which gave him the status of one who draws or leads others, in the language of the sages, or one whose task it was to lead the blind. Gabriel actually preferred the Yemenite synagogue, where they used the touchingly ironic expression to refer to him as the "one who is full of light," another concept bursting with compassion coined by the Jewish sages to spare a blind person disgrace. The boy, who was enchanted by the Eastern melodies, would accompany him.

The girl also offered to be the one who led him along. It was her chance to roam the streets of Tel Aviv, which she was never allowed to do alone. In her gym bloomers and sleeveless top she skipped alongside the old man who was encased in his three-piece suit, and when they lingered at the mouth of the Yarkon on the beach, she used his walking stick to trace the English words he taught her in the sand. When she offered to teach him Hebrew, he refused.

"Why, *Zayde*?"

"Hebrew is a sacred language, and you have brought it down to the level of the everyday."

She didn't understand what he meant, but she was still hurt.

He was "Grandpa No-No," although he never refused her a thing. She was the only one on whom he worked his infamous charm, and his stick became a plaything, especially the shiny silver handle that she would angle toward the sun to make it reflect the light.

"Can you see anything, *Zayde*?" She never lost hope.

The boy suspected that he was faking. Gabriel could already navigate the rooms of the apartment flawlessly, so that it was hard to believe that he couldn't see. The boy never stopped testing him, only to discover that his grandfather detoured round any obstacle that he set in his path, be it a chair, a table, or a stool, as his groping hands or tentative feet always divined it.

"You see, he can see," he would tell the girl triumphantly.

When Gabriel offered to take the children to the cinema, the boy rejected the invitation immediately, but the girl danced with excitement.

Fanny hurriedly appeared to sway Mimi's decision. "A blind man and a child going to a film? It's dangerous."

Her anxious mother agreed, "Who knows what might happen?"

The girl promised that she would be careful and responsible. At that moment she managed to overcome her fear. She wanted so much to see the new Disney movie, *One Hundred and One Dalmatians*.

"It's called, *Of Dogs and Robbers* in Hebrew, *Zayde*."

"Why are you people always changing the names, *maidele*?" He never called the girl by her Hebrew name, but always used Yiddish terms of endearment.

The relatives in Haifa also joined the family debate. Lizzie-Bertha sided with the girl and tried to persuade everyone else. A mission of this weight would contribute to her self-confidence and in the future she would be a woman who would know how to stand up for her rights.

In the end, she succeeded in convincing them, except for the boy who warned that it would end in tears. He had inherited Fanny's outlook on the world.

They traveled to Dizengoff Square by bus. The girl described to Gabriel all the shops and cafes, and the other passengers listened in as well. This time she was careful not to exaggerate, much as she wanted to outshine his beloved New York, and for a change he didn't make any nasty comments about her city.

When they reached the square he turned his cane in the direction of the sound of the water falling in the fountain and asked if there was a statue at the top.

"What kind of statue?" She had heard only of the roaring lion at Tel Hai, but she hadn't seen that yet.

"A woman." Even at her young age she could discern the wistfulness in his voice.

He described the angel with the drooping eyelids who blessed the water in Central Park and endowed it with healing properties. The girl's imagination started to work and she searched for the angel in the jets of water shooting upward, while he cautioned her not to believe in nonsense. Nevertheless, she insisted on dipping her hand in the water and sprinkling it on his eyes.

"If only one day you could really see me," she said.

He hugged her and said that even without eyes he knew exactly what she looked like.

It was the grandest compliment she had ever received.

At the cafeteria at the cinema he bought her Bazooka bubblegum.

While they sat in their seats in the hall, her heart hammering with excitement at the impending rise of the curtain, he recited the list of the Disney animated films. It had never occurred to her that there could be an adult so familiar with *Snow White* and *Pinocchio*, *Fantasia* and *Dumbo* the flying elephant, and *Bambi*, *Cinderella*, *Alice in Wonderland* and *Peter Pan*. She even suspected that her grandfather might be Walt Disney in disguise.

The curtain went up slowly, and the darkness enveloped her as well. He whispered to her that she didn't have to tell him what was happening in the film because he could hear everything, even the footsteps in the background.

Still, she couldn't hold back. She described to him how pretty the animated Anita was, because otherwise he wouldn't understand why Roger fell in love with her. Their matchmaker was Pongo the Dalmatian – his fur white with black spots. He had a hidden motive for bringing them together. He was in love with Perdita, Anita's pet Dalmatian. When they went for a walk in the park, which extended much farther than the strips of grass surrounding Dizengoff Square, the four-legged matchmaker couldn't engineer a way for the two-legged creatures to meet. As a last resort he managed to push the man and the woman into the pond. Anita was angry, but the gallant Roger offered her his handkerchief, and although it wasn't ironed smooth like Gabriel's, but was more like a wet rag, Anita fell in love with him on the spot. Within minutes the couple was married and had moved with the dogs, who were also in love, to a house with lots and lots of rooms, many more than they had.

All this the girl whispered into Gabriel's ear, so she wouldn't disturb the other people in the audience. When the wicked Cruella De Vil entered the picture, she fell silent. She hoped her grandfather's hearing wasn't as sharp as he said, and spared him the descriptions of the villainy and evil of the woman who wanted to slaughter the sweet puppies to make them into a fur coat. All around her people were peeling sticks of chewing gum, and she rose from her seat and wanted to leave in the middle. She didn't touch her Bazooka.

"Don't be afraid, there will be a happy ending," Gabriel held her hand which he had no trouble finding, and added, "If not the Disney stock will fall."

When he laughed it was she who hushed him.

"Did you and Grandma also have a matchmaker?" asked the girl, when the lights went up. She had to inform him about that because his darkness was total. She grasped the silver handle, careful not to let her fingers slip, and used his cane to clear them a path through the aisles. All she could think about now was when she would finally be able to unwrap her gum and reveal the prediction for her future secreted inside. When they emerged into the streaming sunlight Gabriel said, "Safta is waiting for us."

He had recognized Fanny's footsteps, pacing back and forth outside the cinema.

9

Maybe if I push them into the water they'll make up?

If that trick worked in the movie, why shouldn't it work in real life?

How had the argument between the two grownups lasted so long?

Why didn't they learn from the children?

These were the questions that flitted through the girl's mind. Gabriel and Fanny each held one of her hands, while her small body was positioned between them. It wasn't clear who was setting the pace. It may be that the girl deliberately slowed down. She could hear Gabriel's feet matching their steps to Fanny's pattering ones. They spoke in German and while she didn't understand the words, she caught the music between them. That hum that she couldn't name rose to the surface and intensified.

As they passed by the fountain she looked down and saw their faces reflected in the water. A wild head of curls pressed between a man's derby and a woman's straw hat. The mythological Narcissus of Fanny's bedtime story immediately sprang to mind and she decided that the trick of the Dalmatian matchmaker would be too dangerous. It mustn't end in tears, or the boy would tease her forever.

The conversation in German started to bore her, and she closed her fist around the gum that was already soft. If she didn't open it soon it might lose its flavor. She let go of their hands and ran ahead.

Behind her, Fanny and Gabriel's hands found each other. Was it he who felt for hers, or did she grasp his to make sure he wouldn't fall? Whichever it was, this once the timing was flawless.

At that moment, on the strip of grass that surrounds the square named after a woman – Zina, wife of the legendary Tel Aviv mayor – the two came together somehow. The girl didn't even have to push them into the water.

"You waited for me," said Gabriel.

"I was worried. You can't trust children."

"Don't you trust me?"

As expected, her response was a bitter laugh.

"The girl… I know how to take care of her."

"You only take care of yourself."

"I'll leave the house and move to a hotel."

"No."

"It will be good for all of us."

"No. We're family."

Family. The word remained suspended in the air. Ephemeral as the splashes of water that sprayed from the fountain and evaporated.

"You and I are divorced," Gabriel said.

Only the happy cries of the girl in the distance could be heard. She had finally unwrapped her piece of gum.

Eventually Fanny said, "You aren't my enemy. I wanted you to be, but you aren't."

"What do you want me to be?"

Those words also hung in the air, for the girl arrived at that moment, onboard a scooter. A boy she didn't know had agreed to let her ride it in return for her piece of gum. The footboard of the homemade scooter was a simple piece of wood, taken from an orange crate, with two wheels attached, but for her it was a launch pad to the end beyond the end of wherever she would choose. She rode round and round the square ignoring Fanny's panicked cries. She reached for Gabriel's cane to try and block her way.

"Let her be. If she falls, she falls." Gabriel retained his stick and his balance. "We can't save them from anything."

"We?"

It didn't escape Fanny that he spoke in the plural. Others out walking in the square were coming toward them on their way to the cinema, and the girl was approaching them too. Fanny demanded that she return the scooter to its owner. But for some reason she didn't scold her. The girl had the feeling that Gabriel had interceded on her behalf and she was grateful.

Now Fanny tucked her arm in Gabriel's and steered them a path through the other pedestrians. The girl skipped along at their side all the way to the bus stop, now on their left, now to the right of them. Again she chattered non-stop about cafes and shops on Dizengoff Street, and failed to notice that they weren't walking at the same pace. Her grandparents stopped occasionally so that Gabriel could catch his breath, and Fanny took his ironed handkerchief out of his breast pocket and gently wiped the beads of sweat that had gathered on his forehead.

"It's boiling in your country. I'm not sure I can get used to it," he said.

"So you'll have to take off some of your clothes."

That sentence the girl did understand and she thought it was very funny. Her grandfather in khaki shorts and a sleeveless shirt? Not in a million years. Still, she hoped he might give up a few of the silk ties from his fabulous collection, so she could use them to make dresses for her dolls.

When they boarded the bus Fanny guided him from inside and the girl pushed him from behind, reciting the phrase ingrained in all the children during those years, "Respect for the elderly." The passengers gave up the front seats for them, but the girl preferred to stand. It was a good position from which to observe Fanny and Gabriel, who finally seemed to have made up. True, there was no embrace or imminent wedding like there had been for Roger and Anita, but still, there was a truce. Because she was small and couldn't reach the railing, she teetered back and forth all the way home.

That night the girl checked the fortune that came with the Bazooka bubblegum. She hadn't been willing to part with it when she traded the gum for a ride on the strange boy's scooter.

In the dark, next to Gabriel in the folding bed, she strained her eyes to read what her future held. Then she translated it into English for him: "By the age of 21 you'll reach the moon."

"Do you think it will really happen, *Zayde*?"

"I think that you might even reach Mars."

"Is that farther than the moon?"

"Yes."

"Are there people there?"

"No."

"Then I don't want to go."

She thought for a moment and added, "Only if Mommy and Daddy, my big brother and you and Grandma – my whole family – come with me."

The door to the guest room, next to the balcony, was partially ajar. From the balcony the voices of Fanny and the boy could be heard as they prepared for bed.

"Good night, Fanny," Gabriel called out in German. At first she didn't answer. Then, after he raised his voice a little, she responded weakly, "Good night, Gabriel," but she said it in Hebrew.

To the girl it didn't sound like the same thing.

That night she dreamed that she was standing in front of a gigantic piece of Bazooka gum, like a Lego piece colored bright pink that smelled like burnt sugar. She nibbles a tiny taste and to her great disappointment it isn't sweet. Then she removes the piece of paper containing the prediction about her future – it, too, is gigantic, like a winter blanket taken down from the attic – but the spaces between the words keep growing. To find out what the future will bring her, she spreads out the blanket and rides across it on a scooter. Gabriel and Fanny are stuck to the gum and call out to her, "*Maidele*, don't stop," or maybe they're saying "*Maidele*, be careful."

In the morning she couldn't remember whether the dream prediction was the same as the one she had received about the moon, or whether she had accidentally found herself in someone else's dream.

10

In the end, Fanny and Gabriel did need the help of a matchmaker. Not a perspiring professional like the man in Siret so many years before, but another graced with mediation skills, a most pleasant manner, and endless patience, who came forward of his own accord. The volunteer was Mimi's father, the other grandfather, Berl-Dov, the man the boy loved more than anyone else in the world. The only thing he wanted in return was domestic peace. The tension had frayed his daughter's nerves and he was concerned about her psychological state, living inside that family pressure cooker. According to the Yiddish joke, a mother-in-law and daughter-in-law in the same house are like two cats in a sack, but what about a daughter-in-law, a mother-in-law, and a father-in-law all stuck together? That wasn't funny at all.

Yitzhak wasn't sure. To push his parents into an isolated bubble of their own seemed like an insane, even dangerous idea. For his part, he was worried about his mother. Why should she have to deal alone, at this stage of her life, with a person whose capability to hurt others was already an established fact?

His father-in-law tried to persuade him. It was unlikely that, in his present condition, Gabriel would abandon Fanny again, and betrayals were out of the question. Maybe now, finally, when they had both had their fair share of experiences, the time had come for a relaxed marriage of reconciliation as a result of all they both had learned. Not to mention that this was a great mitzvah, although the matchmaker didn't conceal the controversy surrounding the issue of remarrying the same woman after divorcing her. Personally, he ascribed to the ruling by Rabbi Samuel Vital, who enthusiastically supported this commandment, "Especially if she was his first wife, or if he has children from her."

Both those conditions were met.

In the end, Yitzhak gave his blessing to the course of action, and his father-in-law embarked on negotiations between the potential bride and groom. The bride-to-be did not demand a diamond ring, a pre-nuptial agreement, or a contract to formalize her rights. Neither did she demand of the groom that he apologize in public for the pain he had caused her. The only request she made was that the marriage proposal come directly from him. This time she wished to hear his commitment to her with her own ears and not via an intermediary.

Gabriel asked for time to think it over.

"The Blessed Lord has granted you the opportunity to do the right thing and make it up to your family," Berl-Dov urged him, as he presented him with precedents for fulfilling the commandment. Moses himself re-married his divorced wife Zipporah and was re-united with her two sons as well, "for she didn't marry another man." And wasn't it a sign from above that Fanny's Hebrew name was Zipporah?

"That one was a black woman and I am no Moses," responded Gabriel dismissively.

The matchmaker found another high branch to hang himself from, with another example from Moses. Apparently in that family divorcing and remarrying your spouse was a habitual occurrence. Amram sent Yocheved away when Pharaoh decreed the death of every firstborn male of Israel, and only after Moses was born did he marry her again. And by the way, both Yocheved and Zipporah are buried in the Tomb of the Matriarchs in Tiberias. Perhaps we can go there to receive their blessing?

That was out of the question. Paying homage at a gravesite was far from Gabriel's beliefs. In Eastern Europe as well he had laughed at the custom of the *kvitel* note containing a petitionary prayer that was placed near the grave of a revered rabbi in the hope that he would intercede above for the sake of those down below. Not to mention that Israel's tourist sites were of no interest to him and he was not inclined to extraneous travel around the hot and dusty country that it was now his fate to inhabit.

In the end, he agreed to the deal. Yes, in his eyes it was a deal in which neither side was meant to lose out. His way of preventing disappointment was to always expect the worst of people. That was the permanent dispute between him and Manny Greenberg. And now there was no one to remind him that sometimes people surprise you with the goodness they possess.

And so Gabriel chose to respond in the affirmative. After all, what choice did he have? If he had to be chained down, he told himself, at least let it be to a woman he knew. "An old broom knows the dirty corners best," goes the Irish proverb that his lover Mary McMurphy had taught him years before.

At the same time, Fanny's scent, which he had been conscious of when he stood next to her at Dizengoff Square, was pleasant. Her hand in his had been firm yet yielding. Of course he hadn't touched her eyelashes. Were they still so long? "... and do not despise your mother when she is old," he recited the verse from the Book of Proverbs. He preferred not to think about her breasts, for his flesh was also worn out. He had no need of a mirror to know that. It was enough to feel his own body to be aware that old age hadn't simply leapt upon him, but had trampled him.

Better not to wallow in sighs and moans about the ravages of age, which weren't even determined by the principles of reward and punishment. They were simply there, encroaching on the sinners and the pure of heart alike.

All men shriveled up and their once proud and erect members were brought down, regardless of what they did or didn't do in their youth. And all women surrendered to the force of gravity, beautiful or plain, discovering in their mirrors the slackening of chin muscles and the weave of tiny wrinkles invading the areas around their eyelids and mouths, even if they were strictly faithful to only one man. It's a clear and unequivocal plot line that a supreme playwright decreed right from the start. Had she been able to, Fanny would have criticized him sharply for the laziness of his creativity. Why shouldn't people reach their twilight years looking spectacular and desirable, bearing a basketful of passion? What a breathtaking upheaval that would cause in the human drama. The depressing turn of phrase "in his twilight years" would be replaced by "his juicy nights," and "his burgeoning parts," or like the doorknob says in the Disney movie *Alice in Wonderland*, "Nothing's impossible."

Of all things, it was that very film, which had caused his stocks to skyrocket, that sprang to Gabriel's mind just before he proposed to Fanny. Maybe it was because he could hear their carefree grandchildren playing in the yard, as though the rabbit hole was just about to open for them.

The marriage proposal took place by the weeping fig tree, not far from the trash cans. The boy was kicking his ball – he wanted to be a mid-fielder when he grew up – and the girl was playing hopscotch on the sidewalk in front of their house, where she had sketched the game with chalk. The doll with hair had been carefully seated at her side.

Not the most romantic of settings. There wasn't even a flowering shrub to soften the scene, because all that grew in the yard were a few yellow sorrel plants, since the fig tree cast heavy shade. Gabriel did not go down on one knee and he made no proclamations of undying love. He asked clearly and simply, "Fanny, is this arrangement acceptable to you?"

"What if I want to divorce you?"

"I give you my word that I will grant you a divorce whenever you want."

"And after that? Will you propose to me a third time?"

"At least we can use the same ring. You kept the first one, I assume."

"No."

He had hoped that she had passed it on to Yitzhak and that he had married Mimi with it.

"The ring is gone. I got a sack of potatoes for it." That's how Gabriel found out that during the war Fanny had hidden in a whorehouse in Bucharest.

What other revelations would be disclosed along the way? Who were the other men in her life? He had the decency not to ask.

"Black Sorina was a rare soul," Fanny said. "Every morning you should give thanks and say 'Bless Him for creating woman,' because if it hadn't been for her our son wouldn't have survived."

He listened in silence to what she said, and then recited, "A woman of valor who can find?... And gives food to her household and a ration to her maids."

Those verses from the Book of Proverbs were the closest he ever came to a request for forgiveness.

Do you have any regrets?

What mistakes did you make?

If we could go back in time, what would we do differently?

These were the questions that remained unasked.

The fruit of the tree began to rain down on them. As Gabriel brushed it off, he suddenly appeared shaky on his feet.

"I'll buy you a new ring," he told her, as he tried to flick the sticky fruit confetti off his shoulders. Fanny interpreted this promise as well as a kind of apology. A moment later he raised his head and asked, "Is this your Israeli version of a downpour?"

Fanny looked up and discovered the children who had climbed into the branches of the tree. They were shaking the branches vigorously in tandem. The girl hugged her doll in one arm and dropped another handful of sticky fruit straight onto the boy's football, which had rolled to a stop at the foot of the tree. The deluge of fruit had been his idea, to put his grandfather's sight to the test yet one more time. He still suspected him of faking.

"It's just our grandchildren up to mischief," Fanny said.

"We managed to do something good together after all," Gabriel replied.

She described the gruesome twosome to him in vivid detail, the pair of human bats who had taken refuge in the fork of the tree, but mostly their naughty delighted expressions. She didn't leave out the girl's tangled curls or the way the boy gently unraveled them, always checking to make sure he wasn't hurting her. Gabriel listened intently to Fanny's description. It was the first time that she had taken the place of his eyes. He couldn't understand what the children were saying and he never would, for he would never learn the Hebrew tongue.

From his perch in the tree, the boy chuckled, "Look at them, telling old people's secrets."

"They're old so they've had more time to collect secrets."

"You're right. Grandpa really can't see anything. He didn't look up even once."

In their ongoing argument about whether their grandfather was pretending or not she had the upper hand. The boy, who finally had to admit defeat, slid down the tree and kicked the ball toward the trash cans. Both he and the ball were coated in sticky fruit nectar. And the girl celebrated her victory as she squatted on the ground picking the yellow flowers. When she held them out to her grandfather like a bouquet he smelled them right away.

"Taste them *Zayde*?" she asked.

"Are you completely *mishegeneh*?" Fanny scolded. In the free Land of Israel they wouldn't eat weeds from the earth as they had from the cursed dirt of Europe.

Maybe because she had just won the argument with her brother that day she had the confidence to hold her ground. She broke the bulb in two, stood on tiptoe and brought the two halves to Gabriel's lips.

"Sour," he said. To her it was the taste of Wonderland.

The children weren't invited to the wedding.

The only guests were the aunts and uncle and the other grandparents, who traveled from Haifa to attend the modest ceremony at the Tel Aviv Rabbinate. Abandoning the role of matchmaker, my other grandfather now played the part of witness, while my mother and father led Fanny and Gabriel to stand beneath the canopy. There was no wedding gown for the bride and no wedding suit for the groom, sewn specially for the occasion. Just a slim gold ring purchased from the Dizengoff Street jeweler who was also a former Bukovinian. That was one promise that Gabriel kept.

At the meal following the ceremony at the Rabbinate, in a room set off to the side, *leykeh* cake baked by Paula was served and Adom Atik red wine was poured into paper cups by Lizzie-Bertha. The special blessing for one marrying a second wife, "Blessed is the Lord in whose dwelling is joy," was not recited, for a man who is re-marrying the wife he once divorced is not required to utter those words. It seems that the sages who determined the religious laws understood that there is no room for joy when so much time has been wasted.

Also, a man who re-marries his ex-wife is not exempt from a call-up to go to war, as he would be were he to marry a second "new" wife. As far at the Torah is concerned he is permitted to sacrifice his life and run the risk that his secondhand wife may be widowed. Although at Gabriel's age there was no danger of his being asked to serve.

Fortunately, as newlyweds, the couple was entitled to a preferential mortgage. As far as the authorities were concerned they were categorized as a "young couple." Gabriel redeemed some of his Disney stock and used the money to buy a dimly lit apartment in a building on a street not far from our house. The only bright spot was the balcony with a view of the grocery store located two buildings away. The smell of the salted fish in the barrel that stood outside enveloped the entire street.

I live in that area now, and buy my groceries at the same store – although today it's an odorless mini-supermarket – and sneak a glance at the same balcony, which has since been enclosed with shutters. The blind old man and the girl who ceaselessly described to him the wonderland of Tel Aviv aren't there.

11

"Cry a little," Lizzie-Bertha urged Fanny before the wedding.

In those days she was involved in an initiative to set up a shelter for abused women, and she had heard from her friends that tears on a wedding day were a guarantee of good luck. They would be the bride's final tears, as she would have none left to shed during her married life.

Lizzie-Bertha had long since lost faith in the institution of marriage, and Gabriel's abandonment of Fanny had been a decisive factor in her choice never to marry. Unlike those who saw the reunion of the couple as a great mitzvah, she never concealed her opinion that it was pure foolishness. Why choose to return to the same sickbed? It wasn't that she was concerned that her sister, heaven forfend, might be in need of a place in the shelter, but having dubbed Gabriel "the worst husband in the world," she suggested to her colleagues that they establish a therapeutic framework for men like him.

"You're the one who once sent him a letter," Fanny reminded her, before the ceremony at the Rabbinate commenced.

"So that you could be free of him, not so that you could be chained to him again!"

"From now on he will be chained to me," Fanny replied.

That was the moment when Lizzie-Bertha implored her to squeeze out a few tears. If she hadn't managed to convince her to flee the sickbed, at least she could persuade her to cry a few tears for luck. But Fanny didn't cry. Neither did she laugh, or even smile. The rabbi thought that he had never seen a bride and groom with such vacant expressions. Had he not known that they were a divorced couple about to marry again, he would have been certain that they were total strangers. On second thought, perhaps it was the groom's blindness that clouded the atmosphere. Their son hardly radiated joy himself as he prodded his father toward the marriage canopy, so that a fifth pole was added to the four that supported it. The rabbi recited the marriage blessings in a too-loud voice with such exaggerated emphasis that the groom snarled, "I'm blind, not deaf." Then the rabbi was so embarrassed that he forgot to place the glass under Gabriel's foot and it was his son who had to bend down to direct his father's leg.

The smashing of the glass is meant to protect the couple from the evil eye explained the in-law Berl-Dov to the handful of guests. Although this was well-known to all present, he felt the need to say words that befitted a usually joyful occasion and to attempt to infuse some festivity into the proceedings. Meanwhile, the rabbi had no doubt that the demons and detractors wouldn't trouble themselves with a couple reminiscent of Abraham and Yitzhak on their way to the sacrificial altar.

"Best wishes to you on your happy day," read the telegram that Anna and Abe sent from New York, in the banal phrasing characteristic of the United States Postal Service.

"Do you think the marriage will last this time?" asked the sister.

"Maybe this time round she'll be the one to leave him," suggested the brother-in-law. A similar thought – or more precisely a wish – flitted through Lizzie-Bertha's brain on the other side of the ocean.

Clara wasn't party to the guessing game. She stood at her dresser and withdrew from her underwear drawer the Polaroid picture snapped outside a Manhattan cinema. To her surprise it hadn't faded at all, or darkened. She didn't resemble a black woman, but a European matron from years gone by. As she gazed at Gabriel's furious expression, frozen in the photograph, all traces of nostalgia vanished instantly. If he had been such a bitter man when in possession of all his senses, who knew what records he would break now that he was blind. She had no regrets at returning him to the woman who had stood in her way for so many years. She hoped for his sake that the sweetness of grandchildren might mitigate his bitterness and for herself wished only contentment in her solitude.

As she replaced the picture in her drawer she realized that the photographer had a certain flair, for in the likeness of Clara and Gabriel he had managed to suggest something akin to the famous picture of Jackie and John F. Kennedy. Naturally she cast her vote for him in the presidential election, unlike Gabriel who didn't exercise his right to vote. Clara believed that the Kennedy marriage was the epitome of perfection. A happy ending worthy of Walt Disney.

Unlike Anna, she didn't wonder whether Fanny and Gabriel's marriage would hold together the second time around. She walked alone along Fifth Avenue, and when she passed by St. Patrick's Cathedral it was the Christian wedding vows that resonated within her: Till death do us part.

At the conclusion of the ceremony the rabbi asked to speak to Gabriel in private. They stepped aside and he explained that according to matrimonial law a blind man is permitted his wife only after he has recognized her voice.

"She should say something to you before you consummate the marriage," he advised, "so that you know that it is she and no one else."

"I always remember her."

"But you must use signs that the religious law recognizes."

"I know her by her footsteps."

The rabbi pondered the issue. Then he decreed that like the sound of her voice, the pattering of a person's footsteps would do, and there was no danger that instead of Rachel the groom would find Leah in his bed. Then Gabriel embarrassed the rabbi yet again when he said that since in his case it was his eyes that were fatigued (and he made an unexpected pun, using a word that sounded like "Leah") he proposed relying on his sense of smell as well. But since another couple was already waiting to be wed, the flustered rabbi had no time to split hairs in long-winded debate.

"Congratulations Mr. Herzig, I wish you and the new-old Mrs. Herzig a happy life and many years together." And that was the end of the rabbi's briefing about the laws of matrimony.

As he performed his next wedding the rabbi was distracted. He couldn't stop thinking about the biblical verse about Yitzhak, "and his eyes were dim," about the father who failed to recognize his son Jacob disguised as Esau and showered him with blessings that weren't meant for him.

Fanny and Gabriel spent their wedding night in their new apartment. It was still empty, except for a double bed that Yitzhak had pushed up against the wall that very morning, so that Gabriel wouldn't fall out of it while he slept or when he awoke. And there was one other item that Gabriel had insisted on moving to the new apartment right away. It was the big radio that he had brought with him from New York and from which he was never parted. Since there wasn't even a table in the apartment, the radio was placed on the floor in the kitchen, and Gabriel demanded that it be connected immediately to the socket in the wall.

"This is your shortcut to New York?" Yitzhak chuckled.

"New York is the world."

"And Israel is outside the world? Is that what you're saying?"

"You are so innocent Yitzhak. You certainly didn't inherit that naiveté from me."

In protest, the son chose to leave the radio unplugged. For now. That was one way to take advantage of his father's blindness and score points in their ever-present feud.

Fanny brought her small, worn carpet, but she didn't spread it on the floor, for fear that Gabriel might trip over it.

She supported him on the stairs, but once they crossed the threshold he shook off her arm and walked in by himself.

"It's a new place, you might fall."

"It's an empty apartment."

"We can fill it," she whispered, but he was busy groping his way toward the bed. And then he began to undress, folding each item of clothing carefully and placing it in a growing pile, except for the handkerchief that he extracted from the suit pocket without disturbing its sharp creases.

"I am not who I was," he said.

Then he straightened up, and stood exposed before her, completely naked – the parts that were flaccid and shriveled, as well as the few that could still hold themselves erect. In his darkness he felt her eyes scrutinizing every inch of his flesh.

"I am not who I was either," she finally breathed.

"But you have an advantage over me. You can see and not be seen."

She moved closer to him. She didn't remove even one piece of clothing – he noticed that there was no rustling – and she said, "If I close my eyes, I lose the advantage."

Alike in their disadvantages. Equally aligned in the ravages of age.

Fanny and Gabriel should be lauded for having the courage to return to their starting point when so close to the end, even though it was concealed under so many layers of anger and resentment that it was hard to find. Maybe unbeknownst to them it was that courage that united them and left their initial alliance intact. A precarious rope bridge, swinging over an abyss, that didn't snap even when both sides stretched it to the limit.

Fanny felt her way in the space with closed eyes. When her finger met flesh she began to caress the naked Gabriel. He was the only man whose body she knew, and it always succumbed even when his spirt was unwilling. The memory of him was so deeply ingrained in her that she had no need to navigate by sight. She didn't tell him that she loved him. It was her fingertips that conveyed her message in the secret code that only they understood, and mostly it was her hot breath that left its marks on his body. Love is "… a madness most discreet, a choking gall, and a preserving sweet," according to Shakespeare in *Romeo and Juliet*.

During the night Gabriel mumbled in Russian. Fanny, still fully dressed, moved closer but couldn't make out the words, not even something that sounded like a name. When she touched his cheek, bristling with stubble, he curled toward the wall. Then he cried out in German, "They're shelling, get down!" And that she understood.

You will marry twice. Suddenly, as if struck by lightning, she remembered the gypsy's prophesy.

Why hadn't she told her that it would be to the same man?

I don the gypsy's clothes and ask Fanny: "If you'd known, would it have made any difference?"

She doesn't answer me. I imagine she wants to spare me her response.

When morning arrived – Gabriel felt the wave of heat coming through the window – he heard Fanny crying. Since the sound of her weeping was strange to him, the laws of matrimony would not have found it acceptable as a form of identification, but in any case the marriage had already been consummated.

Those were not the last of my grandmother's tears, and they did not bring her luck.

12

I would like to fix things. Why not? Fiction is the contractor who renovates the story by widening its corridors and building additional stories, beyond those permitted according to the building license. It's all in my hands – for better or for worse. So what should determine the ending? What happened, or what might have happened?

It is so tempting to follow in the footsteps of Walt Disney, for whom the happy ending is the most natural thing, dependable and unshakeable. He's the one who gave generations of children like me the "And they lived happily ever after to this very day." Who will stop me from writing the words "The End" in cursive script, shooting off a few fireworks and leaving it at that?

After all, Fanny and Gabriel's love won out in the end, so why rummage around in the truth that lies rotting underneath the romantic union.

In New York, Manny Greenberg announced to the members of the Bukovina club that the Herzigs had ironed out their problems and reached a state of peace and tranquility, amen.

In fact, Fanny and Gabriel's married life was more like her famous recipe for herring that the matchmaker from Siret had touted as one of her virtues. Schmaltz herring with delicate bones, slices of raw onion, sour cream, bay leaves, allspice, a little vinegar, and apple slices. Many loathe the dish, but more than a few are addicted to it despite its problematic odor. Even those who love it recommend that you refrain from exchanging kisses after filling your stomach with it.

Gabriel, who had overcome his distaste for the smell, found a measure of pleasure when he ate it. And when Fanny prepared it, she also derived pleasure from following the familiar recipe. Maybe that should be enough. Herring in cream sauce – isn't that a kind of a repair? Especially if accompanied by a shot of frozen vodka. Russian vodka, of course.

Fanny would buy the schmaltz herring at Dorfman's fish stand in the Carmel Market. She would travel there by bus, gripping her plastic shopping basket, and return with an abundance of treasures with which to prepare her acclaimed dish. When she also bought made-in-Israel "Vodka Gold," Gabriel didn't need the help of his cane to cross the kitchen and pour it down the sink.

"Even your alcohol pretends to be what it isn't," he declared to Yitzhak. "The day you produce alcohol worthy of the name you'll be like all the other nations."

A Zionist rejectionist he had been, and would ever be. Since he perceived the Israeli press as contaminated by political interests, Yitzhak was required to read to him every evening from the stock listings in *The New York Times* – the only newspaper Gabriel trusted. Even though it arrived from America a week after it was published, and the stock market had undergone countless potential fluctuations in that time, it remained his bible as he continued to buy and sell. When Anna and Abe came for a visit – not by boat but on a plane – Gabriel boasted about his clever investment in The Boeing Company. Even years before he had known what was coming and that every man was destined to fly.

The visit of his sister and brother-in-law could also be counted among the things that provided a measure of pleasure. The whole family, including the aunts and uncle from Haifa, gathered for herring in cream sauce and Gabriel downed half a bottle of Smirnoff vodka that the guests had brought. "Made in the USA," Abe announced.

"You haven't changed," Anna told Fanny as they embraced.

"Neither have you," she replied.

They were both lying.

Fanny's hair had turned completely white, and only her long lashes retained their original color.

"That herring again!" the boy groaned, "It's full of bones."

"Learn to swallow them," Gabriel shot back.

The girl spent a long time deboning the fish, for her brother as well, even though he would eat only the raw onion in vinegar and brag that he didn't cry even one tear.

The girl's gift from the relatives from America was an enormous doll, almost as big as she was, whose eyes opened and closed. She loved it so much that her heart almost burst. The boy said that you shouldn't waste love on dolls, and she swore that she would always love him more.

When she asked Gabriel how to say "love" in English, he taught her how to write the word, first in block letters and then in script, and explained that the verb was "to fall in love."

"What does "to fall" mean?"

When he told her, she asked, "So in English, 'love' means falling down *Zayde*? Is that how it is in America?"

"Not only in America." He laughed as he rolled a cigarette with the tobacco that she bought for him at the grocery store.

"And what if you break something, *Zayde*?

"So you break something."

He didn't reply to her next question, "And when do you get up?" but asked her to light a match for him and she obeyed with shaking hand.

"Can a heart also break, *Zayde*?"

"Yes, it's the most fragile organ in the body. You have to be careful *maidele*."

The girl was so proud that she had managed to light a match by herself. She hugged her English notebook to her chest.

"I don't want them to put a cast on my heart," and she insisted that to fall in love in Hebrew was something entirely different.

Gabriel smoked his cigarette down to the end and then he asked her to put it out for him. The girl brought the butt to Fanny so she could throw it in the trash, but she refused to be parted from her notebook.

"The grandchildren are most definitely a source of pride and joy," Anna reported to Clara when she returned to New York.

"How does Gabriel look?"

"Almost black. Their sun is burning hot."

"And Fanny?"

Anna shrugged, and Clara thought of the unattractive woman in the old photograph she had come upon years before in Gabriel's drawer, and wondered whether his blindness was a blessing.

"Does he cheat on her?

"He barely leaves the house, and even then only with his granddaughter."

"The girl is apparently the only woman Gabriel truly loves," Clara told Manny Greenberg. Doris had passed away, and the members of the Bukovina club were tasked with ferreting out whether she might accept him as her husband. Clara was adamant that she remain single.

After the Kennedy assassination, which broke her heart, she sent a letter to Israel and asked if she could come for a visit.

13

Dear Fanny,

I take the liberty of addressing you by your first name and of writing frankly – even though this is not the norm in the German language that we share – because I feel close to you.

You have accompanied me for years. You have been the ghost in my life, despite being a woman of flesh and blood. I have thought about you countless times, tried to imagine what you are like, been angry with you more than once and even wished you ill.

Not anymore.

You must know that it wasn't I who stole your man, since Gabriel belongs only to himself, and will never be the property of any woman.

Had Rabbeinu Gershom not banned polygamy, we might have been able to live side-by-side. Not in a balance of terror, like the Cold War between the United States and the Soviet Union, but in sisterhood and friendship.

Fanny, this is what I feel for you. You are my friend, my sister in adversity, although you are not my affliction. I am not your "Hagar," and you are not my "Sarah." And I have learned to love your Yitzhak like the son I do not have.

The two of us shared one man for many years, for good and for ill. You had much that was bad, and so did I. Gabriel didn't short-change either of us in that respect.

I am sitting on a bench in Central Park opposite the lake and writing to you. The park is the only place in New York that reminds me a little of my home in Europe. Here I have found an island of nature and beauty, and when I sit by the lake I can leave behind some of my sorrow and regret, the mistakes I have made, and all that I have lost. When I look up at the towering buildings that surround the park, I feel as though I live in the future, despite the fact that I have much more past, and perhaps that is the reason that I cling to it increasingly. It's dangerous, I know. You also know that yearnings are a boggy swamp, and I prefer a lake, especially when it's frozen over in the winter and crowded with children on skates. Maybe near your home in Tel Aviv there is also a park where you walk and in which you can see the young life you once had, although you don't have any lake there, and certainly not one that freezes over in the winter.

We had that in Bukovina, but neither of us will return to it, nor will Gabriel. It doesn't exist anymore, apart from on the wrinkled map of our memories.

I beg your forgiveness, Fanny Herzig. And in the final chapter of my life I cannot make do with just words written on paper to fulfill an obligation. The page will only fade or get lost. I want to stand before you, face to face, and hope to hear you say that you forgive me.

As crazy as it sounds, I am a member of your family.

Yours,

Clara Mendel, New York

P.S.

Now there are geese flying over the lake. I watch them as they circle above my head. Are there wild geese in Israel, too?

P.P.S.

Your grandchildren are very sweet. I saw them in a photograph that Yitzhak brought with him when he came to visit. You are blessed to have such pleasure.

Clara's letter was preceded by a meeting with a stranger in the park. He was bearded and his colorful clothes hung loosely on his slim frame as he walked to the edge of the lake where he sat down and smoked a joint.

A hippie. A flower child. The ones who chanted slogans. He looked as though he hadn't bathed in at least two weeks. Since Clara always preferred well-dressed men she moved away from him at once. He turned to face her with his smudge of a beard and when he spoke it was in a husky voice that seemed not to have broken yet.

"Want some, lady?"

"I don't smoke."

"You should. It will do you good. You'll forget everything."

The marijuana smelled sweet. Much better than the tobacco she was accustomed to.

"What do you need to forget so urgently?" she refrained from saying that he had a lot more future than past, and hadn't yet had the time to add regrets, sorrow, mistakes, and loss to his resume.

"How old are you?"

"Eighteen. And don't say, 'When I was your age.'"

She didn't.

"Do you have children, lady?"

"No."

"You're lucky. You won't have to send them to Vietnam."

She knelt beside him and put her hand on his shoulder. To her surprise, the hippie didn't smell. Meanwhile, a goose floated over to them, flapping its wings and scattering droplets.

The hippie pulled a draft notice out of his pocket and held it up to her face.

"I haven't done anything," he said, "I haven't even slept with a woman."

She stopped herself from blurting out, "You have your whole life ahead of you." Neither did she speak of lives that spiral backward, or that stop before they have a chance to begin.

The young man dipped his hand into the water, sending rippling waves out to the goose, but rather than swim away it came toward him with its beak open, as if it wanted to swallow the smoke.

"You, the adults, fuck you all. Why did you make war instead of making love?"

Clara, who for her entire life had wanted only to make love, was not the correct address. Instead of apologizing for who she was and what she was, she reached for the joint and inhaled deeply several times.

She had a slight headache, but the world around her didn't look any better and she didn't forget a thing. When the long-haired hippie stood up the goose spread its wings, spraying them both with water, and lifted off. Soon all the other geese followed it into the air.

Only then did Clara sit down by the water and write her letter.

14

Can three walk together, if they are in agreement?

The ultimate fantasy. Every man's wet dream came true not in a bohemian artists quarter where permissiveness and non-conformism are holy writ, but in an apartment block not far from the grocery store that smelled of salted fish.

Fanny, Gabriel, and Clara broke the taboo and lived together as a threesome for several months. It all took place under the noses of the children who knew nothing of what was going on in real time. The guest was introduced as another auntie from America while the notions "lover," "mistress," "common-law," and "living in sin," were swept firmly under the carpet, and not necessarily Fanny's beloved rug.

What a shame about the timing, Gabriel thought to himself. If this had only occurred when he was younger, when the hormones were raging and the flesh taut and smooth, it might have been a really great party.

At first he had grave misgivings about Clara's visit, and sided with Yitzhak who warned that the tripartite meeting was a recipe for trouble, asking why anyone would add another healthy person to a sick bed already occupied by two. However, Fanny, who hadn't shared the contents of her letter with another soul, insisted that Clara should come.

To her daughter-in-law, who was also resistant to the idea, she said, "And what if it was two men and one woman?"

Mimi replied, "My first husband won't return from the dead," and Fanny was silenced.

The day before Clara's arrival the girl came upon her grandmother sitting and staring at an old photograph.

"Is that the auntie from America?"

"Maybe yes, maybe no."

"Do you know her?"

"Maybe yes, maybe no."

"Does *Zayde* remember her?"

"Maybe yes, maybe no."

"Who took the picture?"

"It was a long time ago."

"So now she looks completely different?"

"Maybe yes, maybe no."

Why can't old people ever give you a straight answer?

Either you know someone or you don't.

Either you remember or you don't.

The girl decided to examine the photograph herself, and she was a little sad to discover that the face of the woman had faded away. All that remained visible were some strands of hair stuck to her temples, creating an empty frame for a face.

"What happened to her, *Safta*?"

Fanny said that you couldn't trust time to preserve everything.

Time, thought the girl, must be the strongest eraser in the pencil case.

She quickly pulled out colored pencils from her schoolbag and drew in eyes for the woman and a nose and a mouth and a mass of yellow hair, just like Sleeping Beauty has in the Disney movie. The necklace didn't need any repairs, for it hadn't faded at all. Still, the girl filled in each pearl. What a shame that *Zayde* couldn't see how nicely she colored.

The photograph had a strange smell, like the cap guns the boys played with on Purim.

There was absolutely no resemblance between Aunt Clara and the woman in the photograph. She wasn't thin and straight-backed, her lips were coated in shiny red lipstick, and she wasn't wearing a pearl necklace. But the disappointment was swept away when she gave the girl a Barbie doll with a tiny waist and long blonde hair. She came with three outfits and tiny high-heeled shoes, so that the girl didn't have to sew dresses for her using *Zayde*'s old ties.

For Gabriel, the aunt from America brought a new tie to add to his collection. It was plain black, with no stars or flowers and the girl didn't covet it at all.

The new aunt and the old grandmother stood face to face and looked surprised.

"You don't look like the picture."

"Neither do you."

Instead of seeming disappointed the two women held each other in a long embrace, and the girl thought she might have spied tears.

"Even though they say they've never met before, I'm sure they know each other," she told her brother. The unholy trinity was of far less interest to him, for he had already crossed over from childhood and was almost a teenager.

Gabriel made the effort to rise from his armchair next to the radio and approach Clara, supported by Fanny and his stick. When Clara kissed his cheeks, inhaling the familiar scent of him, he murmured a verse from the Book of Micah, "Rejoice not over me, O my enemy; when I fall, I shall rise; when I sit in darkness, the Lord will be a light to me."

Clara wasn't revealed as an enemy, and she didn't gloat. This was actually the brightest period in the second marriage of Fanny and Gabriel. For the first time in years his bitterness abated, and some of his old charm was revived. There's nothing like a caress of the male ego to work miracles, Lizzie-Bertha told her friends as she described the rooster being fussed over by the pair of women who held on to him as two people may clutch one another under a prayer shawl.

The friendship that blossomed between the two women was so unexpected, that at times it seemed to Yitzhak that in a different world they would have set up home together and dispensed with the man. However, in this world they took care of him, and the people in the neighborhood became accustomed to the sight of the blind man being guided along one day by the woman with snow-white hair, and on another by the one with hair dyed a deep shade of red.

Fanny and Clara traveled to the market together. They cooked, sewed, embroidered, and sometimes sang the Yiddish songs of Itzik Manger. When Gabriel was glued to the radio, listening to the Voice of America, they spent time outside on the balcony. Even Clara's giggles, which had been an embarrassment to him for so many years, were now a welcome soundtrack playing in the background. He recognized Clara not by her footsteps, but by the sound of her laughter.

One day the two women decided to go to a matinee, to see the 1955 German film *Sissi*. They still had a special place in their hearts for the legendary Austrian queen, as well as for the movie star Romy Schneider who portrayed her in the film. They recruited the girl to babysit Gabriel. Before they left, the girl turned the knob on the radio until she located the *Children's Corner* program on the Voice of Israel, and then she turned up the volume.

"Do you understand anything, Gabriel?" Clara asked.

"No."

"Don't you want to learn Hebrew?" Fanny asked.

"What for? I don't have enough life left to make it worthwhile."

"There's never enough life," Clara said.

The girl laughed. It sounded to her like the most illogical thing in the world.

"What is enough to be worthwhile?" she asked, but the women had already crossed the threshold and she never received an answer.

When they returned from the cinema they found the girl playing Hopscotch in the street, while Gabriel was sitting in the apartment by himself, enjoying a jazz program on the radio.

They went to sit on the balcony, to watch over the girl from above, and she heard them discussing the delicacies set out on Sissi's table in the palace in Vienna. If the queen had ever tasted herring in cream sauce, she wouldn't have sunk into depression, Fanny commented. Then she dictated her recipe to Clara, and her instructions mingled with the jazz blaring from the radio. Gabriel lowered the volume and so he too learned that you need years of experience to achieve the perfect balance between the various and conflicting ingredients.

"The sourness has to learn to live in harmony with the salt, and not allow the sweet to overcome it," Fanny explained.

Clara responded with a compliment: "If you lived in New York, you could be a chef at the Russian Tea Room."

That was the second, "what if" voiced in public. The others were buried beneath the absolution of each family member.

What if Gabriel hadn't abandoned Yitzhak when he was a baby?

What if Manny Greenberg hadn't recognized the picture of Gabriel's son as a young man?

What if Fanny had married the Russian colonel, the Cypriot smuggler, or Meirke Hirsch?

What if Mimi's first husband had survived?

What if the boy and the girl had an older sister?

What if I hadn't written this book?

On the radio, George Gershwin was playing *Swanee.* "Call me Jaqueline's" prophecy on the *Cedric* had come to pass and the song of longing for the river between South Carolina and northern Florida was a hit that sold in the millions. Gabriel, who had chosen the name "George" in homage to the composer, rose from his chair and began to sway to the rhythm of the song, adding the words to the music.

"Somehow I feel, your love is real
Near you I wanna be…"

The sound of the cane meeting the floor increased, accompanied by the rhythmic stomping of his feet. He was so engrossed in *Swanee* that he didn't feel the two women watching him from the balcony.

At that moment Fanny suggested Clara that she never leave.

15

It was the Shalom Tower that destroyed Fanny and Clara's idyll. Israel's first skyscraper – which in 1965 was considered the tallest building not only in the Middle East, but also in Asia and Africa – was the damning bone of contention.

Clara wanted to take Gabriel to visit it.

"It will remind him of New York."

"It will only cause him pain," Fanny protested.

"He will finally feel at home."

"How many floors do you think they built there, Clara?"

"I know it's not the Empire State Building…"

"Only thirty-four floors," Fanny cut her off.

"He won't know. He can't see anything."

"You want us to lie to him?"

"And he hasn't lied to us?"

The lie was for the greater good, Clara reasoned, although it wasn't only for Gabriel's benefit that she wanted to make the trip, for she was hoping that the skyscraper would be a taste of New York. In Israel she discovered that the intensity of her longing for America didn't fall short of her yearning for Bukovina. She was fated to live forever in the spaces between "here" and "there," in that no-man's land of emigrants and immigrants who are forced to deceive themselves, rather than to admit that no land is the Promised Land and no land can be attained.

Behind Fanny's back she suggested to Gabriel that he join her on a trip to the new tower, which had been constructed on the remnants of an old high school whose name she couldn't recall. It had fast elevators and air conditioning, "the best of the world's innovations, in Israel," according to the commercials on the radio. Not to mention the first department store in the country, that took up the entire entrance floor. Gabriel could easily visualize the "Everything you could look for – you'll find what you're looking for," by visualizing the department stores he knew so well from his years in New York. Was he suffering from a lack of skyscrapers?

His bitterness returned. "I won't make do with substitutes," he burst out, accusing Clara of plotting against him with Fanny. Two are worse than one.

He barely managed to extract a cigarette from the silver case sitting atop the radio, and as he groped for the box of matches Clara knocked them savagely away. He heard the box collide with the floor in a far corner of the room.

"You want to punish me, Clara?"

She didn't say a word.

"Because I haven't been punished enough?"

She still wouldn't speak.

Gabriel's memory was so sharp that he recited the verse as if he was reading from an open Bible, "And she shall be his wife, for he hath humbled her; he may not put her away all his days."

Clara said, "I came to Israel because I wanted to make sure that you are in good hands," neglecting to mention the request for forgiveness from the woman, which he had never been capable of articulating.

"You invested in the right stock, Gabriel. It has yielded only profits. You have a family. They didn't throw you to the dogs, even though no one would have blamed them if they had. Apparently someone up there thinks you're an angel." And she turned and left the room, no giggle on her lips.

"Wait, Clara. Wait. I'll go with you to your tower."

But she wasn't there anymore.

The trip to the Tel Aviv skyscraper wasn't mentioned again, but Fanny hadn't forgotten about it. Like Clara, she also worked in secret, only she planned to visit it alone.

Her motivation wasn't the desire to see the height of international innovation in Tel Aviv or to marvel at Zionist progress, but rather something completely practical. Her rug was tattered and worn, and she was hoping to find a substitute for it at the new department store. Not that she meant to throw it away – heaven forfend! It was still the only object that remained from the house in Siret – but she urgently needed something to decorate the floor for a special event. There was to be a family portrait. A member of the "Zionist Youth" youth group that Yitzhak had led, who had recently immigrated to Israel from Bucharest, was a professional photographer who had been asked to present a portfolio of family portraits at a job interview. Since the photographer was single and had no relatives in Israel, Yitzhak volunteered his own family.

A family on loan. The photographer was grateful, and the date was set for the following week.

Late at night, when Clara and Gabriel were fast asleep – he in the double bed and she on the fold-out couch in the living room – Fanny knelt on the floor on the balcony, and measured the width and length of her rug with a measuring tape from Black Sorina's sewing box. It was also an excellent opportunity to trim the frayed edges. The small carpet had almost disintegrated, and the only visible remnant of its original design was in its center. In the faint light cast by a streetlamp Fanny had difficulty making out whether it was a bisected flower or the edges of a pair of wings, and all her efforts to strain her memory to complete the design in her mind came to naught.

She considered taking the carpet with her to the department store, to match it with its successor. First she rolled it up in newspaper and tucked it into her plastic shopping basket. Then she thought better of it. Who knew what might happen to her treasure in the crush she anticipated at the store. Masses of people were streaming to see the sensation that had been erected at the junction of Herzl and Ahad Ha'am streets, and in Israel, she had already learned, people pushed and shoved each other like there was no tomorrow.

The Shalom Tower was less impressive than she had expected, and this despite the fact that it dwarfed all the buildings in the area. A foreign element among the red roofs of the Neve Zedek neighborhood and the shady trees on Rothschild Boulevard, it was a rectangular building with horizontal display windows in front and vertical windows along its sides and it sported light brown mosaic panels. It would lag far behind in any competition with the splendid buildings on Herrengasse Street in Czernowitz. Where was the preponderance of decorations and stone apertures? Where were the adorning plaques telling the story of the history of the people and the nation? And what about lofty statues – if not of mythological gods, at least of Herzl and Ahad Ha'am?

The crowds assembled at the display windows blocked Fanny's view, so that she couldn't see the fancy imported dolls that could move their arms and legs. However, since unlike her granddaughter, she wasn't overly fond of dolls, she wasn't disappointed. More strange elbows poked her in the ribs. People shouted, "Move!" and "You're blocking my view!" and continued to push and shove. It reminded her of the fair in Siret and the legendary acrobat who lay down underneath a cart and emerged unscathed, and she hoped there would be a high barrier around the promised balcony on the roof – the one that wasn't yet open to the public – so that no grief-stricken visitors would jump from the top.

What really impressed Fanny was the escalator in the lobby. She had never seen anything like it. On its two parallel routes it rose and descended, and her gaze was riveted to the stairs that effortlessly emerged and slipped away. What a shame that this wondrous invention hadn't existed when she was traversing the streets of Bukovina with her heavy cart full of bottles of beer. It would have saved her muscle pain and fatigue beyond imagining. The world of the future will belong to those who take shortcuts, she thought to herself. Ulysses' journey will be faster and less grueling, but Penelope's sorrow will remain the same, and neither will be able to deliver their descendants from what cannot be prevented.

Oy, time, time, that which is in the past and that which awaits, why can't you just jump from the tallest tower and leave us be?

Fanny murmured a Yiddish phrase, "When you peek through the holes in the matzah during Passover you can already see the New Year's shofar."

Lost in her musings about the looping motion of the escalator Fanny imagined that she could hear the summons of the shofar – not the long quavering blast of the *teru'ah*, but the three short lilting bursts of *shevarim* – and she lost her balance. She released her grip on her shopping basket and it went tumbling down. Just in time someone reached out and prevented her from falling. It was a soldier in uniform, who like her was riding up the new-fangled Jacob's Ladder. When, with his help, she had regained her balance, she saw that he was barefoot. A pair of military boots tied together by their laces hung across his shoulders.

"Do you know where the entrance is to the department store, ma'am?"

His cheeks were smooth. Barely any wisps of beard.

"What do you want to buy?"

"A new pair of boots. These pinch me and the quartermaster can't get hold of my size."

"So you kept on growing while you were in the army?"

He smiled an embarrassed smile. "It must be from all the training."

"Three years of service is a long time. You may even sprout a beard."

"Are you the grandmother of a soldier?"

"Not yet."

"When will you be?"

"My grandson will be drafted soon."

"And you didn't tell him, 'By the time you grow up there won't be an army?'"

"I'm not one of those people who make promises that can't be kept."

"How many wars have you seen, ma'am?"

"Why do they count backwards when it comes to wars?"

The barefoot soldier shrugged, "What do I know? They don't tell us things like that in the army."

Fanny said, "If we count forward, maybe they won't happen. Tell that to your commanders."

The soldier laughed.

"Do you have a girlfriend?"

He lowered his head shyly.

"I haven't yet met my one and only. Do you think it's all determined from above?"

"When it comes to love my soldier boy, above and below are the same thing."

"How can that be?"

Suddenly the escalator stopped moving. The steps froze beneath them, and Fanny and the soldier waited for long minutes. Nothing happened.

"Do you think this machine – I don't know what it's called – do you think it will start moving again ma'am?"

"Maybe. But it will take time." Fanny kicked the motionless step as if she was trying to awaken a stubborn hibernating animal and declared, "There's no point waiting."

The soldier adjusted the boots across his back and leapt up the frozen escalator. Then he ran back down, gathered up the fallen shopping basket from the bottom of the stairs and carried it over shoulder. Together he and Fanny climbed to the top and arrived at the entrance to the "Everything you could look for – you'll find what you're looking for." She noticed that the soles of his feet were black from the dirt that had already managed to accumulate on the new silver stairs.

"Before they start up this whole *gesheft* again they should give it a good cleaning," she observed, and the soldier laughed. Too bad she couldn't be recruited by the Israel Defense Forces as a Sergeant Major.

Instead of a new rug, Fanny bought the soldier a new pair of army boots. He insisted on taking one size larger than he needed at the moment. If he continued to grow, at least he would have room for his toes. She didn't ask his name, and when he thanked her graciously, he called her "Senora Nona," or "Madame Grandmother" in Ladino, and she told him she hoped he would find love long before he grew a beard. As a bonus for making a purchase during the opening week, Fanny received enough free shoelaces to supply an entire platoon.

"Where's the new carpet?" asked Yitzhak, who was preparing the room for the photographer's arrival.

"I couldn't find a substitute," she replied.

In the family photograph the floor is bare.

16

Does *Zayde* dream?

This question worried the girl, and so she crept stealthily into her grandparents' bedroom when Gabriel was deep in his afternoon nap. That's how she discovered that when he slept his eyes were closed, just like those of a seeing person. She observed him for a long time and he had no idea that she was there. He didn't look blind when he was asleep.

The girl continued to pester everyone with her questions. *Safta* said that *Zayde* was too old to dream, while her mother explained that since he wasn't blind from birth, he had the ability to reconstruct his previous dreams.

"The brain doesn't forget."

"So what does forget?" the girl inquired, but the adults had run out of patience and even her brother thought she was the world's biggest nuisance.

Two days before the photographer was due to come she gathered up all her courage and asked Gabriel himself.

"How do you dream, *Zayde*?"

"I don't understand what you mean." She thought he was being evasive.

"Do you dream in color like regular people, or is everything black for you?"

"Your small head is full of nonsense."

They were alone. Fanny and Clara had gone out to buy flowers, "Because the house should look pretty when the photographer comes." Gabriel sat on a chair by the table, leaning on his cane, and announced that he wouldn't pose for the photograph. It was a waste of time and money, and besides, photographs faded. And even if by some miracle they were preserved, the subjects changed so much that you couldn't recognize them. So why bother? In the end what you have in a picture is a group of strangers.

He told her that he once heard from an Indian woman that her people believed that a camera stole a part of the soul of the person it photographed, but the girl had had her picture taken in the past and didn't feel that anything had been taken from her. In her album she had pictures of herself with the other children in the neighborhood and with her parents and her brother, but she didn't have any pictures of herself with Fanny and Gabriel. And she hadn't found any photographs of his from America. He hadn't brought an album with him, or she would have discovered it by now. She was very talented at snooping in drawers and cupboards.

"*Zayde*, it's important to have your picture taken," she tried to sound grownup as she told him this.

"Why?"

"If you don't, how will I remember you when you aren't here?"

"You don't have to remember anything."

"You don't want me to remember you?"

"Maybe you won't want to."

"*Zayde*, do you only remember what you want to?"

He wouldn't budge. Why should he pose for a picture when he would never be able to see it himself? But the girl wouldn't give in either. She would need a trick to convince him. She placed a shoebox on the table, inside which was her prized collection of paper dolls; she called them her "princesses." She had cut each one out of a newspaper and glued it to a piece of cardboard to reinforce it. "This will be a kind of a game," she announced. She would play the part of the photographer and he would choose which princesses would have their picture taken. As far as she was concerned he could give each one a name and a face from the time when he could still see, or from the vestiges of his dreams.

"You are quite the stubborn little one," he sighed, as he set aside his cane.

She switched on every light in the house, even in the bathroom, since she believed that an abundance of light helped the blind to see. Then she arranged her dolls before him in a row. His eyes were open wide, and he touched the dolls, feeling their contours.

"What do you see, *Zayde*?"

A woman with flaxen hair woven in a braid, who called him Gavril; a dancing woman who called him George; two who referred to him as "*mio amore*, Giorgio;" a woman lounging in a bubble bath; a young lady who played the cello; and another who proffered a gold lighter. And there was also a man, who named him "Horche." The girl felt dizzy and confused. She couldn't catch all the names he murmured.

"Open to me, my sister, my love, my dove, my undefiled," whispered Gabriel, and then he tried to teach the girl a verse from the Song of Songs, "...put in his hand by the hole of the door, and my heart was moved for him."

The girl didn't understand a word, but still she was fascinated. It was like a dream – only it was real.

There was only one more cut-out doll. It was her favorite, from the *Cinema World* weekly, and it had fallen to the floor. The girl retrieved it and tucked it like a cigarette between Gabriel's yellow, tobacco-stained fingers.

"You forgot this one, *Zayde*. She's the prettiest one in my collection."

"*Liebling*."

"What is '*liebling*'?" She moved so close to him that she could see herself reflected in the pupils of his staring eyes.

"Beloved," he said, and she wasn't sure whether or not he was referring to her.

The girl added her to the row of princesses, made the clicking sound of a shutter and proclaimed, "You see, *Zayde*, it's not so bad to have your picture taken."

The scent of the flowers – grassy and pungent – preceded Fanny and Clara's entrance. The room was enveloped in light, and they simultaneously shielded their eyes. The girl waited for a reprimand that never materialized, gathered up her paper dolls and returned them to their shoebox.

"When he wants to, he can see!" she said triumphantly.

17

The light in the room was too dim, and squinting through the lens all the people looked like silhouettes to the photographer who couldn't capture any expression. His immediate challenge was to increase the illumination but even after he had opened all the shutters in the apartment and switched on all the electric bulbs, including in the bathroom, there was no improvement. All he could see through the lens was an unfocused motley group of blurred figures. Even worse, the occasion hadn't infused those present with the demeanor he had hoped for. No sense of elation, no festive atmosphere, no awareness of perpetuating a memory was evoked.

This wasn't the family portrait that would assure him his livelihood. The photographer was ready to pack up his equipment, and it was only Yitzhak's plea, "Give them a little more time. They'll get used to the idea," that kept him from leaving.

The main obstacle was the old man, who fumed non-stop in English and cursed in Yiddish, "*Keesh meer een tuchess*" – (Kiss my ass). It was only when the photographer realized that he was blind that he was overcome by pity and agreed to stay.

The first thing he did was ask the blind man to keep his eyes open. After all, he wasn't blind from birth, and the direct gaze might jog his memory so that facial expressions imprinted in his brain might surface and perhaps even be improved upon.

But the old man refused to cooperate.

"For some reason it's when he closes his eyes that he forgets less," the woman next to him muttered irritably. The photographer noticed that she had prepared for the special event in the appropriate manner, and was wearing her best dress, the one reserved for weddings and funerals. The whiteness of her hair posed a significant challenge. He had to make sure that it wouldn't steal the focus.

"A photograph is a memento for the future," he tried a new tack to convince the obstinate old man.

"What do I care about the future? In any case I won't be in it."

"Isn't it important to you that people know you existed?"

"As if I remember those who came before me?"

"The longer the blind man lives, the more he sees," Clara managed to add one more Yiddish proverb to Fanny's collection before she returned to America. It was on the day before the photographer came.

They exchanged clichéd best wishes for long life, good health, and happy times, and Clara's last words to Fanny were, "Try to save him from himself." They both made a supreme effort to conceal from one another and from themselves that this was the last time they would see each other.

Then Fanny left the apartment and went down to the grocery store so that Clara could take her leave of Gabriel in private. He wouldn't tell her what they spoke of and she would never ask.

Yitzhak had offered to accompany Clara to the airport but she preferred to go alone, in a taxi. He kept his promise to write to her until her dying day, and the nurse in the hospital in New York gently slid an envelope bearing Israeli stamps from between her feeble fingers. Among her possessions they found a Polaroid snapshot whose colors were still bright, which was placed on the coffin at the Jewish funeral home in Manhattan.

And Yitzhak made good on his promise, and brought Florence, his ostracized cousin, back into the family fold, after Abe and Anna passed on. The fact that she was a Catholic Christian didn't make the slightest bit of difference. For him it was and would always be a case of blood being thicker than water.

Florence's parents, who sat shiva for her, are also present in the photograph. To defuse the atmosphere somewhat the photographer employed the family nicknames. At first he placed Tante Anna and Onkel Abe together, on the left side of the sofa, and Fanny and Gabriel on the right. But the symmetrical, Noah's Ark placement of the couples looked so sad, so pitiful – with that arrangement he would only guarantee that he would be unemployed – that he instructed the family to go out onto the balcony, and on the stone platform, in natural light, he sat Gabriel and Fanny in the center, with Anna and Abe on either side, as two supports. Then he positioned Yitzhak and Mimi behind them. She had chosen a black and white checked dress, which afforded him infinite possibilities for playing with the shading, and he focused on the big black button at her neckline that looked like a bullet hole. With great effort he even managed to coax her into a hesitant smile, but not so Yitzhak, who insisted on wearing a formal expression. He towers above everyone in the photograph. In his starched and pressed white shirt, with his arm resting on the railing, he makes sure that no one will fall.

Just a minute, photographer. Don't click the shutter. I don't want to forget the members of the family who are missing. In the alternative photograph, that won't be found in any album, you would see Paula and Lizzie-Bertha on either side of Emil Stein, the man who proved himself to be a steady rock for two women. And Mimi's parents also arrived specially from the afterlife, with Grandfather Berl-Dov, who re-made the match between Fanny and Gabriel, and Grandmother Rochele, whose undying love for her husband is worthy of a book in itself. Both are dressed in traditional *charedi* garb. And a place must be found for Clara Mendel, who, while not an official member of the family has honorably earned the right to be considered a relative.

Just a minute. Just one more delay. I roll out a small carpet and spread it under their feet, the only remnant of that remote town, where not a single Jew is left today, other than in the cemetery. Now, photographer, your photograph will be really wonderful, and it will promise you employment and an income for a long time to come.

You can't see them, but when you look through my lens they are there.

This is the foundation, the photographer told himself as he surveyed the final blocking of that imperfect family. Now we need the most important ingredient of all, the one that will really make the tableau come alive.

Where were the children?

They were still outside. The boy-teen was glued to the radio, listening to the English hit parade broadcast on Radio Ramallah. He wouldn't miss it for any photograph. At least, not before they played the No. 1 song.

The adults waited on the balcony above, while down below he joined The Beatles and belted out the song, *Help*.

The girl, who wouldn't leave his side, translated the words to herself in whispered Hebrew. She was so happy that Grandpa had taught her his language.

"Help, I need somebody. Help, not just anybody. Help."

"Why is the music so happy when the words are so sad?" she asked when the song was over.

The boy-teen replied, "You're mixed-up. It's not sad at all. In the end someone always comes to the rescue."

"Who?"

"Maybe us."

"How can that be?"

"Because we're the ones listening to the song."

The only rescuer the girl knew of was the sunbaked lifeguard on Reading Beach, at the mouth of the Yarkon, but he used a surfboard, not songs. Meanwhile, she was busy trying to make sense of a line from the song.

"What does it mean, 'I just need you like I never done before'?"

The boy-teen said, "We don't always understand everything," and promised her that he would use his allowance to buy the record for the two of them, and then they would listen to *Help* over and over, and together they would solve the puzzle.

From up on the balcony the adults called to them again and again and the brother and sister bounded up the stairs and burst into the photograph.

The boy-teen stood between his parents, leaning forward, smiling all over, as the Beatles continued to play inside his head, from ear to ear. The photographer seated the girl between Gabriel and Fanny. She separated between her grandmother, whose hands were folded in her lap while her neck was encircled by a string of gleaming pearls, and Gabriel in his elegant suit, wearing the black silk tie that was a gift from Clara. Everyone faced the camera, except for Gabriel, whose eyes were trained on his granddaughter, wearing a miniature shiny silk dress and a huge bow in her hair. Eyes squeezed shut, she tilted her face to the side and laughed delightedly.

What did he say to her that she found so funny?

At first, when she skipped onto the balcony, the girl stopped short, frightened by the stranger who had taken over the household and was issuing instructions, and then by the camera that looked to her like the double-edged sword in the hand of the angel that they had just learned about in her Torah class. But what alarmed her more than anything else was the fact that all the people she loved most in the world – with a love that always pierced through her like a dagger – were frozen. Her father, looking exceptionally serious, didn't open his mouth, her brother didn't make a sound, her usually bustling grandmother wearing her pearls, and her sorrowful mother in her checked dress – they were all arrayed in a frozen tableau before the same all-powerful device. Obedient, switched off, inanimate.

Gabriel heard her silent weeping even before he felt the shudders of her small body. She refused to be photographed, tried to run away, and all the while she mumbled the word "help" in Hebrew and in English.

Only Gabriel moved. He leaned toward her and whispered, "Want to hear a secret?"

Her tears were still sliding down her cheeks, but Gabriel made no attempt to wipe them away. In the picture his two hands are spread on his thighs like a pair of wings, and he is turned toward her with eyes wide open. A stranger would never guess that he was blind.

"Your *Safta* saved me," he said.

"How? Did she also sing you a song?"

"She married me twice."

Her tears were forgotten.

"And you, little bunny, will marry us a third time."

And then the girl laughed. The photographer pressed down. One click, and he got the picture he wanted.

Epilogue

That love had every reason to disappear, to fade away, to vanish, to die, and yet, against all the odds, it survived. Even after I transformed Fanny and Gabriel into literary figures and filled in the blanks according to probability or necessity, I realized how much their story had shaken my life. It would be legitimate to describe it as damaged and tainted, as exposing the ugliest aspects of relationships, but I still insist on a love story.

Fanny and Gabriel's second marriage lasted eight years. During the Six-Day War we slowly brought Gabriel down the three floors to the shelter. He cursed the war like he had never cursed before. I learned the crudest and most venomous words in English and Yiddish from him while we sat in the dark and waited for the siren to sound the all clear.

A short time after my brother was called up to serve in the Israel Defense Forces Gabriel suffered a heart attack. Even though he slept on the side of the bed that was against the wall he fell out, and that's when Fanny discovered that Gabriel had left her for good. For a long time she sat on the bare floor, stroking his cold cheek, before she called for my father.

I hold onto a slip of paper as a keepsake, on which some wise original words of my grandmother's are written in Yiddish. I jotted them down when she told me, years ago, "I'm not afraid of death, it's just the road that leads up to it that doesn't appeal to me."

Fanny lived for a long time after Gabriel's demise, and when she died she was nearly ninety.

While we were living in the United States as emissaries for the State of Israel in New York, the only place my grandfather ever considered his home, I gave birth to twins. A boy and a girl. If he had been alive, Gabriel would have celebrated the realization of his dream – descendants who were US citizens. My parents flew over from Israel for the birth. My father asked if the boy's middle name could be "Gabriel," and my mother was aghast. It was my spouse who told me about their impassioned, tearful argument, for I was still in the maternity ward.

My mother said, "He was a terrible father. He abandoned you. Why would you want to memorialize him? He doesn't deserve it!" And my father replied, "He's the only father I have! Blood is thicker than water."

Florence and her husband Jimmy DiMauro were among those invited to the bris at the Jewish Cultural Center in Manhattan. That Catholic Romeo, for the love of whom the Jewish Juliet was torn from her parents' home, wore a skullcap on his head and congratulated us in Hebrew that he had memorized for the occasion. For the baby boy, one of whose names is Gabriel, they brought the gift of a silver spoon from Tiffany's.

A few years ago their two daughters contacted me. In the lobby of a hotel on Broadway I gave my two new, very Christian cousins, Theresa and Joanne, photographs of Anna and Abe, the Jewish grandmother and grandfather they were never able to meet. They examined every detail and pointed out similarities visible only to them.

The young great-grandson of Anna and Abe even came to Israel for a visit. When I met him at a trendy café in Tel Aviv, he explained that he had felt a need to connect to his family roots. He was thrilled by Israel, and especially the Israeli women, and he swore that he would be back.

Just as we were preparing to leave, a waitress approached me with a note, on which was written her name and telephone number, and asked if I could fix her up with the hot guy who was sitting with me. I thought to myself that there are genes that will always resurface.

I visited Fanny before she died. She was an elderly, shrunken woman but her snow white hair was as full and wild as ever and her lashes just as long. Although for a while she had been having only occasional bouts of lucidity, on that day she seemed focused and sharp, all her wits about her. She insisted on a private conversation between the two of us, "Because the heart sees better than the eyes," was one of the remaining Yiddish sayings that popped out of her collection. Her eyes sparkled as she sat me down determinedly on the same jutting balcony where we had all posed so many years before.

"Your man has left you. You're keeping it a secret, but I know."

I told her, "*Safta*, I'm married and my man is with me."

"What shame he has brought upon you. A disgrace to the family. You can hide the truth from the entire world, but you can't hide it from me. I see everything."

"*Safta*, you're confused. It didn't happen to me. I'll have a child soon."

She insisted, "You're an abandoned woman, and you've already given the child away. Why don't you bring him back?"

My explanations were of no avail. She remained stranded in her story.

I remember how I walked the streets of Tel Aviv, the same streets through which I once guided my grandfather, completely beside myself.

Fanny and Gabriel are buried in the Holon Cemetery, but not next to each other. The distance between them remains.

Nava Semel, November 2014 –September 2016

Three young people accompanied me on this journey, intrigued by the spinning of the interwoven paragraphs. Their questions and their curiosity about what preceded them were my inspiration. During the frequent moments when I stumbled they were there, urging me not to give up.

All my gratitude to my twins, Nimi and Ealeal and to her partner Nizan Lotem for the never-ending encouragement and the openness of their hearts. Without them this book wouldn't have been written.